HMAS *cold war warrior* **ONSLOW**

Lindsey Shaw

Senior curator
Maritime technology, exploration and navy
Australian National Maritime Museum

AUSTRALIAN
NATIONAL

MARITIME
MUSEUM

preface

by Mary-Louise Williams

Former Director, Australian National Maritime Museum

Submarines, with their stealth, silence, secrecy and speed, their sinister form, grip the popular imagination like no other type of vessel. It's no wonder, then, that HMAS *Onslow* is one of the Australian National Maritime Museum's most popular attractions.

Onslow, one of six Oberon class submarines of the Australian Submarine Squadron, served from 1969 to 1999 – and then was handed to the museum by the Royal Australian Navy, to join two other ex-RAN vessels, the destroyer *Vampire* and patrol boat *Advance*. *Onslow* is thus part of a unique ensemble of Australian naval history, a collection set unlike any other.

The submarine demonstrates the strong association between the museum and the Royal Australian Navy, one which grows stronger with the years. But *Onslow* represents another very special association, too, between the museum and the crew who handed the sub over after their last tour of duty. When you visit *Onslow* it's their personal belongings – generously donated by those officers and men – that allow us to deliver the authentic feel of a living vessel. And it's their stories of shipboard life that you'll encounter in these pages.

Submariners are a very special breed, as you'll appreciate when you take this opportunity to see and experience for yourself what it's like to live in such cramped quarters for long periods of time, surrounded by the technology of modern naval warfare, often under enemy threat.

We're proud to be able to present such an outstanding museum attraction, and in doing so to increase our visitors' understanding of what it was like to serve in Australia's naval defence forces.

foreword

by Commander John Hodges RAN (Retd)

Former National President, Submarines Association Australia

Little did I realise what an important role HMAS *Onslow* would play in my 21-year-long naval career, when in December 1973, fresh from submarine training in the United Kingdom, I joined *Onslow* as a trainee submarine officer. For the next 12 months I crawled all over *Onslow* learning my new trade. This period reinforced my decision to volunteer for submarine service and my desire eventually to command a submarine. My period of learning in *Onslow* certainly stood me in good stead as I went on to command *Onslow*'s two sister boats – *Otway* and *Ovens*.

When *Onslow* was transferred by the Department of Defence to the Australian National Maritime Museum in 1999, the Royal Australian Navy removed only confidential equipment and the batteries, leaving the rest of the boat intact. Consequently, *Onslow* is one of the few submarines in any museum in the world that is rigged for sea, and she gives every appearance of being ready to sail from Darling Harbour. Her continuing good looks are due in no small part to the efforts of the staff and volunteers at the museum.

As you walk through my former 'home' I ask you to imagine the ship's company of 68 working, eating and sleeping deep below the surface for up to two months at a time. It was certainly exciting and not without inherent dangers as we were all visitors to Neptune's domain!

A tour of *Onslow* at ANMM is an enjoyable and rewarding voyage of discovery, certain both to stimulate and increase the visitor's interest in Australia's submarine history.

introduction

HMAS ONSLOW

HMAS ONSLOW

The Oberon class attack submarines played a vital role protecting Australia for more than 30 years, from 1967 through to 2000. Initially built to replace the British Royal Navy Fourth Submarine Division, which had provided submarine services and training for the Royal Australian Navy after World War II, the Oberons were also a response to concerns about the expansion of the Soviet Pacific fleet. They were commissioned in the middle years of the cold war, a dangerous period of intense military competition and tension between the Communist block under the Soviet Union, and the United States and its allies.

The British-designed Oberons were a product of Britain's World War II submarine experience, and were influenced by the concepts of the German Type XXI electro-boats. Their versatility lay in their ability to be silent and invisible – to watch, listen and collect information without being seen. Using stealth, endurance and agility, these conventionally powered diesel-electric submarines were multi-purpose and undertook many activities including secret patrols, photographic reconnaissance, surveillance, shadowing, and intelligence gathering.

In its 30-year service with the Royal Australian Navy, HMAS *Onslow* clocked up more than 358,000 nautical miles and took part in many international naval exercises, represented Australia on goodwill visits around the world and with its five sister submarines – *Ovens*, *Orion*, *Otama*, *Oxley* and *Otway* – provided the RAN with a formidable submarine force. HMAS *Onslow*'s most secretive work was tracking Soviet submarines moving into the Arabian Gulf from Vladivostok via the Coral Sea and the Great Australian Bight. With HMAS *Ovens*, *Onslow* kept an eye on them, undertaking close-in intelligence collection patrols.

Onslow's story

HMAS *Onslow* was named after the Western Australian town, itself named in 1885 in honour of the then Chief Justice of Western Australia, Sir Alexander Campbell Onslow (1842-1908). Sir Alexander was appointed Attorney General of WA in 1880 and became Chief Justice in 1883. He held that position until his retirement in 1901.

The first *Onslow* was a 900-ton British destroyer which fought with distinction in the Battle of Jutland in 1916. With guns and torpedoes she closed and engaged the German cruiser *Wiesbaden* until she was hit and crippled by Admiral Hipper's flagship the *Derfflinger*. *Onslow* was repaired and eventually returned to active duty to sink the German submarine *U-17* on 25 February 1918. This *Onslow* was scrapped on 26 October 1918.

The second HMS *Onslow* was a 1,610-ton O class destroyer launched in 1941. She participated in convoy escort duties throughout World War II and was involved in sinking the German submarine *U-589*. While carrying out escort duties in the Arctic *Onslow* sighted the enemy, closed and opened fire. The German forces included the pocket battleship *Lutzow*, the heavy cruiser *Admiral Hipper* and six large destroyers. *Onslow* pressed the attack keeping the German capital ships at bay and defending the convoy until reinforcements arrived. *Onslow* was seriously damaged and Captain Sherbrooke severely wounded, losing the sight of one eye. He was later awarded the Victoria Cross. *Onslow* was transferred as *Tippu Sultan* to the Pakistan Navy in 1949

left to right

Chest of valves

Oberons at Sydney's former submarine base, HMAS *Platypus*, with pre-1975 sonar dome configuration

In RIMPAC 98, *Onslow* successfully avoided detection and 'destroyed' the Nimitz class carrier USS *Carl Vinson* – much to the Americans' chagrin!

Onslow at work

Once launched on 3 December 1968 by Her Royal Highness Princess Alexandra, the Honourable Mrs Angus Ogilvy, and commissioned into the Royal Australian Navy on 22 December 1969, HMAS *Onslow* set sail for Australia via the Panama Canal and the first of many naval exercises with the United States Navy off Hawaii.

For the next 30 years HMAS *Onslow* was involved in intense periods of international military exercises operating with aviation, surface, amphibious, allied and special operations forces. *Onslow* has participated in regular deployments to South-East Asia for the

left to right

At sea between Penang and Singapore, 1974

Crew on parade, 1974

Five Power Agreement (Exercise Starfish), local exercises off the Australian east coast (Exercise Kangaroo), the west coast (Exercise Lungfish), our northern waters (Exercise Singaroo), across the Tasman (Exercise Tamex) and in Hawaiian waters (RIMPAC).

During RIMPAC 71, *Onslow* was hit by a US Coast Guard cutter's practice torpedo – the warhead is designed to cut the motor as it nears its target but in this case the mechanism failed. On inspection a small dent was located near the tail section of *Onslow*.

Other highlights include winning the Gloucester Cup in 1977 (the most efficient fleet unit in the RAN – the first such award to a submarine) and winning the submarine squadron fighting efficiency shield six times.

Regular submarine sea training group (SSTG) exercises are undertaken by all submarines, with the boat and its complement being put through extensive work up and training exercises including fighting fires, hydraulic bursts, floods, casualties and electrical failures. These prepare the submarine for action at any given time.

This silent patroller of the deep has also represented the RAN and Australia on many goodwill visits around the world, including the Canadian Navy's 75th anniversary in 1985.

During exercises in South-East Asia an *Onslow* team played rugby against the British Club in Bangkok in 1987. The submarine's complement welcomed Aussie yachtswoman Kay Cottee on board when she returned from her record-breaking solo circumnavigation in 1988. *Onslow* attended many of Hobart's famous annual royal regattas and participated in many open days around the country.

Onslow underwent three major refits in its lifetime, each lasting two years. A refit means the modernisation and updating of equipment, routine replacements, additions and alterations, ultrasonic thickness tests and blasting of the pressure hull, surveys of all equipment and finally testing and trials. Some 6,000 individual activities are undertaken during a major refit.

In 1975–76 major improvements were made to the submarine's combat capabilities – called the SWUP – submarine weapons update program. The first was the installation of the new sonar – named Micro-Puffs – developed by Sperry Gyroscope. The new system, a passive range-finding sonar, allowed the boat accurately to determine the distance from any enemy ship by measuring the time difference that sounds or signals emitted by the ship took to reach the three sonar arrays located forward, midships and aft on the sides of the casing.

The second improvement was the installation of integrated data processing and weapon control systems – called SFCS – submarine fire control system. The system used a digital computer, operated by three men, to process all information from the submarine's sensors and present it on a screen. It could also guide torpedoes to their target.

The third combat system improvement was a replacement attack sonar (CSU3-41). This entailed a redesign of the bow-dome which houses the sonar array.

During its major refit in 1982–84 and after successful test firings by HMAS *Otway* on the Pacific missile firing range in Hawaii, *Onslow* was fitted with sub-Harpoon missiles – becoming the first conventionally powered (i.e. non-nuclear) submarine in the world with an anti-ship missile capability.

above

Efficiency shield, awarded six times

clockwise from below

Commando-launching exercise

Onslow berthed in Western Australia

Battle honours board of vessels named *Onslow*

Propeller and aft diving plane, Garden Island, 2002

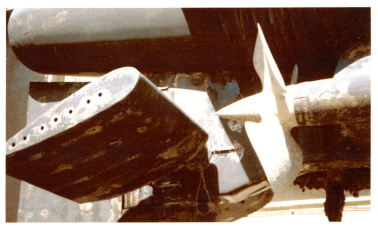

The submarine is a maze of self-contained spaces, each designed to meet a particular need. Every available space is used on a submarine!

a tour of *Onslow*

1

The fore ends

Bow torpedo tubes

The fore ends contained the teeth of HMAS *Onslow* – the torpedoes and missiles. In this space 22 Mk 48 torpedoes and sub-Harpoon missiles could be stowed. The museum currently has four unarmed torpedoes on display – two Mk 8 and two Mk 23 torpedoes. These types of torpedoes were the Oberons' main armament until the major weapons upgrade in the 1980s.

There are six torpedo tubes in the bow section – three on the port side and three on the starboard. The torpedoes and missiles were loaded into this compartment via the forward torpedo loading hatch – the hatch now used for visitor access. They were loaded by crane one at a time then manually manoeuvred into storage position by overhead rails and chains. Hydraulic equipment was used to load the bottom torpedo tubes 5 and 6.

The fore ends is one of the two compartments on the submarine that contain underwater escape towers; the other escape tower is located in the after ends. The built-in breathing system (BIBS) allowed a maximum of 83 to escape from this compartment. Emergency rations of water and barley sugar were located in the nearby lockers.

When extra sleeping accommodation was required (when *Onslow* had trainees on board for example) racks – or bunks – were set up in this compartment among the stowed torpedoes.

At the bulkhead door leading to the accommodation compartment there are some important pieces of equipment. These include racks of the OCCABA equipment (open circuit compressed air breathing apparatus – personal breathing devices for each submariner) and the oxygen generator which uses special long-burning candles. Here too is the submerged signal ejector or SSE which fired pyrotechnics – a red grenade was launched in the case of an emergency, to show the location of the boat. During exercises white or yellow smoke flares were used to reveal its position, and if *Onslow* scored a simulated hit against a target, a green grenade was released. Message containers could also be launched from here.

The CO_2 absorption unit is located under the false flowmesh deck at the entrance to the accommodation compartment. Also beneath the flowmesh is the torpedo store and seaman's store.

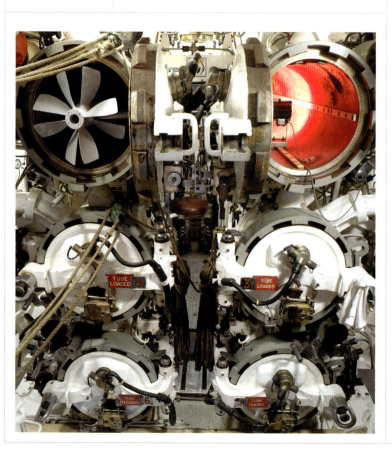

Bulkheads	*Onslow* is divided into five watertight compartments each separated by a bulkhead door. The bulkhead doors isolate compartments and prevent the spread of fire, flooding, gas or poisonous fumes in the event of damage or accident. Intercompartment ventilation could also be shut off by valves to prevent gas leaks.	

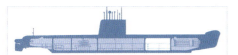

Accommodation compartment

This area contained the forward mess and accommodation for 18 junior sailors – sonar operators, cooks, electronic warfare sailors and radio operators.

Living quarters for submariners are crammed into the spaces left over after the machinery and equipment have gone in, so it's not too surprising that there is little room to move. Racks (bunks) are generally 1.8 m (6 ft) long and 0.6 m (2 ft) wide with just enough room to turn over (in a constrained fashion!). Curtains provided a modicum of privacy and each rack had its own light and air conditioning ventilation outlet. As a third of the men were on watch at any one time, there was just enough room for the others

Racks (bunks) for junior sailors

in the messes. The normal length of a watch was six hours on and six hours off.

Here – and elsewhere throughout the boat – are several groups of bright orange ELSRDs – emergency lifesaving respiratory devices. They were only activated if an evacuation had been ordered by the Captain, providing eight minutes of breathable air in an otherwise smoke-filled or toxic compartment.

There are two batteries – No 1 is underneath this compartment and No 2 is under the control room. Each battery has 224 cells generating 440 volts and each cell contained 93 litres of acid. They lasted six years on average before replacements were required. The batteries

' WON'T BE A MINUTE ... MAKE YOURSELF COMFORTABLE ...'

Accommodation
compartment

powered electric motors driving the propellers, and provided enough power to make 12 knots on the surface and more than 15 knots dived. They also provided power for all lighting and electrical equipment. All 448 cells were removed from HMAS *Onslow* prior to handover to the museum, but 24 have been returned for display.

Along the passageway is a hatchway to a special four-man diving chamber, from which Special Forces divers could leave the submarine for covert operations. They climbed into the space, shut the lower hatch and then opened the upper hatch to swim or climb out when the water equalised the pressure. *Onslow* was the only RAN submarine with this feature. The hatchway was used for normal access and egress for submariners when in port.

Next we encounter the senior sailors' mess which was for the Chief Petty Officers and Petty Officers – 10 of whom slept here while all 13 ate here. It also contains the switchboard for the No 1 battery.

In the galley two cooks served four meals a day – breakfast, lunch, dinner and midnighters (a snack for those coming on or going off watch). Meals were the same for officers and sailors although the officers had a steward to fetch their meals and perform other duties. In the passageway underneath is the coxswain's store for dry-goods – canned and packaged foods. Opposite the galley on the right hand side is the gash ejector. All rubbish was put into special canvas bags called gash bags – made in Australian prison workshops – which were weighted down and then ejected. It sank to the bottom so any debris did not float to the surface and give the submarine's position away. The can crusher is located here, too.

clockwise from
top left

Can crusher outside
the galley

Gash ejector

CO₂ filters

The galley

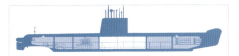

The control room

As you walk along the passageway to the control room the first cabin is the coxswain's grot. The coxswain had three main tasks: victualling (provisioning), keeping discipline and medical services – this was the sick bay too. Three senior sailors lived here. While the original meaning of the term 'grot' has been lost, it is thought that the cabin was once nicknamed the grotto, shortened to grot. There are those who say it's because of the smelly submariners who lived there!

Opposite is the wardroom pantry where the captain's steward prepared meals for the officers. He would get the meals from the galley and set them up here ready for the wardroom.

Some of the lockers in this part of the passageway contained hanging space for the officers' uniforms as well as various ammunitions for pyrotechnics, rifles and small arms. The No 2 battery switchboard is also located in this passageway.

The three racks either side of the wardroom were for the engineer, the steward, the AWA officer (the senior acoustics man), the sonar officer, the executive officer and the navigation officer. The wardroom was used variously as the officers' mess, a briefing room, the ship's office and a mail centre. HQ1 – emergency situations like fire or flood – was controlled from here. Five men could sleep in the wardroom and the table doubled as a dinner table and office desk. Each officer had one drawer and one cupboard for his personal belongings. In addition, there were some hanging lockers out in the passageway.

Fire control alley leads into the control room proper with the black curtain drawn at night so the officers had the same lighting as in the control room. This saved them having to adjust their vision if they were called to duty suddenly.

The control room itself has four main functions:
• attack – the submarine fire control system takes up the first half of the control room
• ship control – the OOW (officer of the watch) panel, diving panel, main and auxiliary blowing (or ballast control) panels and the levers to raise and lower the various masts are situated along the port side
• steering and navigation – evaluation and navigation systems take up the starboard half of the control room
• sonar – has its own room on the starboard side forward of the control room.

anti-clockwise from top left

Coxswain's quarters

Tea-making facilities for the steward

The officers' wardroom

The control room

The control room is the hub of the submarine, the centre of its universe. Lights and gauges showed the states of major hull openings, vents and valves. Diving and surfacing was controlled from here. A submarine's weight at sea continually changes as fuel, stores and weapons are used and as sea density alters. So a constant watch was kept on depth and angle, which could be trimmed (balanced) by transferring water between tanks and adjusting seawater ballast. During action stations, 22 men would be at work in the control room.

At the submarine fire control system (SFCS) the bearing, range, course and speed of targets were calculated and torpedoes and missiles were fired.

Sonar (sound navigation and ranging) provides the submarine with ears to listen for enemy shipping and other submarines.

On picking up a sound the computer in the submarine's sonar fixed the exact direction of the target and sent the information to the submarine fire control system computer for target motion analysis (TMA). This computed the range, course and speed of the target.

The entrance to the conning tower is located in the control room. An 8.5-metre climb leads to the bridge deck located at the top of the fin. Strict procedures were followed in entering or leaving the conning tower after the deaths in 1987 of two sailors on HMAS *Otama* who were still in the conning tower when the boat dived. Sailors' names are entered on the board prior to going to the bridge and removed when they have returned, so no-one is left behind.

clockwise from top left

Fire control system

Sonar operators on board *Onslow*

Diving panel

Evaluation and navigation control

Onslow has a kitchen capable of cooking four meals a day for 64 men over a period of several weeks

Onslow at a glance

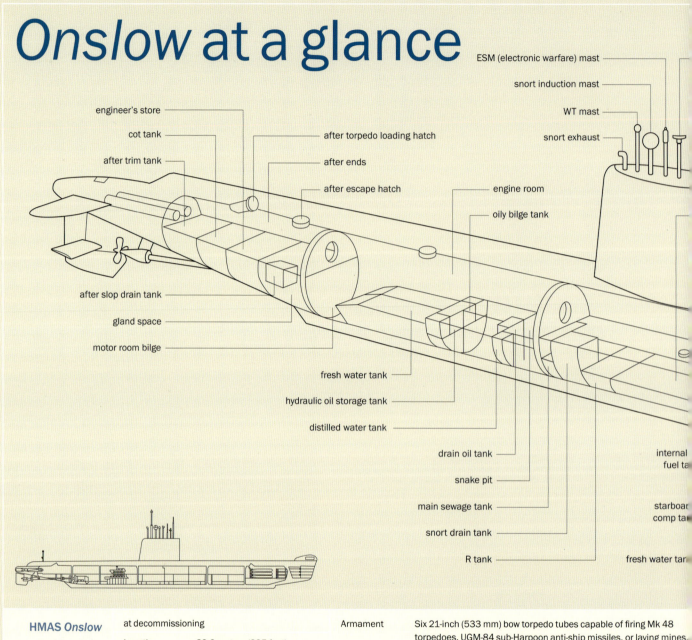

engineer's store
cot tank
after trim tank
after torpedo loading hatch
after ends
after escape hatch
after slop drain tank
gland space
motor room bilge
fresh water tank
hydraulic oil storage tank
distilled water tank

ESM (electronic warfare) mast
snort induction mast
WT mast
snort exhaust
engine room
oily bilge tank
drain oil tank
snake pit
main sewage tank
snort drain tank
R tank

internal fuel ta
starboar comp ta
fresh water tar

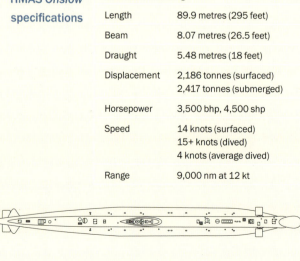

HMAS *Onslow* specifications	at decommissioning	
Length	89.9 metres (295 feet)	
Beam	8.07 metres (26.5 feet)	
Draught	5.48 metres (18 feet)	
Displacement	2,186 tonnes (surfaced) 2,417 tonnes (submerged)	
Horsepower	3,500 bhp, 4,500 shp	
Speed	14 knots (surfaced) 15+ knots (dived) 4 knots (average dived)	
Range	9,000 nm at 12 kt	

Armament	Six 21-inch (533 mm) bow torpedo tubes capable of firing Mk 48 torpedoes, UGM-84 sub-Harpoon anti-ship missiles, or laying mines. Total of 22 missiles and torpedoes.
Machinery	Twin shafts driven by two English Electric main propulsion motors, powered by 440V batteries charged by two 16-cylinder Admiralty Standard Range supercharged diesel generators
Complement	8 officers, 60 sailors, up to 16 trainees*
Builder	Scotts' Shipbuilding & Engineering Co Ltd, Greenock, Scotland
Laid down	26 May 1967
Launched	3 December 1968 by Her Royal Highness Princess Alexandra, the Honourable Mrs Angus Ogilvy
Commissioned	22 December 1969
Arrived	at HMAS *Platypus*, 4 July 1970
Pennant number	60

*When built, the complement was designated as 64

Facts and figures

Oberons have:
- two generators with the capacity to power a town of 30,000
- the equivalent of two road tankers of lube oil
- the equivalent of 94,000 car batteries
- a supermarket of food
- 30 tonnes of fresh water
- 10 tonnes of distilled water
- the air conditioning plant of a small city building
- seven masts taller than telegraph poles
- the equivalent of 12 road tankers of diesel fuel

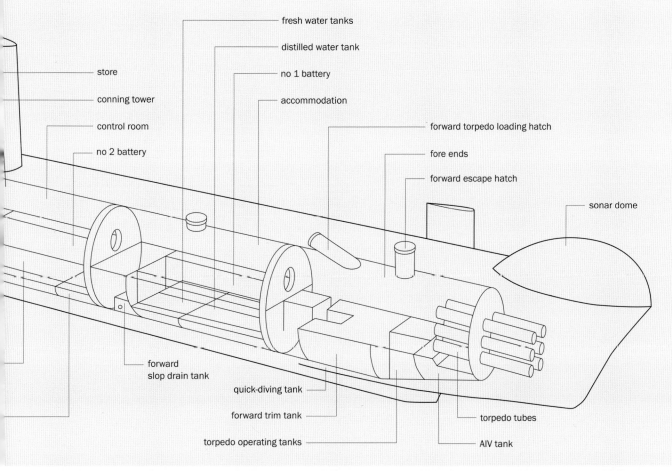

fresh water tanks

distilled water tank

no 1 battery

accommodation

store

conning tower

control room

no 2 battery

forward torpedo loading hatch

fore ends

forward escape hatch

sonar dome

forward slop drain tank

quick-diving tank

forward trim tank

torpedo operating tanks

torpedo tubes

AIV tank

R Sean 'Paddy'
wyer, last
manding Officer
MAS *Onslow*

Serving Commanding Officers				
LCDR C A B Nixon-Eckersall RN	10 Feb 1969 – 16 June 1971	Decommissioning period	30 Sept 1982 – 16 April 1984
LCDR D P B Ryan RN	16 June 1971 – 31 Dec 1971	LCDR D W Mole RAN	16 April 1984 – 28 Oct 1985
LCDR I D G MacDougall RAN	31 Dec 1971 – 7 Aug 1973	LCDR D M Forbes RN	28 Oct 1985 – 6 Mar 1987
LCDR R R H Fayle RAN	7 Aug 1973 – 29 Nov 1974	LCDR B L Beveridge RAN	6 Mar 1987 – 14 Mar 1988
LCDR P W Horobin RAN	29 Nov 1974 – 10 Jan 1975	LCDR J N Edgell RN	14 Mar 1988 – 15 Dec 1989
LEUT A S L Smith RN	10 Jan 1975 – 1 Feb 1977	LCDR B G Anderson RAN	15 Dec 1989 – 4 Mar 1990
Decommissioning period	14 Jan 1975 – 13 Dec 1976	LEUT I R Bray RAN	4 Mar 1990 – 5 May 1990
LCDR A S L Smith RN	1 Feb 1977 – 26 May 1978	Decommissioning period	5 May 1990 – 13 Dec 1992
LCDR G D Anderson RAN	26 May 1978 – 5 July 1979	LCDR I R Bray RAN	13 Dec 1992 – 15 Nov 1994
LCDR K F Pitt RAN	5 July 1979 – 15 Aug 1980	LCDR M A Sander RAN	15 Nov 1994 – 1 April 1996
LCDR J A C Miers RN	15 Aug 1980 – 27 May 1981	LCDR S G Dalton RAN	1 April 1996 – 7 Oct 1997
LCDR A B Parkin RAN	27 May 1981 – 30 Sept 1982	LCDR S P M O'Dwyer RAN	7 Oct 1997 – 29 Mar 1999

The control room

' YOU'RE SUPPOSED TO LET THE HANDLES GO WHEN YOU LOWER THE PERISCOPE !! '

One-man control
– the helm

There are two periscopes in the control room and these are the eyes of the submarine. They were used as night and day lookout when the submarine was at periscope depth, as well as for visual attack. The periscope with the seat is the search periscope. Photographs could be taken through this periscope and in this way harbours, coastlines, oil rigs and surface vessels could be surveyed and recorded. The attack periscope is fitted with a sextant for taking sights of celestial bodies such as stars, for position finding.

The attack periscope is much smaller in diameter at its upper end. This made it more difficult to see, produced less wake, and presented a smaller radar target. It is monocular and magnifies 1½ times or 6 times as required. It was generally only used by the commanding officer.

Onslow originally fixed its position by using the periscope sextant for traditional celestial navigation, the earlier satellite navigation (Satnav) system, and Omega navigation which

was a global, very low-frequency ground-wave navigation system primarily intended for submarines. In a modernisation refit, *Onslow* progressed to the satellite-network global positioning system (GPS) which superseded the earlier systems.

The contact evaluation plot was used for displaying all sensor information when a submarine dived and was also used to record internal states such as changes of routines, changes of course, speed or depth.

The boat was dived and surfaced from the control room by a sailor at the helm – called the one-man control (OMC). 'Diving stations' was piped through the boat 30 minutes before diving and all valves and systems were checked by the XO (executive officer) and reported to the CO (commanding officer) that the boat was opened up for diving. The klaxon was sounded twice to indicate diving was commencing.

Behind the OMC is the officer of the watch panel. This contains the engine telegraphs to the motor room, the start and stop indicators for the diesel engines, and the ballast pump indicator for pumping and flooding water into the internal compensating tanks via the main line.

The closest cabin to the control room is the captain's cabin – the only private space on board. It has hanging space, a small desk and foldaway washbasin as well as a gyro compass, depth gauge, barometer, a safe, and morphine in case of serious accident. Although he had his own space, the commanding officer frequently ate with the other officers in the wardroom. Unlike surface ships, the distance between officers and sailors was not great. It couldn't be, in such a necessarily cramped space where everyone relies on the other to do his job properly – or disaster could strike.

Submariners call the toilets 'traps' and there is a hierarchy to the four on board. The first trap is for urinating only, hence no seat. (Women of the RAN never went to sea on Oberon submarines.) Traps two and three are for sailors; the fourth trap (used by up to 10 men) is for the officers and also has a shower.

The communications centre, where the WT (wireless telegraph) officer worked, is past the captain's cabin. Satellite, low frequency, high frequency and sending and receiving messages were all conducted from here.

Under the passageway is the cool room for food storage.

The senior sailors' washroom was used by 12 to 14 senior ratings and doubled as the photographic darkroom. The junior sailors' washroom was used by up to 50 sailors.

Underneath here (and stretching back to the control room) is the AMS – auxiliary machinery space – which contained the low-pressure blower, hydraulic pumps, fire fighting equipment and air conditioning units. The radar office was also located at this lower level for the electrical warfare officer, and the main safe, where top-secret documents and the boat's cash reserves were kept, was in the radar room. In *Onslow*, the gyro room and what used to be the vegetable locker was turned into an office for the computer terminals and storage for photocopying and stationery supplies.

clockwise from below

Radio room

Officers' heads and washroom

The periscopes

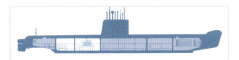

4

The engine room

Onslow was built on the River Clyde in Scotland, so it's no surprise that the boat's two diesel engines are nicknamed Bonnie and Clyde. The engine room was an uncomfortable place to work generating up to 148 decibels of noise and air temperature of around 45°C.

Instant power was provided by the electric motors driven by batteries. The batteries were charged by the 16-cylinder, supercharged diesel engines which functioned as giant generator sets and could recharge the batteries in as little as 25 minutes twice a day. Diesels need air to operate so they can only work when the submarine is on the surface or running at periscope depth (17 metres [56 feet] depth of keel) using the snort mast to provide air. Engine operating gauges gave the engineers information on oil pressures, temperatures, fuel levels and fuel consumption.

Conventional submarines must surface or snort regularly to recharge batteries and release poisonous exhaust fumes. By contrast, nuclear powered submarines can remain submerged almost indefinitely since the nuclear reactor neither requires oxygen nor produces exhaust.

In March 1981 a defect in Bonnie required her to be shut down; but the engine continued running and problems occurred. Within 20 seconds the atmosphere had been sucked from the submarine and CO_2 poisoning was occurring. All but one man made it to safety. Able Seaman Christopher Passlow was found dead outside the senior sailors' washroom. In his memory, the Passlow Shield is awarded annually to the top submarine trainee sailor.

Aft of the engine room is the motor room which contains the main propulsion system controls (speed, stop, start, etc), and from here the batteries and electrical output were monitored.

Underneath here (and stretching back to the engine room) is the lower motor room where the main motors that drive the two propellers are located.

clockwise from below

Builder's plate

The engine room

The motor room

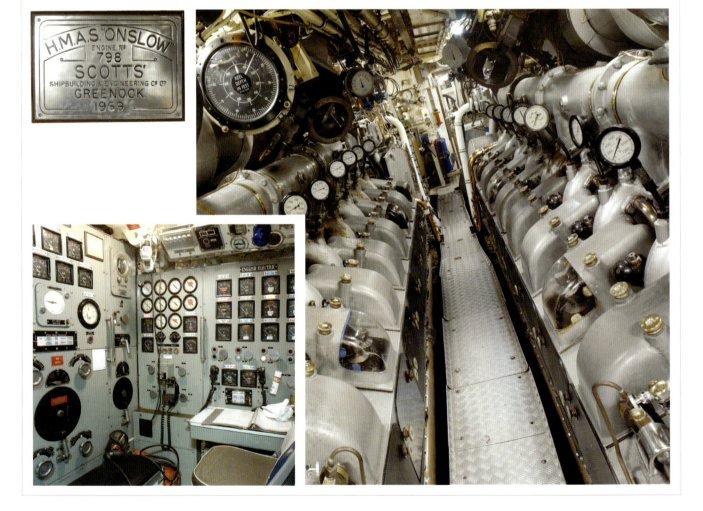

The after ends

This compartment houses the stoker's mess (engineers and motor room sailors), the aft escape tower, the third oxygen generator and second CO_2 absorption unit.

The hydraulic rams for the steering gear and after hydroplanes are also here and beneath the deck are the engineer's store and the stern glands where the propeller shafts exit the hull.

When built, *Onslow* had eight torpedo tubes – six forward and two aft. The after tubes discharged Mk 20 anti-submarine torpedoes but after *Onslow*'s major refit in 1982–84 use of the Mk 20s was discontinued and the after tubes were sealed off. The submariners – never willing to let any space go to waste – found a new use for the tubes. They could each hold 45 dozen cans of beer and being under the water all the time, kept them nice and cold! When the tubes themselves were removed, more space was available for the after mess.

The aft torpedo loading hatch is now the visitor exit point.

After ends accommodation

On the casing

From alongside you can see the exterior of *Onslow* quite well. The main feature is of course the fin (called a sail by the United States Navy). The fin contains the conning tower, the bridge and the seven masts. Reading from fore to aft the masts are: attack periscope, search periscope, radar, ESM (electronic warfare), induction (snort), communication and exhaust.

The dome at the nose covers the main attack sonar array (CSU3-41).

The sonar dome

' BY MY CALCULATIONS, WE MUST BE THROUGH THE ICE BY NOW...'

Onslow has always had the latest in armament. Prior to the sub-Harpoon missiles and Mk 48 torpedoes, *Onslow* had Mk 8 and then Mk 23 torpedoes as primary armament. Two of each are on display in the fore ends.

weapons

UGM-84 sub-Harpoon missile

The UGM-84 Harpoon is a medium-range, all-weather, over-the-horizon, anti-ship missile developed in the USA and able to be fired from surface, sub-surface or air platforms. The encapsulated sub-Harpoon is designed for launch from a submarine. HMAS *Onslow* was the first conventional submarine in the world to be armed with the sub-Harpoon missile.

The capsule is fired by compressed air through the torpedo tube and once clear both the fin and planes deploy. When the broach sensor recognises the capsule is near the surface, it initiates the sequence in which both the nose cap and the aft body are jettisoned and the booster ignited. The booster burns for three seconds and takes the missile out of the water to near cruise velocity at which point the turbojet operates and a turn to the ordered course can begin. It can turn 180° either side of its launch heading then commence descent to cruise altitude. Speed in excess of 500 knots is reached.

At a preset point in its flight the radar seeker is activated into its search and fire control mode. At 'lock on' the missile will descend to a lower altitude dependent on the state of the sea. It can climb to 500 metres (1,700 ft) to avoid detection and give a better angle into the target. Detonation is delayed until the warhead's steel case has penetrated several metres into the target, thus enhancing the probability of secondary explosions. If it fails to acquire the target it will self-destruct.

The missile mounts a 221.6-kg semi-armour-piercing warhead with 100 kg of explosive set off by a contact delay fuse. It carries 45 kg of kerosene-based fuel in the tank in the propulsion compartment.

Length with booster	4.63 metres
Diameter	0.34 metres
Wing span	0.83 metres
Weight with booster	681.9 kg

Mk 48 torpedo

This submarine-launched anti-ship and anti-submarine torpedo, developed in the USA, has been in production since 1972. Wire links it electronically to the operator so it can be continually guided to the target through a two-way communications link with the submarine's fire control system. In active mode it sends sonar pulses out into the water and listens for target echoes, but it can operate in passive mode when it just listens. Detonation can be by contact or 'influence' – where the torpedo detects the ship's movement nearby. The nose section contains the transmitter, receiver and a homing control which processes the signals received and directs the torpedo during homing. Behind the nose section there is either an explosive-loaded warhead (if it's a warshot) or a special data recorder if it is an exercise torpedo used for practice firing. The torpedo is fired from the torpedo tube using compressed air. It can operate at depths of up to 900 metres.

Diameter	533 cm (21")
Length	7.79 m
Weight	1,545 kg
Range	38 km (20.5 nm) active 50 km (27 nm) passive
Speed	102 km/h (55 knots) active 74 km/h (40 knots) passive

Mk 8 torpedo	Designed during World War II, this diesel-driven torpedo was used against surface targets only and was usually fired as one of a salvo of four. The 21" (533 mm) diameter torpedo carried	362 kg of high explosive with a speed of 80 km/h (43 knots) and a range of 4.8 kilometres (2.6 nautical miles).
Mk 23 torpedo	The Mk 23 was a wire-guided, passive homing torpedo designed for anti-submarine use. It was guided in azimuth and depth by the firing submarine until it made a firm acoustic contact with the target. When this occurred the torpedo	was released into autohome to become a passive homing weapon. The warhead carried 90 kg of torpex (torpedo explosive) and was exploded by impact with the target. It was removed from the RAN inventory in 1978.
Mk 5 mine	The Mk 5 was a ground mine for use against surface ships and submarines. They were laid by being launched from the torpedo tubes and were detonated by the movement or proximity of a ship	passing above. The mine carries about 453 kg of high explosive which, depending on the depth, can break the back of a submarine or medium-sized surface ship.

Onslow's torpedo compartment – the fore ends

There are two escape towers on board HMAS *Onslow*. One is located in the fore ends, the other in the after ends. In all escape scenarios the compartment is isolated by shutting the connecting bulkhead door between this compartment and the next.

escape

The three main ways to escape from *Onslow*

1
DSRV – deep sea rescue vehicle

The fore ends can accommodate up to 83 escaping submariners from the disabled submarine. While waiting for the DSRV, the submariners can breathe via the built-in breathing system (BIBS). The DSRV connects with the hatch on the casing and the men can move directly from the disabled submarine into the DSRV.

2
Single man escape

Individual escape suits are located throughout this compartment. Each man will don his SEIE suit (submarine escape immersion equipment) and climb into the escape tower; then the tower is flooded. When the tower is filled with water the top hatch is opened and the submariner automatically shoots to the surface – at a rate of about 30 metres in six seconds. In theory, escape in the SEIE suit can be made from a depth of about 200 metres. The suit provides thermal insulation while floating on the surface and the vivid fluorescent orange colour helps locate the survivor.

3
Compartment or rush escape

This is the most dangerous escape method. Each man is connected to the built-in breathing system; the whole of the compartment is flooded and the upper hatch in the escape tower is opened. High pressure air (HP air) keeps the water level at chest-to-chin height. Each man will take a huge gulp of air, duck into the escape tower and shoot up to the surface – breathing out all the way in an effort to stop his lungs exploding. Depending on the depth, an escaping submariner is likely to reach the surface suffering some kind of air barotraumas (an air embolism).

Escape Training

All submariners do their escape training and refresher courses at the submarine escape training facility (SETF) at HMAS *Stirling* in Western Australia. Prior to its opening in 1989, all submariners were sent to England to do their training at HMS *Dolphin* at Gosport near Portsmouth.

The primary aim of SETF is to train submariners to escape safely from a submarine that has had an accident and is lying on the seabed. The four-day course is part of every submariner's initial training to earn their 'dolphins' – the badge they are presented with when they pass all aspects of submarine training.

While they remain with the submarine squadron, all submariners must undertake a two-day refresher course every three years.

'...THAT'S THE SARDINE'S REVENGE – 60 MEN PACKED IN OIL IN A TIN CAN ...'

Looking up into the escape tower

Five Oberons at HMAS *Platypus*

1 How long can an Oberon stay submerged?

Under favourable conditions, three days. They come close to the surface (periscope depth of 17 metres [56 feet]) and raise the snort mast to let fresh air in.

commonly asked questions

2 Why is a submarine called a boat?

The first submarines were small and called boats, and the word has remained in submarine terminology to this day. In 1578 Englishman William Bourne published details of 'a boate that may go under the water'. The American David Bushnell is credited with the first operable submarine, the tiny *Turtle* powered by the muscle power of a single operator during the American Civil War. It was intended to attach explosive mines to the hull of an anchored ship. In the 19th century the term torpedo was used for bombs and mines sometimes mounted on spars at or below the waterline by craft called torpedo boats. Robert Whitehead developed the self-propelled underwater torpedo in the 1860s and 1870s. By 1900 practicable submersible torpedo-boats had been designed and trialled. The Germans called their submarines *Unterseeboot* (undersea boat) – U-boat for short.

3 What is the origin of the submarine snorkel?

The German Type VIIC submarine was a warhorse of World War II. When the Germans occupied the main Royal Netherlands Navy base at Den Helder in May 1940, they found two almost-complete submarines fitted with a device invented by the Dutch in 1927. It was called the snuiver (sniffer) and allowed bad air to be exhausted from the submarine, and fresh air to be taken in. It wasn't until 1943 and 1944 that anything was done with this invention. The Germans called it the schnorkel (snorter) and built it into their U-boats, allowing them to remain submerged for longer periods as the snorting was undertaken at periscope depth.

4 What did the men do for relaxation?

Sleep. Read. Write. Talk. Play card games. Watch videos and play video games. The TVs and videos you see in *Onslow* are not standard navy issue. Each mess bought its own sound and TV systems. At the captain's discretion, the men were allowed to relax on the casing when at sea. Activities during these times included fishing, swimming, sunbaking and barbequing!

5 Why is *Onslow* painted black and not grey like *Vampire*?

To reduce the possibility of visual detection. Most submarines move in and out of harbour at night, which helps them hide. At periscope depth the black submarine is difficult to see by air or satellite. World War II submarines were mottled grey (camouflaged) because they spent the majority of their time on the surface and this pattern is less visible to a surface ship. *Onslow*'s masts are painted in a camouflage pattern as they are occasionally above the surface.

How deep can an Oberon class submarine dive?

Officially said to be 183 metres (600 ft).
The true depth is classified information,
but up to 300 metres (1,000 ft) may
be possible according to some sources.

How long is the average deployment?

70 days

What is a 'dolphin' badge?

This is the badge awarded to those who pass all
their training and become submariners in the
RAN. The design dates back to 1965 when the
Naval Board recognised the need for submariners
to have their own distinctive insignia. It was
inspired by the dolphins on similar badges
of navies around the world, and the crown
comes from the pre-decimal florin coin. The
badge was produced by Stokes of Melbourne,
well-established manufacturers of service badges
and buttons. The first RAN dolphin badges were
issued in 1966.

How silent is an Oberon?

They have very little acoustic and electronic
noise. Machinery and equipment are insulated
from the hull. They blend well into the background
rumblings and mumblings of the sea.

What do all the initials mean?

You'll have been struck by all the acronyms the
submariners use as shorthand for technical
phrases that are a mouthful – SWUP, SFCS, BIBS,
OCCABA and more.
Here are some more from the submarine world:
SSN – nuclear-powered attack submarine
SSB – ballistic missile submarine
SSBN – nuclear-powered ballistic missile
submarine
SSK – hunter killer submarine
SSG – guided missile submarine

How thick is the pressure hull?

1" (25.4 mm) thick except at the fore ends
which is $1\frac{1}{8}$" (29 mm) and the after ends which
is $1\frac{5}{8}$" (47.6 mm).

Did women ever serve in *Onslow*?

No, but there are now female
submariners serving in the Collins class
submarines that superseded the Oberons.

Did they drink alcohol on board?

No alcohol is consumed by the officers at sea
although, at the captain's discretion, the sailors
may be issued with two cans of beer per day.

What do they wear?

When leaving or entering port, everyone will be
in their summer or winter regulation uniform.
Once at sea they change into black overalls.

15 Could they smoke on board *Onslow*?

Only at the captain's discretion and then only when the engines were running and only at bulkhead 77 (aft). Only six men could smoke at a time.

16 How often do they wash?

At sea, they shower once a week although daily 'bird baths' are taken.

17 Do submariners get extra pay or leave?

They get extra pay but not extra leave. Navy personnel are given five weeks leave per year; this increases to seven if they serve at sea – whether it be in a ship or a submarine.

18 What is 'hot bunking'?

There are often not enough racks (bunks) for each submariner to have as his own and so they share. One will be on duty when the other is off and then they swap – so the bunk is still warm from the previous person. They do however have their own sleeping bags. HMAS *Onslow* had enough bunks for its regular complement of 68.

19 Are any other Oberon class submarines preserved?

HMAS *Ovens* has been transferred to the Western Australian Maritime Museum. Part of HMAS *Otway* is displayed in the NSW country town of Holbrook. HMAS *Oxley* was scrapped but the fin is proudly displayed at HMAS *Stirling* in Western Australia. HMAS *Orion* has been awaiting scrapping since 1996. HMAS *Otama* is in Hastings, Victoria, undergoing preparation to become the centrepiece of a naval memorial park. HMS *Onyx* is on display at Birkenhead, England as part of the Historic Warships Preservation Trust. HMS *Ocelot* is on display at Chatham Historic Dockyard in England.

20 Is there a height restriction to becoming a submariner?

No. You soon learn to duck and weave and to avoid bumping your head if you are tall!

21 How are fresh water and air supplied?

Water was carried in tanks and could also be distilled on board. Under normal conditions an Oberon would snort twice a day for an hour each time, to run the diesel generators to keep the batteries topped-up, and to provide fresh air. In an emergency, all non-essential services were cut and non-essential personnel told to sleep in order to cut down on CO_2 emissions and oxygen consumption.

Emergency oxygen generator

How does a submarine dive?

A submarine has an inner hull (called the pressure hull) and an outer hull. Between the two are ballast tanks.

When the submarine is surfaced, the main ballast tanks are full of air, providing the positive buoyancy necessary to keep the submarine afloat. At the top of each ballast tank is a vent that is shut while the submarine is surfaced. At the bottom centreline of each ballast tank is a flood port that is always open to the sea. As long as each vent (at the top) is shut, the pressure from the air in the tanks prevents the water from filling up the tanks.

The submarine dives when the vents are opened by sailors at the diving panel in the control room. The trapped air is released (vented) and the seawater enters through the flood ports. As the main ballast tanks fill with water, the submarine becomes heavier than the water it displaces and it submerges. The fore and aft diving planes angle the submarine downward so that it can dive faster. The submarine can float underwater by adjusting the ballast until it weighs the same amount as the volume of water it displaces. This is called neutral buoyancy.

To surface, the vents for the main ballast tanks are shut and compressed (high pressure) air is forced back into the tanks. As the air expands, it forces the seawater back out through the flood ports, causing the submarine to weigh less than the water it displaces. Positive buoyancy has been reinstated. This forces the submarine to rise to the surface. To ensure the bow of the submarine rises first, water is blown out of the forward ballast tanks. The diving planes also angle the submarine upward so that it rises quickly.

YOU DIVED THE BOAT **HOW** !!

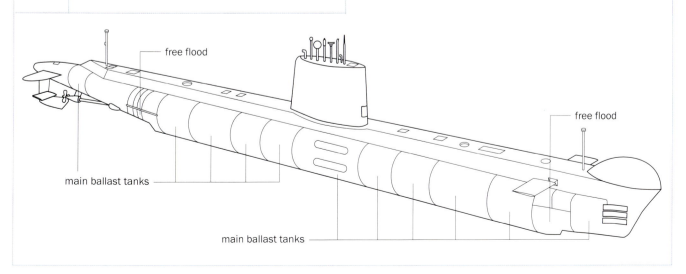

picture credits

All colour photography by Andrew Frolows, Australian National Maritime Museum, unless otherwise credited

Royal Australian Navy (RAN) photographs reproduced courtesy of the Navy

Cartoons reproduced courtesy of the artist Sandy 'Hi Rob' Freeleagus

Front cover
RAN

Page 3
RAN

Page 5
RAN

Page 6
USS *Carl Vinson* photograph by RAN
left: David Horne
right: John Hodges

Page 7
right and bottom left: RAN

Page 12
right: RAN

Page 23
bottom: RAN

Page 28
ANMM collection

back cover

Onslow's badge and motto *Festina Lente* (Hasten Slowly)

below

Onslow cap tally

HMAS *Onslow*: cold war warrior

© Australian National Maritime Museum Sydney 2005
Reprinted 2013

Author Lindsey Shaw, senior curator, maritime technology, exploration and navy, ANMM

Editor Jeffrey Mellefont, ANMM

Designer Jeremy Austen, Austen Kaupe

Printed in Australia by Pegasus Print Group, NSW

Technical advice kindly provided by John C Jeremy and John M Hodges. Any errors remaining are solely the responsibility of the publisher.

ISBN-13 978-0-9751428-4-4

National Library of Australia Cataloguing-in-Publication data

Shaw, Lindsey, 1957 –
HMAS *Onslow*: cold war warrior

1. *Onslow* (submarine). 2. Submarines (ships) – Australia.
3. Submarine warfare.
I. Australian National Maritime Museum II. Title

359.938320994

This work is copyright. Apart from any use permitted under the *Copyright Act 1968*, no part may be reproduced by any process without prior permission from the Australian National Maritime Museum.

Australian National Maritime Museum
2 Murray Street Sydney NSW 2000 Australia
telephone: +61 2 9298 3777 facsimile: +61 2 9298 3670
www.anmm.gov.au

Ro

A Sketchmap History
of the Caribbean

MACMILLAN
CARIBBEAN

Macmillan Education
Between Towns Road, Oxford OX4 3PP
A division of Macmillan Publishers Limited
Companies and representatives throughout the world

ISBN–13: 978-0-333-53623-0
ISBN–10: 0-333-53623-1

Text © Robert Greenwood 1991
Design and illustration © Macmillan Publishers Limited 1991

First published 1991

Printed in Thailand

2010 2009 2008 2007 2006
18 17 16 15 14 13 12 11 10

Contents

Preface

This book attempts to cover the Caribbean Examination Council's History syllabus economically. It follows the thematic approach required by the syllabus but concentrates on the salient points of each theme only.

The approach to each topic has three parts: map, written passage, notes. Each part re-enforces the other, but each part can be studied separately as in revision. The map focuses the student's attention on the topic (where a map is inappropriate a chart or table is used). The written passage follows the factual approach required by the syllabus and should give the student enough information to assist in essay-writing. The notes extract the main points of the topic for the student.

The book will serve as a basic textbook for the syllabus but also as a revision aid because it will refresh the student's memory of the topic at a glance. The notes especially are intended to give the student what he needs to know concisely. By referring from the note to the written passage which precedes it he can obtain the factual detail required. For a student who wishes to flick through the book for final revision, the maps, charts and tables can be used by themselves. However, the three parts used in conjunction are recommended if this book is to be of greatest use.

Robert Greenwood
Kamuzu Academy, Malawi

Theme 1: The Amerindians and the Europeans

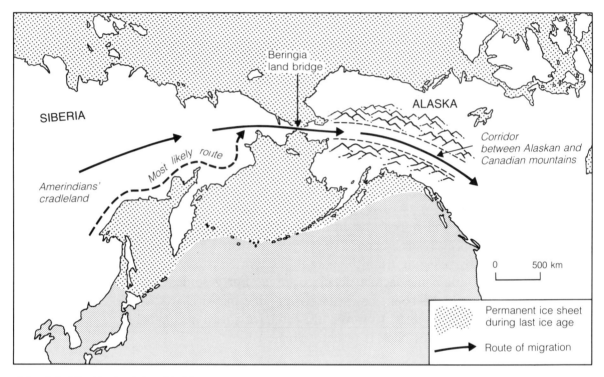

Map 1.1: The Beringia land bridge

Map 1.1: The Beringia land bridge

About twenty-five to twenty thousand years ago the world was in the grip of the last Ice Age. At this time mongoloid people from East-Central Asia began to migrate out of their cradleland north and eastwards towards the Bering Strait. They were following the herds of deer which were their livelihood. Their route was probably close to the east coast of the land mass of Asia. There are two explanations as to how they crossed into the continent of America:

a) Twenty-five thousand years ago the Plain of Siberia was connected to Alaska by an isthmus, i.e. the Bering Straits were above sea level – the Beringia land bridge.

b) The peak of the last Ice Age occurred at this time and the migrants crossed the Bering Straits on ice, i.e. an ice bridge.

'Mongoloid' is applied to these people because their cradleland was roughly where Mongolia is, an area on the western boundary of China and in Asiatic Russia south of Lake Baikal. Today 'mongoloid' is applied to the Eskimos and Amerindians are classified as a separate race on account of biological differences. However, Amerindians are more nearly homogeneous than the inhabitants of any other large land mass. If they entered the continent as recently as twenty thousand years ago there has not been enough time for differences to have evolved. North-eastern America was settled about the same time as the extreme south of South America, about ten thousand years ago.

Notes

1 Amerindians are mongoloid people, possibly descended from the Ainu.
2 Their ancestors were nomadic hunters from East-Central Asia.
3 They migrated into America about twenty-five to twenty thousand years ago.
4 Siberia and Alaska were joined either by the Beringia land bridge or by an ice bridge over the Bering Straits.

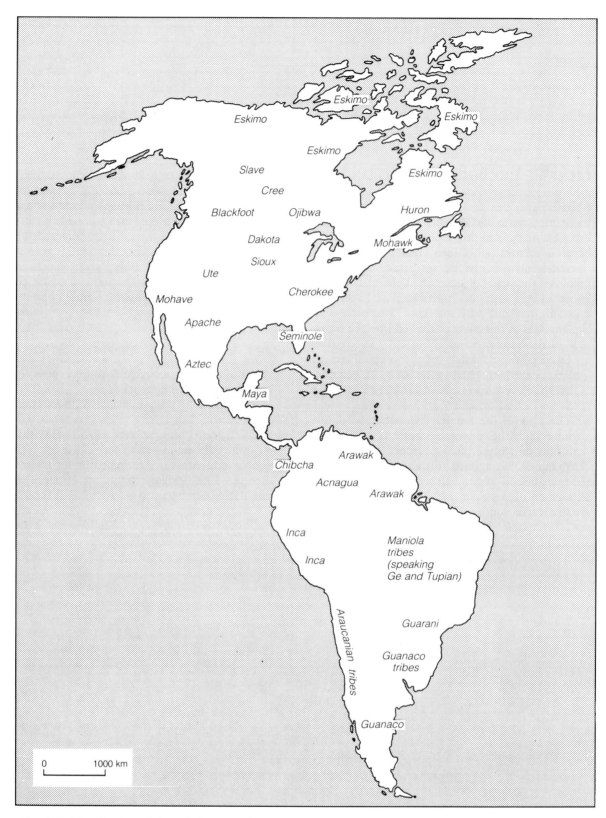

Map 1.2: Distribution of Amerindian peoples

Map 1.2: Distribution of Amerindian peoples

Amerindians immigrated into America twenty-five to twenty thousand years ago in successive waves. By ten thousand years ago some had settled as far south as Cape Horn. North-eastern America, a much shorter migration, was only reached about the same time because the ice cap took a long time to recede.

By the time of the Spanish Conquest most Amerindians were still nomadic. Eskimos and North American Indians were almost all nomadic. In Central and South America were the notable exceptions, the Aztecs, Mayas and Incas. From their centre in Cuzco in modern Peru the Incas expanded north and south to form an empire where their people long ago adopted a sedentary style of living based on the cultivation of maize (probably about two thousand five hundred years ago). The classical period of Inca civilization can be taken as AD 0–1000.

Population figures for Amerindians at the Spanish Conquest differ widely from a low figure of 5 million to a high figure of 100 million. So really we have no idea. Some historians settle on a figure of 30 million for North and South America combined, and agree that the Incas were the single most numerous people with a population in the whole empire at its height of about 6 million.

A simple illustration of how homogeneous Amerindians are is through appearance and physical characteristics; brown-skinned, straight black hair, absence of body hair, narrow, almost slit eyes, high cheek-bones and common blood groups.

Notes

1 Mongoloid characteristics are shown by brown skin, straight, black hair, absence of body hair, slightly slit eyes, high cheek-bones.
2 Not enough time has elapsed for pronounced local differences to appear.
3 By ten thousand years ago North and South America were widely inhabited.
4 It is impossible to give an accurate figure for the Amerindian population of the Americas at the time of the Spanish Conquest.
5 With the exceptions of the Aztecs of Mexico, the Maya of Yucatan and the Incas of Peru, Amerindians were nomadic hunters and fishermen at the time of the Spanish Conquest.
6 The Incas were the largest single group and perhaps their total population in the early sixteenth century was 6 million.

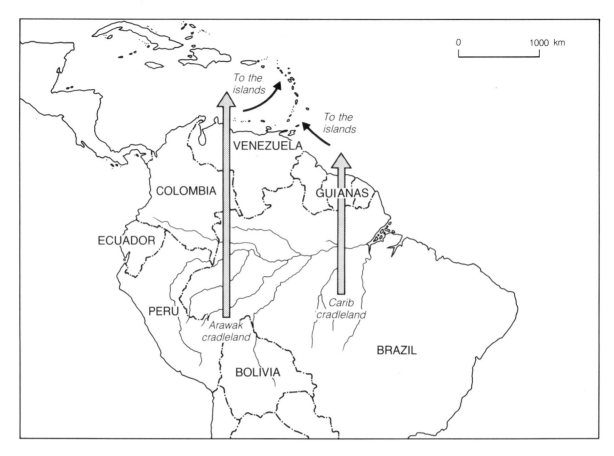

Map 1.3: Arawak and Carib migrations into the West Indies

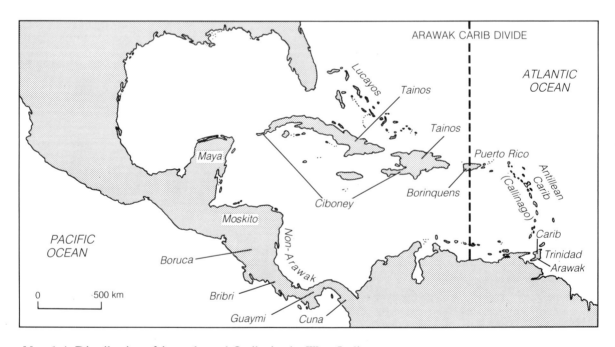

Map 1.4: Distribution of Arawaks and Caribs in the West Indies

Maps 1.3 and 1.4: Arawak and Carib migrations into the West Indies and their distribution in the West Indies

Map 1.3 shows the ancestors of the West Indian Arawaks and Caribs coming from the tropical rain forests of South America, the cradleland of the Arawaks being to the west of that of the Caribs. The evidence for these conclusions from language and mythology is strong, for example the belief that the sun and moon emerged from a cave is a very strong mythological link between the areas.

The South American Arawaks inhabited the northern and western Amazon Basin as far as the foothills of the Andes (the Campa Arawaks). They were sedentary farmers but were not influenced by the Incas. They also hunted and fished. Our map shows them migrating northwards to the coastal region of Venezuela where they embarked for the West Indies. Their migration may have been more to the north-east and their embarkation point the coastal region of the Guianas. In the West Indies they are known as the Antillean Arawaks, or Taino (Tainos). They cultivated maize and manioc around small villages (up to 3000) and hunted and fished. They belonged to the Arawakan language group, the same linguistic group as the South American Arawaks.

The Antillean Arawaks reached the West Indies before the Caribs, but being peaceful were driven out of the islands as the Caribs arrived. Eventually the Arawaks occupied the Greater Antilles and the Caribs the Lesser Antilles with one or two exceptions, notably that of Puerto Rico and Trinidad which were divided between Arawaks and Caribs, and some Caribs who were found in Eastern Hispaniola.

The ancestors of the West Indian Caribs probably came from an area between the Amazon River and the Guianas. Again the link between Antillean Caribs and South American Caribs is language – the Cariban linguistic group. The South American Caribs had a typically tropical forest lifestyle, growing manioc and hunting with the blowpipe. The Antillean Caribs became sea-loving and expert fishermen and navigators. They were also much more warlike than the Arawaks. Cannibalism was common to both the Antillean Caribs and their South American ancestors.

It is simple to think of the northern coastal regions of South America as being the stepping-off point for both the Antillean groups, and that their migration through the West Indies was by 'island-hopping' from south-east to north-west.

Notes

1   'Arawak' and 'Carib' are language classifications from the linguistic groups 'Arawakan' and 'Cariban' respectively.
2   Mythology, especially in the case of the Arawaks, also provides links with the mainland ancestors.
3   Arawaks in both the islands and the mainland lived in villages of up to 3000 inhabitants, cultivating manioc and maize and hunting and fishing. They were peaceful. The word for Antillean Arawaks, 'Taino' means 'peace'.
4   Caribs hunted and fished with great skill. The South American Caribs cultivated a little and in the islands the Antillean Caribs cultivated even less. They were aggressive and cannibalism was practised in both areas. The word 'Carib', is derived from a word meaning 'cannibal'.
5   Arawaks and Caribs migrated north from the tropical forest regions of South America, the Arawaks migrating west of the Caribs. The northern coastal region of South America was the 'stepping-off' zone for the islands.
6   The Lesser Antilles were the first islands to be settled by both groups.
7   The Arawaks arrived in the islands first. As the Caribs arrived they drove out the Arawaks.
8   The Arawaks in the Bahamas, the Lucayos, were the least aggressive of all.
9   By the time of Columbus the Arawaks were occupying the Greater Antilles and the Caribs the Lesser Antilles.
10   Puerto Rico and Trinidad were divided between Arawaks and Caribs.
11   Puerto Rican Arawaks, 'Borinquens', were relatively warlike probably due to the proximity of Caribs in the eastern part of the island.

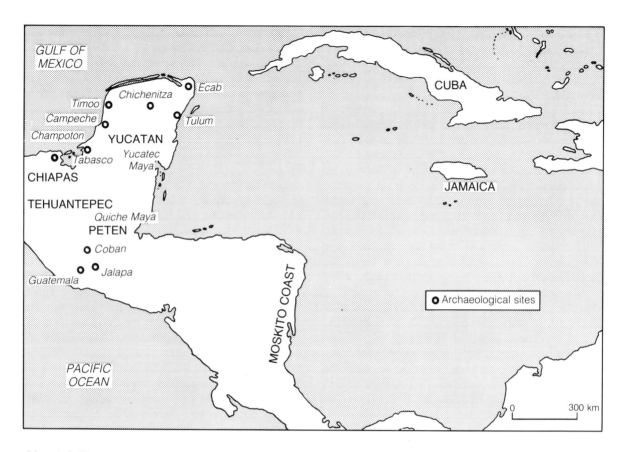

Map 1.5: The Maya empire

Map 1.5: The Maya empire

The Maya are a Central American people geographically and historically bound up with the Caribbean because of their civilization in the Yucatan Peninsula. However, they extended into non-Caribbean areas of Southern Mexico and Guatemala and their descendants still occupy these areas today. Their highly civilized life can be contrasted with the relatively primitive lives of the Arawaks and Caribs.

Mayan civilization flourished from the third to the sixteenth centuries AD. The first recorded date is AD 292. The Maya were conquered by the Spaniards in AD 1541. The classical period of Mayan civilization was from AD 300 to AD 900. After this latter date the Maya were invaded by the Itza in about AD 1000.

Temples like pyramids, tombs, stelae (columns), carvings, pottery and wall-paintings are the notable archaeological remains. The Maya built their dwellings in wood and thatch, but their public buildings, which were largely ceremonial, in limestone and cement with bone and jade for decoration. The cities were full of monuments with nobles' houses nearby and peasants' houses in forest clearings. These cities were located in Yucatan, Peten, Copan, Chiapas and the Usumacinta Valley. Probably the most famous site is Chichen-Itza, Yucatan, but Coban has famous temple sites.

Chichen-Itza was a complete city with a population of perhaps 10 000 in the classical period. Its public buildings were made of limestone blocks and were placed around pavemented squares. The pyramids had temples on top with carved altars. The stelae of notable architectural design had hieroglyphic inscriptions. Another notable achievement in this field was the use of the corbelled arch.

The Maya could read and write but only three of the books written in hieroglyphics remain and scholars as yet cannot read them. They were probably copied from the glyphs cut in the stelae of the ancient cities. The Maya excelled in mathematics and astronomy. Their numbers changed their value when they changed position and they also knew the use of zero, comparable achievements to ancient Babylonian mathematics. They used the solar year which was fairly accurate and which was divided into eighteen months of twenty days, giving a year of 360 days. There was also a sacred year of 260 days. The combinations of the sacred year and the solar year introduced complications too difficult to consider here.

Notes

1 Mayan civilization flourished in the Yucatan Peninsula between 0 and AD 1500, but the classical period was between AD 300 and 900.

2 It declined with the Itza invasion of AD 1000 and collapsed on the Spanish conquest of AD 1541.

3 Chichen-Itza is the most famous site as a complete city. Other sites are temple sites, and yet other sites have not been reclaimed from the bush or discovered at all.

4 The Mayans built their houses in wood and thatch and their public buildings in limestone blocks and cement.

5 They carved in jade, stone and bone.

6 Hieroglyphic instructions on stelae which have been copied into books tell us that the Maya could read and write, but as yet these hieroglyphics have not been deciphered by scholars.

7 Mayan mathematics and astronomy were brilliant. They moved numbers to the left and right to change their value and they used zero. They had an accurate solar calendar and their dating was accurate but complicated due to their use of different calendars.

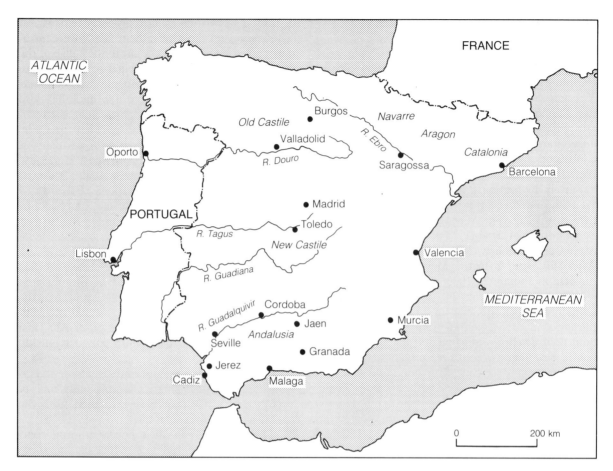

Map 1.6: Spain

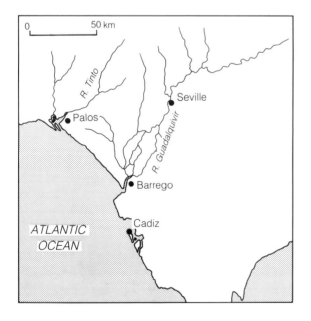

Map 1.7: The position of Seville, Cadiz and Palos

Map 1.6: Spain

The Moors conquered Spain in AD 711 and in medieval times it was a Moorish dominion. Under the Moors science, literature, philosophy, agriculture and architecture flourished. However, Christian kingdoms in the north were growing strong enough to challenge the Moors and by AD 1300 only Granada in Southern Spain remained under the Moors. The Christian kingdoms were disunited until the marriage of Ferdinand of Aragon and Isabella of Castile in 1479. Their combined strength drove out the Moors in 1492. The following century, 1500–1600, has been called 'the Golden Century of Spain', referring to the treasure reaped from the New World and Spain's domination of Europe. In fact Spain's dominant position in Europe and the world lasted for one hundred and fifty years. Charles I of Spain (Charles V of the Holy Roman Empire), 1516–1556, was the most powerful ruler in Europe. The decline of Spain did not begin until after the death of Philip II, Charles's son, in 1598.

Columbus's explorations were sponsored by Isabella of Castile and it was Castile which was active in the exploitation of the New World. The Crown demanded a monopoly of colonial trade. All trade had to pass through Seville and be in the hands of Castilians. Only Castilians were meant to settle in the New World. A government department, the *Casa de Contratacion* (House of Trade), was set up in Seville in 1503 to handle all the exports and imports of the colonies. However, Castile could not handle all the commerce of the New World and had to import goods to re-export to the Indies. The attempt and failure to maintain a Castilian monopoly probably encouraged other European countries to supply the Spanish Indies.

Notes

1 Spain had been dominated by the Moors until AD 1300.
2 Spain became a united country by the marriage of Ferdinand and Isabella in 1479 and the conquest of the Moors in Granada in 1492.
3 Spain was the leading power in Europe from 1500 to 1600. Its decline can be dated from the death of Philip II in 1598.
4 Colonial trade and settlement was the monopoly of Castile.

5 The *Casa de Contratacion* in Seville controlled all colonial shipping and trade.
6 The failure of Castile to carry out all its commitments with regard to the colonies made the entry of other European countries into the trade possible.

Map 1.7: The position of Seville, Cadiz and Palos

Seville in the Andalusia region was built on the estuary of the River Guadalquivir, but 110 km from the sea. Therefore its port facilities were limited, for instance large galleons could not reach Seville because of a bar across the river at San Lucar; ships could not turn round in the narrow waters at Seville, and only a few ships could dock at the same time. Columbus had to sail from Palos because of congestion at Seville. Below Seville the Guadalquivir ran through marshes which made navigation difficult. Therefore Seville was not a good choice as the port to handle all shipping to and from the New World.

However, it became the highest populated city in sixteenth century Spain with about 150 000 inhabitants by 1588. Of course, it was also the richest because of all the gold and silver imports from the New World and all the commerce brought there by the *Casa de Contratacion*. It became a banking centre for Europe. Officially Seville did not give way to Cadiz as Spain's chief port until 1717.

Notes

1 The Crown of Castile directed that Seville was to handle all shipping to and from the New World.
2 In 1503 the *Casa de Contratacion* was established in Seville to control all the imports and exports of the New World.
3 In the sixteenth and seventeenth centuries Seville benefited from her monopoly to become the largest and richest city in Spain.
4 Seville was not a good port and gave up its position as Spain's leading port to Cadiz in 1717.
5 Columbus was forced to use Palos in 1492 for his first voyage to the Indies.

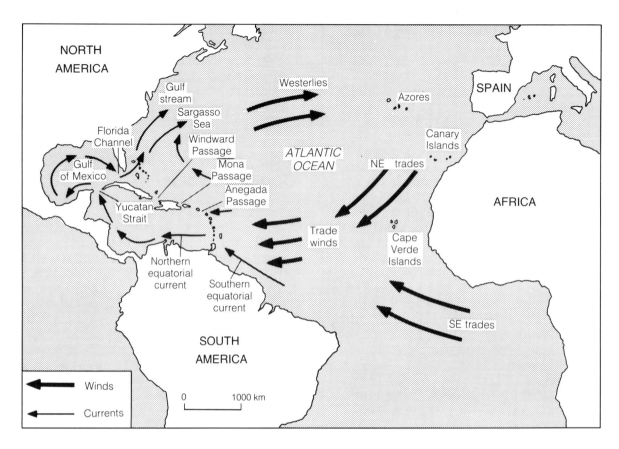

Map 1.8: Winds and currents of the Caribbean

Map 1.8: Winds and currents of the Caribbean

Winds

For about three hundred days of the year the trade winds blow into the Caribbean. They are caused by the high pressure on the Equator sucking in the cool air from the Arctic, but as the earth rotates from west to east, the air currents are turned towards the west where the earth has its greatest circumference, that is at the Equator. Their strength is consistent and never more than fourteen knots so they did not endanger sailing ships. The sailors knew them as 'fair weather winds' and they were ideal for ships sailing from the coasts of Africa into the Caribbean.

Further north westerlies blow from west to east across the Atlantic. These winds are less reliable and consistent than the trade winds, and when they are strong can cause much trouble to wooden sailing ships. However, they were the right winds to carry ships back to Europe from the New World.

Currents

Flowing into the south of the Caribbean are two currents which merge about the Lesser Antilles. These are the South Equatorial Current and the North Equatorial Current, although part of the North Equatorial Current does circle northwards east of the islands and turn towards Florida. These currents move at between five and eight knots and maintain this speed as they circle the Caribbean in a clockwise direction. They made east to west navigation in the days of sail relatively easy but west to east almost impossible except in the north Caribbean.

Flowing out of the Caribbean between Florida and Cuba is the Gulf Stream which follows the coast of North America until it turns eastwards and enters the North Atlantic Current. The Gulf Stream is a warm current moving at between five and eight knots and assists ships sailing back to northern Europe from the Caribbean.

Notes

1 Trade winds bringing fair weather blow into the Caribbean for eighty per cent of the year.
2 At under fourteen knots they never endangered sailing ships.
3 They are interrupted by storms and hurricanes. The hurricane season is between mid-July and mid-October.
4 On leaving the Caribbean to the north sailing ships met the westerlies to take them back to Europe.
5 The Southern and Northern Equatorial Currents merge on entering the Southern Caribbean and flow round the Caribbean in a clockwise direction.
6 The Gulf Stream helps ships back to Europe from the Northern Caribbean.

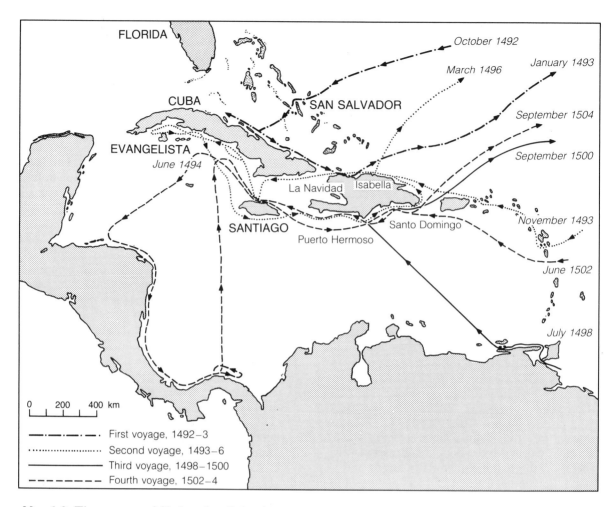

FLORIDA

October 1492

March 1496

January 1493

CUBA

SAN SALVADOR

September 1504

EVANGELISTA

September 1500

June 1494

La Navidad   Isabella

SANTIAGO

Santo Domingo

November 1493

Puerto Hermoso

June 1502

July 1498

0   200   400 km

—·—·—·— First voyage, 1492–3
·············· Second voyage, 1493–6
———— Third voyage, 1498–1500
– – – – – Fourth voyage, 1502–4

Map 1.9: The voyages of Christopher Columbus

Map 1.9: The voyages of Christopher Columbus

Christopher Columbus undertook these voyages in the belief that the world was round and that therefore he could sail west and reach the East. He underestimated the circumference of the world and thought that he would come to Japan or China after sailing west some 3000 miles. He was ridiculed by some but persuaded Isabella of Castile to sponsor him. His 'contract' with Isabella gave him the title of 'Viceroy' of all the lands he discovered and a tenth share of their wealth. All the lands would belong to the House of Castile and be settled by Castilians only.

Columbus made four voyages, the first of which is the most famous. He sailed in three ships, the *Santa Maria*, his flagship and the *Pinta* and *Nina*. Altogether there were about ninety crew. He sailed from Palos and made his first landfall on 3 August 1492 in the Canary Islands establishing the route to the west. After sailing for over eight weeks he came to land at San Salvador in the Bahamas. He thought he had reached an outlying island of the East and spent two weeks looking for Japan before landing on Cuba at the end of the month. The primitiveness of the people he met, among other things, should have told him that he had not found the East. He left a colony, 'La Navidad', on Hispaniola, the first European settlement in the New World. He sailed for Spain in January 1493. Ferdinand and Isabella were pleased with Columbus and began making preparations for another voyage. They urged Pope Alexander VI to demarcate the discoveries of Portugal and Spain.

Columbus's second voyage showed that he was a better navigator than administrator. The colony of La Navidad had been destroyed and his new colony of 'Isabella' was not well sited. Ill-treatment of the Arawaks began and Caribs were enslaved. The Spaniards mutinied because they found so little gold and were expected to do manual labour. Massacres of Arawaks followed and the forced labour systems began. However, Hispaniola was established as the centre of the Spanish Empire in the Indies and Columbus's brother, Bartholomew, founded the capital of Santo Domingo.

By the third voyage Ferdinand and Isabella began to regret having given Columbus such wide powers. Columbus faced two rebellions in Hispaniola, one from the *cacique*, Gaurionex, and the other from a Spaniard, Francisco Roldan. Reports of these troubles went back to Isabella and Bobadilla was sent out to arrest Columbus.

Columbus obstinately claimed that he had discovered the East although by this time most others doubted him. With greatly reduced powers and commanded not to visit Hispaniola, Columbus was allowed to make a fourth voyage. He went beyond the islands to Central America trying to find a passage through to the East. He failed to do so and in spite of his orders he ran foul of Ovando who had been sent as Governor of Hispaniola.

In the year of his return Columbus lost his best supporter, Isabella. He was discredited by contemporaries and allowed to die in relative poverty and obscurity in 1506.

Notes

1 Columbus was Genoese.
2 He studied Portuguese navigation and cartography at Lisbon.
3 He tried to sail for Portugal but his ideas were not accepted.
4 He sailed for Spain because Isabella of Castile was willing to risk a relatively small outlay in order to beat the Portuguese to the East.
5 Columbus made four voyages for Spain: first 1492–93 in which he reached the Bahamas in the West Indies and established a colony in Hispaniola; the second, 1493–96, in which he explored the coasts of Hispaniola, Cuba and Jamaica and failed as a colonial administrator; the third, 1498–1500, in which he reached the coast of South America at the mouth of the Orinoco and was sent home in chains from Hispaniola; and the fourth, 1502–4, in which he explored the coast of Honduras and Panama and still protested that he had reached Asia.
6 He was a great captain who used the winds and currents of the Atlantic and Caribbean and charted the Caribbean accurately by the standards of the day.
7 His initial good intentions towards the natives soon turned to harshness and great cruelty.
8 He gave the New World to Spain but did not receive his just rewards and acknowledgement from his contemporaries.

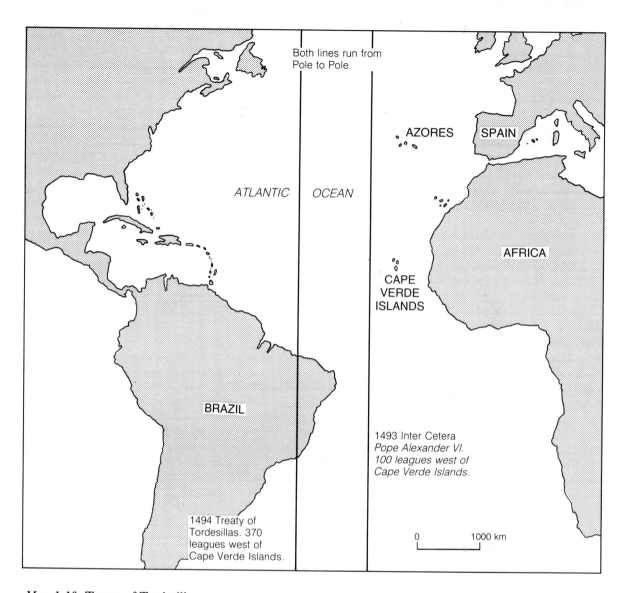

Both lines run from
Pole to Pole.

AZORES   SPAIN

ATLANTIC   OCEAN

AFRICA

CAPE
VERDE
ISLANDS

BRAZIL

1493 Inter Cetera
Pope Alexander VI.
100 leagues west of
Cape Verde Islands.

1494 Treaty of
Tordesillas. 370
leagues west of
Cape Verde Islands.

0   1000 km

Map 1.10: Treaty of Tordesillas

Map 1.10: Treaty of Tordesillas

The Portuguese (Bartholomew Dias) had rounded the Cape of Good Hope in 1487. At the time of Columbus's first voyage in 1492 the Portuguese were in the middle of a ten-year respite in their voyages of exploration. However, it did seem as if the Portuguese had found a way round Africa to the East. When Columbus claimed that he had reached the East by sailing west, both Portugal and Spain were claiming the East. Clearly a decision had to be made about these conflicting claims.

The matter was put to the arbitration of the Pope as Head of the Roman Catholic Church to which all European countries belonged at that time. The Pope, Alexander VI, simply divided the world into two halves with a line from the North Pole to the South Pole, 100 leagues to the west of the Cape Verde Islands. The Portuguese were to keep to the east of this line and the Spanish to the west. Both countries could claim any lands in their sphere not already claimed by another Christian prince.

The Pope's decision pleased Ferdinand and Isabella because it limited the Portuguese in the Atlantic. King John II of Portugal wanted more room for his voyages round Africa and was unlike-ly to keep to the decision. The representatives of Portugal and Spain met in Tordesillas in Spain in 1494 and maintained the division of the world into two spheres but they moved the line of demarcation further west to 370 leagues west of the Cape Verde Islands. Thus the Portuguese would find the eastern part of Brazil in their sphere following Cabral's discovery of 1500. Pope Julius II reaffirmed the Treaty of Tordesillas in 1506.

Notes

1 The Portuguese were exploring a sea route round Africa to the East.
2 Columbus, believing the world to be round, was sailing west to claim the East for Spain.
3 In 1493 both countries claimed the East.
4 The Pope, Alexander VI, issued a Bull, *Inter Cetera* dividing the world between Portugal and Spain by a line 100 leagues west of the Cape Verde Islands.
5 In the Treay of Tordesillas, 1494, Portugal and Spain moved this line of demarcation to 370 leagues west of the Cape Verde Islands.
6 All unclaimed lands to the east of this line were Portuguese, and to the west were Spanish.

Theme 2: European settlement and rivalry_____

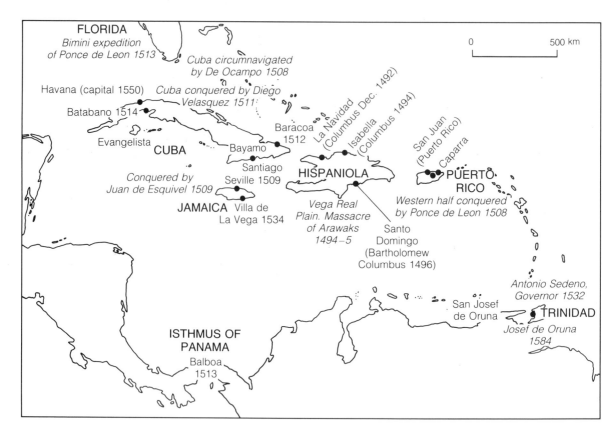

Map 2.1: The Spanish conquest of the Indies

Map 2.1: The Spanish conquest of the Indies

Hispaniola

Christopher Columbus acted as the conquistador of Hispaniola, especially on his second expedition, 1493–96. He abandoned La Navidad and built Isabella, the first European-built town in the New World. From Isabella the exploration and conquest of the interior was undertaken. Alonso de Ojeda was sent to find gold but brought back very little. Later Columbus himself, having left his brother, Diego, in charge of Isabella, took 400 armed men into Vega Real where he met little opposition from the Arawaks who merely stared at the Spaniards. He built a fort called St Thomas in the Cibao mountains to the south of Vega Real.

Then Columbus was away for four months exploring Cuba. In his absence the Arawak *caciques*, except for Guacaganari, had revolted. Caonaba, a Carib chief, attacked St Thomas but was captured by Alonso de Ojeda. Thereafter the slaughter and enslavement of Arawaks began. Columbus had given up his humanitarian attitude towards the Arawaks and suggested enslaving them. Queen Isabella always resisted this and began to look on Columbus with disfavour.

In 1495 Columbus and Ojeda campaigned against the Arawaks in Central Hispaniola and subdued them, building forts in the conquered territory. Then Columbus imposed a heavy tribute on the conquered people. By October 1495, he had 'conquered' Hispaniola.

Puerto Rico

Juan Ponce de Leon, Lieutenant-Governor of Eastern Hispaniola, was allowed by Ovando to explore Puerto Rico in 1508 with the intention of colonising the island. In 1509, after much confusion, Ponce de Leon was confirmed as Governor of Puerto Rico.

He set up his first colony at Caparra but soon moved to Puerto Rico (later San Juan). The conquest was difficult as the Arawaks of Puerto Rico were used to fighting the Caribs in the east of the island. Ponce de Leon required reinforcements from Hispaniola before he could complete the conquest of the western half.

When he was replaced as Governor in 1513 he went on his famous Bimini expedition to Florida.

Jamaica

Diego Columbus wanted Jamaica to be settled by his own nominee so that it would not fall into the hands of a rival. He appointed Juan de Esquivel Governor in 1510. Esquivel founded Seville on St Ann's Bay on the north coast. The settlement lasted until 1519 and then declined. It gave place to Villa de la Vega (Spanish Town) which became the capital in 1534.

The Arawaks in Jamaica were peaceful and did not put up any resistance. Their rapid decline in numbers was due to ill-treatment, despair and suicide. It could hardly be called a 'conquest' by Esquivel. Jamaica's function was at first just to serve as a farm to supply the other Spanish colonies.

Cuba

In 1508 Sebastian de Ocampo proved Cuba to be an island by sailing round it, but he did not attempt a conquest. Diego Columbus sent Diego Velasquez to conquer Cuba in 1511. Again, it could hardly be called a 'conquest'. It began with the massacre of Arawaks at Caonas which Bartholomew de las Casas witnessed and thereafter the island was easily taken over.

The first city, Baracoa, was established in 1512. Santiago de Cuba had an excellent harbour and acted as capital for a short time before Bayamo,

which was inland, took over. Then attention switched to the western end of the island. Velasquez founded Batabano in 1514 and from there the citizens crossed to the north coast to build Havana. Havana could control the exit from the western Caribbean and the Gulf of Mexico and it had a good harbour. Ships called there before the return voyage to Europe. It became the capital of Cuba in 1550.

Trinidad

For many years the Spanish failed to colonise Trinidad because of the hostility of both the Arawaks and the Caribs who were used to fighting each other. Antonio Sedeno abandoned his colonisation attempt in 1532. Trinidad became one place where the Spanish Crown permitted enslavement because of the attitude of the Indians, many of whom were removed from the island.

In 1584 Josef de Oruna brought Spanish rule to the north-western part of the island and founded the town of San Josef de Oruna which was near modern Port-of-Spain.

Notes

1   'Conquistadores' is applied to those who extended Spanish authority to the islands, but they cannot be compared to Cortes and Pizarro.
2   Columbus acted as a conquistador in Hispaniola with help from others like Alonso de Ojeda.
3   Ponce de Leon 'conquered' Puerto Rico; Juan de Esquivel, Jamaica; Diego de Velasquez, Cuba; and Antonio Sedeno attempted the conquest of Trinidad.
4   In many cases, e.g. Jamaica and Cuba, there was little or no resistance from the Arawaks yet even so the conquests proceeded with great cruelty, enslavement and massacre.
5   Puerto Rico and Trinidad resisted the conquistadores more readily because the Caribs and Arawaks there were used to fighting each other and this had made the Arawaks more warlike than in the other islands.
6   The Greater Antilles were conquered quickly between 1494 and 1513.
7   The islands became the springboard for the conquests of some of the mainland territories.

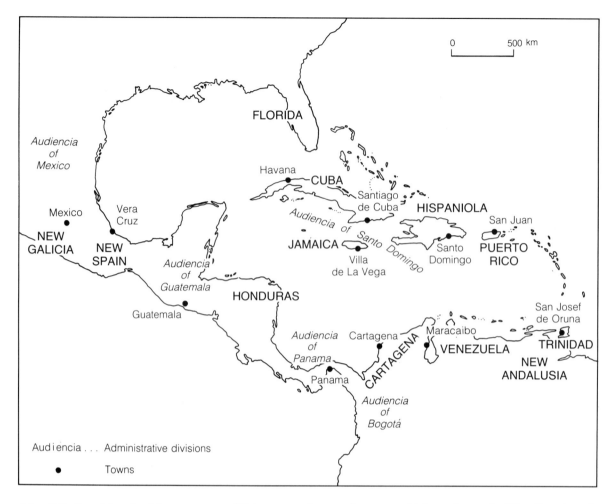

Map 2.2: Spanish colonial government (This map embraces the parts which made up the Vice-Royalty of New Spain in 1535 – Mexico, Central America, West Indies, Colombia and Venezuela).

Map 2.2: Spanish colonial government

The Spanish used the conciliar system of government (i.e. through councils) to govern their Empire in the New World. The King of Spain, as an absolute monarch, ruled the Empire but he needed the help of the councils. Three main ones, the Council of Castile, the Council of Finance and the Council of the Indies, were involved in colonial government.

The Council of the Indies dealt directly with the colonies. It was set up by King Ferdinand in 1511 and reorganised by Charles V in 1524. It appointed the colonial officials and approved colonial laws. Most of its work was legal as the King ruled and the Council judged whether the rule was being obeyed by officials and subjects.

Spanish colonial government was systematised through the administration of Diego Columbus, which the authorities considered needed checking. Two formal, direct checks on a governor were the *residencia* conducted by three judges from Spain at the end of a governor's term of office, and the *visita* carried out by an official from Spain during a governor's term.

The Empire was divided into ten *audiencias* (five of the early ones are shown on the map). The Audiencia of Santo Domingo was the chief one from 1511 to 1793. It was another check on the administration of the governor in its function as a court of appeal, but it was also an administrative unit. It was appointed from Spain and reported directly to the Council of the Indies. Therefore Viceroys and Governors had no control over it. In its administrative capacity the *audiencia* carried out the Viceroy's orders, i.e. they were executive councils.

In 1535 it was felt that Santo Domingo could not fairly control the mainland as well as the islands so the Spanish Empire in the New World was divided into two Viceroyalties, those of New Spain (Mexico, Central America, the West Indies, Colombia and Venezuela) and, in 1551, Peru (all South America except for Colombia and Venezuela). Under the Viceroys of these huge areas were provincial governors and *alcaldes* (mayors of towns).

The ordinary citizens were governed locally by municipal governments called *cabildos*. They governed the towns and the countryside surrounding them. The officials of the *cabildos* were called *regidores* and were nominated by the captains-general. They were rarely elected. Their military duties were emphasised in the keeping of law and order. The *cabildos* were the mainstay of Spanish colonial government.

Notes

1 The conciliar system of government was used to help the King.
2 Decisions were very slow as each matter had to pass through several councils and the King for approval and then be relayed to the Indies.
3 The Royal and Supreme Council of the Indies dealt directly with the Empire.
4 The system of government in the Indies was established mainly in the governorship of Diego Columbus between 1509 and 1523.
5 Many of the features of Spanish colonial government show checks on the powers of Viceroys and Governors.
6 *Audiencias* were legal bodies appointed from Spain to check on a governor's administration, but they were also administrative units acting as councils to carry out the orders of Viceroys and Governors.
7 The *cabildos* or municipal governments dealt with the day-to-day running of the Empire and controlled the subjects by enforcing law and order.

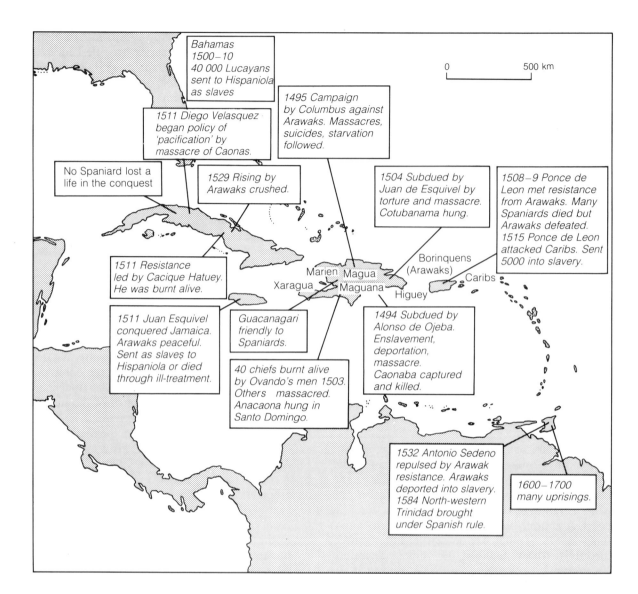

Map 2.3: The extinction of the Arawaks

The labels on the map read:

Bahamas 1500–10 40 000 Lucayans sent to Hispaniola as slaves

1495 Campaign by Columbus against Arawaks. Massacres, suicides, starvation followed.

1511 Diego Velasquez began policy of 'pacification' by massacre of Caonas.

No Spaniard lost a life in the conquest

1529 Rising by Arawaks crushed.

1504 Subdued by Juan de Esquivel by torture and massacre. Cotubanama hung.

1508–9 Ponce de Leon met resistance from Arawaks. Many Spaniards died but Arawaks defeated. 1515 Ponce de Leon attacked Caribs. Sent 5000 into slavery.

1511 Resistance led by Cacique Hatuey. He was burnt alive.

1511 Juan Esquivel conquered Jamaica. Arawaks peaceful. Sent as slaves to Hispaniola or died through ill-treatment.

Guacanagari friendly to Spaniards.

40 chiefs burnt alive by Ovando's men 1503. Others massacred. Anacaona hung in Santo Domingo.

1494 Subdued by Alonso de Ojeba. Enslavement, deportation, massacre. Caonaba captured and killed.

1532 Antonio Sedeno repulsed by Arawak resistance. Arawaks deported into slavery. 1584 North-western Trinidad brought under Spanish rule.

1600–1700 many uprisings.

Borinquens (Arawaks) Caribs

Marien Magua
Xaragua Maguana
Higuey

0   500 km

Map 2.3: The extinction of the Arawaks

It is difficult to estimate the population of Arawaks in the Indies before the coming of the Spaniards. In the Bahamas, Cuba, Hispaniola, Jamaica, Puerto Rico and Trinidad together it was probably under one million. (Bartholomew de las Casas's estimate of three million in Hispaniola alone must be a wild exaggeration). However, the speed with which the Arawaks were killed cannot have been exaggerated as fifty years after the coming of Columbus there was hardly an Arawak left in the Greater Antilles.

To take Hispaniola as an example of the genocide which took place under Spanish rule: suppose there were 250 000 Arawaks in 1492. Their widespread slaughter began in 1494 when Columbus took a party of 400 well-armed men into the interior. In the following year the *caciques*, with the exception of Guacanagari, revolted. Alonso de Ojeda captured and killed the Carib *cacique*, Caonaba, and killed his followers when they attacked the fort at St Thomas in the Cibao mountains. Columbus sent another 500 to Spain as prisoners. In October, 1595, he began a campaign against the hostile *caciques*, enslaving thousands in Vega Real and killing thousands more, allowing bloodhounds to tear many to pieces. He then imposed a heavy tribute on the conquered who retaliated by refusing to grow crops in the hope that the Spaniards, through lack of food, would be forced to leave. Instead the Spaniards attacked them and killed more. Others who were driven into the mountains starved to death or committed suicide. By 1546 there was probably not an Arawak left in Hispaniola. Sir Walter Raleigh certainly found none in 1591.

In Cuba there was no resistance from the local Arawaks at first. Higuey, a *cacique* from Hispaniola, gave some resistance, and was burnt alive. However, Velasquez adopted the policy of 'pacification' which entailed the massacring of certain communities in order to make others submit more readily. He began with the massacre at Caonas which Bartholomew de las Casas witnessed. Not one Spaniard was killed in the conquest of Cuba and after 1531 there was no further resistance.

In Jamaica the Arawaks were quickly wiped out. They were peaceful people and easy for the Spaniards to capture and send to Hispaniola as slaves. Those who remained were treated so badly that they lost the will to live and committed suicide by drinking cassava juice. By 1600 there were too few left to provide labour for the Spaniards and when the English attacked Jamaica in 1655 there were no Arawaks left.

There was fierce fighting between the Borinquen Arawaks and the Spaniards in Puerto Rico. Ponce de Leon gradually overcame them in the western part of the island. In 1515 he began to enslave the Caribs of the eastern part and deported them to the Lesser Antilles. With this Indian resistance the Spanish Crown permitted attacks and enslavement which hastened the extinction of both Arawaks and Caribs in Puerto Rico.

The Lucayan Arawaks in the Bahamas were shipped as slaves to Hispaniola to work in the mines. This showed how quickly the labour force in Hispaniola had been depleted. Between 1500 and 1510 40 000 were sent to Hispaniola leading to the rapid depopulation of the Bahamas.

Only in Trinidad did the Arawaks and Caribs survive the period of Spanish colonisation in any numbers. By the end of the sixteenth century they still had not been subdued in the south-eastern part of the island. However, they were destroying themselves in internal warfare. Again, because of their resistance to the Spaniards, the Crown allowed their enslavement and deportation. Yet in the seventeenth century there were Indians fiercely resisting the Spaniards in Trinidad.

Notes
1 In most cases docile, subsistence-living people came up against ruthless conquerors and were wiped out.
2 They were completely unused to the forced labour that the Spaniards imposed upon them.
3 This forced labour was introduced about 1498 under the systems of *repartimiento* and *encomienda*, the one being the division of Indians for labour and the other being a grant of land which included the Indian labour on it.
4 The Crown protected the Indians at first but could do little to change the attitudes and actions of the settlers in the islands. Later the Crown sanctioned attacks on the Indians and their enslavement in cases of resistance to Spanish authority.
5 Bartholomew de las Casas was known as 'the Apostle of the Indies' because of the work he did to try to save the Indians and his two books, *A Brief Account of the Destruction of the Indians* and *A History of the Indians* in which he told metropolitan Spaniards what was being done to the Indians in the islands.

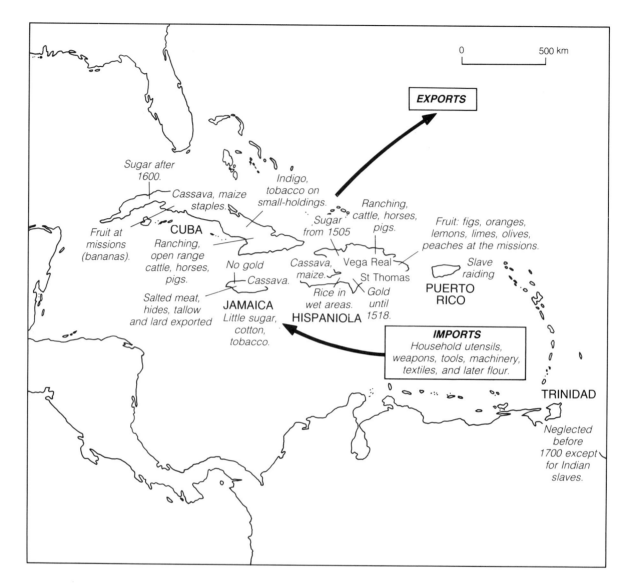

0   500 km

EXPORTS

Sugar after
1600.

Cassava, maize
staples.

Indigo,
tobacco on
small-holdings.

Ranching,
cattle, horses,
pigs.

Sugar
from 1505

Fruit: figs, oranges,
lemons, limes, olives,
peaches at the missions.

Fruit at
missions
(bananas).

CUBA

Ranching,
open range
cattle, horses,
pigs.

No gold

Cassava,
maize.

Vega Real

St Thomas

Slave
raiding

PUERTO
RICO

Cassava.

Rice in
wet areas.

Gold
until

Salted meat,
hides, tallow
and lard exported

JAMAICA

Little sugar,
cotton,
tobacco.

HISPANIOLA 1518.

IMPORTS
Household utensils,
weapons, tools, machinery,
textiles, and later flour.

TRINIDAD

Neglected
before
1700 except
for Indian
slaves.

Map 2.4: Economic development under the Spanish

Map 2.4: Economic development under the Spanish

The West Indies complemented Spain in the trading system at the beginning of the sixteenth century. The Indies were to provide raw materials for the mother country and be a market for the mother country's manufactured goods in accordance with mercantilist theory.

Columbus and the early settlers wanted gold and the profits from trade in Indian slaves. Gold was a disappointment. In Jamaica, Cuba and Puerto Rico there was little or none and the gold in Hispaniola was all but exhausted. Gold production in Hispaniola did rise to 500 000 ducats by 1517, but by that time there, and in the other islands, economic development had taken a different turn. Trade in Indian slaves had been condemned by Isabella as early as 1494. Hopes of quick and easy profits had come to nought.

The second phase of economic development had already begun while some were still pinning their hopes on gold. On his second voyage Columbus took livestock to the Indies and, under Ovando's governorship, they increased in number. Therefore the second phase was ranching which suited the hidalgo class who emigrated from Spain in the expectation of lands, large herds and little work themselves. There were no serious cattle diseases and the grasslands were abundant. The *reparti-miento* system, introduced in 1498, and backed up by the land grants under *encomienda*, gave the settlers the labour they needed. While the Indian populations survived, Indians did the manual work and provided the Spanish with the staple foods, at first cassava and maize, for the Spanish could not afford to import flour for the first hundred years and wheat could not be grown successfully. Large grants of land were known as *hatos* (ranches) and smaller grants were *estancias* (small-holdings). From the earliest years private ownership of land was permitted. A circle made by a radius from a fixed point determined the boundaries of a ranch and the open range system was universal. Horses, cattle, pigs and sheep quickly multiplied and ran wild but were periodically rounded up for branding and slaughter. The wild livestock was known as *cimarrones* and the hunting of it was known as *monteria*. It became so popular that the countryside was strewn with carcasses. The import of livestock was not necessary after 1515.

The islands were soon producing meat far in excess of their needs and the surplus was salted for export. Jamaica lay on the route between Cartagena and Havana and supplied the passing ships. Cuba supplied the ships en route to Europe. Cattle yielded other products like hides and skins, tallow for making candles and treating ships' timbers, and lard.

When it became clear that there was no gold in Jamaica and little in Cuba, these two islands became like huge ranches, especially Jamaica where the Spanish population dwindled while the herds multiplied. Cuba's economy was more diversified as a large class of small-holders developed alongside the large ranch owners. The small-holders and artisans were the foundation of the Cuban nation and the backbone of the future tobacco industry.

The third phase in economic development was the sugar industry. Sugar cane was introduced by Columbus but it was not crushed into sugar until 1505, and not milled until 1515 when Gonzalo Velosa built the first *trapiche* (horse-drawn mill). In that year the first boxes of sugar were exported to Spain and by 1541 there were forty mills in Hispaniola exporting about 4000 chests of sugar. Up to that time the sugar industry in the Indies was localised in Vega Real in Hispaniola and had not taken off in the other islands. However, after 1600 Cuba overtook Hispaniola in sugar produc-tion. Jamaica had scattered fields of cane but no real sugar industry.

Of the other crops tobacco also made a slow start and only really developed in Cuba in the last quarter of the sixteenth century. Production was by small-holders who provided their own, highly-skilled labour. The missions were responsible for the introduction of other crops such as rice, figs, olives, lemons, limes, oranges, peaches and bananas. The fruits grew in the walled orchards of the monasteries which were soon copied by the houses of the richer colonists. Wheat never did well in the Indies and the settlers relied on cassava and maize, at first provided by Indians.

The imports had to come from the mother country and consisted of weapons, tools, household utensils, machinery, hardware and textiles. At first very little that was not of immediate practical use was imported.

The idea that the colonies and the mother country existed for their mutual benefit necessitated a close control of trade and the *Casa de Contratacion* was set up in Seville in 1503 to do this. All ships, goods and settlers to and from the Indies had to pass through this port and the imports and exports were carefully recorded.

Notes

1 The Indies were expected to export gold, livestock products and tropical crops to Spain and import manufactured goods from Spain.

2 Gold was almost exhausted by the coming of Columbus and only Hispaniola exported significant quantities before 1519 when Mexican production began.

3 Staple foods were grown by the Indians and supplied to the Spanish. Cassava was the most important staple, followed by maize. Flour was too costly to import at first.

4 Ranching became the dominant industry. The social structure, the absence of cattle diseases and the abundant grasslands all suited ranching.

5 Sugar became an export crop in Hispaniola in the first half of the sixteenth century, but after 1600 Cuba overtook Hispaniola in sugar production.

6 An infant tobacco industry developed in Cuba between 1575 and 1600.

7 Missions experimented with exotic fruits and crops. Most of the tropical fruits flourished in the Indies, especially bananas and citrus fruits.

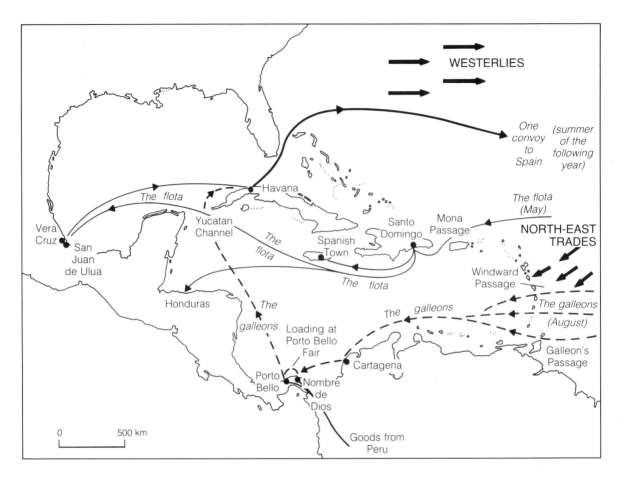

Map 2.5: Spanish trade routes

Map 2.5: Spanish trade routes

Christopher Columbus established the routes to and from the Caribbean which made the best use of the winds and currents; out by the trade winds and the equatorial currents and home by the westerlies. These routes were sanctioned by the *Casa de Contratacion*. The whole shipping system between Spain and the Indies was organised strategically by Pedro Menendez de Aviles between 1567 and 1574.

From 1543 Spain sent two fleets to the Indies every year. The *flota* set out from Seville in May bound for San Juan de Ulua, the port for Vera Cruz and Mexico. It passed through the Mona Passage, called at Santo Domingo in Hispaniola and then went on south of Cuba and through the Yucatan Channel to Mexico. Ships left this convoy for Jamaica and Honduras, but the *flota* reassembled in Havana by February of the following year for the return to Spain.

The galleons set out in August bound for Nombre de Dios and Porto Bello. They entered the Caribbean by the Galleons' Passage between Trinidad and Tobago or by the Windward Passage further north. They called at Cartagena on the Spanish Main for goods from Venezuela and New Granada before loading at Nombre de Dios and the Porto Bello Fair where the bullion from Peru arrived after its voyage up the Pacific Coast of South America and its mule train passage across the Isthmus. The Porto Bello Fair lasted for about six weeks and could be held back if the galleons had not yet arrived.

From there the galleons made for Havana where the *flota* was usually waiting. At Havana they picked up the provisions for the return voyage to Spain in the spring or early summer of the year after they had set out from Spain.

Pedro Menendez de Aviles devised a system for protecting these convoys and their valuable goods in Caribbean ports. His main aim was to bring the bullion safely back to Spain and he devised three main ways to ensure this:

a) the convoy system whereby the ships protected each other,

b) squadrons of fast ships called *armadillas* patrolling the shipping lanes of the Caribbean,

c) fortification of the ports of Cartagena, Santo Domingo, San Juan and Havana.

His system was so successful that only three fleets were lost between 1567 and 1700.

Notes

1 Columbus established the routes which took advantage of the winds and currents of the Atlantic and Caribbean.

2 The *Casa de Contratacion* was in overall control of trade and shipping from 1503.

3 The *flota* left Seville in May bound for Mexico.

4 The galleons left Seville in August bound for Panama.

5 The two fleets reassembled at Havana to make the return journey to Spain in one convoy a year after they set out.

6 Pedro Menendez de Aviles was in charge of shipping between 1567 and 1574 and he successfully worked out the means for protecting these valuable fleets.

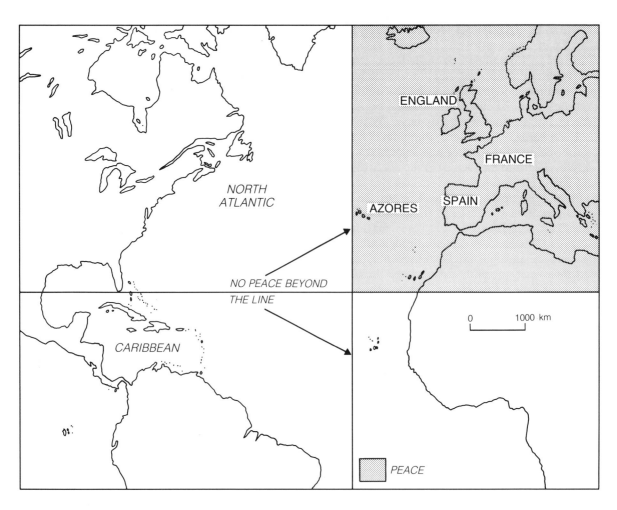

Map 2.6: 'No Peace Beyond the Line'

Map 2.6: 'No Peace Beyond the Line'

Charles of Spain was elected Holy Roman Emperor in 1519 arousing the jealousy and anger of Francis I of France. In 1523 he declared. 'I should like to see the clause in Adam's will that excludes me from a share of the world'. Francis obviously thought that he had a right to send ships into the Caribbean and French pirates operated there throughout the century, apart from short periods of peace like those established by the Treaty of Crespy in 1544 and Cateau-Cambrésis in 1559. In the peace talks for the latter there seems to have been an unwritten agreement that peace would not apply to an area north of the Tropic of Cancer and west of the most westerly of the Azores. These were the 'Lines of Amity' which were formalised later. Spain could not accept the French right to trade and lands in the Americas and France would not be denied this right.

France was a Roman Catholic country yet would not accept the Pope's division of the world in 1493. England was a Protestant country by Elizabeth's reign and in 1580 Queen Elizabeth openly contested Spain's exclusive right to the Americas (which sailors had been secretly ignoring for most of the century) when she received Sir Francis Drake after his circumnavigation. Elizabeth implied that Spain was the aggressor by denying foreigners access to the Americas and that if Spain wanted 'No Peace Beyond the Line' she could have it!

Notes

1 An unwritten agreement existed from the mid-sixteenth century that European countries would fight each other in the Caribbean even during times of peace in Europe.
2 The dividing line beyond which there would be no peace was north/south through the most westerly of the Azores.

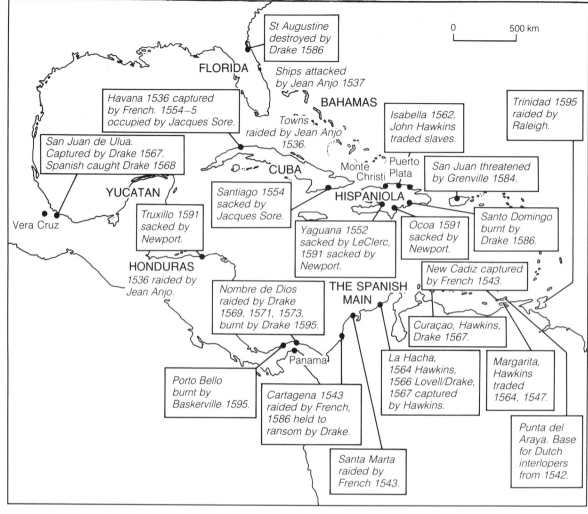

Map 2.7 labels:

St Augustine destroyed by Drake 1586

Ships attacked by Jean Anjo 1537

FLORIDA

Havana 1536 captured by French. 1554–5 occupied by Jacques Sore.

BAHAMAS

Towns raided by Jean Anjo 1536.

Trinidad 1595 raided by Raleigh.

Isabella 1562, John Hawkins traded slaves.

San Juan de Ulua. Captured by Drake 1567. Spanish caught Drake 1568

CUBA

Monte Christi

Puerto Plata

San Juan threatened by Grenville 1584.

YUCATAN

Santiago 1554 sacked by Jacques Sore.

HISPANIOLA

Santo Domingo burnt by Drake 1586.

Vera Cruz

Truxillo 1591 sacked by Newport.

Yaguana 1552 sacked by LeClerc, 1591 sacked by Newport.

Ocoa 1591 sacked by Newport.

HONDURAS 1536 raided by Jean Anjo.

Nombre de Dios raided by Drake 1569, 1571, 1573, burnt by Drake 1595.

THE SPANISH MAIN

New Cadiz captured by French 1543.

Curaçao, Hawkins, Drake 1567.

Porto Bello burnt by Baskerville 1595.

Panama

Cartagena 1543 raided by French, 1586 held to ransom by Drake.

La Hacha, 1564 Hawkins, 1566 Lovell/Drake, 1567 captured by Hawkins.

Margarita, Hawkins traded 1564, 1547.

Santa Marta raided by French 1543.

Punta del Araya. Base for Dutch interlopers from 1542.

Map 2.7: Sixteenth-century pirates

Map 2.7: Sixteenth-century pirates

The distinction between peaceful traders, smugglers and pirates in the sixteenth century was a fine one, and many French, Dutch and English merchants who went to the Caribbean came away as 'pirates', at least in the eyes of the Spanish.

English and French merchants sailed to the Caribbean after visiting Brazil from 1499 and 1503 respectively. In 1540 an English vessel, the *Barbara*, came to the West Indies from Brazil and captured a Spanish ship off Hispaniola, an act of piracy.

However, at this stage French pirates were more active and more successful. After a few years of capturing Spanish ships and settlements in the Caribbean, the French realised that it was not necessary to risk the voyage across the Atlantic, but that they could lie in wait for the Spanish treasure fleets in European waters. From 1512 French pirates were using Bordeaux and the Portuguese ports as their bases, often backed by a wealthy Bordeaux merchant named Jean Anjo. He provided Jean Fleury with the ships with which he captured Cortes's treasure fleet from Mexico in 1523. In 1536 a French ship captured Havana and in the following year Jean Anjo himself captured Spanish ships between Florida and the Bahamas and then raided towns in Hispaniola, Cuba and Honduras. One year before the Treaty of Créspy the French pirates turned their attention to the Spanish main, capturing Nueva Cadiz on Cubagua, Santa Marta and Cartagena. Then a peaceful interlude of eight years followed the Treaty.

The most famous French pirates were François

LeClerc and his lieutenant, Jacques Sore. They were Huguenots whose hatred of Catholicism added to their hostility towards the Spanish. In 1552 LeClerc laid waste Yaguana and other towns in Hispaniola and on the Spanish Main. Two years later Jacques Sore sacked Santiago de Cuba and Havana, spending a few months there destroying the symbols of Catholicism and torturing and killing Catholic priests. Hostilities were suspended between the French and Spanish by the Peace of Cateau-Cambrésis in 1559.

Dutch interlopers had been going to Punta del Araya to quarry rock salt from 1542. The Spanish tolerated them at first but when they turned to attacks on Spanish ships and towns, the Spanish had to look on them as just other pirates.

When England became Protestant in the reign of Edward VI, 1547–53, relations with Spain deteriorated. John Hawkins posed as a peaceful trader, trading under a local licence at Isabella in 1562 but he was prepared to fight and the licence was probably granted under the implied threat posed by the English ships. Hawkins lost all the cargo he gained here so when he went back to the Indies in 1564 with seven ships he made it clear that he would attack if trade was refused. He was able to trade at Margarita, Sante Fé, Borburata and Rio de la Hacha peacefully. However, when John Lovell and Francis Drake sailed back to the Caribbean in Hawkins' ships in 1566 they were treated with hostility at La Hacha and had 100 slaves confiscated. This incident contributed to Drake's hatred of the Spanish.

In 1567 Hawkins and Drake went back to the Spanish Main and traded peacefully at Margarita and Curaçao, but they attacked La Hacha, capturing it easily. On their way home they met a storm after passing through the Yucatan Strait and decided to put into San Juan de Ulua for repairs. They were caught there by a Spanish treasure fleet and only two ships escaped. This was another incident which made Drake never forgive the Spanish, especially when he learnt of the ill-treatment of English prisoners and survivors in Mexico. Drake therefore planned an attack on Nombre de Dios to capture the mule train from Panama. In 1569 and 1571 he made reconnaissance voyages, establishing a secret base and making friends with the local maroons. He carried out a successful raid on the mule train in 1573, capturing gold and burying much silver.

England and Spain were officially at peace but in 1580 Elizabeth declared that English ships would sail in the Caribbean and she would feel entitled to claim any lands in the Spanish sphere. Then in 1585 war was declared and Drake was sent with thirty ships to the Caribbean with the object of inflicting as much damage, and capturing as much treasure, as possible. He captured Santo Domingo in 1586 and burnt it in order to squeeze as much ransom money as he could out of the city. He did the same at Cartagena but in both cases the ransom obtained was disappointing, not even covering the costs of the expenditure. Many English lives were lost through disease.

Drake was engaged in home waters next, notably against the Armada in 1588. The Spanish were weak in the Caribbean at this time but the English also lacked money for expeditions. An exception was Christopher Newport's which sacked Yaguana and Ocoa in Hispaniola and Truxillo in Honduras in 1591.

Drake's last voyage was in 1595. His objective was a Spanish treasure galleon in San Juan harbour but he delayed in sailing across the Atlantic, missed the prize at San Juan and sailed on to the Spanish Main where he captured La Hacha and Santa Marta and burnt Nombre de Dios. In January 1596 Drake died of dysentery off Porto Bello which was burnt by his successor, Baskerville.

In spite of all these famous successes by English, French and Dutch pirates, the Spanish treasure fleets still reached Spain unharmed and there is more excitement and romance about this period than permanent damage to the Spanish Empire.

Notes

1 Peaceful traders turned to piracy because of a) the temptations of gain; b) Spanish hostility; c) religious differences; d) commissions from their monarchs.
2 French pirates were most active in the reign of Francis I, 1515 to 1547, because of his personal hatred for Charles V, and up to the Peace of Cateau-Cambrésis in 1559.
3 English pirates were active after Edward VI turned England Protestant between 1547 and 1553, and then again in the reign of Elizabeth from 1558.
4 England did not officially declare war against Spain until 1585 but undoubtedly Hawkins and Drake were encouraged in their enterprises by Elizabeth.
5 In spite of the activities of English, French and Dutch pirates, very little damage was done to the Spanish Empire and Spanish shipping in the Caribbean in the sixteenth century.

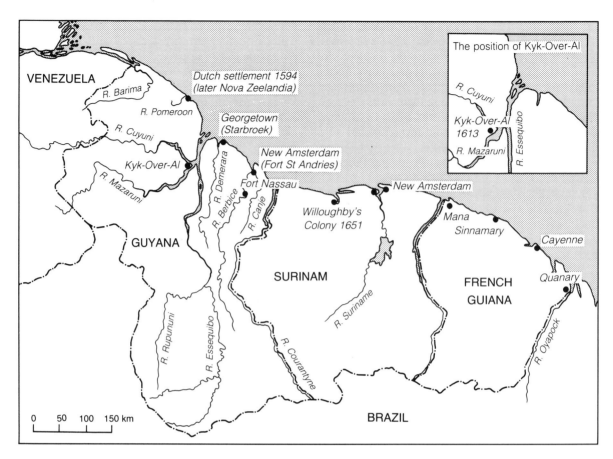

Map 2.8: The Wild Coast

Map 2.8: The Wild Coast

The first non-Spanish settlements in the Caribbean area were on the Wild Coast, that part of South America between the rivers Orinoco and Amazon. The Spanish lay to the north, the Portuguese to the south, but the inhospitable land in between had been left to the aggressive Caribs.

Sir Walter Raleigh was drawn to this coast in 1595 by the *El Dorado* legend which on this occasion placed *El Dorado* up the Orinoco River ruling a city called 'Manoa'. Raleigh came with four ships, captured San Josef de Oruna, capital of Trinidad, imprisoned the governor and claimed Trinidad for England. Then he took one hundred men up the Orinoco in search of gold. Of course, they did not find *El Dorado*, but he was favourably impressed with the land and sent two of his captains back in the following two years, Laurence Keymis in 1596 and Leonard Berry who explored the rivers Oyapock and Courantyne in 1597. Still no settlement was made.

In 1604 Charles Leigh founded the first colony at Mt Howard on the Oyapock but left within a year. From 1609 to 1613 the colony was re-occupied by Robert Harcourt. A third attempt in the Oyapock region was made by Roger North in 1620 but like the others he admitted failure.

Success was achieved by the Dutch in 1613 with the Kyk-Over-Al settlement at the junction of the Essequibo, Cuyuni and Mazaruni rivers. The founder was William Usselinx who was determined to make the settlement permanent. His success was based on a) good Dutch/Indian relations; b) subsistence agriculture; c) tobacco as a cash crop; d) hard work, thriftiness and Protestant crusading zeal. About this time the Dutch also settled up the rivers Courantyne, Pomeroon, Oyapock and Amazon, but they neglected the coastal strip.

From 1616 to 1664 the Dutch colonies were governed by Adrian Groenwegen who continued the ideals of Usselinx and the Kyk-Over-Al colony was so successful that the rival Dutch West Indies Company colony had to ask to join in with Groenwegen's older colony.

The Dutch were driven from Brazil in 1654 and thereupon concentrated on Guiana which they renamed 'Nova Zeelandia' in 1657. Immigration increased and sugar plantations worked by slaves began, especially in Nova Zeelandia. The other colonies were really trading stations although nonetheless permanent because of their subsistence farming and good relations with the Indians.

Notes

1. Non-Spanish settlement began on the Wild Coast, or 'Guiana' as it was then spelt.
2. Three English colonies, the most famous being Mt Howard, on the Oyapock River all failed.
3. The Dutch succeeded with a colony called Kyk-Over-Al up the Essequibo River in 1613.
4. The 'father' of the Dutch colonies was Adrian Groenwegen who was Governor of Kyk-Over-Al for forty-eight years.
5. The Dutch grew their own food, worked hard, sold tobacco, kept friends with the Indians and were determined to establish Protestantism.

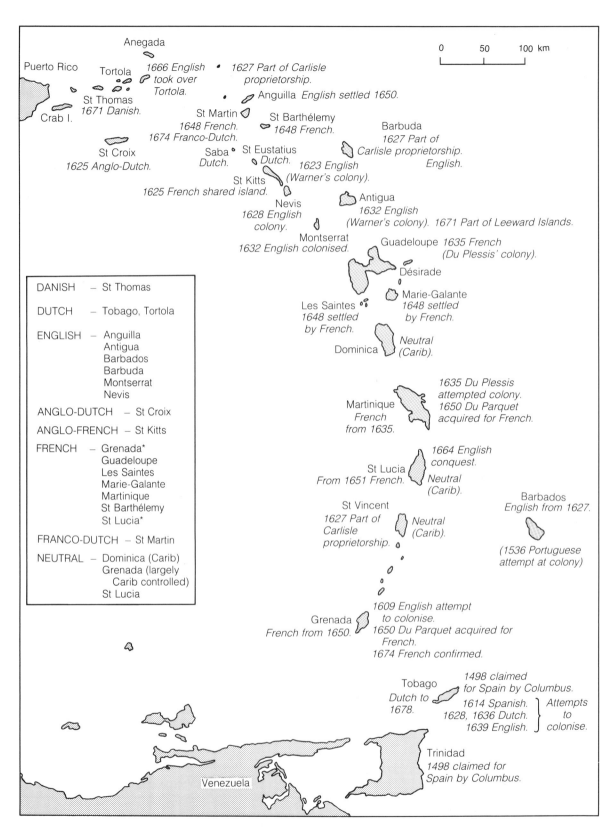

Map 2.9: Non-Spanish island colonies in the seventeenth century

Anegada

Puerto Rico   Tortola   1666 English   • 1627 Part of Carlisle
                          ℘ took over   proprietorship.
                          Tortola.
St Thomas   ℘ Anguilla English settled 1650.
Crab I.   1671 Danish.   St Martin ℰ   St Barthélemy   Barbuda
                          1648 French.   ℰ 1648 French.   1627 Part of
St Croix   1674 Franco-Dutch.   Carlisle proprietorship.
1625 Anglo-Dutch.   Saba ° St Eustatius   English.
                          Dutch. ℰ Dutch. 1623 English
                          St Kitts   (Warner's colony).
                    1625 French shared island.   Antigua
                          Nevis   1632 English
                          1628 English   ℰ (Warner's colony). 1671 Part of Leeward Islands.
                          colony.
                    Montserrat
              1632 English colonised.   Guadeloupe 1635 French
                                                      (Du Plessis' colony).
                                              Désirade

                                          Marie-Galante
                              Les Saintes °℘   1648 settled
                              1648 settled   by French.
                              by French.
                                  Dominica ℰ Neutral
                                              (Carib).

DANISH   — St Thomas   1635 Du Plessis
                                                      attempted colony.
DUTCH   — Tobago, Tortola   Martinique   1650 Du Parquet
                                     French   acquired for French.
ENGLISH   — Anguilla   from 1635.
               Antigua
               Barbados   1664 English
               Barbuda   St Lucia conquest.
               Montserrat   From 1651 French. Neutral
               Nevis   (Carib).
                                                                Barbados
ANGLO-DUTCH — St Croix   English from 1627.

ANGLO-FRENCH — St Kitts   St Vincent
                                     1627 Part of   Neutral
FRENCH   — Grenada*   Carlisle   (Carib).
               Guadeloupe   proprietorship. ℰ
               Les Saintes   (1536 Portuguese
               Marie-Galante   attempt at colony)
               Martinique
               St Barthélemy
               St Lucia*

FRANCO-DUTCH — St Martin   1609 English attempt
                                     Grenada   to colonise.
NEUTRAL   — Dominica (Carib)   French from 1650. 1650 Du Parquet acquired for
               Grenada (largely   French.
                 Carib controlled)   1674 French confirmed.
               St Lucia
                                              Tobago   1498 claimed
                                              Dutch to   for Spain by Columbus.
                                              1678.   1614 Spanish.   ⎫ Attempts
                                                          1628, 1636 Dutch. ⎬ to
                                                          1639 English.   ⎭ colonise.

                                                          Trinidad
                                                          1498 claimed for
                                  Venezuela   Spain by Columbus.

0   50   100 km

Map 2.9: Non-Spanish island colonies in the seventeenth century

In the sixteenth century the Dutch, English and French had challenged Spain's exclusive right to the Indies and the Caribbean with acts of piracy. When they did attempt settlements, they made sure that they kept well clear of Spanish lands, as in the Guiana and Virginia settlements. In the seventeenth century this was largely true of the non-Spanish settlements on the Eastern Caribbean islands: they sought colonies in islands unoccupied by the Spanish although between 1624 and 1644 the Dutch and English did attempt to put colonies in Trinidad and Tobago.

The Spanish had neglected the Lesser Antilles because: a) The Greater Antilles were larger and a better prospect economically; b) Once installed in the Greater Antilles, the Lesser Antilles held little appeal because of the very difficult voyage to the windward; c) The Lesser Antilles were occupied by aggressive Caribs whom the Spanish kept clear of.

Colonisation by non-Spanish countries was haphazard and was initially left to individuals. Governments did not direct it. This was especially true in the case of England until the 'Western Design' led to the colonisation of Jamaica. In France Cardinal Richelieu, the first minister of Louis XIII, did take an interest in colonies and encouraged the formation of *La Compagnie des Îles d'Amérique* in 1635 of which de Poincy was the Lieutenant-General. However, in the Caribbean de Poincy was left to his own devices in finding the colonies for France. The Dutch West India Company was formed in 1621 at the conclusion of the twelve-year truce with Spain to establish permanent settlements but the company's activities in the Caribbean were not directed from home and were only put under central control with Pieter Stuyvesant in 1643.

The Dutch concentrated in the East Indies, not the West Indies, and as a small country had few settlers to send to West Indian islands so their policy was to set up trading stations. In 1636 they realised that they lacked manpower to establish large colonies and they decided to concentrate on small, unoccupied islands which they hoped they would not have to defend. Their colonies fell into two groups, three islands off the Venezuelan coast dominated by Curaçao, and three islands in the Leewards dominated by St Eustatius (Tortola, originally Dutch, soon passed to the English).

In the seventeenth century the English colonies were also scattered, apart from a small concentration around St Kitts, the 'Mother Colony' of the English islands. Barbados was 500 miles south of St Kitts, and very isolated to the windward of the Windwards which left it untroubled by foreign attacks. 1000 miles to the west of St Kitts was Jamaica, the largest English colony, and exceptional in that it was taken from the Spanish by conquest and was the only non-Spanish colony in the Greater Antilles in the seventeenth century.

The French dominated the Windwards to a greater extent than the English dominated the Leewards. The French had interests from Guadeloupe in the north to Grenada in the south, but like the English their first colony was on St Kitts. From 1627 to 1660 France made a big drive for colonies in the West Indies in which Martinique and Guadeloupe were colonised as well as other islands in the Windwards. However, in two cases, Dominica and St Vincent, the French had to yield occupancy to the Caribs, and in two others they were only nominally in control as the Caribs could not be dislodged completely. These were St Lucia and Grenada. In the following century this state of affairs was recognised by the term 'Neutral Islands'.

Notes

1 The Dutch, English and French kept clear of the Spanish lands and made for islands not occupied by the Spanish.
2 These islands were the Lesser Antilles which the Spanish had neglected in favour of the Greater Antilles and the mainland.
3 Colonisation by non-Spanish countries was not directed from home but left to individuals on the spot.
4 In the seventeenth century the English dominated the Leewards while the French dominated the Windwards.
5 The Dutch colonies were intended to be trading stations.
6 The Caribs remained in control of Dominica and St Vincent and kept the French within narrow bounds in St Lucia and Grenada.

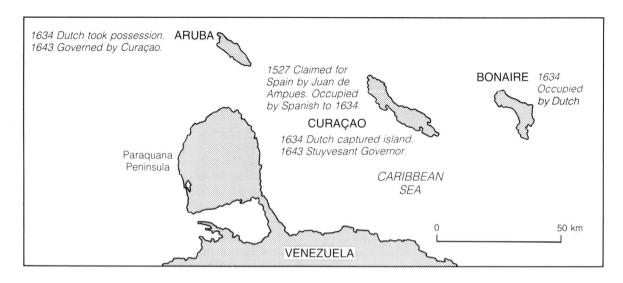

Map 2.10: The Dutch island colonies

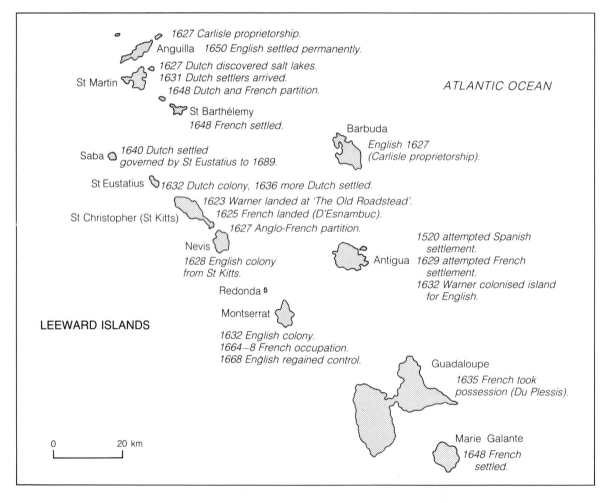

Map 2.10a: The Dutch and English island colonies

Map 2.10: The Dutch island colonies

Alonso de Ojeda discovered Aruba, Curaçao and Bonaire in 1499 but no settlement was made. Another Spaniard, Juan de Ampués, claimed Curaçao for Spain in 1527 and the Spanish occupied it for over a hundred years. The Dutch truce with Spain ended in 1621 and soon the Dutch contested places in the Caribbean. In 1634 they drove the Spanish from Curaçao and, with the exception of an English period between 1805 and 1816, the island has been Dutch ever since. The 1634 expedition also occupied Aruba and Bonaire. The Arawaks were peace-loving and lived alongside the Dutch in these islands. Intermarriage has led to the disappearance of pure Arawak stock.

In 1643 Pieter Stuyvesant became Governor-General of the Dutch West Indies and the government of the southern group of islands was centralised in Curaçao. At that time the Dutch dominated the world's carrying trade and Stuyvesant knew that as the other non-Spanish colonies developed, Dutch shipping and ports would reap the benefit by supplying their imports and carrying away their exports. By the Treaty of Munster, 1648, Spain recognised the Dutch West Indies and the Dutch right of trade and navigation in the Caribbean.

The Dutch called their other group of colonies the 'Windwards' because they were to the windward of the Curaçao group. They were inhabited by Caribs when the Dutch arrived. In 1627 the Dutch discovered natural salt lakes on St Maarten and in 1631 they decided to make a settlement there. This annoyed the Spanish as salt was a valuable commodity in Europe then so they recap-tured the island. Stuyvesant led an expedition in 1644 which failed to regain the island but in 1648 the Spanish left and the Dutch and the French partitioned St Maarten, the Dutch taking the south, the French the north, and the two sharing the salt lakes.

In 1632 the Dutch colonised St Eustatius in order to win the trade of the Leeward islands. In 1636 more settlers arrived and St Eustatius became the base from which other islands could be colonised. Its government was under a patron until 1682 when it became a colony under the Dutch West Indies Company. Settlers from St Eustatius colonised Saba in 1640 and Saba was governed by St Eustatius until 1689. (Tortola was Dutch until 1666 when the English took over and it became part of the English Virgin Islands group).

Notes

1 The Dutch dominated the carrying trade in the seventeenth century and wanted island colonies which could capture the trade of the English and French islands.
2 Curaçao was the chief Dutch island colony and it became an important entrepôt in the carrying trade of the Caribbean.
3 St Eustatius was well placed to capture the trade of St Kitts and the other English Leewards.
4 Pieter Stuyvesant directed Dutch colonial policy in the Caribbean from 1643.
5 He saw that the Dutch could supply the English and French colonies with their needs and with Dutch expertise in tobacco and sugar cultivation.
6 The Dutch 'windwards' were in the Leewards from the English point of view.

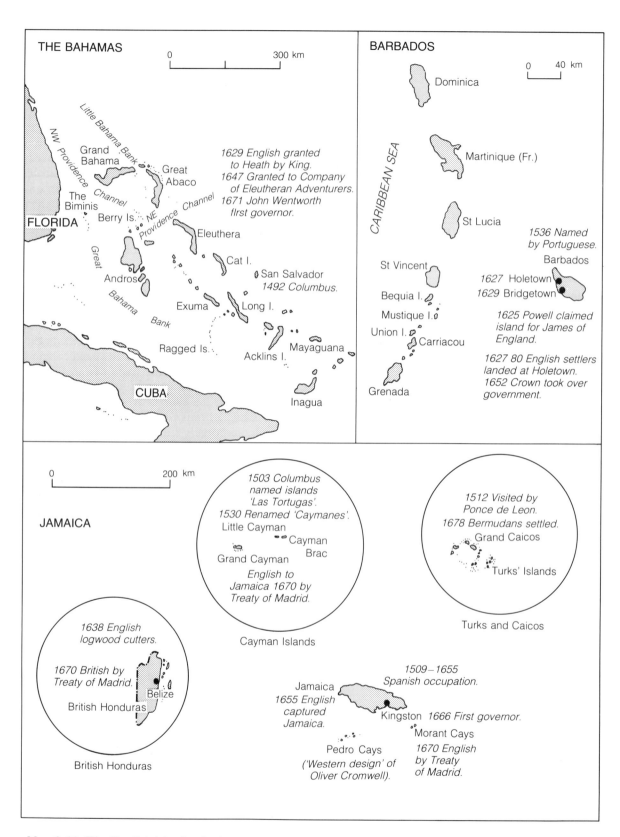

THE BAHAMAS

0   300 km

1629 English granted
to Heath by King.
1647 Granted to Company
of Eleutheran Adventurers.
1671 John Wentworth
first governor.

NW Providence Channel
Little Bahama Bank
Grand Bahama
Great Abaco
The Biminis
FLORIDA
Berry Is.
NE Providence Channel
Great Channel
Eleuthera
Cat I.
San Salvador
1492 Columbus.
Andros
Great Bahama Bank
Exuma
Long I.
Ragged Is.
Acklins I.
Mayaguana
CUBA
Inagua

BARBADOS

0   40 km

Dominica

CARIBBEAN SEA

Martinique (Fr.)

St Lucia

1536 Named
by Portuguese.

St Vincent

Barbados

1627 Holetown
1629 Bridgetown

Bequia I.
Mustique I.
Union I.
Carriacou

1625 Powell claimed
island for James of
England.

1627 80 English settlers
landed at Holetown.
1652 Crown took over
government.

Grenada

JAMAICA

0   200 km

1503 Columbus
named islands
'Las Tortugas'.
1530 Renamed 'Caymanes'.
Little Cayman
Cayman
Brac
Grand Cayman
English to
Jamaica 1670 by
Treaty of Madrid.

Cayman Islands

1512 Visited by
Ponce de Leon.
1678 Bermudans settled.
Grand Caicos

Turks' Islands

Turks and Caicos

1638 English
logwood cutters.

1670 British by
Treaty of Madrid.
Belize
British Honduras

British Honduras

1509–1655
Spanish occupation.

Jamaica
1655 English
captured
Jamaica.
Kingston 1666 First governor.
Morant Cays

Pedro Cays
('Western design' of
Oliver Cromwell).

1670 English
by Treaty
of Madrid.

Map 2.11: The English island colonies

Map 2.11: The English island colonies

Having failed to establish permanent settlements on the Wild Coast, the English turned their attention to the Lesser Antilles. The first English island colony, St Kitts, was founded by Thomas Warner, an English captain who had given up in Guiana in 1622 and was exploring the Eastern Caribbean. He was attracted by St Kitts and the friendliness of its Carib chief, Tegramond. In January, 1624, he returned with settlers and they started building at Old Road. In 1625 Warner returned to England to obtain a charter from Charles I and the help of a wealthy patron. Thus St Kitts is known as the 'Mother Colony' of the English islands, not only because it was the first colony but also because it gave rise to the other island colonies of Nevis, Montserrat and Antigua. The proprietorship (whereby an influential patron was given tenure of the colony) was given to the Earl of Carlisle. Nevis, Montserrat and Antigua were included in the same proprietorship as St Kitts. Anthony Hilton of St Kitts went to Nevis in 1628 with other settlers. In the same year other refugees from Barbuda arrived. The first English settlers went to Montserrat in 1632 and, apart from 1664 to 1668 when the French held it, Montserrat has been British ever since. Antigua had attracted the Spanish in 1520 and the French in 1629, but neither had stayed. In 1632 Warner sent a colony from St Kitts and after much trouble from the Caribs they survived.

Two other islands in the Leewards which the English settled were Anguilla and Barbuda. Anguilla was settled permanently from 1650, surviving a serious Carib raid from Dominica in 1656. In 1628 the Earl of Carlisle granted Barbuda to Captain Littleton but he quickly abandoned it due to Carib hostility and moved to Nevis. Barbuda was included in Sir Charles Wheeler's commission as Governor-in-chief of the Leeward Islands in 1671.

Five hundred miles south of St Kitts was Barbados. Perhaps it had been visited three times by English ships to and from the Wild Coast before 1625, but none had attempted settlement. The first certain English visitor was Captain John Powell on his return from Pernambuço. In 1625 he claimed the island for King James I of England. Powell was in command of one of Sir William Courteen's ships. Courteen sent him back with 80 settlers in 1627. They built Plantation Port and called the settlement 'Jamestown' which is now Holetown.

King Charles I was confused about the geography of the Caribbean (perhaps he confused Barbados with Barbuda) but whatever the case he gave the island to the Earl of Pembroke instead of to the Earl of Carlisle in 1628. Carlisle sent an expedition to take the island in 1629 and these settlers founded Bridgetown. Lord Willoughby bought the proprietorship from Carlisle's son and held it to 1652. Barbados was the centre of government for all the English Windward Islands at first.

During the governorship of Captain Henry Hawley from 1629 to 1640 the Barbados Parliament was founded. Hawley was known as a 'ruffian' and was unpopular so he gave the planters a parliament in 1639 thinking that they would support his governorship, but far from doing that they deposed him in 1640. The Barbados Parliament was the earliest representative body in the British West Indies.

The English colonisation of Jamaica in 1655 is referred to as an 'afterthought' because the capture of Hispaniola was the original objective of Cromwell's 'Western Design'. However, Cromwell had been badly advised and the force of 6000 under Admiral Penn and General Venables was a rabble. When this force failed to capture Santo Domingo they dared not go on to Cuba nor return to England so they captured Jamaica where the Spanish were weak and probably could not raise more than 500 fighting men. The English took Passage Fort in Kingston Harbour and the Spanish came there day after day for a week to surrender. Other Spaniards retreated to the north coast to await help from Cuba, but the help never came. Eventually the English, under d'Oyley, won a decisive battle at Rio Nuevo in 1658 and Jamaica was theirs. D'Oyley became the first English Governor of Jamaica, from 1656 to 1662. By the Treaty of Madrid, 1670, the Spanish recognised English possession of Jamaica. Included in this were the Cayman Islands which then acted as a haven for pirates and buccaneers and had no permanent settlement until the next century.

The Virgin Islands were also haunts of pirates and not settled until some English captured Tortola from the Dutch in 1666. The islands were used for sugar, indigo and cotton cultivation. Some planters were attracted to Virgin Gorda for this purpose in 1680.

There were no permanent settlements in the Turks and Caicos Islands in the seventeenth century except for some Bermudans raking salt in 1678, but pirates of all nations considered these islands strategically well placed to catch Spanish treasure ships from Havana to Spain.

(For the English at Grenada and St Lucia in the seventeenth century see Map 2.12: The French island colonies.)

Notes

1 The English turned their attention to the Lesser Antilles after failing to make permanent settlements on the Wild Coast.
2 Both St Kitts and Barbados were first visited, and the ideas for colonies conceived, by captains returning from voyages to the Wild Coast.
3 St Kitts was the first English colony in the West Indies and is known as the 'Mother Colony' of the English islands.
4 The Crown did not involve itself in the government of the colonies at first but granted proprietorships under which a patron took control of the islands in return for payment of a sum of money to the Crown.
5 Cromwell's 'Western Design' was to drive the Spanish out of the West Indies by first capturing Hispaniola and then the other important Spanish possessions.
6 Having failed to capture Hispaniola the expedition turned to Jamaica and captured it easily between 1655 and 1658.
7 In the seventeenth century the Cayman Islands, the British Virgin Islands and the Turks and Caicos were bases for pirates and buccaneers.

Map 2.12: The French island colonies

In 1625 d'Esnambuc, in a badly damaged French pirate ship, sought refuge in St Kitts to carry out repairs and then asked the English if he could settle. The French helped the English drive off Carib attacks in 1625 and 1626 which brought an end to Carib aggression. In 1627 d'Esnambuc and Warner made an agreement to partition the island, the French taking the ends Capesterre and Basseterre, the English the middle, and both nationalities sharing salt lakes, fish ponds, harbours and roads.

D'Esnambuc was supported by Cardinal Richelieu who formed the Company of St Christopher but this company in fact did little to help and went bankrupt in 1635. Thereupon Richelieu formed a new company, the Company of the Isles of America, which sent de Poincy to St Kitts in 1639 as Lieutenant-General for all the French islands.

Before his death in 1635 d'Esnambuc had sent du Pont to found a colony in Martinique. He drove the Caribs into the eastern part of the island and started a successful colony on the west coast. Du Parquet continued his good work by planting tobacco and allowing free trade which helped the port of St Pierre to prosper. In 1650 the Company of the Isles of America sold Martinique to the du Parquet family.

De l'Olive and du Plessis were sent to Martinique in 1635 but did not stay as they were given a hostile reception by the Caribs. They went straight on to Guadeloupe where they landed with 400 settlers and claimed the island for France. Du Plessis soon died and the settlement was left under the control of de l'Olive who showed great cruelty towards the Caribs. De Poincy replaced de l'Olive but the Company did not like the replacement and installed Houel as Governor. Houel was Governor from 1643 to 1660 and eventually bought the island and adopted the title 'Marquis of Guadeloupe'. He was a very successful governor and under him the island prospered.

De Poincy, Lieutenant-General of all the French islands from 1639 to 1660, was a very important figure. He directed French colonial expansion in the West Indies enthusiastically, from St Croix in the Virgin Islands in the north to Grenada at the south of the Windwards. The Spanish had driven the Dutch and English from St Croix in 1650. De Poincy drove out the Spanish almost immediately and the French held St Croix from 1650 to 1696 when they left. St Martin was already occupied by the Dutch when de Poincy sent a French settlement there in 1648 but by the Treaty of Mt Concordia they agreed to partition

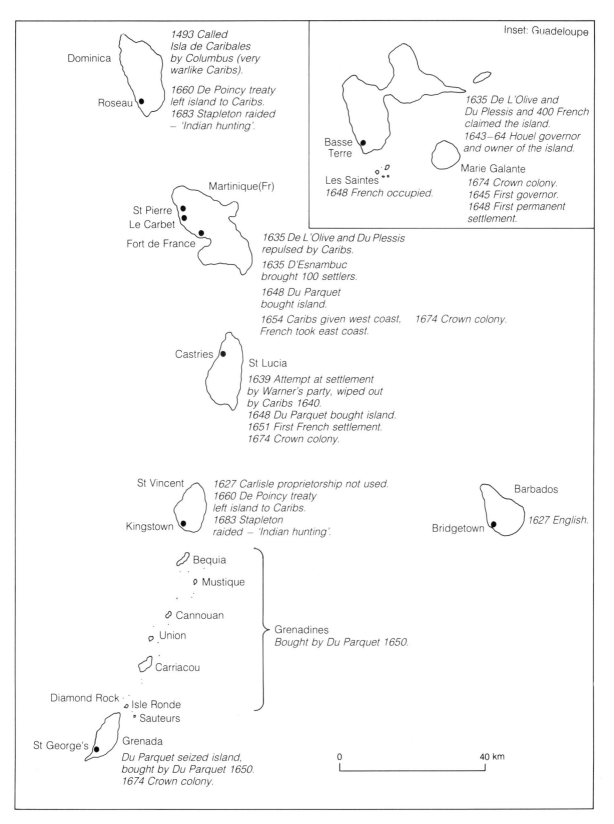

Dominica

1493 Called
Isla de Caribales
by Columbus (very
warlike Caribs).

1660 De Poincy treaty
left island to Caribs.
1683 Stapleton raided
– 'Indian hunting'.

Roseau

Inset: Guadeloupe

Basse
Terre

1635 De L'Olive and
Du Plessis and 400 French
claimed the island.
1643–64 Houel governor
and owner of the island.

Marie Galante
1674 Crown colony.
1645 First governor.
1648 First permanent
settlement.

Les Saintes
1648 French occupied.

Martinique(Fr)

St Pierre
Le Carbet
Fort de France

1635 De L'Olive and Du Plessis
repulsed by Caribs.

1635 D'Esnambuc
brought 100 settlers.

1648 Du Parquet
bought island.

1654 Caribs given west coast,   1674 Crown colony.
French took east coast.

Castries

St Lucia

1639 Attempt at settlement
by Warner's party, wiped out
by Caribs 1640.
1648 Du Parquet bought island.
1651 First French settlement.
1674 Crown colony.

St Vincent

1627 Carlisle proprietorship not used.
1660 De Poincy treaty
left island to Caribs.
1683 Stapleton
raided – 'Indian hunting'.

Kingstown

Barbados

Bridgetown   1627 English.

Bequia

Mustique

Cannouan

Union

Grenadines
Bought by Du Parquet 1650.

Carriacou

Diamond Rock
Isle Ronde
Sauteurs

St George's   Grenada
Du Parquet seized island,
bought by Du Parquet 1650.
1674 Crown colony.

0   40 km

Map 2.12: The French island colonies

the island. The French colonised St Barthélémy which had not previously been occupied, in the same year. Under Houel, Governor of Guadeloupe, the first Governor of Marie-Galante was appointed in 1645, but the island was not settled until 1648. Les Saintes and Désirade were also occupied from Guadeloupe in the same year.

Du Parquet was the force behind the colonisation of the Windwards by the French. In 1605, 67 English settlers had been abandoned on St Lucia by the crew of their ship and 19 survivors from Carib attacks managed to reach the Spanish Main. In 1637 Warner sent some settlers to St Lucia but they deserted. In 1638 130 Bermudans settled but the colony was abandoned in 1640. Willoughby then decided to buy St Lucia from the Caribs but the French pre-empted him by occupying the island as soon as the English had left. The Caribs resisted fiercely but more French settlers arrived in 1651 and in spite of the murder of the French Governor, de la Rivière in 1654, the French remained. In 1664 1000 Englishmen from Barbados joined by 600 Caribs captured St Lucia and thereafter the French and the English struggled for control of the island.

In 1650 du Parquet bought Grenada from the Company of the Isles of America. There had been a short-lived English settlement there in 1609 which had been driven off by the Caribs. After du Parquet's purchase the French made a settlement at St George but the Caribs resisted so fiercely that the French never had firm control of the island in the seventeenth century and they even suggested exchanging it for the English part of St Kitts in the Treaty of Breda, 1667. In 1674 Grenada became a French Crown Colony.

The French were interested in Dominica and St Vincent but did not attempt colonisation seriously because of the hostility of the Caribs. By a Treaty made by de Poincy in 1660 Dominica and St Vincent were made Carib islands.

The Company of the Isles of America had administered all the French island colonies through its Lieutenant-General in St Kitts. However, due to impending bankruptcy, the Company was forced to sell off the colonies to the existing governors as proprietary colonies, e.g. Houel of Guadeloupe bought Guadeloupe, Marie-Galante, Désirade and Les Saintes in 1649; du Parquet bought Martinique, St Lucia, Grenada and the Grenadines in 1650; de Poincy, on behalf of the Knights of Malta, bought St Kitts, St Martin, St Croix and St Barthélémy in 1651. The Proprietary system ended in 1674 when Louis XIV made them all Crown Colonies.

Notes

1 The St Kitts' Colony, founded by d'Esnambuc in 1625, was the first French colony in the West Indies.

2 Cardinal Richelieu, first minister of Louis XIII, supported French colonisation through the Company of St Kitts and the Company of the Isles of America.

3 French colonial expansion in the West Indies was directed and vigorously encouraged by de Poincy, Lieutenant-General of all the French colonies.

4 a) In the Virgin Islands and the Leeward Islands the French held colonies in St Croix, St Martin, St Barthélémy and St Kitts.
   b) In the Guadeloupe group they held Guadeloupe itself, Marie-Galante, Désirade and Les Saintes.
   c) In the Windward Islands the French claimed St Lucia, Grenada and the Grenadines.
   d) The French left Dominica and St Vincent to the Caribs.

5 The French colonial companies owned the islands at first, then they were owned by proprietors and finally, in 1674, they belonged to the Crown.

Theme 3: Sugar and slavery_____

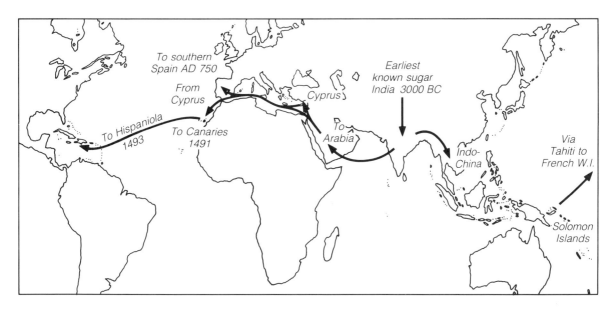

Map 3.1: How sugar reached the West Indies

Map 3.1: How sugar reached the West Indies

The earliest known cultivation of sugar cane and its propagation into sugar is in India about 3000 BC. There is a written reference to sugar in a Hindu Holy Book of about 800 BC and the first reference in European literature is from Nearchos, a general who travelled with Alexander the Great to India between 327 and 325 BC.

From India sugar propagation went eastwards into Indo-China and westwards with the Arabs into Arabia in about AD 100. The Arabic word, *sukkar*, is the derivation for our word, 'sugar'. The Arabs took sugar cultivation to all parts of the Mediterranean world where they had interests and where it was hot enough (above 62° Fahrenheit), including Southern Spain by the eighth century AD.

However the shoots of the type that Columbus took to the West Indies are believed to have come from Cyprus by way of the Canary Islands to Hispaniola on his second voyage in 1493. He also transported some Canary Islanders to supervise the cultivation in the West Indies.

At this time sugar was used by Europeans and Arabs as a sweetener for drinks and was scarce in Europe until the late-seventeenth century. It remained expensive until the late-eighteenth century in Europe.

(Sugar also originated independently in the Solomon Islands in the South Pacific. This type of cane probably came by way of Tahiti to the West Indies in the late-eighteenth century).

Notes

1 The type of sugar cane which Columbus introduced to the West Indies in 1493 originated in India about 3000 BC.
2 It came to Europe by way of Arabia and was known to the Spaniards in the eighth century AD.
3 The sugar taken to Hispaniola in 1493 came directly from Cyprus to the Canary Islands in 1491 and from the Canary Islands to Hispaniola.
4 Some Canary Islanders were also transported to help in cultivation.

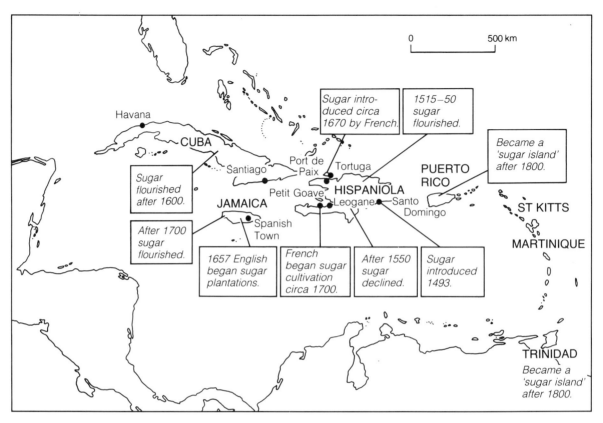

Map 3.2: Islands which did not experience the sugar revolution

Map 3.2: Islands which did not experience the sugar revolution

In West Indian history the term 'sugar revolution' strictly refers to the change from tobacco to sugar cultivation which took place in the mid-or late-seventeenth century in the Eastern Caribbean islands, and the social changes that went with it.

The Greater Antilles had been settled by the Spanish between 1493 and 1511. However, these islands remained under-populated for about two centuries so there was plenty of land for diverse farming. Sugar was not grown to the exclusion of other crops and ranching and large sugar estates existed alongside ranches and small-holdings. Therefore the social changes concomitant with the sugar revolution did not happen under the Spanish: white small-holders increased in number and the white population rose as the black rose; tobacco production increased and quality improved; ranching was actually detrimental to sugar cultivation as the cattle trampled the crops and ate them.

Sugar was introduced into Hispaniola in 1493 and by 1515 was being exported. By 1541 there were 40 sugar mills in Hispaniola, but from about 1550 the decline began as ranching grew in importance and large areas of land went out of sugar cultivation. Slaves were in less demand and some escaped to become maroons. It was a long time before there was a revival of sugar in Hispaniola. It happened about 1700 around Petit Goave on the west coast of Hispaniola when the French established their colonies there. St Domingue became a prosperous sugar colony which rivalled Jamaica and outstripped Martinique and Guadeloupe. However, what happened in St Domingue cannot be called a 'sugar revolution' as it was not a question of sugar replacing what had gone before and changing an economy. It was the foundation of a new colony.

Cuba took over from Hispaniola as the chief Spanish sugar-producing island after 1600 and remained so thereafter, but it was not to the exclusion of other crops. The sugar industry in Cuba developed slowly between 1550 and 1650, but tobacco also flourished in this period and small-holders grew in number as did urban artisans. Ranching also flourished as Cuba was large enough and under-populated enough for there to be large ranches, sugar estates and small-holdings.

The Spanish neglected Jamaica. Sugar grew in isolated areas but was not exported. The English arrived in 1655 but most of those who settled at first were not interested in planting. They were army deserters, buccaneers and drifters. It took a few years, up to about 1670, before its potential as a sugar island was exploited, but even then sugar was never grown exclusively.

Puerto Rico and Trinidad did not become great sugar islands until the nineteenth century, owing to the difficulties of settlement and the dominance of Cuba. Rising world demand for sugar turned their economies over to that crop.

Notes

1 'Sugar revolution' should only be applied to the change from tobacco to sugar cultivation which took place:
   a) In the mid- to late-seventeenth century.
   b) In the Eastern Caribbean islands belonging to the English and French.
   c) Where the monoculture of sugar became the rule.
   d) Where the social changes were equally revolutionary, e.g. small-holdings were swallowed by large estates; indentured servants were dispossessed; black slaves dominated the populations by a ratio of at least 10 to 1.
2 There was no 'sugar revolution' in the Greater Antilles because:
   a) Sugar cultivation and production developed slowly.
   b) Sugar was never cultivated to the exclusion of other farming.
   c) White urban and rural populations always remained a large proportion of the total population.
   d) Cuba was so large that for two hundred years the Spanish hardly needed another source of sugar.

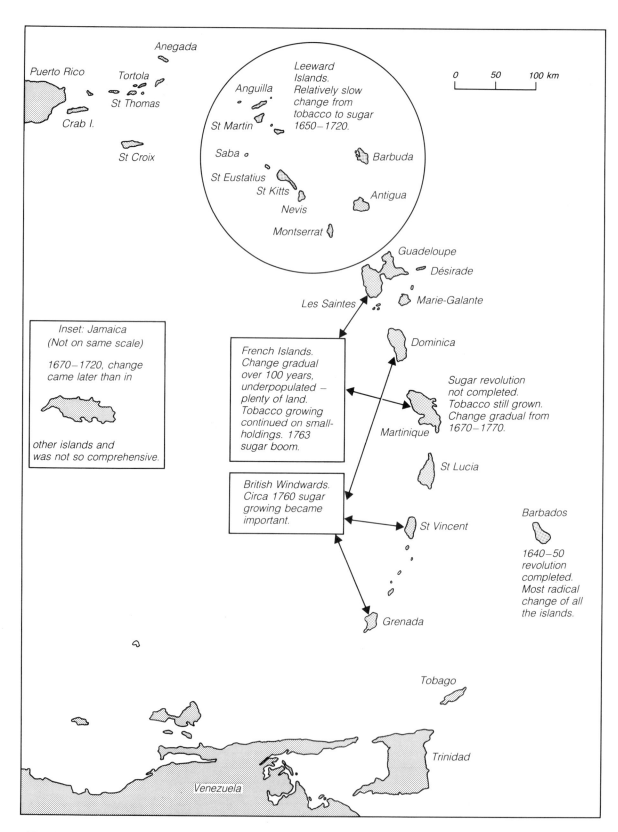

Anegada

Puerto Rico

Tortola
St Thomas

Crab I.

St Croix

Anguilla

St Martin

Saba ∘

St Eustatius

St Kitts

Nevis

Montserrat

Leeward
Islands.
Relatively slow
change from
tobacco to sugar
1650–1720.

Barbuda

Antigua

0   50   100 km

Guadeloupe

Désirade

Marie-Galante

Les Saintes

Dominica

Inset: Jamaica
(Not on same scale)

1670–1720, change
came later than in

other islands and
was not so comprehensive.

French Islands.
Change gradual
over 100 years,
underpopulated –
plenty of land.
Tobacco growing
continued on small-
holdings. 1763
sugar boom.

British Windwards.
Circa 1760 sugar
growing became
important.

Sugar revolution
not completed.
Tobacco still grown.
Change gradual from
1670–1770.

Martinique

St Lucia

Barbados

1640–50
revolution
completed.
Most radical
change of all
the islands.

St Vincent

Grenada

Tobago

Trinidad

Venezuela

Map 3.3: The Eastern Caribbean sugar revolution

Map 3.3: The Eastern Caribbean sugar revolution

The change from tobacco to sugar cultivation in the Eastern Caribbean was so far-reaching that it can be termed a 'revolution'. Not only did the cash crop change, in some cases within ten years, but also land tenure, land prices, social structure and racial composition changed in these islands.

In the early seventeenth century tobacco from Virginia in North America began to reach the European market. By 1627 Virginia exported over 225 000 kg of tobacco to England. Virginian tobacco surpassed West Indian tobacco in quantity and quality so demand for West Indian tobacco fell dramatically and its price was so low that many West Indian tobacco planters went out of business.

At the same time there was a growing demand for sugar which was still an expensive luxury in Europe. The Eastern Caribbean islands had climates suitable for sugar cultivation and land available as tobacco became uneconomical. However, they lacked the capital, expertise and labour. These could be provided by the Dutch who were losing their hold of Brazil to the Portuguese. The Dutch made the sugar revolution possible because they put up the credit when the English and French planters could not raise the capital; they provided the expertise in sugar cultivation which they had learnt in Brazil; they imported the slave labour in their ships; and they carried away the sugar for export. The English colonies in particular were unable to start sugar by themselves as they were not supported by governments or wealthy companies.

Barbados, between 1640 and 1650, epitomises the sugar revolution. Before 1640 tobacco was being grown on small-holdings averaging about four hectares. There were about 12 000 small-holders. When the price of tobacco fell these small-holders could not support their families on their incomes nor could they afford to expand because they could not raise the capital. They were forced to sell up and leave and their lands became available for sugar estates. In Barbados about 60 hectares was the minimum size of a sugar estate which could yield an adequate income so the average land holding changed from 4 hectares before the revolution to 60 hectares after; the average land price from £6 per hectare to £80 per hectare. White society changed from 12 000 independent small-holders to 750 planters. The nature of society changed from a free citizenry to a slave population, and racially from white to black as about 40 000 additional African slaves were imported to work on the sugar estates. All this happened in under a generation.

In the Leeward Islands the sugar revolution began as that in Barbados was ending and it was never so dramatic. For example St Kitts was mountainous so its land could never be given over completely to sugar cultivation. Other islands changed to sugar more slowly as whites still managed to make a living by other occupations. After fifty years the sugar revolution was still not complete in the Leewards. The radical demographic changes were not complete until the end of the eighteenth century. The white population actually increased in this period reflecting very little emigration and some natural increase.

Jamaica probably would have had a sugar revolution if it had been a British colony from the start. However the English did not arrive until 1655 and sugar cultivation did not 'take off' until after 1670. Therefore Jamaica did experience the sudden changes found in the Eastern Caribbean islands, but not to the same extent. And of course, we must not forget that there was no tobacco cultivation to be replaced.

The English Windward Islands turned to sugar after the period of the sugar revolution. Dominica, St Vincent and Grenada were not securely British until the Peace of Paris in 1763. Settlers had begun to cultivate sugar before then but the insecurity brought about by the eighteenth-century wars made investment in sugar estates far too risky.

There was a sort of sugar revolution in the French islands although the chief French colony, St Domingue, started off as a sugar island. In Martinique and Guadeloupe the change to sugar cultivation came very slowly over a hundred years, from 1670 to 1770. It was never complete as tobacco continued to be grown. White small-holders remained and small land-holdings were possible as the price of land did not rise very much. More land was available in the French islands than in the British. African slaves were not imported to the same extent as the French supply was difficult. Consequently without the hands sugar cultivation was held back and the ratio of blacks to whites, at 6:1 in Martinique, was much lower than that of the English islands.

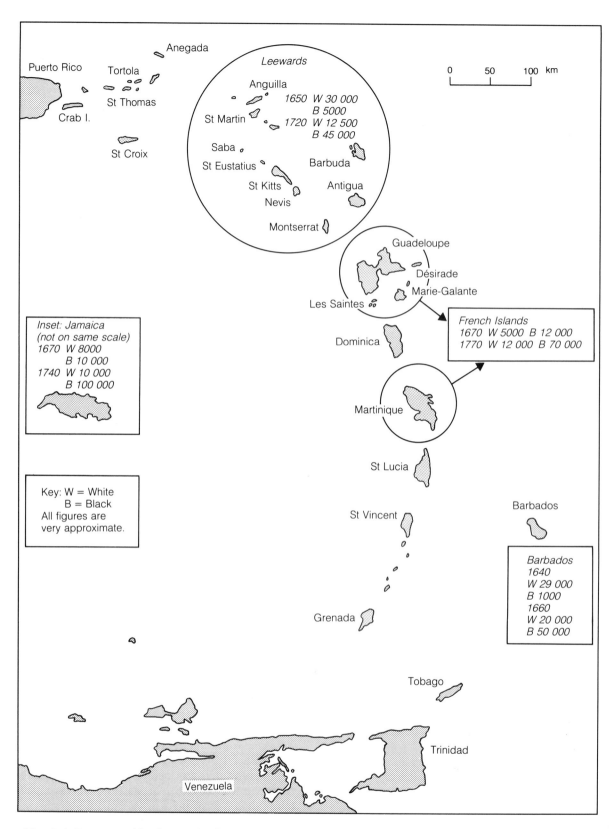

Map 3.4: Demographic changes in the sugar revolution

Notes

1 West Indian tobacco prices fell when tobacco from Virginia, in greater quantity and of better quality, began to be sold in Europe.
2 The Dutch, who were losing their colony of Brazil between 1624 and 1654, helped the English and French colonies begin sugar cultivation with capital, expertise, slaves and transport.
3 Barbados changed from tobacco to sugar in the decade 1640 to 1650, the epitome of the sugar revolution.
4 Concomitant changes were the increase in size of land holdings; fall in numbers of land owners; increase in land prices; polarisation of society into white planters and black slaves; and a black to white ratio of at least 10:1.
5 The Leeward Islands experienced the sugar revolution later than Barbados. It lasted longer but was not so complete.
6 Jamaica rapidly became a sugar island after 1670 but sugar was not replacing anything.
7 St Domingue became the leading sugar producer of the French islands but it was a new colony.
8 Martinique and Guadeloupe experienced gradual revolutions over the period 1670 to 1770, but these were incomplete as tobacco-growing and small-holding remained.

Map 3.4: Demographic changes in the sugar revolution

A century from 1640 to 1740, covering the sugar revolution in most areas, would show the following trends:
a) A decline in the white population.
b) An increase in the black population.
c) A decline in the number of landowners.
As the white population was free and the black population slave, society changed from free to slave.

These trends are shown by population statistics from different islands. Barbados demonstrates all these trends most clearly:

Year	White	Black	Landowners	
1639	29 000	1000	7000	
1645	39 000	7000	12 000	(Sugar revolution begins)
1666	18 000	52 000	760	(Sugar revolution over)

The decline in the white population by over 50 per cent in the later part of the revolution reflects the dispossessed white small-holders emigrating elsewhere to seek their livelihood. The most startling trend is the decline in landowners from 12 000 to 760 reflecting the swallowing up of small-holdings by sugar estates. The black to white ratio of 3:1 after the sugar revolution seems surprisingly low. The ratio grew larger later as the white population remained relatively static while the black population increased rapidly.

Jamaica presents a different picture as it had not been a colony of small-holders.

Year	White	Black	
1673	8000	10 000	(Sugar revolution begins)
1723	8000	83 000	(During sugar revolution)
1741	10 000	100 000	(Sugar revolution over)

Sugar cultivation took off after 1670 and immediately more slaves were brought in. Between the first two years quoted the black population rose by over 800 per cent. The black to white ratio of 10:1 after the sugar revolution reflects the small white population before sugar which remained constant in spite of the sugar revolution.

The Leewards figures show how slow the demographic changes were.

Year	White	Black	
1654	30 000	5000	(Before the sugar revolution)
1707	8000	25 000	(During the sugar revolution)
1724	12 500	45 000	(After the sugar revolution)

There was a dramatic decline in the white population at the outset of the sugar revolution followed by a natural increase in the white population while the black population increased steadily as sugar cultivation was introduced slowly.

Figures from Martinique show the contrast between the French islands and the English:

Year	White	Black	
1670	5000	12 000	(Before the sugar revolution)
1700	7000	23 000	(During the sugar revolution)
1770	12 000	70 000	(After the sugar revolution)

Martinique, a comparatively large island, was underpopulated. The fact that the white population increased during the sugar revolution reflects an increase in the number of small-holders because tobacco growing increased. The black population grew very slowly reflecting a gradual changeover to sugar cultivation in the French islands. Overall these figures show that the sugar revolution in the French islands was neither so dramatic nor so complete as in the English.

Notes

1 As a result of the sugar revolution a) the white population declined, b) the black population increased, c) the number of landowners decreased, d) society changed from free to slave.

2 In Barbados all the above trends occurred.
3 In Jamaica there had not been a small-holder society. The white population remained constant while the black population increased tenfold.
4 In the Leewards the black population increased slowly showing that the change to sugar was gradual and imcomplete.
5 In the French islands the white population actually increased because small-holding increased. The black population increased very slowly in comparison with the English islands because the French source of slaves was unreliable.

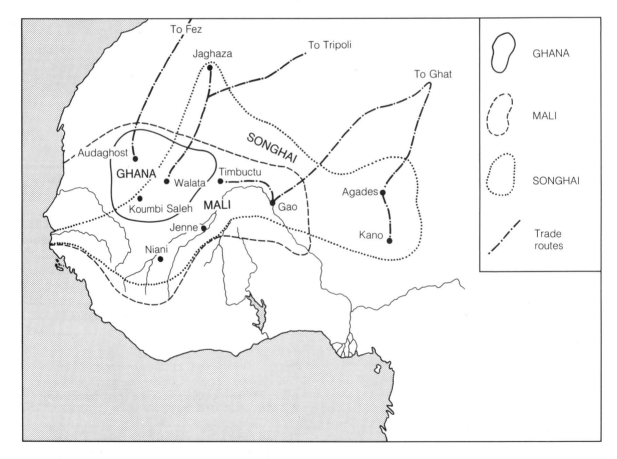

Map 3.5: The empires of the Western Sudan

Map 3.5: The empires of the Western Sudan

Between AD 800 and 1600 three empires, Ghana, Mali and Songhai, arose in the Western Sudan, the savannah belt between the forests to the south and the desert to the north. There was plenty of water so sedentary living was possible. The crops grew well and relatively large communities developed. Movement was easy in the savannah and these communities were organised for trade. Salt was the key to this trade. People in the forests needed the rock salt from the desert mines like Taghaza. In exchange they gave gold, slaves and kola nuts.

Ghana flourished between AD 800 and 1240. Its centre was at Koumbi Saleh which was about 200 miles north of modern Bamako. The Soninke people of Ghana began the gold trade by which the gold of West Africa reached North Africa and Europe. The Berbers from the desert brought the salt in exchange. Inevitably slaves were carried on these routes as well as gold.

Mali, an empire of the Mandinka people, was founded by King Sundiata when he conquered Ghana in 1240. It flourished between then and 1500. At first its centre was at Niani but then it moved north to Jenne near the internal delta of the River Niger. It became Moslem and included Timbuctu, the famous centre of Islamic learning in West Africa. As a larger trading empire than Ghana, Mali was responsible for the spread of Islam in West Africa.

From 1400 Mali began to decline as subject people began to break away. At first the Tuareg, then the Woloff and finally the Mossi rebelled and Mali came to an end. In 1513 it was conquered by a ruler from the Songhai empire of Gao. This empire became easily the largest in the Western Sudan, completely embracing the whole geographical area of Mali and lands further east. It had its centre in Gao on the great bend of the Niger. It flourished from the time of Sonni Ali's conquest of Timbuctu in 1464 to the Moroccan invasions of 1591.

From the point of view of Caribbean history, these empires are important in that they were organised for trade and some of that trade was in slaves. Slaves became increasingly important as Arab demand for slaves grew. However, this slave trade was directed to the north and was in African hands, not southwards to Europeans on the West African coast. It was the Portuguese who changed the direction of the trade, helped by the forest states of Benin, Oyo, Dahomey and Ashanti.

Notes

1 Trading empires grew up in the West African savannah belt between AD 800 and 1600.
2 The three most famous empires in chronological order of domination of the trade were Ghana, Mali and Songhai.
3 The trade was based on salt from the desert in exchange for gold from the forests, but slaves were carried as well.
4 In this period the trade was directed to the north.
5 When the Portuguese arrived on the coast the direction of the trade changed to the south to the coast.
6 Slaves then became the reason for this trade.

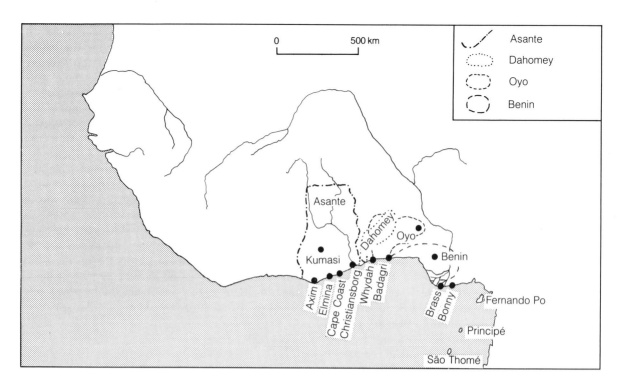

Map 3.6: The forest states of West Africa

Map 3.6: The forest states of West Africa

The forest states, Benin, Oyo, Dahomey and Asante, took advantage of the European demand for slaves. In the period of the slave trade they were never ruled by Europeans but tolerated European forts on the coasts of their territories.

From the arrival of the Portuguese in 1472 Benin began to grow strong. It acted as the middleman between Yorubaland and the coast. At first the Portuguese took the slaves to their islands in the Gulf of Guinea but early in the sixteenth century the demand for slaves in the West Indies arose. The Portuguese bought the slaves with guns. With these guns the Bini captured more slaves and so the cycle developed. However, the temptations of wealth from the slave trade led to internal wars and about 1700 Benin declined.

Oyo was another Yoruba state which enjoyed a short period of domination in the slave trade, but it was not deeply involved in it. Its centre was too far from the coast and then, between 1750 and 1800, the Fulani captured its source of slaves to the north of the River Niger. Oyo was squeezed out of the trade by coastal states which did not have the same disadvantages.

One of these states was Dahomey whose capital, Abomey, was not far from the coast. Dahomey took up the slave trade soon after 1700 when it captured the great slave port of Whydah. The Fon of Dahomey used the guns they obtained from the sale of slaves to expand into Yorubaland. At the turn of the next century, however, King Agaja, under pressure from the abolitionists, gave up slave trading.

The Asante became the greatest slave traders of all beginning in the seventeenth century and continuing until long after the others had stopped. Kumasi, their capital, was far from the coast, but the Asante drove to the coast to reach the Dutch at Elmina and the English at Cape Coast. Certainly the Asante wanted guns with which to conquer their neighbours. The Asante stopped slave trading only when the British conquered them in 1874.

These empires, with the exception of Oyo, owed their strength to the slave trade. The guns they obtained from selling slaves enabled them to expand, but it is debatable whether the slave trading was the motive force behind their expansion.

Notes

1 The Portuguese reached Benin in 1472 and soon encouraged the Bini to bring them slaves.
2 The first slaves were taken to the Portuguese islands in the Gulf of Guinea.
3 Oyo was an ancient empire of the Yoruba and played little part in the slave trade except for the period 1700 to 1750.
4 The Asante empire became the greatest slave-trading empire in the forest zone.
5 The slave trade grew as these empires grew but whether it caused the growth is debatable.

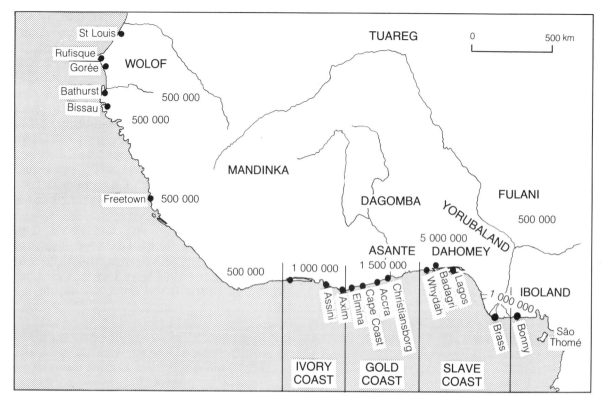

Map 3.7: Sources of slaves in West Africa

Map 3.7: Sources of slaves in West Africa

Slaves were taken almost entirely from the forest zone of West Africa. This is a densely populated belt of forest between 150 and 300 km deep from the coast. The people lived in forest clearings, growing their subsistence crops which were usually those introduced from South-East Asia like bananas, yams and coco-yams before 1500, and those from the New World like maize, cassava and pineapples after 1500. The people were peaceful farmers accustomed to raids in the past from the more warlike pastoralists of the savannah empires of Ghana, Mali and Songhai.

In the European slave trade the slaves came from the eastern part of the forest zone in the greatest numbers. The Guinea Coast to the west of the Niger delta probably yielded about 5 million slaves in the whole period of the slave trade. Inevitably it became known as the 'Slave Coast'. The great slave ports of Whydah and Badagri were on this coast. Only about 1 million slaves were taken from the delta as access was difficult.

In the first two centuries of the slave trade the 'Gold Coast' yielded many slaves as the Portuguese and Dutch concentrated their efforts there. The earliest European fort, Elmina, built by the Portuguese in 1482 and taken over by the Dutch in 1637, was on this coast. Throughout the whole period probably about 2½ million slaves came from this part of the coast.

Further west very few slaves were taken in comparison, probably only about 2 million between the Ivory Coast and Senegambia in the whole period. The French had their main sources of slaves here and they were difficult to exploit particularly from the hinterland behind St Louis, Rufisque and Gorée, their famous slave ports. The Wolof peoples, including the feared Jolof tribe, resisted the slave raiders fiercely.

The savannah lands beyond the forest zone did not attract slave raiders. The distance from the coastal ports was too great but also the populations were less dense and were the more warlike pastoralists who put up resistance to the raids. Thus the savannah was hardly affected by the slave trade.

Notes

1 The forest zone is a belt between 150 and 300 km deep along the coast of West Africa.
2 It was densely populated by subsistence farmers who lived in forest clearings.
3 The 'Slave Coast' between Whydah and the Niger Delta yielded about 5 million slaves between 1500 and 1850.
4 The sources of slaves for the French in the Senegambia were not easy to exploit because the people offered more resistance.
5 Regions beyond the forest zone were not exploited because of the greater distances from the coastal ports. Also their people were pastoralists and more warlike and the populations less dense.

Map 3.8: The triangle of trade of the North Atlantic

The Spanish policy of exclusivism, i.e. that no foreigners could enter the trade of the Indies, had to be relaxed when her colonies began demanding slaves because Spain had no source of African slaves. Therefore, in 1515 Spain granted an Asiento to Portugal who already had forts on the West African coast from Arguin Island to Fernando Po and had demonstrated the effectiveness of African slave labour in the islands of São Thomé, Principe and Fernando Po in the Gulf of Guinea.

Portuguese ships from Lisbon carried manufactured goods to forts like Elmina where they took on slaves for Brazil and the West Indies to sell to the Spaniards. This established the first two sides of the triangle – manufactured goods from Europe to West Africa and slaves from West Africa to the Americas. The third side was back to Portugal. From Brazil they would bring sugar, tobacco and cotton, but from the Spanish islands they did not want to come back empty-handed. The Spanish kept their monopoly over treasure and the Portuguese were left to find whatever cargoes they could.

The Asiento lapsed in 1580 but the Portuguese were still the main suppliers of slaves to the Span-ish. The Dutch had temporary control over the north-eastern corner of Brazil from 1624 to 1654 but the Portuguese were secure in the south from where the Spanish bought their slaves.

The profits to be made from the triangle of trade attracted the Dutch, the greatest commercial shipping nation in the world at that time. From 1624 to 1654 they had their own sugar estates in the north-eastern corner of Brazil and thus their own demand for slaves. This led them to acquire forts in West Africa like Arguin Island, Axim, Badagri and Elmina for varying periods in the seventeenth century. However, their colonial policy was really based on the carrying trade and after they lost Brazil their part in the triangle grew instead of declining. They established island trading posts like Aruba, Bonaire and Curaçao for the Windwards' trade and Saba, St Eustatius and St Martin for the Leewards' trade. From 1600 to 1670 the Dutch dominated the slave trade. They took West African slaves to Paramaribo in Surinam or to Curaçao to deliver them directly to the English and French planters. Then the same ships brought English and French sugar and tobacco for the voyage back to Europe, the third side of the triangle. The Dutch regularised the trade on this leg of the voyage.

In the Dutch Wars, 1652 to 1678, the English and the French broke the Dutch monopoly of the carrying trade. Then for a short period, 1670 to 1713, the French dominated the slave trade. The French ports of Bordeaux and Nantes grew powerful from this trade. Their ships called at St Louis, Rufisque and Gorée in Senegambia, and Whydah on the Slave Coast, carrying the slaves to Fort de France in Martinique and later to Port au Prince in St Domingue. (The British transported more slaves to Guadeloupe in their four years of occupation from 1759 to 1763 than the French had done before.)

The English domination of the slave trade from 1713 to 1807 was greater than that exercised by any country previously. Ships from the ports of Bristol and Liverpool carried textiles, guns and other metal goods to ports all along the coast of West Africa from St Louis to Lagos in Nigeria. They dominated the forts of the Slave Coast and Gold Coast. The price of slaves rose in the English period due to the frequent wars in the first sixty years of the eighteenth century making the trade very profitable. The English carried their slaves to Bridgetown, Barbados, and Kingston, Jamaica, as well as to North American ports like New Orleans and Charleston. On the return from the West

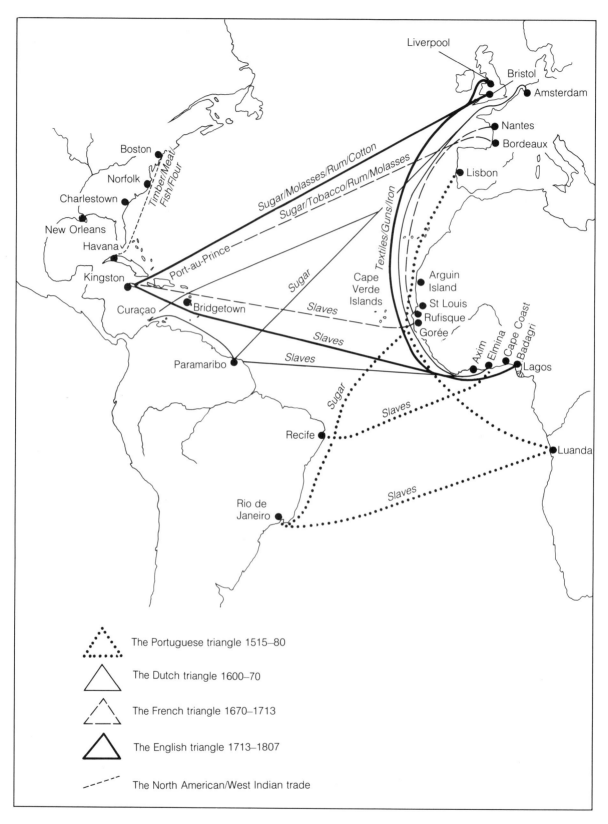

Map 3.8: The triangle of trade of the North Atlantic

Indies they carried sugar, rum, molasses, cotton and tobacco.

At first English companies such as the Royal Africa Company and the South Sea Company insisted on a monopoly to ensure profits sufficient to cover the considerable risks they were taking as wars were so frequent. Inevitably these abnormal profits attracted other merchants and the trade became a free-for-all in the eighteenth century. The merchants of Liverpool were expecting profits in excess of 50 per cent in a year's trading. This was an aggregate profit made up of the separate profits gained on each leg of the trade after costs had been taken off.

It was essential for the ships to complete the triangle quickly and a round trip in a year was possible. The bigger merchants had ships at sea and in port at all times of the year so the profits kept coming in regularly. However, the triangle was very hard on the ships and their working life was only about ten years so depreciation was a very large cost.

The key to the triangle of trade was the notorious 'middle passage', the voyage from West Africa to the West Indies. Slaves were packed into ships called 'slavers', the largest carrying over 700 slaves. Cruel and insanitary conditions prevailed and a 30 per cent death rate was common. This cut profits, but better conditions would have increased costs. In the West Indies the slaves would be 'refreshed' on islands like Carriacou in the Grenadines by giving them exercise and feeding them with fruit and fish before 'oiling' them for sale.

The middle passage was known as the 'nursery of seamen' because the speed of the voyage and the danger of revolt made the sailors efficient, tough and brutal. They did not like the middle passage but their experience from it served the British navy well in the Napoleonic Wars.

The triangle of trade exploited the winds and currents of the North Atlantic first worked out by Columbus centuries before. From West Africa to the Caribbean the ships were driven by the trade winds and carried by the equatorial currents. From the Caribbean to Europe they were driven by the westerlies and carried by the Gulf Stream.

In the nineteenth century the slave trade was abolished so the middle passage and the triangle went out of existence. The coming of steam meant that ships could sail to and fro across the North Atlantic regardless of the winds and currents.

Notes

1 The slave trade was the key to the triangle.
2 Spain had to relax her policy of exclusivism as she had no source of slaves.
3 The Asiento, 1515 to 1580, allowed Portugal to supply slaves to Spanish colonies.
4 Portugal began a triangle from Lisbon to Elmina, Elmina to Recife and Recife back to Lisbon.
5 The Dutch formalised the triangle by establishing the goods carried on the third leg of the voyage, sugar and tobacco to Europe.
6 The French dominated the slave trade from 1670 to 1713.
7 The English dominated the slave trade from 1713 to 1807.
8 Merchants expected profits in excess of 50 per cent per year from the triangle of trade.
9 There would have been no triangle but for the middle passage from West Africa to the West Indies.
10 On this passage as many slaves as possible were packed into each ship in cruel and insanitary conditions which made the death rate very high.
11 The slaves were 'refreshed' in the West Indies before being sold.
12 The abolition of the slave trade abolished the middle passage and brought the triangle of trade to an end.

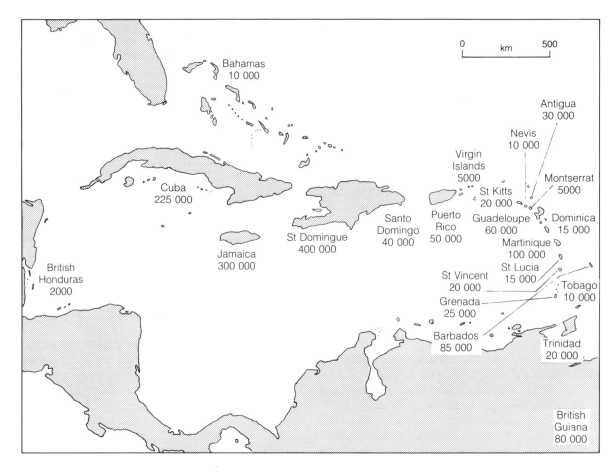

Map 3.9: Approximate numbers of working slaves and their distribution in the West Indies in the nineteenth century (Total: 1 500 000)

Map 3.9: Approximate numbers of working slaves and their distribution in the West Indies in the nineteenth century

It is very difficult to give accurate figures for the numbers of slaves working on sugar plantations as a result of the sugar revolution. Figures of black populations, in themselves approximate, include all slaves, whether working in sugar or not, women and children and with the children, in the British islands at least, one parent a slave made the children slaves. We have incomplete figures for the numbers of slaves shipped out of West Africa but the death rate on the middle passage makes the numbers arriving in the West Indies even more uncertain. The death rate on the plantations was also high. If one in three died on the middle passage, and a further one in three died in the first three years in the West Indies, we can conclude that most of the new slaves imported were replacing those who had died. Therefore the growth in slave populations was largely due to natural causes in the West Indies.

From the British islands we have figures on the number of slaves emancipated in the period 1833 to 1838, and the compensation paid to the owners. These are probably better figures to work on but we must allow for the fact that owners would exaggerate their claims wherever possible. Only working slaves would qualify for compensation. Therefore the figures on the map are very approximate but a better guide to the relative slave populations between the islands.

The very large number of working slaves in St Domingue occurred because the western part of Hispaniola had been neglected before the French took over. The French found large areas of vacant land on which they could begin sugar plantations with thousands of imported slaves. St Domingue at first rivalled, and then outstripped Jamaica in slave population and sugar production. This made the collapse brought about by the Haitian Revolution dramatic. Sugar production declined very quickly and about 200 000 black lives were lost in fighting between 1791 and 1803.

Santo Domingo, the eastern end of Hispaniola, remained a backwater. It had been neglected by the Spanish after its initial period of importance, was conquered by the French under Leclerc in 1801, claimed independence from Spain twice (1821 and 1844) as the Dominica Republic, and was then brought under Spain again in 1861. During all these upheavals the economy was neglected, sugar cultivation not developed and very few slaves imported relative to the size of the country.

Cuba, the largest island and the biggest sugar producer in the nineteenth century had a low slave population relative to its neighbours, Jamaica and St Domingue. Cuba had a large free peasant class and a large indentured labour force and so did not rely on slave labour to the same extent in its sugar production. Puerto Rico bears comparison with Cuba. By the time Puerto Rico turned to large-scale sugar production in the nineteenth century, the slave trade was ending. The Puerto Rico sugar industry was based on free peasant and indentured labour and the few slaves were soon emancipated.

Jamaica bears comparison with St Domingue in that it had been neglected by the Spanish and from the beginning of British rule sugar cultivation was based on slave labour on relatively large estates by the standards of the British islands. Tens of thousands of slaves were imported very quickly and the slave population was soon very high.

Slave populations in the Windwards are low by comparison not only because the islands are smaller than Jamaica, but also because ownership of the islands was disputed throughout the eighteenth century and consequently planters were unwilling to risk their capital in sugar production. However, Martinique, the largest French sugar-producing island before the rise of St Domingue, was stable throughout the wars and imported thousands of slaves in the early period. Guadeloupe's slave population would have remained very low if it had not been for the British occupation of 1759 to 1763 which turned it into a sugar island.

Barbados had gained a large slave population before the end of the seventeenth century. The fact that it did not increase much after that was due to the completeness of its sugar revolution and its small size. Similarly the Leewards were all too small in size and some too mountainous to allow large-scale sugar cultivation and the large slave populations which went with it.

Notes

1 Population figures for slaves are very approximate because the slave trade figures are approximate, the death rates only guessed at and the emancipation figures probably exaggerated.

2 Slaves working on plantations were but a fraction of the black populations.

3 Islands like Jamaica and St Domingue started their colonial periods under the British and French as sugar islands and quickly had large slave populations.

4 Islands like Cuba and Puerto Rico had well-established settlers and peasants and did not rely so heavily on slave labour as did Jamaica and St Domingue.

5 Santo Domingo was undeveloped and the upheavals it went through in the eighteenth and nineteenth centuries meant that it could not develop large-scale sugar production. Therefore its slave population was very low relative to its size.

6 Political instability in the eighteenth century hindered the development of the Windwards as sugar islands and their slave populations remained low. Martinique was relatively stable and so imported thousands of slaves for its sugar industry.

7 Barbados completed its sugar revolution in the mid-seventeenth century and before the end of the century had a large slave population relative to its size which did not increase very much thereafter.

8 The Leewards were too small and some too mountainous for large-scale sugar cultivation and their slave populations were low in comparison with Barbados.

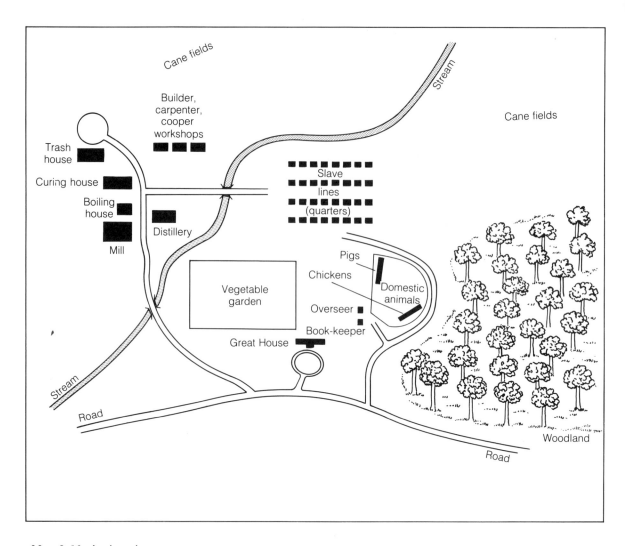

Map 3.10: An imaginary sugar estate

Map 3.10: An imaginary sugar estate

Part 1: The physical layout

Typically a sugar plantation was divided into three because it aimed at being self-sufficient. One division was the canefields, the cash crop. Another was woodland to provide timber for fuel to heat the boilers and for construction. The third was for farming to produce as much as possible for all who lived on the estate, half being set aside for producing food for the slaves. Cattle, pigs and poultry were kept and vegetables and fruit were grown.

Of course the slaves were far and away the biggest group on the estate. They lived in 'lines' of mud and wattle or timber huts away from the whites for security and because the whites did not wish to have an ever-present reminder of the condition of slavery. Where there was enough land, as in Jamaica, slaves were allowed to have 'grounds', plots of their own, but they were usually on marginal land.

The factory consisted of a mill, a boiling-house (often attached to the mill), a curing house, a trash house and a distillery. These were located close to each other as the processes were in a chain. These were the first buildings on the estate as there could be no sugar production without them. By the nineteenth century water-power was commonly used to drive the mills so they were located near streams which could be diverted into a mill-race.

Self-sufficiency also applied to the maintenance of all buildings, machines and transport on the estate. Estates employed builders, carpenters, coopers and blacksmiths. All these artisans needed workshops which ideally would occupy a central position.

The vegetable garden and orchard were located near the whites' habitation as they offered a pleasant aspect. The enclosures for domestic animals were usually near the slave lines as the animals were tended by the old slaves or young children. Cattle grazed on the verges of canefields or the banks of irrigation channels.

Offices were necessary for the records which had to be kept of the crop, production, maintenance, labour and accounts. All the clerks working in these offices were under the book-keeper whose house would be nearby in the white location and of a size befiting his high status in the plantation hierarchy.

The overseer's house was likely to be next both in grandeur and position to the planter's. The overseer was in charge of all the labour, a very responsible position requiring much experience in sugar cultivation and production.

The planter's house was known as the 'Great House', in the British West Indies. It would have easy access to the road and the outside world, acting as the symbol and entrance to the plantation. It would be in a prominent position, perhaps on a hill commanding a view over the whole plantation. At the foundation of the estate the planter's house was of secondary importance after the factory. It was just to serve as a roof over the planter's head while he established the plantation. As the profits came in, so the planter would aggrandise his house, enlarging and embellishing it. The Great House reflected the prosperity of the estate. Perhaps it would have classical columns, grand staircases and balconies and fine woodwork.

Notes

1   Self-sufficiency in a plantation meant a) all personnel connected with the plantation lived on the plantation, b) the cash crop and the production processes were on the same site, giving each plantation its independence, c) subsistence farming – meat, dairy, eggs, vegetables and fruit were alongside the cash crop.
2   Slaves lived in lines away from the whites.
3   The factory was the first building on the plantation as it was essential for production.
4   Workshops for maintenance and offices for records were also needed.
5   The houses of the whites reflected their status with the planter's house, called the 'Great House', being the grandest.
6   The three divisions of the plantation were the canefields, the woodland and the farm.

Part 2: The role of the slaves

British slavers docked at ports like Bridgetown, Barbados, St George's, Grenada or Kingston, Jamaica. The captains wanted to get rid of the slaves as quickly as possible so sometimes a 'scramble' was held on deck whereby at the sound of a bell or the firing of a gun, prospective buyers rushed on to buy the slaves on the basis of 'first come, first served'. At other times the slaves were disembarked and sold in an auction on the dock.

The usual policy was to split up tribal and family groups although this may have already been done in West Africa as the slaves embarked for the middle passage. Planters did not want to buy slaves who could communicate with each other as they were suspicious of them plotting a revolt. Separation from their friends just added to the slaves' bewilderment and fear.

Planters inspected slaves with three categories of labour in mind – domestic, factory and praedial (field). Slaves fresh from Africa, known as 'Guinea Birds', would have to be trained. The usual practice was to put the newly arrived slaves under experienced slaves to learn the tasks they were to perform and to learn the new language. This was a shock to the new slaves, and inevitably, with all the frightening experiences between leaving their homes in West Africa and servitude on a West Indian plantation, many gave up hope, lost the will to live, succumbed to disease or died from the strain of hard labour and cruelty. The first three years were the testing time in which about one in three slaves died in the West Indies. Thereafter the death rate was still high but life expectancy did increase considerably after the first three years.

In the previous section we saw that the land of the sugar estate was in three divisions, canefields, woodland and farm, and that the buildings were factory, workshops, offices and houses. These divisions demanded different types of slaves, praedial, factory and domestic. Domestic slaves enjoyed better conditions and were exposed to the culture of their masters. Factory slaves learnt skills under supervision. Workshop slaves were artisans and highly prized as skilled builders, carpenters, mechanics and coopers. Praedial slaves had none of these advantages. Their work was merely physical and very hard. Their hours were long and their direct contact with a superior was only with a black slave driver who applied the whip frequently.

Most of the slaves on the plantation were praedial slaves. Their work was seasonal in a cycle from August to July. In August the canefields were prepared for the new crop. This activity was known as 'holing' which involved digging the soil to a depth of 25 cms in metre squares. It was very hard work especially if scrub and roots had first to be cleared with machetes. Other slaves applied manure to the newly dug soil. Then the cane shoots, known as 'ratoons', were planted. The work became easier for the next two months involving weeding round the old canes, pushing back the soil into the holes as the new canes grew, and stripping the outer leaves from the canes which was known as 'trashing' in Jamaica. Weed-

ing and holing could have been done mechanically but labour intensive methods were cheaper and the planters wanted to keep the slaves occupied at all times.

In November crop time began. This involved many operations and was the busiest time on the plantation in most departments. The canes had to be cut by machete, a back-breaking job as they had to be cut low down and they were very hard and heavy being full of juice. Then the cut canes had to be loaded onto ox-carts and transported to the mill as quickly as possible (certainly within 48 hours) so that the canes did not dry out at all. At the mill the canes had to be fed into a crusher one by one, a very slow process. After passing through the rollers the crushed canes were carried away to the trash house.

From then on the operations involved the juice. From the rollers the sucrose ran in a trough to a big copper clarifier in the boiling house where it was heated with white lime. The stirring of the sucrose as it was being heated was a semi-skilled operation under the supervision of an overseer who would decide on the quality of sugar desired. The purified juice then went through four boilers each one hotter than the last and the juice became thicker and thicker. By the time it was in the fourth boiler it was sugar crystals and molasses. The molasses were drained off through holes in small barrels. They were so thick that this operation lasted for three weeks. The residue was called 'muscavado'. The molasses could be boiled again to make a sugar known as 'peneles' which was used for making rum. The molasses were put into hogsheads and taken to the harbour for export.

In crop time the slaves worked in shifts doing long hours but there was so much work that crop time lasted many months being completed by July. Then the praedial slaves removed the remains of the old crop from the ground and the cycle would began again.

The daily routine of praedial slaves varied according to the season. In holing time they worked from sunrise to 9 o'clock when they had breakfast. Then they worked from about 9.30 a.m. to noon when they had lunch, their main meal of the day. After a rest they had another four to five hours labour before sunset. In crop time praedial slaves worked even longer hours, starting before sunrise and finishing after sunset, with less time for meals.

In crop time factory slaves worked in shifts of nine hours each but each one overlapping the preceding one by one hour so that there were three shifts in twenty-four hours. As a factory slave usually worked two shifts per day, it meant that the hours were very long.

This was the sort of labour which led to the early deaths of so many slaves. Of course, the planters did not want them to die, but they also wanted to extract as much labour from them as was possible.

Notes

1 Planters bought slaves with a view to their suitability for work either in the fields, or the factory or houses.

2 Praedial slaves had the hardest life with no 'fringe' benefits and were treated cruelly.

3 Factory slaves had the chance of learning some skills in the sugar-manufacturing process.

4 Domestic slaves were in a privileged position and were treated more favourably than other slaves.

5 Slaves in the workshops were referred to as 'artisans' and their skills were indispensable to the running of the estate.

6 Labour performed by praedial slaves varied according to the season which followed a cycle from August to July.

7 From August to November their operations consisted of holing, planting, weeding, replacing soil and stripping off the outer leaves from the canes.

8 Planters would not mechanise any of these operations because a) slave labour was cheaper, and b) they wanted to keep the slaves occupied.

9 Crop time began in November and could last until July.

10 Factory operations consisted of crushing, purifying, boiling, stirring, separating off the muscavado and putting molasses into hogsheads.

11 Praedial slaves worked from sunrise to sunset in holing time but longer hours in crop time with shorter breaks.

12 In crop time the factory worked non-stop with the slaves working two shifts of nine hours each.

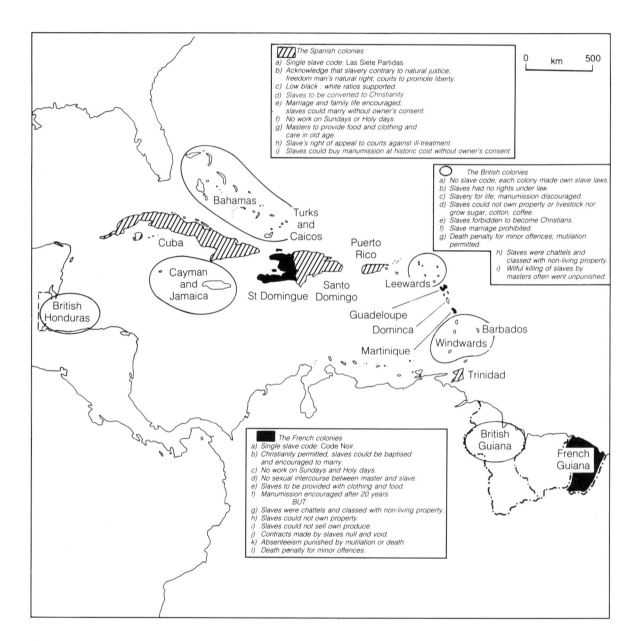

The Spanish colonies
a) Single slave code: Las Siete Partidas.
b) Acknowledge that slavery contrary to natural justice; freedom man's natural right; courts to promote liberty.
c) Low black : white ratios supported.
d) Slaves to be converted to Christianity
e) Marriage and family life encouraged; slaves could marry without owner's consent.
f) No work on Sundays or Holy days.
g) Masters to provide food and clothing and care in old age.
h) Slave's right of appeal to courts against ill-treatment.
i) Slaves could buy manumission at historic cost without owner's consent.

The British colonies
a) No slave code; each colony made own slave laws.
b) Slaves had no rights under law.
c) Slavery for life; manumission discouraged.
d) Slaves could not own property or livestock nor grow sugar, cotton, coffee.
e) Slaves forbidden to become Christians.
f) Slave marriage prohibited.
g) Death penalty for minor offences; mutilation permitted.
h) Slaves were chattels and classed with non-living property.
i) Wilful killing of slaves by masters often went unpunished.

The French colonies
a) Single slave code: Code Noir.
b) Christianity permitted, slaves could be baptised and encouraged to marry.
c) No work on Sundays and Holy days.
d) No sexual intercourse between master and slave.
e) Slaves to be provided with clothing and food.
f) Manumission encouraged after 20 years.
        BUT:
g) Slaves were chattels and classed with non-living property.
h) Slaves could not own property.
i) Slaves could not sell own produce.
j) Contracts made by slaves null and void.
k) Absenteeism punished by mutilation or death.
l) Death penalty for minor offences.

0   km   500

Bahamas
Turks and Caicos
Cuba
Puerto Rico
Cayman and Jamaica
St Domingue   Santo Domingo
Leewards
British Honduras
Guadeloupe
Dominca
Martinique
Windwards
Barbados
Trinidad
British Guiana
French Guiana

Map 4.1: Contrasting slave conditions in the British, French and Spanish colonies *circa* 1750

Map 4.1: Contrasting slave conditions in the British, French and Spanish Colonies *circa* 1750

In theory basic conditions for slaves differed considerably according to the colonial power, but in practice these differences would be harder to detect on the spot. The slave was the property of his master throughout the Caribbean territories and in his day-to-day life would be treated very much the same whatever the nationality of his master. For example an humanitarian master in Barbados, an island with a severe slave code, could treat his slaves more humanely than a harsh master in Hispaniola with a more liberal slave code. So slave conditions were very much at the whim of the individual master.

The generalisation is that slaves were treated better in Spanish and French colonies than in British because: a) Spanish and French metropolitan governments directed the conditions of slaves throughout their colonies with a detailed slave code whereas each British colony made its own slave laws without guidelines from the Mother Country, b) France and Spain were Catholic countries and the Catholic Church was more active in safeguarding the welfare of slaves, c) racial lines were not clear, and racial prejudice not so deep in the French and Spanish colonies as in the British. Miscegenation was certainly more common in the Spanish colonies and the French colony of St Domingue.

In the French colonies there was a single slave code, the *Code Noir*, issued in 1685, which lasted until 1804. It was strongly influenced by the Catholic Church. In the Spanish colonies the slave code, *Las Siete Partidas*, was the same code as had been in force for European slaves in the late Roman Empire and it had been drawn up by a Christian, the Emperor Justinian. In complete contrast the British Government offered no slave code and left it to the colonies to make their own laws. There was no interference by the Established Church, the Church of England, on behalf of the slaves in British colonies. Indeed, that church was on the side of the planters.

Contrasts between slave conditions under the three nations can be made under the following headings: Legal position of slaves; Christianity; Owner's responsibilities; Punishments.

Legal position of slaves

In British and French colonies slaves were defined as 'chattels', moveable property like non-living things. They were part of the estate and were usually sold with the estate. They had no rights under law and could do nothing without their owner's consent. They could not make contracts or give evidence in court as both would be 'null and void'. In Spanish colonies in some matters slaves were allowed to act without their owner's consent, e.g. to marry or to obtain their manumission. In the British and French islands slaves could not own property or sell their own produce. In practice, however, this law was lax and slaves frequently had personal possessions and sold their own produce in Sunday markets. The aim of this law was to protect the planters from competition from slave-produced crops so sugar, cotton and coffee were specifically named and other crops were exempt as it was to the master's advantage for his slaves to supplement their diets with other food crops.

In the Spanish colonies the government acknowledged that slavery was contrary to natural justice and that liberty was a natural human right. Therefore a Spanish slave could expect support from the courts and could even appeal to the courts in the event of ill-treatment. In the British colonies a slave could not go to court against his master because a slave was not allowed to give evidence. Prosecutions against slave owners had to be made by the civil authorities and the courts were likely to take the side of the slave as they were part of the establishment, the plantocracy.

Manumission, the right of the slave to obtain

his freedom, was discouraged in the British colonies, encouraged with conditions in the French, and positively encouraged in the Spanish because liberty was the natural right. The British discouraged it as a dangerous precedent; that masters would free their slaves to avoid having to care for them in their old age; that manumitted slaves would be a burden on society; that manumitted slaves would encourage other slaves to revolt. In the British colonies a slave tended to be a slave for life and manumission was ringed with difficulties. The master had to pay the civil authorities a deposit to ensure that the freed slave would not be a drain on public funds. Also the deposit would make the master less willing to dodge his responsibilities. In the British colonies a manumitted slave had to wear a badge and could not easily move from parish to parish. He was not allowed to work alongside a slave. In practice manumission was not so desirable as wage labour paid so little it seemed preferable to remain a slave where everything was found.

In the French colonies manumission was encouraged after twenty years of labour and there were no restrictions placed on a manumitted slave. In the Spanish colonies a slave could buy his manumission without his owner's consent at the historic cost, that is the sum his master originally paid for him.

As well as not being able to own property or sell certain produce, slaves did not own their own labour. The master owned it and only he could hire out his slave's labour. However, skilled slaves, known as 'artisans', were allowed to work for money and to keep some or all of it for themselves especially in the years just preceding emancipation when planters were anxious to keep their artisans. They were known as 'jobbing slaves'.

Christianity

The attitude to slaves becoming Christians shows the biggest differences between the British, French and Spanish positions. In the British colonies the conversion of slaves was forbidden although the Crown had ordered it in the seventeenth century. The colonial legislatures felt that the Christian teachings of brotherhood and equality before God were incompatible with slavery. They felt that conversion would undermine slave societies and as there was no opposition from the Church of England, Christianity was officially denied to slaves. Nonconformist missionaries who preached to and converted slaves were often out-

lawed, as the Quakers in Barbados, and as emancipation drew nearer missionaries were often persecuted. However, in practice Christianity could not be suppressed as the slaves demanded it and as they could not receive it from the Church of England, they took it wherever they could find it or practised Christian cults of their own. Individual Christian masters sometimes allowed their slaves to become Christians but such masters were regarded with suspicion by the other planters.

In the Spanish colonies slaves had to be converted to Christianity by law and all the sacraments of the Church were open to slaves. There was to be no work on Sundays and Holy Days in the Spanish colonies. The French colonies adopted an intermediate position with regard to Christianity. Conversion was permitted but was not compulsory. Slaves could receive the sacraments but the Church did not always make it easy for the slaves. Again, no work was allowed on Sundays and Holy Days. Baptism provides a good illustration of the relative attitudes: in the Spanish colonies it was compulsory; in the French it was permitted; in the British it was forbidden.

Slave marriage was another issue which brought out different attitudes. In the British colonies slave marriage was not possible in theory as under law a slave could not enter into any contract. In practice it was discouraged as it was felt that it would give a slave the independence and security of family life which would undermine subservience. In the French colonies slave marriages were encouraged. In the Spanish colonies it was emphasised that marriage was a natural human right and slave marriages were consecrated by the Church. The civil authorities tried to insist on a minimum proportion of females to make marriages more common.

Owner's responsibilities

The three colonial powers had most in common in the matter of the obligations a master had for his slaves' welfare. Masters were expected to provide four of the five basic necessities of life; food, clothing, shelter and good health. The fifth, the right to education was denied. Up to a third of the land of an estate could be set aside for slaves' subsistence. The trade between the North American colonies and the British West Indies was based on the slaves' need for protein – fish. It was to a master's advantage to feed his slaves well. To this end slaves were allowed to supplement their diet with what they could grow on their own 'grounds'. Masters were not obliged to provide grounds but in practice a tenth of the cultivable land in a British colony could be taken up by slaves' grounds. The same was true in French and Spanish colonies where more land was available than in most of the British islands. Masters also provided clothing, usually two sets made of a coarse cloth sometimes known as 'Osnaburg'. Masters gave slaves materials with which to build their houses which were usually mud-and-wattle huts. Masters accepted the obligation to care for their slaves in old age or sickness. On the larger estates hospitals were provided. The motive could have been self-interest in the case of health – healthy slaves would provide more work. In the French and Spanish colonies old slaves were frequently set free and they could subsist more easily than in the British colonies where land was scarcer.

Officially slaves were denied education in the British colonies but this law was difficult to enforce. There were two conflicting opinions: one was that uneducated slaves were more subservient; the other was that educated slaves gave better service. However, it really depended on the status of the slave. An artisan slave or a domestic slave was often allowed, even encouraged to read and write, but a field slave was denied this advantage.

Punishments

Slavery was confinement and unpaid labour. Therefore imprisonment and fines were inapplicable. Slave punishments were almost always corporal. The punishments were usually administered by the estates and not by the civil authorities.

Slave punishments were extremely severe because it was felt that leniency would show weakness. The death penalty was given for minor offences, as in Barbados in the seventeenth century for stealing goods of value more than a shilling.

The death penalty was inflicted in most cruel ways, for example by being torn limb from limb by oxen, by being hung, drawn and quartered, or by being burnt to death. In some British colonies mutilation was permitted, as in Jamaica for running away for more than a month a foot could be cut off. A hand was frequently cut off for stealing. In the early days of colonial Barbados castration of slaves was a common punishment. However, in the French and Spanish colonies torture and mutilation were expressly forbidden. The most common punishment throughout the Caribbean was lashing (whipping) and 39 lashes was the usual minimum but considered inadequate. The maximum could be 150 but this was often exceeded and cases of over 300 lashes are recorded. Death under the lash often resulted.

Notes

1 Slave conditions depended as much on the master as on the colonial nationality.
2 The French slave code was the *Code Noir*, the Spanish *Las Siete Partidas*. There was no British slave code.
3 The French and Spanish generally treated their slaves better than the British did.
4 Manumission was encouraged by the French and Spanish but not by the British.
5 Conversion of slaves to Christianity was forbidden by the British but it was the Spanish law to convert. Conversion was permitted by the French.
6 All three colonial powers had similar obligations towards the slaves' welfare. Education was denied them.
7 Slave punishments were almost always corporal and very severe. Lashing was most commonly used.

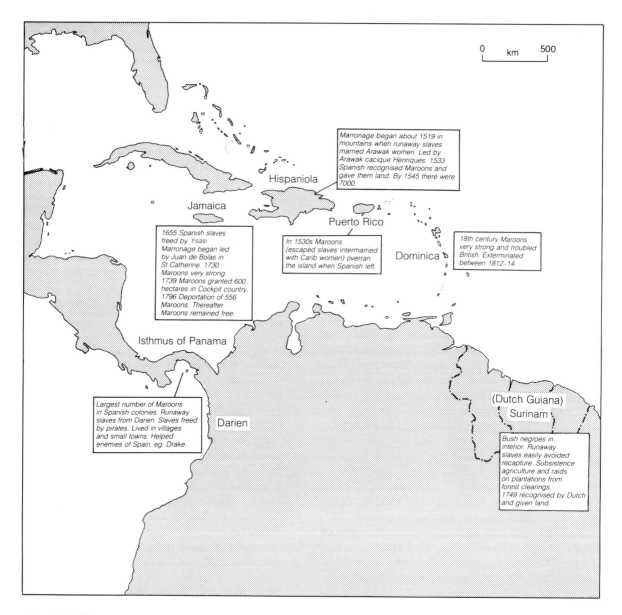

Map 4.2: Marronage

The following text appears within the map:

Marronage began about 1519 in mountains when runaway slaves married Arawak women. Led by Arawak cacique Henriques. 1533 Spanish recognised Maroons and gave them land. By 1545 there were 7000.

Hispaniola

Jamaica

Puerto Rico

1655 Spanish slaves freed by Ysasi Marronage began led by Juan de Bolas in St Catherine. 1730 Maroons very strong. 1739 Maroons granted 600 hectares in Cockpit country. 1796 Deportation of 556 Maroons. Thereafter Maroons remained free.

In 1530s Maroons (escaped slaves intermarried with Carib women) overran the island when Spanish left.

Dominica

18th century Maroons very strong and troubled British. Exterminated between 1812–14.

Isthmus of Panama

(Dutch Guiana) Surinam

Largest number of Maroons in Spanish colonies. Runaway slaves from Darien. Slaves freed by pirates. Lived in villages and small towns. Helped enemies of Spain, eg. Drake.

Darien

Bush negroes in interior. Runaway slaves easily avoided recapture. Subsistence agriculture and raids on plantations from forest clearings. 1749 recognised by Dutch and given land.

0   km   500

Map 4.2: Marronage

In the Spanish colonies

Slaves began to escape very soon after they were introduced into Hispaniola. They ran away to the mountains of the interior to join those Arawaks who had fled from the Spanish cruelty of *repartimiento*. They intermarried with Arawak women and came under an Arawak *cacique* called 'Henriques' by the Spanish. Thus they were called *cimarrones* ('dwellers on the mountain tops') from which the English word 'maroons' is derived. They were important enough to be given a treaty by the Spanish in 1533 which granted them land and freedom. By 1545 they were 7000 in number.

Puerto Rico was almost abandoned by the Spanish in the 1520s and 1530s and left to maroons who had intermarried with local Carib women or Carib women from the Leewards. These African slaves were relatively newly arrived and hardly knew the condition of slavery. Their presence made it more difficult for the Spanish to re-occupy the island.

Most escaped slaves from the Spanish territories found their way to the Isthmus of Panama which was mountainous and covered with dense jungle. The original maroons came from Darien to the south and they were joined by slaves set free by the pirates. They hated the Spanish and sided with their enemies, such as Francis Drake in his raids on the Isthmus between 1571 and 1573. These maroons lived in villages of which about three might even be called towns. Drake found one maroon town fortified and inside the walls were three streets and fifty-five houses.

(From 1650 to 1694 maroons in Brazil had their own independent black republic, known as the Palmares Republic. It was recognised by the Portuguese in 1678 but later they captured it and killed its leader. With a population of 200 000 it greatly overshadowed the maroon settlements of the Caribbean).

Notes

1   Slaves who escaped into the mountains were called *cimarrones* hence the English word 'maroons'.
2   Most escaped slaves from the Spanish colonies went to the Isthmus of Panama where they sided with Spain's enemies such as Francis Drake.
3   The maroons frequently caused local riots and uprisings against colonialists.

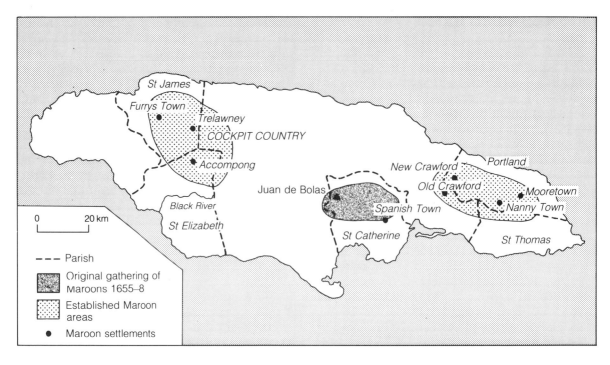

Map 4.3: The maroons of Jamaica

Map 4.3 The maroons of Jamaica

In the British colonies

In defence against the English in 1655 the Spanish commander, Ysasi, freed about 1000 slaves who joined with the existing maroons to make a force of about 2000 to help the Spanish. At first they were operating from St Catherine against the English garrison in Spanish Town under a leader called Juan de Bolas (a mountain is named after him). Then they blocked the English on the overland route to Rio Nuevo enabling Ysasi to land there peacefully.

The English drove out the Spanish but the maroons did not surrender and threatened the English thereafter in three ways: a) they encouraged slaves to revolt and join them either actively or just by their presence nearby; b) they raided plantations especially those close to maroon areas; c) they took advantage of any weakness in British defences as when British forces left Jamaica on expeditions; and, d) they were potential allies of Britain's enemies.

The maroons left St Catherine and settled in the eastern and western parts of the island. In the east

their settlements were New Crawford, Old Crawford, Nanny Town and Moore Town in the parishes of St Andrew, Portland and St Thomas. In the west they were Furrys Town, Trelawney Town and Accompong and all through Cockpit Country between Trelawney and Accompong in the parishes of Hanover, St James and St Elizabeth. In the early eighteenth century the settlements had famous leaders, in the east Quao and Cuffee and in the west Cudjoe, Accompong and Johnny who were prepared to challenge the British. At the end of the ensuing war, The First Maroon War, the western maroons were granted 600 hectares of land between Trelawney and the Cockpits for ever. Separate but similar agreements were made with the Accompong maroons and those in the eastern settlements.

The eastern maroons were relatively peaceful thereafter but those in St James would not be restricted by their land grant and pushed into Cockpit Country and south into St Elizabeth keeping north of the Black River. A Second Maroon War ensued after which over 500 western maroons were deported. The remainder accepted their conditions resentfully and lived thereafter quietly in Trelawney.

Dominica

Dominica was neglected by the Spanish, British and French due to the hostility of its Caribs so it naturally became a haven for maroons, runaway slaves who married Carib women. At the Peace of Paris, 1763, the British took over Dominica ending its status as a 'Neutral Island'. The maroons were a nuisance to the British, being ready to side with Britain's enemies in that century of wars. As a result of the help these maroons gave to the French (who supplied them with guns) in the War of American Independence and Napoleonic Wars, the British exterminated them between 1812 and 1814.

In Surinam (Dutch Guiana) and Berbice

It was very difficult for the Dutch to keep slaves on the plantations of the Coastal Belt with such extensive bush and forests inland and easy access to it by the rivers. Indeed some African slaves hardly experienced plantation labour before they ran away to the bush to resume their African-style subsistence living. They also enjoyed raidng the European plantations of the Coastal Belt so they did not go too far into the interior. Consequently they became known as 'The Bush Negroes of Surinam'.

They lived in forest clearings with their houses surrounded by plots of eddoes and yams and the plots surrounded by groves of plantains. These villages were often fortified with moats, concealed pits and stockades, and organised on military lines for raids on the European plantations. When the authorities retaliated the Bush Negroes could always retreat further into the interior beyond the rapids which their pursuers would not pass.

Eventually the Dutch recognised the independence of the Bush Negroes in the interior on condition that they would not raid the coastal plantations. They kept pcacc for thirty years but rose up in the French Revolutionary Wars and their leaders were executed. Those in West Demerara and Berbice survived to independence from Holland and nowadays their population is put at over 40 000.

Notes

1   The Spanish freed slaves in Jamaica to help in the fight against the British.
2   When the Spanish were driven out the maroons remained, established in their own villages, and continued to threaten the English.
3   There were two maroon wars. After the first the maroons were given land grants but after the second 500 maroons were deported.
4   Dominica, through colonial neglect, became a haven for maroons. They were exterminated between 1812 and 1814 by the British for siding with the French.
5   Runaway slaves in Surinam were called 'The Bush Negroes of Surinam'.
6   The Dutch recognised their independence on condition that they ceased raiding the plantations. There are now over 40 000 of them.

1843 Series
of slave
revolts in
Matanzas.

1791 Slave rising at Cap Français
turned into slave and mulatto
revolt and the Haitian revolution.

1522 First slave revolt
in Caribbean. Some
Spanish killed.

1733 Serious revolt.
Slave conditions very bad.
40 whites killed. French
from Martinique suppressed
revolt.

1685 Slave
revolt in which
some whites were
killed.

Cuba

1687 Slave revolt,
surprising in view of
good conditions. Suppressed
brutally.

Jamaica

Hispaniola

St John

Antigua

1760 Tacky's rebellion
in St Mary. Spread
throughout Jamaica.
60 White's killed,
400 slaves killed,
600 slaves deported.

Puerto
Rico

Nevis

Guadeloupe

Belize

Martinique

1765 Revolt by slaves
deported from
Jamaica after Tacky's
rebellion.

1732–9
First Maroon War
1795–6
Second Maroon War
1831 'The Baptist War'.
Samuel Sharpe instigated
a strike. Rebellion
followed, 50 000 slaves
in revolt.

1725 revolt
plotted

1770, 1771, 1774 Slave revolts,
black : white ratio 20:1 so
revolts serious. Brutally suppressed

1822, 1824 Revolts at Cabet.
1833 Serious revolt at Grande Anse

Barbados

Providence
Island

Tobago

1639 First slave revolt
in British West Indies.
Surprising for a
Puritan settlement.

1649 Revolt was result of
poor slave conditions and high
black : white ratio.
1816 Revolt provoked by registration
bill, whites blamed missionaries.

Trinidad

Berbice

1763 Coffy's
rebellion. Poor
slave conditions.
Coffy was a
moderate leader and
wanted partition
like Surinam.

0   500 km

Map 4.4: Resistance and revolt

Map 4.4: Resistance and revolt

There were approximately fifty slave revolts in the Caribbean between 1515 and 1833, of which only three were successful: a) The Maroon Revolt in Jamaica which the British failed to suppress between 1655 and 1658, again in the First Maroon War, 1732 to 1739, and yet again in the Second Maroon War, 1795 to 1796; b) The Bush Negroes of Surinam throughout the colonial period; and, c) The Haitian Revolution, 1791 to 1804.

These three cases of successful resistance took place where land was plentiful and sometimes mountainous, remote and difficult to penetrate. In most of the Caribbean colonies slave revolts could never succeed because of the close physical limits of a small island. There was nowhere to hide and remain free. Therefore we must conclude that in most cases the slaves revolted knowing that they would ultimately fail. Two points emerge from this: a) the desperation of the slaves, and b) the explanation of why there were so few revolts.

Some revolts that failed

The first slave revolt in the Caribbean was in 1522 as soon as slaves began to outnumber the whites in sufficient numbers to give hope of success. In this revolt in Hispaniola success could only have been achieved if the rebels could have reached the maroons in the interior, but after killing several Spaniards they were hunted down and executed. At about the same time there were several revolts in Puerto Rico coinciding with the departure of the whites so they cannot be called successful. The rebels were left to become maroons who were gradually rounded up when the Spanish began to recolonise the island. The Spanish were wary of slave revolts in their colonies and took the following precautions: a) slave : white ratios were controlled; b) one-third of slaves imported had to be women; c) no slaves from the Joloff tribe could be imported as they were prone to revolt. However,

the main reason for relatively few revolts in the Spanish territories was that slave conditions were better and slaves were protected by the Church.

In the British islands the first revolt was in Providence (Santa Catalina) off the coast of Nicaragua on the route between Panama and Havana. It was a surprise for two reasons. Firstly whites outnumbered slaves by five to one. Secondly Puritans usually treated their slaves well. However, this could not have been the case on Providence as the slaves revolted in 1639 against impossible odds.

There were slave revolts in Barbados in spite of the impossibility of the rebels ever managing to escape retribution. The sudden change in the slave : white ratio brought about by the sugar revolution encouraged some slaves to revolt when food became scarce in 1649. Also in Antigua in 1687 strength in numbers after the sugar revolution prompted a serious revolt even though slave conditions were relatively good.

St John in the Virgin Islands experienced a serious slave revolt which nearly succeeded in 1733. The Danes had come to St John in 1716 and were very few in number. They treated their slaves very badly. Forty whites were murdered and the remainder had no chance of putting down the revolt. However, a successful revolt would have had serious repercussions in other islands and so they sent forces to put down the revolt in St John. Englishmen from Tortola and St Kitts failed to do so but a French force from Martinique eventually crushed the rebels.

Slave revolts were more common in Jamaica than in the Leewards and Windwards for five reasons: a) the slave : white ratio was higher; b) land was more extensive and wild areas offered refuge; c) the presence of the maroons was a reminder of success; d) the estates were larger and vigilance could not be so thorough; e) slave conditions were the worst. There were slave revolts in Jamaica in 1685, 1754, 1760, 1765, 1776, 1777, 1795, 1803, 1807, 1823, 1824 and 1831, (the frequency increased as emancipation drew nearer). These revolts were apart from the Maroon Wars.

Tacky's Rebellion of 1760 and the 'Baptist War' of 1831 are two good examples.

Tacky was a Gold Coast slave who led a revolt among other Akan peoples in St Mary which eventually spread to other slaves regardless of tribe. At the outset fifty whites were killed. The militia was mobilised and the help of the maroons was enlisted. Tacky and many of his men were killed. Another 400 were killed or executed in the rounding-up operations and 600 were deported to Honduras where they were blamed for a revolt in 1765 in an otherwise peaceful colony.

The 1831 'Baptist War' arose out of a strike called after Christmas by Samuel Sharpe, 'Daddy Sharpe'. He did not plan a revolt as it would be against his religious principles as a member of the Baptist Church, but a spark turned the smouldering impatience for freedom into the fire of revolt. The slaves knew that emancipation was coming and thought that the whites were delaying it. Conditions in St James, where the revolt began, were particularly bad, but by January 1832, it had spread into five other parishes and 50 000 slaves were involved. The aim of the slaves was destruction not the killing of whites, and in fact only 15 whites lost their lives. The militia acted quickly before December 1831 was out, but not ruthlessly as in January a pardon was offered to slaves who would surrender. Most did so, but others continued fighting in St James and Trelawny where most of the killing took place. 400 slaves lost their lives in the fighting and 100 were executed. It was called the 'Baptist War' because the whites blamed Samuel Sharpe and William Knibb, both prominent Baptists, for inciting the revolt.

The 1763 revolt in Berbice and Surinam nearly succeeded as it was so widespread and the whites so weak and unprepared. Coffy, the leader who gave his name to the revolt, was an artisan slave who was a moderate and only wanted the partition of Berbice on the lines of Surinam. He would be 'Governor' of the slaves in the interior while the whites stayed in the coastal belt. However, others wanted to kill all the whites and make the whole of Berbice an independent black state.

The revolt began in February 1763, on the Canje River and by March had spread to the Berbice River. The whites had only 12 soldiers and 12 sailors to oppose the rebels. Fort Nassau, the key to the colony, was threatened and could easily have been taken at this stage of the rebellion. Most whites were prepared to surrender the colony to the slaves. However, Coffy hesitated to attack Fort Nassau. Van Hoogenheim, the Governor, was determined not to surrender and called up re-inforcements of 100 soldiers from Surinam. Coffy asked Van Hoogenheim for partition but was told to wait for a decision from Holland which would come in April. In the meantime Gravesande, the Governor of Essequibo planned to relieve Berbice with a force of Indians from Demerara. They would attack the slaves in the rear while British forces from Barbados and Dutch reinforcements from Holland would attack up river. Coffy made his attack on the plantation Dageraad, the whites' stronghold, too late and was beaten. He committed suicide. The revolt continued until September when ships brought the forces up the Berbice River while the Indians from Upper Demerara attacked the slaves in the rear. Some slaves were killed and others escaped into the forests.

Notes

1   In the three hundred years before emancipation there were about 50 slave revolts of which only three were successful.
2   Most of the Caribbean colonies were small islands from which there was no escape and there was no refuge within the islands. Successful revolts took place in Haiti, Jamaica and Surinam where there were wide tracts of mountainous, bush or forest land.
3   Slaves revolted knowing that they would be recaptured and probably executed which suggests how desperate they were with servitude.
4   Revolts were comparatively rare in the Spanish colonies as slave conditions were better and the authorities took steps to reduce the likelihood of revolts.
5   Slave revolts in the Eastern Caribbean islands were relatively uncommon because there was no chance of success.
6   Revolts were most common in Jamaica where slave conditions were very bad.

7 Revolts became more frequent as emancipation drew nearer and the slaves became impatient for freedom.

8 The plantocracy accused the missionaries of inciting the slaves to revolt in the British islands.

9 Slave revolts were suppressed ruthlessly with killings, executions and deportations to deter other slaves from revolting. The different nations helped each other in suppressing slave revolts.

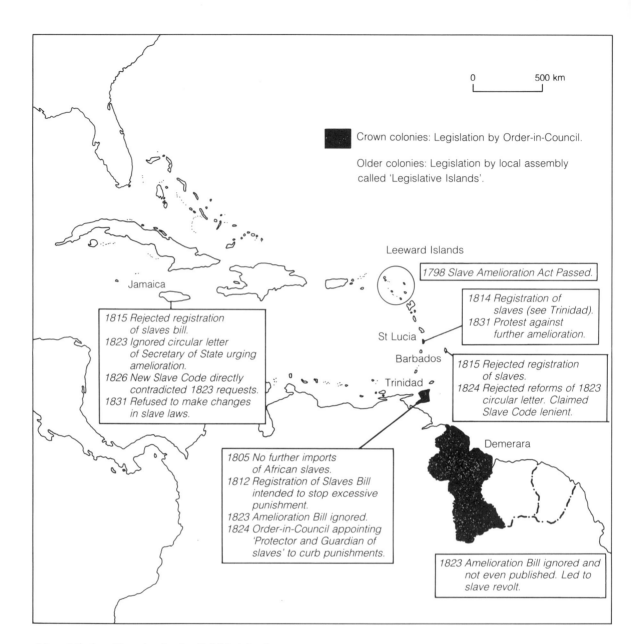

0 ——————— 500 km

Crown colonies: Legislation by Order-in-Council.

Older colonies: Legislation by local assembly called 'Legislative Islands'.

Leeward Islands

1798 Slave Amelioration Act Passed.

1814 Registration of slaves (see Trinidad).
1831 Protest against further amelioration.

Jamaica

1815 Rejected registration of slaves bill.
1823 Ignored circular letter of Secretary of State urging amelioration.
1826 New Slave Code directly contradicted 1823 requests.
1831 Refused to make changes in slave laws.

St Lucia

Barbados

1815 Rejected registration of slaves.
1824 Rejected reforms of 1823 circular letter. Claimed Slave Code lenient.

Trinidad

Demerara

1805 No further imports of African slaves.
1812 Registration of Slaves Bill intended to stop excessive punishment.
1823 Amelioration Bill ignored.
1824 Order-in-Council appointing 'Protector and Guardian of slaves' to curb punishments.

1823 Amelioration Bill ignored and not even published. Led to slave revolt.

Map 4.5: Amelioration in the British islands

Map 4.5: Amelioration in the British islands

Amelioration is the policy of making slave conditions better. The abolitionists supported this policy both as an end in itself and as a half-way step to complete emancipation. They wanted the slaves to be treated better, to have less severe punishments and to be allowed human rights such as marriage and Christianity. They felt that if the planters would accept amelioration first it would be easier to bring in emancipation later. However, the planters were opposed to amelioration seeing it as the 'thin end of the wedge' which would lead to emancipation. They compared their slave conditions favourably with the conditions of seamen, manual labourers in Britain, transportees to Australia and the urban poor, and slave justice with the justice meted out by British courts. They also resented the interference in their internal affairs by the British Parliament and the humanitarians in Britain.

The British Government did have the right to legislate for its Crown Colonies, those recently-acquired colonies of St Lucia, Trinidad and Demerara, by Order-in-Council. The planters in these colonies did not like this but had to accept that it was constitutional for them. The older colonies, called the 'Legislative Islands' had their laws made by their own assemblies and they firmly rejected any bills or suggestions coming from the British Parliament such as amelioration. A few planters did believe that if they adopted amelioration measures the humanitarians would drop their demands for emancipation. However, most of the planters, especially the Jamaican planters, reacted to the prospect of emancipation by making their slave conditions worse, not better.

Amelioration was put forward intermittently in the first thirty years of the nineteenth century. Its obvious failure convinced the abolitionists that complete emancipation was the only answer to the attitude of the planters and colonial assemblies. The Leewards had passed a Slave Amelioration Act in 1798. They and Barbados claimed that their slave conditions were very good and did not need further amelioration. In 1812 and 1814 Registration of Slaves Bills were passed for the Crown colonies by Orders-in-Council to control new imports of slaves and stop excessive punishments but the older colonies would not consider such bills.

In 1823, urged on by Wilberforce and Buxton, Lord Bathurst, Secretary of State for the Colonies, made a determined effort to put amelioration into effect throughout the British West Indies. He was supported by the West Indies Committee in Britain who hoped that it would make the humanitarians drop their demands for emancipation. A circular letter was sent to the Legislative Islands suggesting less severe punishments, religious instruction, marriage and stable family life for slaves and the right to possessions. The response of the Legislative Islands was negative, in fact the Jamaican Assembly published a new Slave Code in 1826 directly contradicting the circular letter. Even the Crown Colonies ignored the suggestions and in Demerara they were not even published.

By 1830 the failure of amelioration was obvious. The attitude of the planters to their slaves had hardened, the slaves were revolting and missionaries were being persecuted. All these things convinced people in Britain that complete emancipation must be passed by the British Parliament.

Notes

1 Amelioration was the policy adopted by the humanitarians, and from 1823 by the British Government, to improve conditions for slaves.
2 Amelioration lasted for the first thirty years of the nineteenth century.
3 Planters and colonial assemblies rejected amelioration and the Crown Colonies ignored it.
4 Some islands like the Leewards and Barbados claimed that their slave conditions were already good enough.
5 Jamaica made its slave conditions harsher, not better.
6 The failure of amelioration convinced the British Parliament that complete emancipation was the only answer.

Spanish

French

British

Spanish (Cuba)

1815 Congress of Vienna. Spanish promised to end slave trade. Not carried out.
1820 Spain formally agreed to stop slave trade.
1865 Spain abolished slave trade.

Emancipation:

1840 Slaves imported after 1820 agreement to be freed. Independence coupled with emancipation in Cuba.
1868 Emancipation of some estates.
1878 Treaty of Zanjon: gradual emancipation.
1880 Emancipation without compensation.
1886 Emancipation complete.

British

1772 By Mansfield's judgement slavery made illegal in England.
1787 Sierra Leone founded for freed slaves.
1778 Society for effecting the abolition of the slave trade.
1789 Parliamentary campaign against slave trade begun by Wilberforce.
1802 Parliamentary campaign reopened.
1805 Slave trade prohibited in Guiana, St Lucia, Trinidad.
1807 Slave trade abolished in British empire.
1823 Society for gradual abolition of slavery. Amelioration policy.
1830 Amelioration failed.
1833 The Emancipation Act.
1834 (August) Slavery abolished.
1834–8 Apprenticeship system. 668 000 slaves set free with compensation of £16 500 000.

Bahamas

Turks and Caicos

Cuba

1822 Boyer freed slaves.

Dominican Republic

Leewards

Caymans and Jamaica

British Honduras

Haiti (St Domingue)

Puerto Rico

1873 Slavery abolished.

Guadeloupe

Martinique

Dominica

Windwards

Barbados

1794 Slavery abolished.
1803 Slavery reintroduced by Napoleon.
1803 (November) Independence declared.
1804 'Haiti' replaced 'St Domingue'. Slavery abolished finally.

Trinidad and Tobago

British Guiana

French Guiana

0   500 km

French

1803 Napoleon reintroduced slavery.
1815 Slavery retained by Bourbon kings.
1834 La Société pour l'Abolition de l'Esclavage founded.
1836 Slavery abolished in France.
1838 Emancipation defeated. Slaves began to flee to British islands for freedom.
1847 Société demanded immediate emancipation.
1848 (April) Emancipation passed. No apprenticeship period. Over 200 000 slaves freed in Martinique, Guadeloupe and Cayenne. Over 100 000 000 francs in compensation.

Map 4.6: Abolition and emancipation in the Caribbean

Map 4.6: Abolition and emancipation in the Caribbean

'Abolition' refers to the stopping of the trade in slaves and 'emancipation' to setting slaves free. The two go together in history as abolition was a step towards emancipation. For the humanitarians emancipation was the goal but it could not be achieved without the intermediate step of abolition. The campaign faced opposition, but less for abolition than emancipation, so they thought it would be easier to tackle abolition first before the more difficult task.

In Britain and France the campaign was led by humanitarians, men concerned about the welfare of their fellow men. Emancipation was achieved by persuading the metropolitan governments to pass laws abolishing slavery. However, in Spain and her colonies the situation was different. The Roman Catholic Church had always been humanitarian but the state and public opinion believed that slavery was a necessary evil for the economies of Caribbean countries. A sugar boom in the second half of the eighteenth and first half of the nineteenth centuries in Cuba and Puerto Rico did not help the cause of abolition and emancipation. Spain was unlikely to abolish slavery in the colonies therefore independence from Spain became a pre-condition for emancipation.

The British colonies

In 1750 slavery was still legal in England with about 10 000 African slaves there. In 1772 Lord Chief Justice Mansfield declared slavery illegal in England, the first victory for Granville Sharp in his crusade against slavery. He then turned his attention to the slave trade. In 1787 The Society for Effecting the Abolition of the Slave Trade was formed which worked through William Wilberforce, a member of Parliament, who made abolition and emancipation his life's work thereafter. The Parliamentary campaign began with Wilberforce's first speech against the slave trade in 1789, but the first bills were easily defeated. The abolition of the slave trade passed by Denmark in 1792 helped the cause in Britain, but then the French Revolution made people frightened of the excesses of reform so the campaign was set back for a decade. When it began again in 1802 the movement was stronger and progress towards abolition accelerated. In 1805 an Order-in-Council prohibited the slave trade in Guiana, St Lucia and Trinidad. In 1806 the Abolition Act began its successful passage through Parliament and the slave trade was abolished throughout the British Empire in 1807.

Those whose only goal had been abolition then dropped out of the movement. Those who remained proceeded slowly as the opposition was formidable. They suggested amelioration as an intermediate measure. The group formed in 1823 actually called itself 'The Society for the Gradual Abolition of Slavery' and adopted the policy of amelioration. By 1831 the planters and local assemblies had made it clear that they would never voluntarily improve the conditions of their slaves. The British Government convinced them that emancipation was inevitable and so they set about achieving concessions such as compensation and apprenticeship which would soften the blow.

At the point of success Wilberforce was dying, so Thomas Fowell Buxton took over the cause and steered the Emancipation Act through Parliament. It was passed in August 1833 to take effect in August 1834. 668 000 slaves were set free and compensation of £16 500 000 was paid to slave owners in the British West Indies at an average of £25 per slave. The period of apprenticeship was intended to last until August 1840, but some islands gave immediate freedom in 1834 and in others apprenticeship was not a success so was brought to an end in August 1838. Freedom for slaves in the British colonies had repercussions throughout the Caribbean.

The French colonies

The French Revolution of 1789 brought emancipation for slaves at the stroke of a pen throughout the French Empire but the colonies ignored the decree except in the case of St Domingue. Commissioners were appointed from France to enforce the decree freeing slaves in 1792 and it was carried out by the local assembly in St Domingue in 1794.

Napoleon made slavery legal again in 1803 and slavery was retained on the restoration of the Bourbons in 1815. In St Domingue this had no effect as metropolitan France was incapable of bringing back slavery there.

At the Congress of Vienna, 1814 to 1815, France promised to abolish the slave trade but did not formally pass abolition through the French Assembly until 1818. Even then it was not effective. Laws passed in France were resisted by local planters and Cayenne, Guadeloupe and Martinique carried on much as before.

The French also proposed amelioration before emancipation. In 1832 manumission was made easier by abolishing the tax levied on planters for each slave manumitted. In 1833 the registration of slaves was made compulsory and the branding and mutilation of slaves was prohibited.

Victor Schoelcher led the crusade against slavery in France. He was a humanitarian but not associated with any particular church. The movement in France was secular, supported by intellectuals and workers. In 1834 *La Société pour L'Abolition de L'Esclavage* was formed. In 1836 slavery was made illegal in France but the 1838 emancipation was defeated easily in the French Assembly. By this time slaves in the British islands were free and slaves from the French islands were trying to escape to the British. In 1838 Schoelcher decided to abandon amelioration and press for immediate emancipation with no apprenticeship. A national petition of 1847 seemed to be effective as the French Assembly passed the Emancipation Bill in 1848 and slaves were set free throughout the French Empire. Over 200 000 slaves were freed in Cayenne, Guadeloupe and Martinique and over 100 000 000 francs compensation was paid.

In the Spanish colonies

The Spanish colonies experienced a sugar boom after 1750 which lasted into the nineteenth century as the British and French abolished slavery thus weakening their competition with Spanish, slave-produced sugar. The Spanish imported more slaves in the nineteenth century than before, in some years 10 000 went to Cuba alone. The Spanish authorities were only concerned about the increase in the black:white ratio and not with the humanitarian aspect of the slave trade. In spite of promises at the Congress of Vienna, the Reciprocal Search Treaties of 1817 and 1835 and their own Abolition Law of 1820, the Spanish continued to import slaves, sometimes under the flag of the United States. However, in 1865 the Spanish abolished the slave trade effectively because: a) the creoles in Cuba feared the sudden rise in the slave population, b) there was pressure on the metropolitan government to abolish the slave trade, c) foreign pressure, especially from Britain, was having an effect, and d) the abolition of slavery in the United States made it impossible for Spanish traders to hide under the American flag.

In the Spanish Caribbean colonies Spanish rule was necessary to keep the slaves in check and therefore the plantocracy wanted colonial rule. The liberals wanted independence and emancipation but even they were worried by what emancipation had brought in Haiti. Others were worried about the economic effects of emancipation on Spanish sugar production.

In Cuba in 1868, Cespedes, the revolutionary leader, freed slaves on his estates. Then began the Ten Years War for independence. The Treaty of Zanjon brought this war to an end. In 1880 Spain ordered emancipation and by 1886 it was fully carried out.

The Haitian Revolution brought emancipation to the Spanish half of Hispaniola. In 1801 Toussaint L'Ouverture occupied Santo Domingo and the slaves were set free. Slavery was restored when LeClerc brought the Spanish part of the island under France. Spanish rule was restored by the revolt of 1808 and in 1821 another revolt brought independence from Spain. In 1822 Haiti was invaded and President Boyer ruled the whole island. He brought emancipation to St Domingue.

Slavery continued for most of the nineteenth century in Puerto Rico and the importation of slaves actually increased then. In 1869 the island was given the status of province of Spain with some autonomy. By general consent slavery was abolished in 1873.

Notes

1 'Abolition' is the stopping of the slave trade and 'emancipation' is the ending of slavery.
2 Abolition was a step towards emancipation.
3 In Britain humanitarians who led the campaign for abolition and emancipation were associated with churches like the Quakers, Baptists and Methodists.
4 In France the movement was behind that of Britain. It was not associated with churches but with intellectuals and workers.
5 In Spain economic considerations outweighed humanitarian because Spain thought that slave labour was necessary to keep the Spanish sugar industry competitive.
6 Britain abolished the slave trade in 1807 but it only became really effective in 1811.
7 France abolished the slave trade in 1818 but the loss of St Domingue and the Revolutionary Wars had already curtailed French slave trading.
8 The Spanish continued the slave trade until 1865 in spite of their abolition law of 1820.
9 In the British colonies emancipation was re-

sisted by the planters and local assemblies until 1831 when they accepted that it was inevitable and they asked for concessions like compensation and apprenticeship.

10 The French passed emancipation with compensation in 1848 but with no apprenticeship.

11 Emancipation in the Spanish colonies was linked to independence movements.

12 Emancipation in Cuba came shortly after the end of the independence struggle in 1878.

Theme 5: The French Revolution and St Domingue

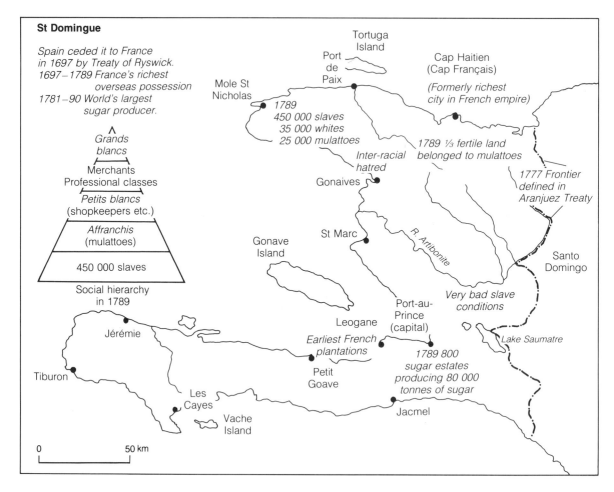

St Domingue

Spain ceded it to France in 1697 by Treaty of Ryswick.
1697–1789 France's richest overseas possession
1781–90 World's largest sugar producer.

Grands
blancs

Merchants
Professional classes

Petits blancs
(shopkeepers etc.)

Affranchis
(mulattoes)

450 000 slaves

Social hierarchy
in 1789

Tortuga
Island

Port
de
Paix

Cap Haitien
(Cap Français)

(Formerly richest city in French empire)

Mole St
Nicholas

1789
450 000 slaves
35 000 whites
25 000 mulattoes

*Inter-racial
hatred*

1789 ⅓ fertile land belonged to mulattoes

Gonaives

*1777 Frontier
defined in
Aranjuez Treaty*

St Marc

R. Artibonite

Gonave
Island

Santo
Domingo

*Very bad slave
conditions*

Port-au-
Prince
(capital)

Leogane

Lake Saumatre

*Earliest French
plantations*

*1789 800
sugar estates
producing 80 000
tonnes of sugar*

Jérémie

Petit
Goave

Tiburon

Les
Cayes

Jacmel

Vache
Island

0   50 km

Map 5.1: St Domingue before the French Revolution

Map 5.1: St Domingue before the French Revolution

St Domingue was divided into classes socially, legally and racially which caused deep hatred, especially the racial divisions. The 35 000 whites were divided into three social classes. The *grands blancs* consisted of the very rich planters and the top civil and military officers. Below them came the whites of the merchant and professional classes whom the *grands blancs* looked down on. The lowest white social class was the *petits blancs* who were the artisans and shopkeepers. These three divisions were further complicated by the attitude that a person born in France was superior to a locally-born white (a creole). Legally all three classes of whites enjoyed rights and freedoms above any person of colour, blacks or mulattoes.

By the *Code Noir* of 1685 mulattoes had been given the rights of free men but these had been eroded by subsequent laws. Thus in St Domingue mulattoes were called *affranchis* which means 'free from slavery'. However by 1789 they could not hold civil or military office, carry firearms or even wear the same clothes as whites but they could own property and slaves which put them on the side of the whites on some issues. Indeed one third of all the fertile land in St Domingue belonged to mulattoes. Their colour confused them; over slavery they were against the blacks, but in conscription to labour on the roads they were aligned with the blacks.

At the bottom of the social scale were the 450 000 black slaves who had been imported rapidly into St Domingue by the French in the sugar boom even at a rate as high as 30 000 per year. Numbers were important and little regard was paid to selection or conditions. Their death rate was the highest in the Caribbean but disregarded by the planters who merely imported more from Africa. Consequently a high proportion of St Domingue slaves were African-born and the distinction between them and creole slaves was important. In St Domingue slaves were made to work harder, treated more cruelly, worse fed and given worse conditions than elsewhere in the Caribbean which brought much deeper racial hatred there.

This was the background in St Domingue against which we must consider the impact of the French Revolution and its ideas of 'liberty, equality and fraternity'. We can compare the *grands blancs* to the French aristocrats, the privileged class who supported the King. The mulattoes were the bourgeoisie, the middle class who resented the privileges of the nobles. The slaves were the mob who had nothing to lose and who wanted to exterminate the whites. However, colour complicated the issue in St Domingue. In France in 1789 there was no group to correspond with the mulattoes of St Domingue.

Notes

1 There were deep class divisions in St Domingue in 1789.
2 Racial hatred was more acute than elsewhere in the Caribbean because slaves had been imported with no thought to their conditions or treatment.
3 Mulattoes had lost the status they had been granted by the *Code Noir* yet many were very prosperous and were great landowners and slave owners.
4 St Domingue society had parallels with French society but colour introduced an issue not present in France.

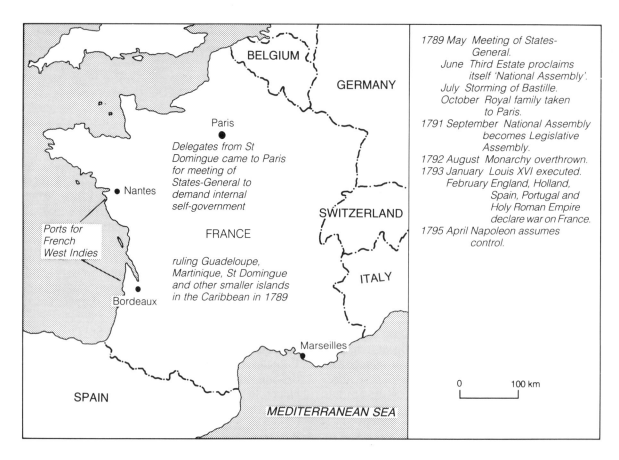

Map 5.2: The French Revolution

The map contains the following labels and text:

BELGIUM

GERMANY

Paris

Delegates from St Domingue came to Paris for meeting of States-General to demand internal self-government

Nantes

Ports for French West Indies

FRANCE

SWITZERLAND

ruling Guadeloupe, Martinique, St Domingue and other smaller islands in the Caribbean in 1789

ITALY

Bordeaux

Marseilles

SPAIN

MEDITERRANEAN SEA

0   100 km

1789 May Meeting of States-General.
June Third Estate proclaims itself 'National Assembly'.
July Storming of Bastille.
October Royal family taken to Paris.
1791 September National Assembly becomes Legislative Assembly.
1792 August Monarchy overthrown.
1793 January Louis XVI executed.
February England, Holland, Spain, Portugal and Holy Roman Empire declare war on France.
1795 April Napoleon assumes control.

Map 5.2: The French Revolution

Louis XIV, 1643–1715, had been an absolute monarch who brought prestige to the French crown. His successors, Louis XV and Louis XVI had allowed the aristocracy (the nobles) to assume powers and privileges in government and judiciary which they were never entitled to under law. At the same time the bourgeoisie (the middle class) had become much more prosperous and resented the privilege of the nobility. The monarchy had lost its prestige appearing weak in the face of nobility.

The Revolution was inevitable because the real state of affairs in France and the way of life were so different to what the law intended. It came in 1789 because of the financial crisis the monarchy was in. The richest classes in France paid no taxes so the monarchy was cutting itself off from its biggest source of funds. The monarchy was bankrupt because of the expense of French participation in the War of American Independence, the extravagance of the court and the inefficiency in financial administration. The King tried to solve this problem by calling a body which had not been used since 1614, the States-General. Louis XVI hoped that it would find a way out of the crisis. He expected the meeting to be dominated by the First Estate, the Nobles, but the Third Estate, the Commons, refused to vote by estates and insisted on voting as one body. After six weeks of stalemate the Third Estate called itself the National Assembly and signed the Tennis Court Oath not to disperse until its reforms had been granted. So the Revolution began.

The violence started when Louis decided to ignore the financial crisis and dissolve the National Assembly. This led to the storming of the Bastille, a symbol of repression and persecution. The peo-ple formed the National Guard. The rest of France followed the example of Paris and the peasants attacked the chateaux of the nobles. The King was suspected of plotting counter-revolution and in October 1789, he and his family were brought to Paris and placed under house arrest.

Slowly the news of events in France reached the overseas possessions. Those who supported the King were known as 'royalists' and their opponents were 'revolutionaries'. The people in the colonies were bewildered. They did not know whether they were being ruled by the King or by the Assembly. They did not know whether the ideas of 'liberty, equality and fraternity' would be applied to slave societies. The decrees coming out of France confused them further as they were often contradictory.

Notes

1 Between 1713 and 1789 the French monarchy had declined in power and prestige.
2 The nobles took advantage of this by assuming more powers and privileges, the chief of which was exemption from paying taxes.
3 The bourgeoisie wanted political power to reflect their new importance in society and they were bitter towards the privileged classes.
4 The monarchy was facing bankruptcy in 1789 and resorted to calling an archaic body, the States-General, to solve the crisis.
5 The nobles expected to dominate the States-General but the Third Estate was determined to bring reforms and became the National Assembly.
6 In the colonies the people did not know whether they were under the King or the Assembly.

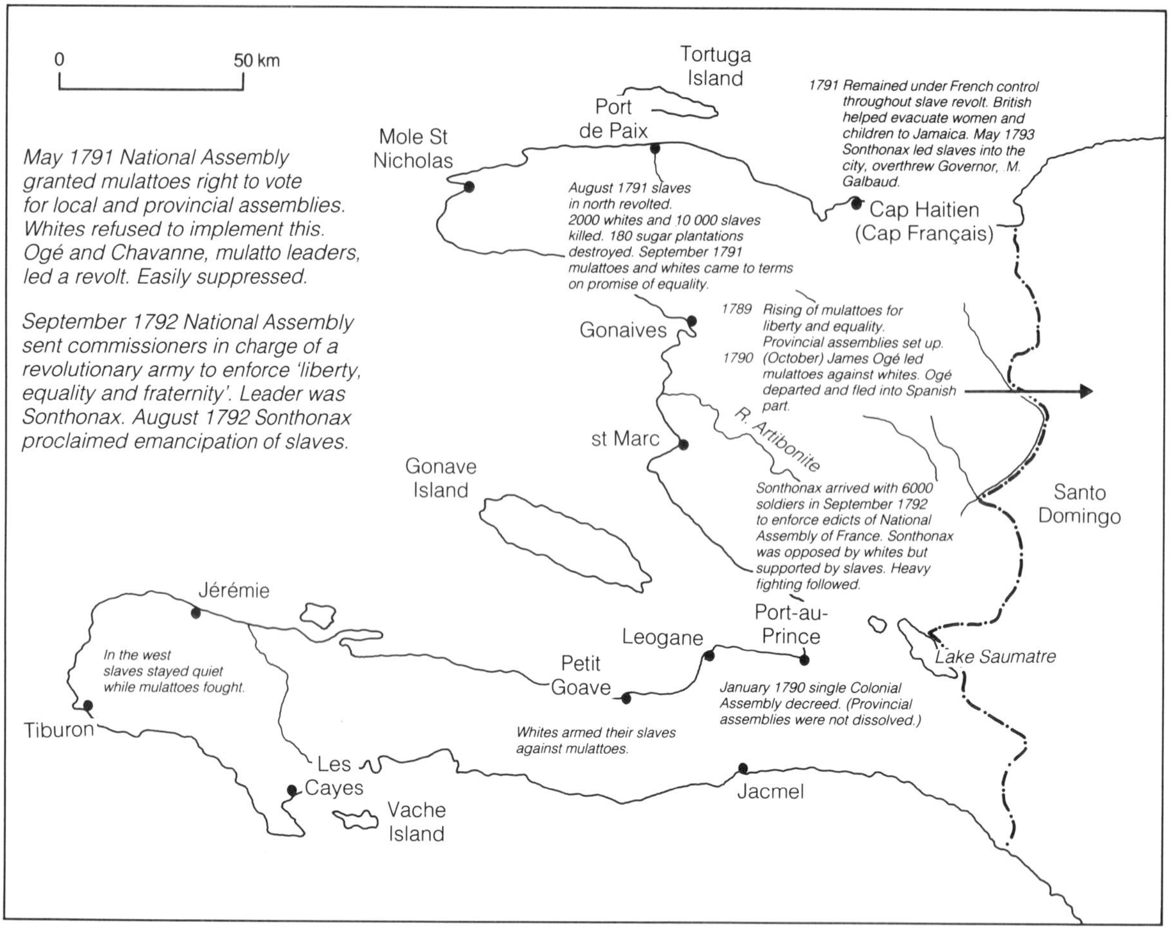
0
50 km
Tortuga
Island
Port
de Paix
Mole St
Nicholas
1791 Remained under French control throughout slave revolt. British helped evacuate women and children to Jamaica. May 1793 Sonthonax led slaves into the city, overthrew Governor, M. Galbaud.
May 1791 National Assembly granted mulattoes right to vote for local and provincial assemblies. Whites refused to implement this. Ogé and Chavanne, mulatto leaders, led a revolt. Easily suppressed.
August 1791 slaves in north revolted. 2000 whites and 10 000 slaves killed. 180 sugar plantations destroyed. September 1791 mulattoes and whites came to terms on promise of equality.
Cap Haitien
(Cap Français)
September 1792 National Assembly sent commissioners in charge of a revolutionary army to enforce 'liberty, equality and fraternity'. Leader was Sonthonax. August 1792 Sonthonax proclaimed emancipation of slaves.
Gonaives
1789 Rising of mulattoes for liberty and equality. Provincial assemblies set up.
1790 (October) James Ogé led mulattoes against whites. Ogé departed and fled into Spanish part.
R. Artibonite
st Marc
Gonave
Island
Sonthonax arrived with 6000 soldiers in September 1792 to enforce edicts of National Assembly of France. Sonthonax was opposed by whites but supported by slaves. Heavy fighting followed.
Santo
Domingo
Jérémie
Port-au-
Prince
Leogane
Lake Saumatre
In the west slaves stayed quiet while mulattoes fought.
Petit
Goave
January 1790 single Colonial Assembly decreed. (Provincial assemblies were not dissolved.)
Tiburon
Whites armed their slaves against mulattoes.
Les
Cayes
Jacmel
Vache
Island

Map 5.3: The impact of the French Revolution in St Domingue

Map 5.3: The impact of the French Revolution in St Domingue

St Domingue sent delegates to the meeting of the States-General of May 1789, aware of the crisis of the monarchy. However, news from France took weeks to reach St Domingue and often by the time decisions had been implemented they were revoked by subsequent decrees causing much frustration and confusion in St Domingue. The French Revolution had a much greater impact in St Domingue than in other parts of the French Empire because of the class structure and racial hatred.

In St Domingue the first response to the message of 'liberty, equality and fraternity' from their brothers in France came from the mulattoes. In 1789 they rebelled against the restrictions placed on them but were soon quietened by concessions from the whites. Provincial Assemblies were set up and were not dissolved when Louis XVI sent a decree in January 1790, ordering a single Colonial Assembly. This Assembly gave mulattoes equality with whites as regards service in the militia which again appeased the mulattoes until October when James Ogé, a mulatto educated in France, returned to St Domingue with arms. He was joined by another mulatto, Chavannne, in a revolt against the whites. It failed and they fled to the Spanish part of Hispaniola whence they were handed back to the French and executed.

A decree of the National Assembly of May 1791, gave equality to all free-born persons of whatever colour and gave mulattoes the right to elect members for local and provincial assemblies. The Governor refused to enforce the decree when the whites resisted it. Mulattoes with slave mothers were not to be classed as free. The mulattoes rose in a much more serious rebellion. Round Cap Haitien the mulattoes were joined by slaves and together they massacred about 2000 whites, destroyed 180 sugar estates and 900 coffee and indigo plantations. About 10 000 blacks and mulattoes were killed or executed. In the west mulattoes and whites were also fighting each other but in the south the whites armed their slaves and the mulattoes kept peace.

Thereafter the whites accepted the May 1791, decree, but then another decree threw matters into confusion in September revoking the May decree. The mulattoes were completely disillusioned with the whites and, allied with the slaves, they began the killing again. White women and children had been evacuated from Cap Haitien with the help of the British from Jamaica and later men also took exile.

The National Assembly changed its decision yet again in April 1792, and gave equality to all free men. St Domingue was to have assemblies with members elected by whites and coloureds. The National Assembly sent out commissioners with 6000 soldiers to enforce the decrees. The leader, Légér Felicité Sonthonax, arrived in St Domingue in September 1792, and being opposed by the whites drew his support from the slaves, promising them liberty and booty. There was much fighting in the north. Sonthonax led his forces into Cap Haitien forcing many more whites to evacuate to Jamaica, Cuba, the United States and Britain where they appealed for military help. In August 1793, Sonthonax, who was almost a dictator, declared emancipation for the slaves. The British, who had not so far intervened in the revolution in St Domingue, were moved to a declaration of war against France by the execution of Louis XVI in January 1793. They decided to send an army to St Domingue. This arrived in September.

Notes

1 News from France took a few weeks to reach St Domingue.
2 Decrees were often revoked by subsequent decrees which bewildered the people of St Domingue especially the mulattoes who did not know whether they had been given equality with the whites or not.
3 The mulattoes became disillusioned with the whites and, helped by the slaves, rose against the whites.
4 Most of the killing and destruction was in the north around Cap Haitien.
5 The National Assembly sent out Sonthonax with other commissioners and revolutionary soldiers to enforce the decrees.
6 The whites opposed Sonthonax so he joined forces with the blacks.
7 The execution of Louis XVI in January 1793, made Britain declare war on France and send forces to St Domingue in September.
8 In August 1793, Sonthonax emancipated all the slaves in St Domingue.

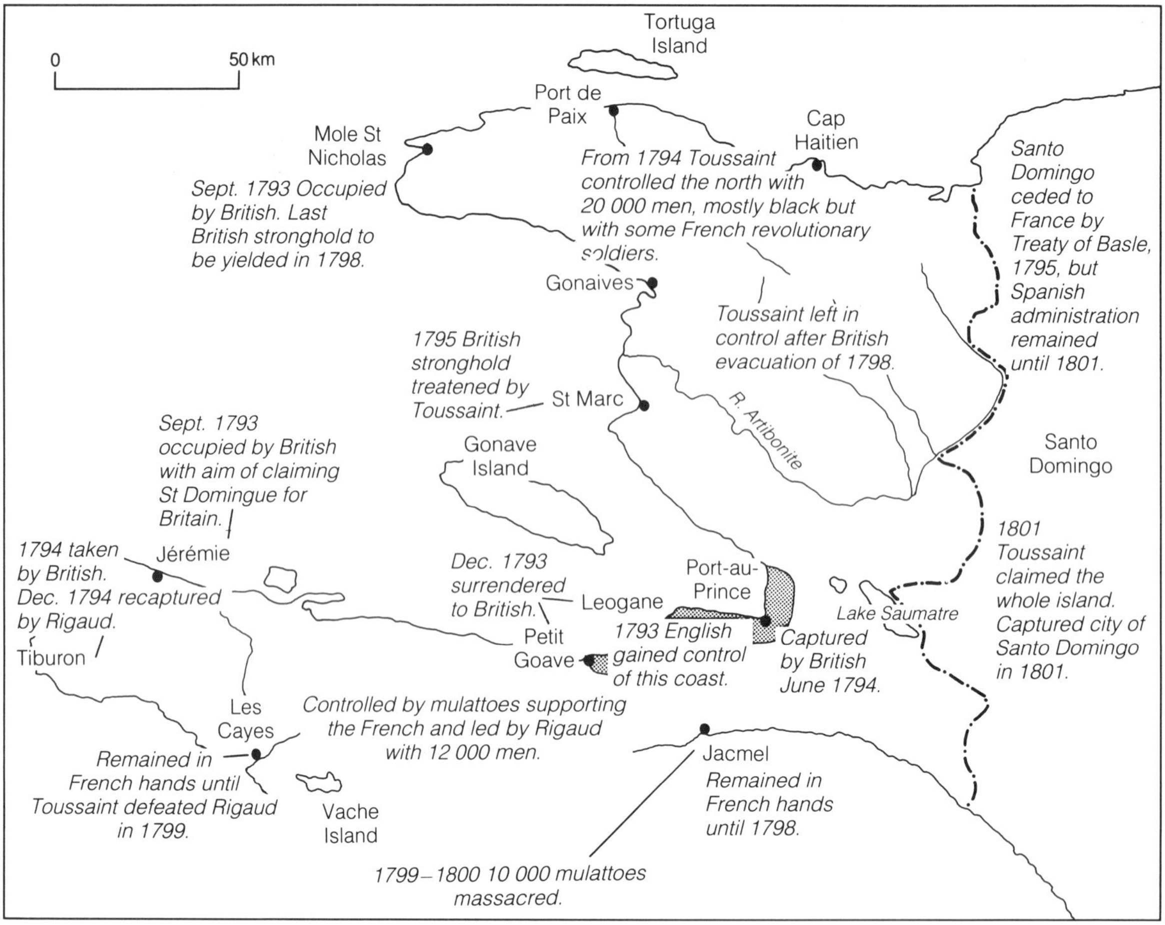

0
50 km
Tortuga Island
Port de Paix
Cap Haitien
Mole St Nicholas
Sept. 1793 Occupied by British. Last British stronghold to be yielded in 1798.
From 1794 Toussaint controlled the north with 20 000 men, mostly black but with some French revolutionary soldiers.
Santo Domingo ceded to France by Treaty of Basle, 1795, but Spanish administration remained until 1801.
Gonaives
Toussaint left in control after British evacuation of 1798.
1795 British stronghold treatened by Toussaint.
St Marc
R. Artibonite
Sept. 1793 occupied by British with aim of claiming St Domingue for Britain.
Gonave Island
Santo Domingo
1801 Toussaint claimed the whole island. Captured city of Santo Domingo in 1801.
1794 taken by British. Dec. 1794 recaptured by Rigaud.
Jérémie
Dec. 1793 surrendered to British.
Leogane
Port-au-Prince
Lake Saumatre
Tiburon
Petit Goave
1793 English gained control of this coast.
Captured by British June 1794.
Les Cayes
Controlled by mulattoes supporting the French and led by Rigaud with 12 000 men.
Remained in French hands until Toussaint defeated Rigaud in 1799.
Vache Island
Jacmel
Remained in French hands until 1798.
1799–1800 10 000 mulattoes massacred.

Map 5.4: The revolutionary wars in St Domingue, 1793–8

Map 5.4: The revolutionary wars in St Domingue, 1793–8

Even those in Britain and other countries who sympathised with the revolutionaries in France, could not condone regicide, and the execution of Louis XVI brought about the revolutionary wars. Whites in Jamaica were also in favour of war in order to stop the unrest in St Domingue spreading to the slaves in Jamaica. Royalist planters in St Domingue led by M. de Charmilly invited the British to occupy St Domingue.

At first a force of 900 from Jamaica landed at Jérémie in September 1793, where they were welcomed by the French. By January 1794, Mole St Nicolas, Leogane and Tiburon were occupied. The British were soon weakened by disease but so were the French revolutionary forces under the mulatto, General Rigaud. The British were able to control the land around Port-au-Prince. In June 1794, the British occupied Port-au-Prince itself. More troops arrived to replace those lost in the fighting and from disease and in May 1795, General Williamson was appointed Governor of St Domingue although the British were far from controlling the island.

There were five forces operating in St Domingue: British supporting the Royalists; General Rigaud with a revolutionary army of 12 000 French, mulattoes and blacks in the south; Toussaint L'Ouverture leading 20 000 blacks and some French in the north; Spanish who had been allied to the British but then conducted their own campaign; and bandit escaped slaves who terrorised everyone.

In the south Jacmel and Les Cayes had always been occupied by French revolutionary forces and in December 1794, Rigaud recaptured Tiburon. From these ports the revolutionaries were able to disrupt shipping from Jamaica, but then the Second Maroon War in 1795 stopped any more reinforcements coming from Jamaica. As the British had lost at least 20 000 men from yellow fever and about the same number in the fighting, the war was turning against them. Then the decree of the Assembly of February 1794, confirming the emancipation of the slaves put Toussaint and all the blacks on the revolutionary side. He recaptured all that he had lost in the north by defeating the Spanish. Then he turned against the British and drove them across the Artibonite River and threatened St Marc. General Maitland, now commander of the British forces, decided to withdraw from all the towns under British occupation as he had insufficient forces in good health. He made terms with Toussaint on the condition that Toussaint would protect the remaining French in these towns. In April 1798 the British evacuated Port-au-Prince and other towns apart from Mole St Nicolas and Tortuga Island which were evacuated in October. The British withdrawal left Toussaint to take control of St Domingue and the Revolutionary Wars were over but a new war with Napoleon was soon to begin.

Notes

1 When war with France was declared in 1793, Britain decided to occupy St Domingue.
2 French Royalists welcomed British occupation and soon the British controlled most of the towns of the south except Jacmel and Les Cayes.
3 Disease (yellow fever) killed more on the British side than the fighting, and it also killed many on the revolutionary side.
4 By 1794–5 the situation was confused in St Domingue because of many different forces in spite of the fact that the British claimed the territory.
5 Toussaint exerted his control from the north and in 1797 the British decided to withdraw. This was completed by 1798.
6 Toussaint was in control of most of St Domingue in 1798.

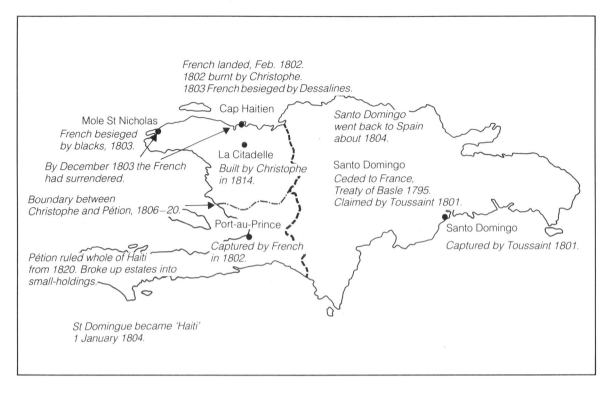

Map 5.5: Haitian independence

Map 5.5: Haitian independence

Toussaint L'Ouverture quickly gained control over St Domingue after the British evacuation. He defeated the mulatto leaders Rigaud and Pétion, but unfortunately Dessalines, one of Toussaint's lieutenants, turned the defeat into a massacre of about 10 000 mulattoes in the south. Toussaint was not able to stop this until 1800.

In 1801 Toussaint declared himself Governor-General for life over the whole island of Hispaniola because the Spanish part had been ceded to France by the Treaty of Basle in 1795. He reinforced this claim by sending in soldiers to capture Santo Domingo in 1801. 2000 Spaniards fled to South America.

Meanwhile Napoleon had come to power in France. He was determined to reoccupy the French West Indian colonies. In December 1802, he sent 20 000 veteran soldiers to St Domingue under the command of his brother-in-law, General LeClerc, with the mulatto generals, Rigaud, Pétion and Boyer, who had been in France after their defeat by Toussaint. Napoleon hoped that Toussaint would co-operate with France and prob-

ably Toussaint would have done if his rule had been recognised but Napoleon would not accept another ruler in the French Empire. Henri Christophe, another of Toussaint's lieutenants, would not allow LeClerc to land peacefully at Cap Haitien. The blacks burnt the town. In February 1802, LeClerc declared war on Toussaint and the fighting began. The French quickly captured Port-au-Prince and Santo Domingo and by May, 1802, most of the fighting was over. Peace negotiations were opened with Toussaint, Dessalines and Christophe. On their surrender they were promised amnesty for their armies and the rank of general in the French army for themselves. However, the French betrayed Toussaint, captured him and deported him to France where he died in 1803.

Dessalines and Christophe knew then that they could not trust the French so they rallied their armies again and were determined to wipe out the French completely. The French army had been weakened by an outbreak of yellow fever in November 1802, which took 40 000 lives including that of LeClerc. The blacks also suffered about 60 000 deaths from the diseases but for them reinforcements were easier to obtain especially as they had a real fear of the reintroduction of slavery in St Domingue (it had already been reimposed in Guadeloupe).

General Rochambeau succeeded LeClerc. His situation was hopeless as the British resumed the war against France and blockaded all the ports of Hispaniola so that the French could not receive supplies or reinforcements. The blacks captured all the towns and cities except for Santo Domingo, Cap Haitien and Mole St Nicolas. In November 1803 Dessalines had Rochambeau trapped in Cap Haitien. Rochambeau knew that the blacks would kill all his army so he sailed out and surrendered to the British. In December 1803, the French garrison at Mole St Nicolas also surrendered at sea to the British.

Dessalines was now the leader of what had become the 'Haitian Revolution'. He adopted the name 'Haiti' as it was the old Arawak name and meant 'land of mountains'. In January 1804, he proclaimed the independent republic of Haiti. In May he was made Governor-General for life and in October was crowned 'Emperor Jacques I', Emperor of Haiti. He massacred all the remaining whites in the country, but was himself assassinated in 1806 as he had made many enemies by his great cruelty.

The eastern part of Hispaniola reverted to Spain and Henri Christophe succeeded as ruler of Haiti. In 1811 he was crowned 'King Henri I'. He built himself a huge fortress palace at La Ferrière called 'La Citadelle', an amazing feat of construction. However he could only rule the northern part of Haiti. Pétion was President of the southern half and the two parts were at war with each other from 1812 to 1814 when they made temporary peace fearing that on the restoration of the monarchy in France there would be another French invasion. Louis XVIII did try to persuade Christophe and Pétion to accept French rule but they refused.

Christophe had tried to restore the plantation economy in the north by inviting whites to return. He forced the blacks to work on plantations like slaves and was extremely cruel. After an attempted revolution against him he committed suicide in 1820 leaving all of Haiti to Pétion. Pétion was under pressure from the blacks to break up the plantations into small-holdings which he did but it meant that the export trade could never be revived. However, Pétion maintained Haiti's independence which was recognised by France in 1825 and Britain in 1826.

Notes

1 By 1801 Toussaint was well in control of St Domingue having overcome the mulattoes.
2 He was supported by two lieutenants, Dessalines and Christophe.
3 Napoleon would not accept another ruler in the French Empire so he sent an army under LeClerc to recapture St Domingue.
4 In 1802 LeClerc fought Toussaint's armies and quickly recaptured most of St Domingue.
5 The French broke their promise to Toussaint, captured him and deported him to France where he died in 1803.
6 Dessalines and Christophe restarted the fighting and this time the French were in a hopeless position as 40 000 of their soldiers had died from yellow fever.
7 The British had also declared war on Napoleon and they blockaded all the ports of St Domingue.
8 By December 1803 the French had surrendered.
9 Dessalines proclaimed the independent republic of Haiti in 1804.
10 Haiti was eventually recognised by France in 1825 and Britain in 1826.

Theme 6: The problems of emancipation

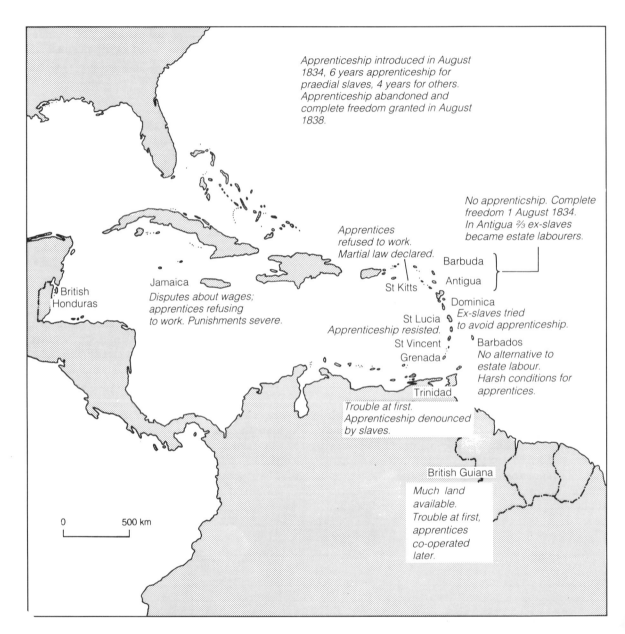

Apprenticeship introduced in August 1834, 6 years apprenticeship for praedial slaves, 4 years for others. Apprenticeship abandoned and complete freedom granted in August 1838.

No apprenticeship. Complete freedom 1 August 1834. In Antigua ⅔ ex-slaves became estate labourers.

Apprentices refused to work. Martial law declared.

Jamaica
Disputes about wages; apprentices refusing to work. Punishments severe.

British Honduras

Barbuda

Antigua

St Kitts

Dominica

St Lucia
Apprenticeship resisted.

Ex-slaves tried to avoid apprenticeship.

St Vincent

Grenada

Barbados
No alternative to estate labour. Harsh conditions for apprentices.

Trinidad

Trouble at first. Apprenticeship denounced by slaves.

British Guiana

Much land available. Trouble at first, apprentices co-operated later.

0   500 km

Map 6.1: The apprenticeship system

Map 6.1: The apprenticeship system

The apprenticeship system was proposed by James Stephen, a member of the Society for the Abolition of Slavery and adviser to the Colonial Office on West Indian affairs. He was probably sincere in his belief that ex-slaves would need time to adjust to freedom, to looking after themselves, to handling money and to supporting families. In April 1833, a period of twelve years' apprenticeship was suggested but it was soon cut down to six.

Apprenticeship meant that an ex-slave would continue working for his master for six years in the case of a praedial slave, and four years in the case of all others, that is complete freedom would be delayed until 1 August 1840 and 1 August 1838 respectively. The apprentice would work for forty hours (or forty and a half hours) per week without pay and the remaining hours with pay, but not more than forty-five hours per week in total. There would be no work on Sundays. In return the employers would provide food and clothing. By saving out of his wages a slave could buy his freedom before his period of apprenticeship was over.

Apprenticeship was passed by the British Parliament along with compensation to owners freeing their slaves, but apprenticeship had also to be passed by each colonial legislature. There could be no alternative to apprenticeship, i.e. no continuation of slavery, but colonies could dispense with apprenticeship altogether and grant immediate freedom or could cut short the period of apprenticeship.

The real reason for the apprenticeship condition, and why the planters accepted it, was to delay complete emancipation and to give them a few more years of free labour. Planters resented having to pay any wages at all as they were not used to a cash system but a credit system. They did not use the period of apprenticeship to adjust to a cash system, in fact West Indian banks did not open until after apprenticeship had ended. Planters tended to try to treat their apprentices as if they were slaves and to squeeze more work out of them than they had done formerly. In Jamaica especially there were disputes about wages with planters trying to make apprentices work longer hours than laid down. On the estates planters still enforced discipline and always looked for opportunities to punish so that they could re-introduce conditions of slavery in the workhouses, called 'Houses of Correction'. The treadmill was a new form of punishment introduced into the British West Indies in this period. Consequently special magistrates, or 'stipendiary' magistrates were appointed along with apprenticeship to prevent abuses to the system. They were to listen to complaints of ill-treatment, inadequate wages, food or clothing. On the other hand they were also to listen to planters' complaints when apprentices refused to work. Generally-speaking the special magistrates favoured the apprentices but they were not popular with them as they regarded apprenticeship as a device to withhold freedom and the magistrates as upholders of the system. The magistrates were not popular with the planters either because they thwarted their attempts to return to pre-1833 labour conditions. However, it is usually accepted that special magistrates were the one good thing to come out of the apprenticeship period.

Slaves probably did need a period of time to adjust to freedom although the authorities in Barbados and the Leewards considered that their slaves were advanced enough to fend for themselves. However, apprenticeship was not wage labour and the apprentices still had their food and clothes found for them. They were not given any practice in supporting themselves and they handled very little money. They certainly did not need a period of six years under these conditions. At the outset Antigua disagreed with apprenticeship and gave immediate emancipation for the slaves in August 1834. There was little alternative but estate labour in Antigua so almost at once two-thirds of the ex-slaves became wage labourers producing 10 per cent more sugar than before emancipation. Barbuda also enjoyed immediate freedom but it was a proprietary colony and freedom was conferred by the proprietor, not because the planters disagreed with the apprenticeship system.

By 1838 apprenticeship was considered a failure. The reason for its premature abandonment, however, was because once artisan slaves were freed on 1 August 1838, freedom had to be given to praedial slaves as well because the artisans would not work with people still denied their freedom. The French and Spanish colonies did not copy the British experiment of apprenticeship.

Notes

1 Apprenticeship was proposed by James Stephen in 1833 on the grounds that slaves would need time to adjust to freedom.

2 Ex-slaves had to continue working for their masters for six years in the case of praedial slaves and four years in the case of all other slaves.

3 The first forty hours per week were to be unpaid and all subsequent hours paid.

4 Masters were to provide food and clothing for apprentices.

5 The real reason for apprenticeship was to delay full emancipation and to give planters a few more years free labour.

6 Special magistrates were introduced to protect the interests of the ex-slaves. They did such a good job that they were retained long after apprenticeship was over.

7 In general, islands where there was little or no alternative to estate labour adapted to apprenticeship fairly well.

8 Islands and British Guiana where there were vacant acres, bush and Crown Lands had difficulties administering apprenticeship.

9 The end of the apprenticeship period was brought forward by two years so that all ex-slaves had complete freedom on 1 August 1838.

10 In general the apprenticeship system was a failure and its period not a happy one.

Table 6.1: British sugar islands c.1839.

Classification by size	Colony	Area in sq km	Population density per sq km	% change in sugar production after emancipation	Wages
Small	Antigua	280	125	Up 10	1/6
	Barbados	430	250	Up 140	10d
	St Kitts	296	85	Down 15	9d
Large	British Guiana	215 000	0.5	Down 45	2/–
	Jamaica	11 500	27	Down 65	1/6
	Trinidad	4 800	4.5	Up 15	2/6

Table 6.1: Wage labour after emancipation

The slaves had hated labouring on sugar plantations and the condition of slavery and apprenticeship. When freedom was achieved on 1 August 1838, their first thoughts were for a new way of life away from the plantation. However, the reality for most was that there was nowhere to go, no alternative way of subsisting or earning a living. Also as apprenticeship had not prepared them for fending for themselves, they had to offer their labour for wages on the plantations they had hoped to leave behind.

The planters were not prepared for wage labour. In apprenticeship they had not adjusted to a cash economy. Generally they resented paying wages for labour which had been free and at first they did not realise that if the wages they offered were not attractive, no labour would be forthcoming. At first the wages they offered, e.g. 7½d per day in Jamaica, were far too low and had to be raised immediately to a more attractive level. They also had to attract labour with food, clothing, shelter and grounds as fringe benefits, often without charging rent for house and grounds.

These generalisations cover the whole of the British West Indies. There were differences between the large and small territories and Table 6.1 invites us to draw conclusions about these differences.

The small territories had high population densities and land was scarce. Subsistence farming was not an alternative to estate labour. Planters knew that the ex-slaves would have to offer their labour for wages at whatever rate the planters would give, therefore wages were low. On the other hand,

sugar production increased immediately after emancipation which shows that wage labour with its incentives for harder work was more efficient than slave labour.

Antigua provides a good example. With a population density of 125 per sq km there was little land outside the plantations, and what there was was infertile. In Antigua fishing for subsistence was taken up by some ex-slaves, but two-thirds of the ex-slaves were working for wages by 1839. A smaller labour force was producing more sugar than before emancipation. Wages were relatively low at 1/6d per day but the highest of the small territories because there had been no apprenticeship in Antigua and the planters wanted to maintain the good employer/employee relations that had been established.

Barbados had the highest population density and the least land available. At first wages, at 9d per day, were the lowest in the British West Indies but they had to rise to 10d because of the proximity of Trinidad with its abundant land and high wages.

St Kitts' population density was not as high as the other small territories but land outside the plantations tended to be mountainous and infertile, unsuitable for subsistence. No alternative to plantation labour led to very low wages there.

In the large islands there were sometimes alternatives to plantation labour. Crown lands, unused fertile land and bush contributed to the supply of land on which ex-slaves could subsist or grow cash crops. Relatively large towns offered the possibility of trading, working for wages in construction and other trades, or even crime. Therefore the ex-slaves did not have to return to the plantations in the same way that they did in the small territories. Sugar production went down sharply after emancipation as labour left the estates. To attract labour back to the estates planters had to offer high wages and good fringe benefits.

British Guiana had Crown lands which the British Government was willing to sell to ex-slaves. In the interior there were thousands of acres of savannah and virgin bush. Ex-slaves also pooled their resources to buy plantations up for sale when the owners could not adjust to the cash economy. Sugar production fell by 45 per cent after emancipation. Wages, at 2/- per day, were relatively high.

The situation in Jamaica was complicated. There was land outside the plantations but little of it was Crown land. The unused land tended to be mountainous and infertile. Jamaican planters were unwilling to sell land to blacks, therefore the possibilities for subsistence farming or growing cash crops like sugar were not as great as in British Guiana. However, on the other hand, resistance to their former life and treatment was much stronger on the part of ex-slaves in Jamaica and they did all they could to find alternative ways of living such as 'higgling' or labouring. Sugar production fell by 65 per cent. In spite of the difficulty in obtaining wage labour, planters would not offer high wages. At first they had even suggested 7½d per day. They started at 1/- per day in 1838 but had to increase to 1/6d, still the lowest wage rate in the large territories.

Trinidad was relatively underdeveloped as the British had only been in occupation for three or four decades. Sugar production actually rose slightly after emancipation and probably would have quickly risen more but for the difficulty in obtaining labour. At 2/6d per day, wages in Trinidad were higher than elsewhere in the British West Indies.

Notes

1 There was strong resistance towards plantation labour after emancipation but many ex-slaves had no alternative.

2 Possible alternatives were subsistence farming or growing cash crops but these depended on the availability of land.

3 Possible sources of land were Crown land, unused land or estate land up for sale.

4 Towns offered other alternatives in the form of trade or labouring.

5 In the small territories there was little or no alternative to wage labour on plantations.

6 In the small islands sugar production generally increased after emancipation.

7 In the small islands wages were relatively low, ranging from 9d to 1/6d per day.

8 In the large territories there was some prospect of subsistence farming as land was available.

9 In the large territories sugar production generally fell sharply after emancipation.

10 In the large territories wages were relatively high, ranging from 1/6d to 2/6d per day.

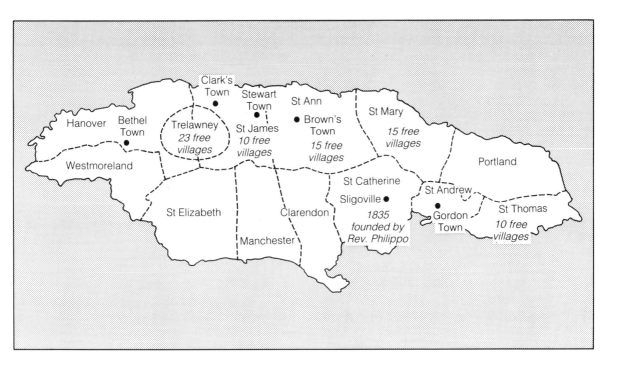

Map 6.2: The free village movement

Map 6.2: The free village movement

William Knibb, a Baptist missionary in Jamaica, urged ex-slaves to set up 'free villages' on Crown land during the apprenticeship period. He was supported by another Baptist minister, the Rev Philippo. These two gave the impetus to the free village movement. Knibb favoured Crown land although there was little available in Jamaica as it would confer secure title to the land and make the ex-slaves completely independent of the planters. He also acknowledged the possibility for ex-slaves to pool their resources and buy unused estate land but Jamaican planters were usually reluctant to sell to blacks. This was the usual way of acquiring land in British Guiana. Missionary societies, Baptists, Quakers and Moravians, all supported the ex-slaves in the free village movement and often helped with the finance in Jamaica.

The attitude and actions of the planters also hastened the Free Village Movement. The planters resented the ending of their supply of free labour and turned against the ex-slaves. In 1838 the Jamaican Legislature passed the Ejection Act whereby ex-slaves no longer working on the estate could be evicted from their homes within a week. The Trespass Act followed this by permitting the arrest and imprisonment of any ex-slave still found on the estate after being ejected. These acts forced ex-slaves unwilling to work for wages on plantations to seek land of their own.

The old maroon towns offered places for ex-slaves to go but these were already overcrowded in the previous century. Yet most free villages in Jamaica were set up in the same area, that is the parishes of Hanover, St James, St Ann and St Elizabeth, in particular in Trelawney in St James where twenty-three villages were established. Unfortunately the land was not good, being mountainous and infertile or marginal land on the fringes of estates.

In Jamaica the price of land around 1840 ranged from £4 to £10 per acre, the average price paid by ex-slaves being about £6. Two to three acres was the minimum for subsistence. Some managed to afford as much as ten acres. Starchy subsistence crops like cassava, sweet potatoes and corn made the Free Village Movement possible. Later bananas made a big contribution to the diet. Ackee, arrowroot, avocado pear, guava, paw-paw, pineapple, breadfruit and vanilla were other crops which helped to vary the diet. Small stock – chickens, goats and pigs were also reared. The Lebitz-type water tank provided water for the home and for irrigation.

Missionary influence meant that the first and chief buildings in every village were the chapel and the schoolroom with the homes grouped around them in the English-village style. The names chosen for the villages reflected missionary and humanitarian influences, e.g. 'Bethany', 'Bethel', 'Clarkson', 'Buxton', 'Wilberforce' and 'Sturge'.

In 1835 the Rev Philippo founded Sligoville outside Spanish Town with a chapel and a school-room. By 1840 it had one hundred families and was known by its founder as 'the first town to rise on the ruins of slavery'. In 1840 William Knibb helped to establish Sturge Town, named after Joseph Sturge, a Quaker from Birmingham in England. Seventy families lived around a church and a school. Knibb referred to it as 'Our little Birmingham'. Also in 1840 the Moravians founded Maidstone. In 1844 the Baptist Mission, through William Knibb, contributed £1700 19s for the land on which Granville was founded.

By 1840 there were two hundred free villages in Jamaica with eight thousand households and nineteen thousand inhabitants. By 1859 there were fifty thousand households confirming the success of the free village movement. Then 40 per cent of the arable land in Jamaica consisted of small-holdings owned by blacks constituting an independent yeoman class in Jamaica which Knibb had dreamed of.

There were similar movements elsewhere in the British West Indies. In Antigua, where land was scarce, independent households established themselves on the fringes of the estates. In St Lucia and Dominica the independent households tended to be scattered in the hills and relatively isolated. However, the other large-scale movement was in British Guiana. There independent communities of ex-slaves were known as 'Negro Colonies'. Such communities were much more easily formed than in Jamaica as land was plentiful and planters were willing to sell off estates or parts of estates to blacks. Unlike Jamaica the Negro Colonies were not assisted by missions but formed and financed by ex-slaves pooling their resources. They some-times established themselves on the banks of the Berbice and Demerara rivers as the Bush Negroes had done. The Golden Grove estate in Demerara was bought for $1716 by fourteen labourers and the Perseverance Estate was bought for $2000 by one hundred and nine. The class of black house-holders grew even faster than in Jamaica. By 1838 three-quarters of the twenty thousand freed slaves owned their own land.

In Trinidad Negro Colonies were found in the Montserrat Ward in the interior, otherwise inde-pendent blacks squatted on land around Port-of-Spain. The movement never became strong in Trinidad in spite of there being much Crown land.

Notes

1   Ex-slaves wanted their own land to enable them to subsist independently of the planta-tions which they hated.
2   The missions were supportive in these aims and in Jamaica would help with finance.
3   In Jamaica the planters hastened the move-ment by evicting ex-slaves who would not work for wages.
4   Unfortunately the ex-slaves tended to find that the only land they could afford or plan-ters would sell to them, was marginal land or infertile, mountainous land.
5   Most 'free villages' were located in Trelawney and those parishes in the west and north-west of the island.
6   Subsistence crops like cassava, corn and sweet potatoes made the Free Village Move-ment possible.
7   Diet was supplemented by fruits and some-times meat from chickens, goats and pigs.
8   The chapel and the schoolroom were the chief and central buildings of the free village.
9   Negro Colonies grew very fast in British Guiana where Crown land, unused estate land and virgin land were available.
10   In British Guiana land was obtained by labourers pooling their resources and little financial help came from the missions.
11   The free village movement gave rise to an independent yeoman class in the British West Indies, especially in the larger islands.

Map 6.3: Immigrant labour, 1841–1917

Soon after emancipation it was clear that the plantation system could not continue on the labour supply of ex-slaves especially in the larger territories, British Guiana, Jamaica and Trinidad. The British Government and the ex-slaves were strongly opposed to long-term contracts so that the labour supply was almost on a day-to-day basis. The planters were desperate for labour and tried many sources of supply from 1838.

European labour schemes were tried between 1834 and 1841 but failed because whites from Northern Europe succumbed to tropical diseases and refused to do work formerly done by slaves. Portuguese labourers from Madeira did go in large numbers to British Guiana (30 000 to BG; 36 000 to BWI in all) attracted by higher wages, but Madeira was not large enough to sustain a sufficient flow of labour for the needs of West Indian plantations and the scheme died out after 1850. Likewise Malta was too small to send all but a few hundred labourers.

Free labour from Africa was regarded with suspicion as slavery re-introduced. Indeed the French imported 17 000 prisoners from the Congo up to 1859 much like the slave trade. Those imported to the British colonies were freed slaves or descendants of freed slaves from Sierra Leone or slaves rescued from illegal slave ships. Between 1841 and 1862 36 000 Africans were imported under this scheme, but Africans soon became suspicious and stopped volunteering.

Therefore in one way or another all these schemes had proved unsatisfactory. The planters were looking for a large supply of labour which would yield a steady flow under secure contracts of at least five years. The Far East, in particular India and China, had huge peasant populations which might be attracted to the West Indies. The British Government had to be persuaded to accept such schemes and even become actively involved in them because India was part of the British Empire.

China was not as satisfactory as India because it was as far as possible from the West Indies by ship and was not part of the British Empire. Two attempts, one by Trinidad in 1806, and the other by British Guiana in 1844, proved false starts. However, in 1852 thousands of Chinese began to be imported through the Portuguese port of Macao in Southern China. This was the main source until 1859 when a 'family scheme' (Macao had supplied no women) was begun from the provinces of Kuangtung and Fukien through the Chinese ports of Canton and Amoy. At first it was to British Guiana but Trinidad joined in the scheme in 1864. In all 20 000 Chinese came to the British West Indies up to 1893. It was a small but regular flow. Chinese immigration, however, could not satisfy the planters' demands because Chinese were physically unsuited to plantation labour and often refused to labour on the grounds that they had been deceived as to the nature of the work before leaving China. The Chinese Government would not co-operate in the schemes and the British Government was not involved in China administratively. The biggest drawback was the expense of importing a Chinese in comparison with an Indian. It was 60 per cent more.

From the point of view of numbers and steady flow Indian immigration was much better. 416 000 came in all and the flow lasted from 1844 to 1917. The first immigrants went to British Guiana in 1838 on the personal initiative of one planter but the scheme was immediately attacked by the Anti-Slavery Society and the Indian Government suspended it until it was satisfied with the conditions in British Guiana. Before 1848 most of the Indians were drawn from the slums of Bombay, Calcutta and Madras which remained the ports of embarkation from British India. After 1848 more peasant farmers from the famine-struck provinces of Agra-Oudh and Behar were taken.

As India was part of the British Empire the British Government had an interest in both the exportation and importation of Indians. In 1848 it began giving loans to West Indian Governments for the costs of importation (at £15 per immigrant from India). It supervised the conditions in the West Indian colonies. In 1876 it was not satisfied with conditions in non-British territories and it banned the exportation of Indians to all but Guadeloupe, Martinique and Surinam. In 1886 Surinam became the only non-British territory allowed to import labour from British India.

Between 1844 and 1917 239 000 Indians went to British Guiana, 134 000 to Trinidad, 33 000 to Jamaica and over 10 000 to the Eastern Caribbean islands.

All the immigrant labour schemes were based on contracts. Before 1848 contracts were signed on arrival in the territory. This proved unsatisfactory as when the immigrants were confronted with plantation labour they refused to sign. Planters wanted contracts to be signed on embarkation and

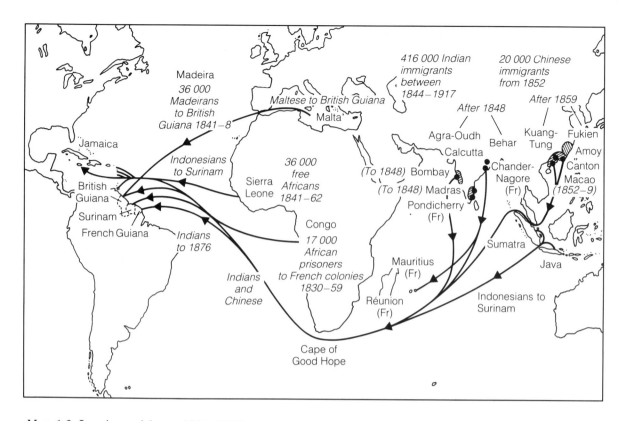

Map 6.3: Immigrant labour, 1841–1917

in 1848 the government agreed to this but only one-year contracts. Planters wanted five-year contracts and the Government gave way to this in 1850. The contract laid down that the labourer had to work seven hours per day in the field or ten hours per day in the factory, every day of the week except Sundays and holidays at a wage rate of 1/- per day for a man and 8d per day for a woman or boy under the age of sixteen. The employer had to provide rent-free housing for the whole contract and food at 4d per day for the first three months of the contract. Medical services also had to be provided. On completion of the contract the immigrant could insist on repatriation. West Indian Governments did not want this because of the expense involved. They wanted labourers to 're-indenture' (sign a new contract). Before 1848 most immigrants asked for repatriation and West Indian Governments were hard pressed to find the money. They decided to make residence more attractive and repatriation unattractive. Free land was commonly offered after 1870. Repatriation could only be given after ten years of residence from 1854 and after 1895 the immigrant had to contribute to the cost of his return passage.

The Chief Justice of British Guiana called immigrant labour schemes 'The New Slavery' in 1871 because a) immigrants were deceived as to the nature of the work and living conditions; b) they were confined to their estates and could not move freely even in their own time; c) they were denied normal family life as so few women were imported; d) they were brutally punished for breaches of labour laws and punishments frequently re-imposed conditions of slavery; e) all means were tried to make the labourer re-indenture; f) the whole establishment from government officials to planters, especially the courts, were against the immigrants.

The success or failure of immigrant labour depends on one's point of view. West Indian Governments spent $20 000 000 on the scheme between 1838 and 1917 and must have thought the expense justified. The sugar industry kept going throughout the nineteenth century and sugar production actually increased in British Guiana and Trinidad, but so did it in Barbados where there was no immigrant labour. Indians in the British West Indies would definitely deem it a success. Its detractors concentrated on the social divisions caused in the host territories by immigration, e.g. racial and religious segregation.

Notes

1 After emancipation planters were desperate to find new sources of labour.
2 European labour schemes failed because Europeans would not be labourers in black societies and they also succumbed to tropical diseases.
3 Free African labour was suspected of being the slave trade re-introduced.
4 20 000 Chinese came to the British West Indies under immigrant labour schemes between 1852 and 1893 but the distance made the scheme expensive and the Chinese did not prove suitable labour.
5 416 000 Indians were imported between 1844 and 1917, before 1848 from the slums of the cities and after 1848 from famine-hit areas in the north.
6 The British Government supervised both ends of the Indian immigration scheme.
7 The British Government gave loans to West Indian Governments towards the costs of the scheme.
8 The planters did not want contracts signed on arrival but five-year contracts signed on embarkation.
9 Immigrant labourers had to work seven hours a day, six days a week for 1/- per day.
10 Employers had to provide housing, food (to start with) and medical services.
11 Repatriation was offered in the contract but West Indian Governments resisted it as they wanted re-indenture.
12 Immigrant labour created racial divisions in West Indian society.

Table 6.2: Problems of the BWI sugar industry after emancipation

Territory	Sugar production Tonnes		Cost of production per cwt 1848 prices	Price of sugar London Market per cwt		Labour supply	Technology and mechanisation
British Guiana	1828 1846 1851 1861 1882 1894	40 000 23 000 38 000 62 000 124 000 102 000	25/-			Local labour 2/-p.d. 239 000 Indians 30 000 Madeirans 14 000 Africans 12 000 Chinese	Steam engines Vacuum pans
				1846	22/6		
Jamaica	1832 1856 1882 1894	70 000 22 000 33 000 20 000	22/7d			Local labour 1/6 p.d. 33 000 Indians 10 000 Africans 5 000 Chinese	No mechanisation Ploughs and harrows
				1856	37/5		
Trinidad	1832 1838 1846 1882 1894	6 000 7 000 7 500 55 000 47 000	25/-			Local labour 2/6 p.d. 134 000 Indians 8 000 Africans 3 000 Chinese 2 000 Madeirans	Steam engines Vacuum pans 1871 First central in BWI
				1881	21/-		
Antigua	1830 1856 1882 1894	9 000 11 500 13 000 12 000	15/4$\frac{1}{2}$			Local labour 1/6 p.d. 2000 Madeirans	No mechanisation Ploughs and harrows slowly introduced
				1896	11/-		
Barbados	1830 1856 1882 1894	15 000 35 000 48 000 51 000	15/4$\frac{1}{2}$			Local labour 10d No immigrant labour	No mechanisation Ploughs and harrows slowly introduced 1888 Scientific Research Station
St Kitts	1830 1856 1882 1894	5 500 4 500 11 000 11 500	16/2			Local labour 9d 1200 immigrant labour – all sources	Centralised production, c.1870
Cuba	1815 1828 1860 1894	35 000 70 000 350 000 over 1 000 000	12/-			Slave labour to 350 000 1886 124 000 Chinese	Steam mills from 1819 Steam engines Vacuum pans Enclosed furnaces Centrals
BWI Total	1860 1894	200 000 260 000					

N.B. All production figures are approximate. p.d. = per day

Table 6.2: Problems of the BWI sugar industry after emancipation

Table 6.2 shows increases in sugar production in the British West Indies (BWI) after emancipation with the exception of Jamaica. This seems to hide the problems that existed. In the last two sections we have seen the labour problem and how it was overcome. Now we must examine other problems.

Before emancipation the plantation economy had managed with very few cash transactions. Labour was not paid so planters did not have to meet wage bills every week. Planters obtained their supplies, both industrial and domestic, on credit they had with their Liverpool and London merchants against the sale of their sugar crop each year. Therefore very little money was in circulation and there were no banks. In 1837 English merchants set up two banks, the Planters' Bank in Jamaica and the West India Bank in Barbados with branches throughout the islands. Planters then combined credit transactions through their merchants abroad with cash transactions through their banks at home. When planters' bank balances were healthy they could meet their bills, but when sugar prices fell and costs remained the same, their bank balances tumbled and they had to sell up. Eventually the banks collapsed.

The greatest proportion of the costs of production was wages, ranging from a wage bill of £20 per 100 workers per week in Barbados to £60 in Trinidad, because sugar production was labour intensive. The table shows that where wages were highest, e.g. 2/6d per day in Trinidad, production costs at 25/- per cwt were highest, and where wages were low, e.g. 10d per day in Barbados, production costs were low at 15/4½ per cwt. In the larger sugar colonies the prices obtained on the London Market in 1846–8 did not cover costs of production. The estates were running at a loss. Losses could be sustained for one or two years but persistent losses forced estates to close down. This problem was made worse by increased production. The more sugar offered on the London Market, the lower the price. After 1846 Cuba began selling more and more on the London Market further depressing prices.

The British Government added to the problems of BWI planters by the Equalisation of Sugar Duties Act of 1846. In the 1840s free trade was being urged strongly by the Manchester School so that British consumers could buy in the cheapest markets. Hitherto, BWI producers had been protected against foreign competition and low prices by duties placed on sugar from non-British territories. At 12/- per cwt Cuba could undercut BWI prices by at least 3/-. Although the 1846 Act would remove duties gradually over the next eight years by 1854 foreign-produced sugar could enter Britain completely free of duties. The BWI sugar industry was already struggling against high costs and low prices. The 1846 Act gave a test of its survival.

From the 1830s BWI sugar estates had been running into debt. Emancipation increased the numbers in debt and the Sugar Equalisation Act made matters even worse. And as planters sold their estates so the price of land fell. Planters could not sell off part of their estates to cover debts. Buyers would not buy estates encumbered with debts as they would be responsible for those debts. Sugar production was severely hampered by land going out of production in this way. In 1833 St Lucia allowed states to be sold without the buyer taking on the debts. The British Government thought there were benefits in this and passed the Encumbered Estates Act in 1854. However, this Act brought further problems. Creditors, i.e. the Liverpool and London merchants, had first claim on such estates and when they acquired them they sold off the sugar as quickly as possible to recover their debts without caring for the administration of the estates. Similarly if they sold the estate to a new owner they forced him to sell off the sugar at low prices to repay the creditor so that there was little chance of making a profit. Therefore by removing the profit incentive potential buyers were discouraged and so was investment even if a buyer was found.

A very serious problem was that the BWI sugar industry would not move with the times. In many of its field operations sugar production had to be labour intensive but better tools would increase output per man. Ploughs and harrows were only introduced slowly into the British West Indies even when labour-saving methods became essential after emancipation. Antigua did not have a pitchfork or a wheelbarrow in 1846.

BWI planters were conservative and wanted each plantation to carry out all its own production processes. In 1897 Barbados still had 440 separate factories in a very small island. The 'central' would have economised in production costs yet the first central in the British West Indies did not appear until 1871 in Trinidad. Most BWI sugar-producing territories were too small for the economies of scale to be achieved, but this did not apply to centrals. Production in all territories justified centrals. The Eastern Caribbean islands, with the exception of Trinidad, were too small to justify railway networks feeding the estates but even if size had not ruled them out, probably conservatism, desire for independence and lack of investment would.

BWI planters also resisted developments in factory processes. Triple crushing of cane produced 90 per cent sucrose yet British planters continued with a single crushing. Refined sugar fetched far higher prices in European markets yet British planters still sold on the London Market to British entrepreneurs who did the refining in Britain.

The sugar industry in British Guiana and Trinidad was largely developed in the nineteenth century and as their planters were not so conservative modern methods could be incorporated at the outset. Also their acute labour difficulties encouraged them to adopt labour-saving methods. Therefore sugar production in these two territories was more mechanised and progressive than in the other British territories.

From the 1820s and 1830s BWI sugar production suffered from foreign competition. Indian and Mauritian sugar was allowed into Britain at the same rates of duty as BWI sugar. However, the most serious competition in the nineteenth century came from Cuba and Louisiana which had so many advantages over the British West Indies: a) Louisiana had slave labour to 1865 and Cuba to 1886; b) both territories could expand their industries cheaply and easily because of their vast areas of virgin land. In many of the British colonies the soil was exhausted; c) Cuba had mountains and fast-flowing streams for water power. However, many of Cuba's advantages were man-made: a) Cuba's sugar industry had been mechanised from 1819 when the first steam mills were introduced; b) pipes running from these steam engines carried heat to vacuum pans which boiled juices at lower temperatures; c) the most advanced machinery was imported from France and the USA; (d) Cuba's large estates enabled economies of scale to be achieved; e) lower costs meant higher profits which attracted investment; f) Cuba could sell in both the London and New York Markets. After the Sugar Equalisation Act Cuba could compete more than favourably on the London Market and by 1864 was selling 150 000 tonnes there. If prices were depressed in London she could sell in New York.

The Ten Years' War, 1868 to 1878, in Cuba removed Cuban competition for a time, but a new competition, that of European beet sugar emerged. This was even more serious and the table shows how sharply sugar prices fell when this sugar reached the market. The price had dropped to 11/- per cwt before the end of the century.

Notes

1 Before emancipation there was little money in circulation in the BWI as planters conducted most of their transactions on credit through London merchants.

2 The first banks in the BWI collapsed when planters' bank balances fell due to high costs and falling prices.

3 After emancipation labour costs became a high proportion of production costs because sugar production was labour-intensive.

4 Prices on the London Market were often too low to cover production costs.

5 The Equalisation of Sugar Duties Act, 1846, ended protection against foreign-produced sugar and led to the collapse of many BWI estates.

6 Plantations with debts could not be sold easily.

7 The Encumbered Estates Act, 1854, merely transferred control of encumbered estates to London creditors which was not good for the future running of the estates.

8 When sugar plantations were not making a profit they were unlikely to attract investment.

9 BWI plantations, with the exception of those in British Guiana and Trinidad, were backward because of the conservatism of the planters and the lack of investment.

10 Competition with Cuba and Louisiana became very great after the Sugar Equalisation Act, forcing many British estates to close.

11 At the end of the nineteenth century competition from European beet sugar forced prices down sharply to as low as 11/- per cwt in 1896.

Map 6.4: Alternative crops

The reliance on one crop like sugar is known as 'monoculture'. It was a dangerous economic base for most of the British West Indies. The introduction of different crops is known as 'diversification' and was expected to make the economic base more secure as the other crops could back-up sugar if anything went wrong with that crop. In the nineteenth century falling world sugar prices brought just the situation where alternative crops were needed.

British colonisation in the seventeenth century had started with tobacco as the cash crop but this quickly changed to sugar in the sugar revolution and the monoculture of sugar began. However, in some islands from the outset cotton played a minor role as a cash crop. In the eighteenth century cotton was being exported by Barbados, Antigua, St Kitts, Nevis and Montserrat, and during the War of American Independence it was introduced into the Turks and Caicos. When sugar slumped in Barbados in 1787 cotton proved a useful back-up crop. During the Napoleonic Wars, 1802 to 1815, 70 per cent of Britain's cotton imports came from the British West Indies, therefore cotton was an obvious alternative to sugar in the nineteenth century difficulties.

Coffee was always grown in Jamaica and the Windward Islands and in Jamaica during the wars of the eighteenth century was an important back-up to sugar. When these wars were over Dominica, St Lucia, St Vincent and Grenada developed coffee as a cash crop. The Spanish had grown coffee in Trinidad and the British took over 130 plantations there in 1897. Coffee was considered a better alternative to sugar in the Windwards than was cotton in the Leewards.

Cacao had also been introduced by the Spaniards. From the Greater Antilles it was transplanted to the British islands but on a small scale until the nineteenth century. Along with arrowroot, ginger, indigo and pimento it was known as a possible alternative if anything should threaten the sugar industry.

Emancipation gave a great boost to the cultivation of alternative crops because small-holders using a high proportion of their limited land for subsistence needed high-yielding cash crops for their remaining land. At this time ginger and pimento became important in Jamaica, nutmegs in Grenada, arrowroot in St Vincent and limes in Dominica and Montserrat. The crops which had always been considered received renewed attention, e.g. cacao in Trinidad, coffee in Jamaica and the Windwards and cotton in Barbados and the Leewards.

The BWI sugar industry was in such difficulties by 1882 that a Royal Commission was appointed to recommend ways of improving production and to suggest alternatives to sugar. The Report was pessimistic about the future of sugar but overoptimistic about alternative crops of which fruit, spices, cacao and coffee were mentioned. Between 1882 and 1896 the price of sugar fell from 21/- to 11/- per cwt and the British Government sent another Royal Commission, called the 'Norman Commission' after its chairman, Sir Henry Norman. Its report was also pessimistic about sugar and strongly recommended diversification except for Antigua, Barbados and St Kitts which could produce sugar at competitive prices, especially if centrals were built. Of the alternative crops it emphasised the importance of fruit.

Bananas were the most important cash fruit crop in the British West Indies. Bananas had been transplanted from Hispaniola to Jamaica by the Spaniards but the British introduced the *Gros Michel* variety from Martinique which was superior. The export of bananas began in 1866 but was made regular two years later when Lorenzo Dow Baker, an American sea captain, took his first cargo to Boston. In 1880 he founded the Boston Fruit Company and established banana plantations near Port Antonio and Port Morant. This company was taken over by the United Fruit Company in 1899 and it dominated the Caribbean banana industry until 1930. This alternative crop was so successful that it made up 50 per cent of Jamaica's exports by 1912.

Rice was introduced by Indian and Chinese immigrants. They were experts in its cultivation and grew not only enough for their own subsistence but also for export. British Guiana was the principal producer and by 1919 was able to export 11 000 tonnes. The coastal lowlands were especially suited to rice growing and the rice fields were frequently bordered by coconut palms.

The remaining alternative crops struggled against foreign competition in the export markets with the following exceptions: sea-island cotton from Barbados, St Vincent and the Leewards had a specialised market in luxurious, high-priced garments which was exploited after it failed to compete with Egyptian and United States cotton in the 1920s; coconuts in Trinidad did especially well when copra prices rose in the 1914–18 War, encouraging Trinidad to start other plantations;

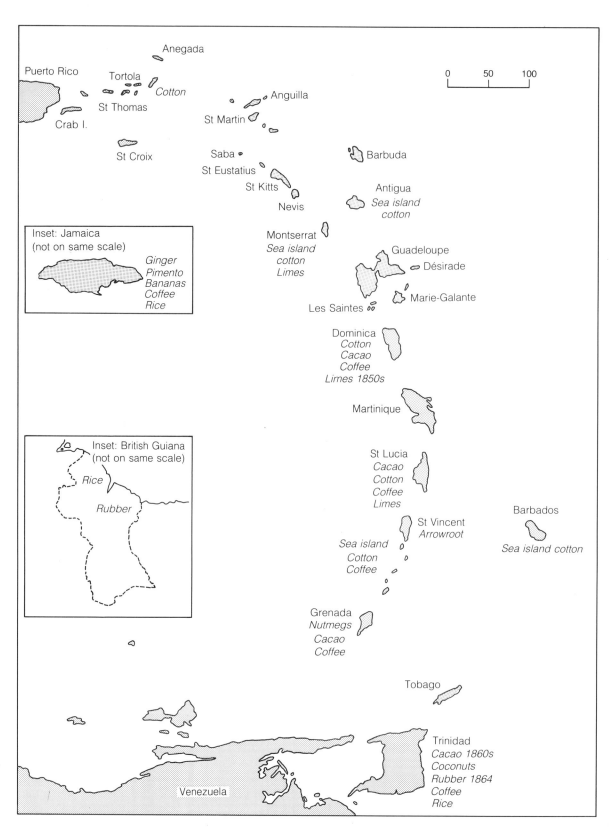

Anegada

Puerto Rico

Tortola
St Thomas   *Cotton*

Crab I.

St Croix

Anguilla
St Martin

Saba
St Eustatius
St Kitts
Nevis

Barbuda

Antigua
*Sea island
cotton*

0   50   100

Montserrat
*Sea island
cotton
Limes*

Guadeloupe
Désirade

Les Saintes

Marie-Galante

Inset: Jamaica
(not on same scale)

*Ginger
Pimento
Bananas
Coffee
Rice*

Dominica
*Cotton
Cacao
Coffee
Limes 1850s*

Martinique

St Lucia
*Cacao
Cotton
Coffee
Limes*

Inset: British Guiana
(not on same scale)

Rice

Rubber

St Vincent
Arrowroot

*Sea island
Cotton
Coffee*

Barbados

Sea island cotton

Grenada
*Nutmegs
Cacao
Coffee*

Tobago

Trinidad
*Cacao 1860s
Coconuts
Rubber 1864
Coffee
Rice*

Venezuela

Map 6.4: Alternative crops

rubber also experienced high prices at the beginning of the twentieth century and Trinidad and British Guiana benefited for a decade until the world price fell in 1914 with Malaysian rubber reaching the world market; cacao grown in Trinidad on Indian small-holdings also flourished sufficiently to become Trinidad's chief export in 1920. Cacao was also grown in Dominica, St Lucia and Grenada.

Limes from Dominica and spices from St Vincent and Grenada had such small markets that they were not viable alternatives. Synthetic flavouring replaced lime juice in drinks. No other spice island could compete with Zanzibar and East Indian islands so St Vincent and Grenada could not rely on spices for export revenue. Similarly cacao could not compete in world markets once the Gold Coast's production was begun.

Notes

1 The monoculture of sugar put BWI economies in a dangerous position at the mercy of world market prices.

2 Other cash crops were known and grown in the British West Indies, but only cotton in Barbados and the Leewards and coffee in the Windwards had played an important part as an alternative crop before the nineteenth century.

3 Falling sugar prices in the nineteenth century made governments realise the need for alternative crops.

4 Emancipation gave a boost to alternative crops as they could be cash crops for small-holders.

5 The Royal Commissions were appointed in 1882 and 1896 respectively to make recommendations for BWI economies.

6 Both reports were pessimistic about sugar and recommended alternative crops.

7 Bananas were a particularly successful alternative crop for Jamaica.

8 Other alternative crops like cacao, rubber and cotton did well for a short time but by the 1920s had been forced out of world markets by superior foreign production.

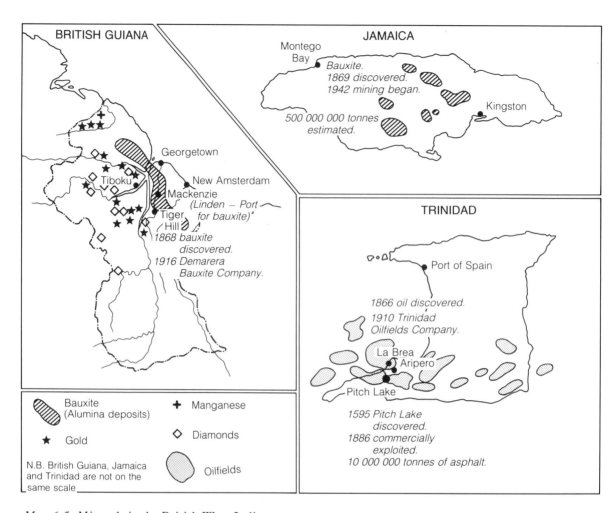

BRITISH GUIANA

Georgetown

New Amsterdam

Tiboku

Mackenzie
(Linden — Port
for bauxite)'

Tiger
Hill

1868 bauxite
discovered.
1916 Demarera
Bauxite Company.

JAMAICA

Montego
Bay

Bauxite.
1869 discovered.
1942 mining began.

500 000 000 tonnes
estimated.

Kingston

TRINIDAD

Port of Spain

1866 oil discovered.

1910 Trinidad
Oilfields Company.

La Brea
Aripero

Pitch Lake

1595 Pitch Lake
discovered.
1886 commercially
exploited.
10 000 000 tonnes of asphalt.

Bauxite
(Alumina deposits)

Manganese

Gold

Diamonds

N.B. British Guiana, Jamaica
and Trinidad are not on the
same scale

Oilfields

Map 6.5: Minerals in the British West Indies

Map 6.5: Minerals in the British West Indies

The Royal Commissions of 1882 and 1896 concentrated on agricultural products. In British Guiana, Jamaica and Trinidad minerals also offered some alternative source of wealth. The presence of minerals had been known in the mid-nineteenth century, but exploitation did not begin until the late-nineteenth century and early twentieth, and in the case of bauxite in Jamaica, not until the Second World War. (Most minerals in the British West Indies existed in quantities too small for commercial exploitation).

Trinidad exploited two minerals commercially. In 1595 Sir Walter Raleigh discovered the Pitch Lake at La Brea. It was used locally for two and a half centuries for caulking ships. In 1886 the Trinidad Government gave A.L. Barber a concession for £10 000 per year to exploit the asphalt from the lake. In 1925 the concession was transferred to the Trinidad Lake Asphalt Company for £24 000 per year. The Pitch Lake covers 110 acres and is 285 feet deep and is thought to contain at least 10 000 000 tonnes of asphalt from a source of fresh crude oil.

Nearby oil was first discovered on the Aripero Estate in 1866 by Captain Darwent of the Paria Petroleum Company. In 1908 an oil well was sunk on the western edge of the Pitch Lake of La Brea. In 1910 The Trinidad Oil Fields Company was formed and oil was exported to the United States. By 1936 oil was earning £4 000 000 per year making up 50 per cent of Trinidad's export earnings. Oil has been the most successful alternative revenue earner to sugar in the British West Indies as it now makes up 80 per cent of Trinidad's exports. (To-day there are 38 oil fields offshore and on land. The biggest is the Amoco Field which lies between 3 and 50 miles off the south-east coast).

British Guiana had three minerals which were exploited commercially, bauxite, diamonds and gold. The presence of bauxite was discovered in 1868 along the Demerara River. These deposits were later found to stretch from south-east to north-west between the Demerara and Berbice rivers and beyond in both directions. In 1916 an American, George Mackenzie, founded the Demerara Bauxite Company and exports began in 1917, too late to catch the high demand of the First World War. However, British Guiana benefited from the high prices in the Second World War and bauxite made up 40 per cent of export earnings. The Demerara River is navigable as far as Linden where the bauxite can be loaded.

Diamonds were found in alluvial deposits along the Mazaruni, Cuyuni and Potaro rivers. Alluvial gold was found along the same rivers and in the Rupununi area. The commercial exploitation of these minerals has only occurred recently and on a very small scale.

In Jamaica bauxite was discovered as long ago as 1869 but not exploited commercially until 1942 when prices were high in the Second World War. There are very rich deposits of bauxite in the centre of Jamaica and this area had made Jamaica the world's biggest producer by the late 1950s with 20 per cent of the world's bauxite.

Notes

1 Most of the minerals in the British West Indies exist in quantities too small to exploit commercially.

2 Although their presence was known in the 1860s, commercial exploitation did not begin until the turn of the century.

3 Trinidad exported asphalt and later oil which has become the most successful alternative to sugar.

4 British Guiana exported bauxite, diamonds and gold, the latter two on a very small scale.

5 Jamaica began the export of bauxite in 1942 and now produces 20 per cent of the world's supply.

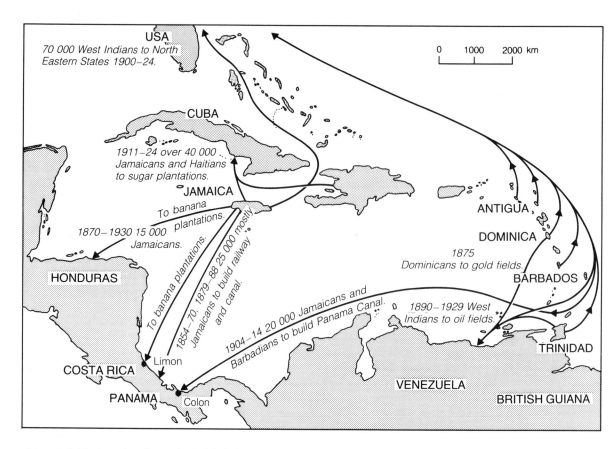

USA
70 000 West Indians to North Eastern States 1900–24.

0   1000   2000 km

CUBA
1911–24 over 40 000 Jamaicans and Haitians to sugar plantations.

JAMAICA
To banana plantations.

1870–1930 15 000 Jamaicans.

To banana plantations.

1854–70, 1879–88 25 000 mostly Jamaicans to build railway and canal.

HONDURAS

ANTIGUA

DOMINICA

1875 Dominicans to gold fields.

BARBADOS

1890–1929 West Indians to oil fields.

1904–14 20 000 Jamaicans and Barbadians to build Panama Canal.

Limon

COSTA RICA

PANAMA   Colon

VENEZUELA

TRINIDAD

BRITISH GUIANA

Map 6.6: Emigration from the British West Indies, 1854 to 1929

Map 6.6: Emigration from the British West Indies, 1854 to 1929

After emancipation many ex-slaves without land, homes or families looked for somewhere to go to start a new life. However, most of the neighbouring lands still had slavery so at first emigration was confined to the British Caribbean, e.g. from Barbados to British Guiana or Trinidad in search of higher wages.

The decline of sugar increased the pressure to emigrate as economies went into depression. After emancipation West Indians expected better lives. Also racial prejudice and discrimination brought social tensions as blacks found that freedom had not been accompanied by equality.

At first only men emigrated, leaving the women and children behind, perhaps to start new families in their new countries or to repatriate money to maintain their old families hoping one day to return to them. In some cases, e.g. when emigration was to the United States, the emigrant would send for his wife and family when he felt established.

Large-scale emigration to countries outside the British Caribbean began in 1854 when 2000, mostly Jamaicans, went to work on a railway across the Isthmus of Panama. This project provided work in the 1850s and 1860s. From 1882–8 the first attempt by Ferdinand de Lesseps to build a Panama Canal attracted 25 000 emigrants, again mostly Jamaicans. The death toll was so high that the project had to be abandoned. The United States bought the rights for a canal from Ferdinand de Lesseps under the Hay-Pauncefort Treaty of 1801. Scientists by this time had begun to overcome yellow fever and work began in 1904. In the next twenty years another 20 000 West Indians, mostly Jamaicans and Barbadians, went to Panama. Wages were 4/- per day and much of the earnings was repatriated to Barbados and Jamaica. (Today 60 000 people in the Canal Zone claim descent from West Indian immigrants).

In the 1880s American companies started banana plantations in Costa Rica and Honduras and demand for labour could not be satisfied locally. Many Jamaicans emigrated there chiefly around the port of Limon in Cost Rica. Some stayed permanently, others temporarily repatriating their money. This demand for labour lasted until 1930.

With the abolition of slavery in Cuba in 1886 the expanding sugar industry was in desperate need of labour. Over 100 000 British West Indians went there from Jamaica and Barbados (also many thousand Haitians) to work on sugar plantations, mostly in the period of the Cuban sugar boom between 1911 and 1921. In 1924 many immigrants were deported from Cuba which exacerbated unemployment in their native lands.

Between 1900 and 1924 over 70 000 British West Indians emigrated to the United States usually to settle permanently. At first they went to the banana port of Boston, but later to industries in Baltimore, New York and Philadelphia. The peak came in 1924 when 11 000 emigrated in one year. In 1925 unrestricted immigration into the United States ended.

In 1875 the Venezuelan gold fields attracted labour from Dominica. Emigrants from the Eastern Caribbean went to the Venezuelan oil fields between 1920 and 1929.

Up to the 1920s emigration had relieved hardship and unemployment in the British West Indies. Much money had been repatriated to Barbados and Jamaica from Panama and the United States. On the other hand the British West Indies, especially Jamaica, lost thousands of able-boiled men. When emigration came to an end in the 1920s the safety valve for social discontent disappeared and social tensions in the next decade became acute.

Notes

1 After emancipation there was some emigration from the Eastern Caribbean to Trinidad and British Guiana, attracted by higher wages.

2 While slavery existed in neighbouring countries emigration outside the British Caribbean was not likely.

3 The depression brought on by falling sugar prices increased the pressure to emigrate.

4 Some emigrated permanently, others in order to repatriate money to families left behind.

5 All emigration came to an end by the end of the 1920s for various reasons.

6 Emigration had provided a safety valve for social tensions and when it was removed social disturbances broke out in the 1930s.

Theme 7: The United States and the Caribbean_____

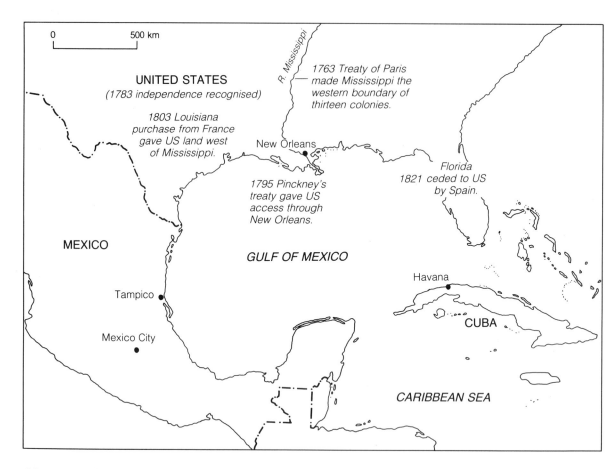

0   500 km

UNITED STATES
(1783 independence recognised)

1763 Treaty of Paris made Mississippi the western boundary of thirteen colonies.

R. Mississippi

1803 Louisiana purchase from France gave US land west of Mississippi.

New Orleans

Florida 1821 ceded to US by Spain.

1795 Pinckney's treaty gave US access through New Orleans.

MEXICO

GULF OF MEXICO

Havana

Tampico

CUBA

Mexico City

CARIBBEAN SEA

Map 7.1: United States' access to the Caribbean

Map 7.1: United States' access to the Caribbean

The United States became a new nation in world affairs by the Treaty of Paris, 1783. Britain, France and Spain as colonial powers in the Caribbean, feared the impact the United States would have on their colonies. Therefore immediately on US independence these three countries tried to restrict the influence that the United States might be able to exert in the Caribbean. France and Spain wanted to confine the United States east of the Appalachians. Britain and France restricted US trade to their Caribbean colonies. However, US relations with Spain were the most important because Spain was ruling Florida and Louisiana at the end of the eighteenth century which cut the United States off from the Gulf of Mexico and the Caribbean. In the Treaty of Paris, 1763, Spain had recognised the western boundary of the Thirteen Colonies as the Mississippi. After independence the United States needed the Mississippi to carry all the needs for her westward expansion but Spain closed the port of New Orleans at the mouth of the Mississippi to American traffic. Therefore the United States had no outlet to the Gulf of Mexico and with no coastline either, she could play no part in the Caribbean.

The United States remained neutral in the French Revolutionary Wars but concluded Pinckney's Treaty with Spain in 1795 which opened New Orleans to US shipping and access to the Caribbean. Then the United States obtained coastline on the Gulf of Mexico west of the Mississippi River through the Louisiana Purchase of 1803 by which the United States paid France $15 000 000 for Louisiana. Spain still held the coastline east of the Mississippi. Florida with its peninsula would take the United States into the Caribbean and very close to Cuba. Thomas Jefferson, the US President, failed to obtain Florida in 1805 but after the 1812–14 War with Britain, in which Spain had been Britain's ally, the United States was able to persuade Spain to give up Florida instead of paying compensation for war damages of $5 000 000. Spain ceded Florida to the United States in 1821.

Thus by 1821 the United States had a coastline on the Gulf of Mexico stretching from about 80 degrees to 95 degrees west, the major port of the Gulf, New Orleans, to serve her westward expansion, and a peninsula to carry her influence into the Caribbean. Only Cuba was blocking the United States from further penetration into the Caribbean.

Notes

1 Britain, France and Spain were worried about US influence on their colonies following her independence in 1783.
2 Relations with Spain were most important to the United States because Spain held Florida, Louisiana and the port of New Orleans, cutting the United States off from the Gulf of Mexico.
3 The United States gained access to the Gulf of Mexico by being granted the use of New Orleans under Pinckney's Treaty, 1795, obtaining a Gulf coastline by the Louisiana Purchase of 1803, and a peninsula into the Caribbean by the cession of Florida in 1821.

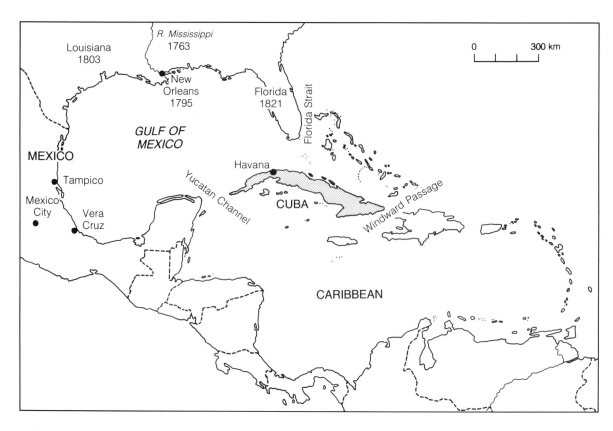

Map 7.2: Cuba's strategic importance to the United States

Map 7.2: Cuba's strategic importance to the United States

Cuba lay across the mouth of the Gulf of Mexico blocking the United States' access to the Caribbean. Thomas Jefferson acknowledged the strategic importance of Cuba to the United States in 1809 but thought that as Spain was a declining colonial power, Cuba would 'gravitate' towards the United States. Cuba commanded the important shipping lanes of the Yucatan Channel and the Florida Strait. Havana, capital and main port of Cuba, was the key port in the Spanish trade system.

Notes

1 Cuba lay across the entrance to the Gulf of Mexico.
2 It could control the Yucatan Channel and the Florida Strait.
3 Havana, the main port of Cuba, was the key port in the Spanish trade system.

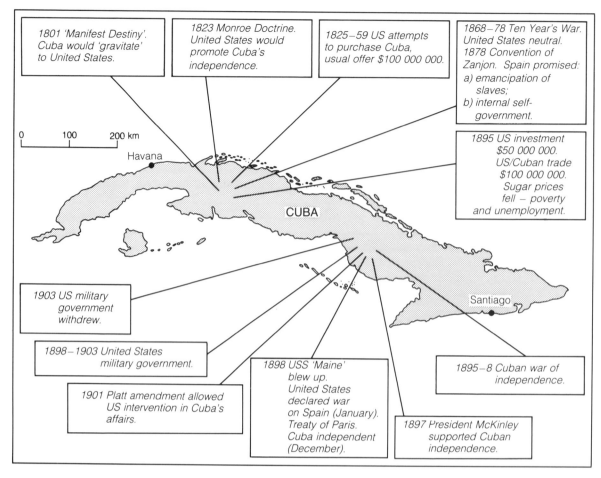

1801 'Manifest Destiny'. Cuba would 'gravitate' to United States.

1823 Monroe Doctrine. United States would promote Cuba's independence.

1825–59 US attempts to purchase Cuba, usual offer $100 000 000.

1868–78 Ten Year's War. United States neutral. 1878 Convention of Zanjon. Spain promised:
a) emancipation of slaves;
b) internal self-government.

1895 US investment $50 000 000. US/Cuban trade $100 000 000. Sugar prices fell – poverty and unemployment.

1903 US military government withdrew.

1898–1903 United States military government.

1901 Platt amendment allowed US intervention in Cuba's affairs.

1898 USS 'Maine' blew up. United States declared war on Spain (January). Treaty of Paris. Cuba independent (December).

1897 President McKinley supported Cuban independence.

1895–8 Cuban war of independence.

Map 7.3: The United States and Cuba, 1801 to 1903

Map 7.3: The United States and Cuba, 1801 to 1903

Thomas Jefferson put forward the idea of 'Manifest Destiny' in 1801 saying that it was natural and inevitable that the United States would dominate the Americas and that an independent Cuba would 'gravitate' towards the United States. In 1823 part of President Monroe's inaugural speech known as the 'Monroe Doctrine' was aimed at Cuba. He warned European colonial powers that the United States would consider any further colonisation in the Americas, suppression of independence or reclaiming colonies which had won independence, as unfriendly acts towards the United States. Therefore we can assume that the United States expected Cuba to gain independence from Spain and would encourage it. Then by Manifest Destiny the independent Cuba would gravitate towards the United States. If Spain tried to prevent Cuba's independence, that would be a hostile act towards

the United States and justify US intervention against Spain.

This attitude worried Britain. British ministers, Canning in the 1820s and Palmerston in the 1840s, tried to persuade the United States to support the existing position in the Caribbean of no change in the status of Cuba as a colony of Spain, but the United States repeatedly refused to agree. For example in 1852 Britain called a convention between herself, France and the United States to guarantee the existing status of Cuba but the United States rejected the convention and it was obvious that she wanted to take over Cuba.

From 1825 to 1859 US policy concentrated on the purchase of Cuba. In 1825 they asked for Cuba as security for a loan to Spain. It was refused. In 1848 President Polk offered $100 000 000 for Cuba. It was refused. Then the United States tried to destabilise Cuba by allowing ex-Cubans to make raids on Cuba from US bases in order to make Spain want to be rid of Cuba. In 1852 President Pierce offered $100 000 000 hinting he would go up to $130 000 000 if necessary and that the alternative to purchase was conquest. He wanted to know what the reaction of Britain, France and Spain would be to conquest. In 1854 the United States called a meeting in Ostend. Pierce offered $120 000 000 for Cuba. Pierce's opponents issued the 'Ostend Manifesto' which showed how strongly the three European countries rejected the United States' designs on Cuba.

The last serious attempt to purchase Cuba was in 1859. Thereafter the United States resorted to economic, diplomatic, ideological and military methods to take over Cuba:

a) Economic: From 1868 the United States dominated Cuba's economy taking 83 per cent of her exports. US investment in the mechanisation of the sugar industry resulted in the record crop of over one million tonnes in 1894. By 1895 US investment was $50 000 000 and the trade turnover between the two countries was $100 000 000. Cuba was dangerously dependent on the United States. American investors demanded protection for their investments in Cuba. This gave the United States reason for military intervention in Cuba.

b) Diplomatic: The United States remained neutral in the Ten Years' War, 1868–78, but in the Convention of Zanjon, 1878, the United States insisted that Spain should grant emancipation to slaves and internal self-government for Cuba. Cuba was very slow in granting emancipation and failed to grant internal self-government. This gave another reason for military intervention.

c) Ideological: The United States had thrown off colonialism in 1783 and was the champion of freedom and opposed to imperialism. However, when Britain, France and Germany made their imperialism clear at the Berlin Conference, 1884–5, the United States felt justified in some imperialism of her own on the grounds that other powers were threatening her peace and security. Thus the United States' conscience was clear for military intervention.

d) Military: In 1897 McKinley, who supported independence for Cuba, became President. In January 1898, the United States accused Spain of blowing up the USS *Maine* in Havana harbour with a mine. They demanded Spain's withdrawal from Cuba and when Spain refused, declared war. The US admiral, Sampson, sunk the Spanish fleet, and the general, Shafter, enforced the surrender of the Spanish

army at Santiago. In the Treaty of Paris, 1898, Spain recognised the independence of Cuba.

The United States occupied Cuba militarily from 1898 to 1903 in order to 'americanise' Cuba before her complete independence. The second military governor, General Wood, benefited Cuba by improving roads, building bridges, schools and hospitals, improving the telephone and telegraph systems, deepening Havana harbour and introducing a public health programme. He finally ordered elections for a convention to draft a constitution for the independent Cuba. The United States' Congress thought that independence was coming too soon, i.e. before Cuba had been 'americanised'. In 1901 the Platt Amendment was a compromise to Cuban independence by giving the United States close control over Cuban affairs after the military withdrawal, of, for example, foreign affairs, finance, health and sanitation, military and naval bases and the right to intervene to preserve peace and security. The Cuban Convention rejected the Platt Amendment but the United States would not withdraw until it was written into the constitution. In 1903 it was accepted.

Notes

1 Manifest Destiny was the idea that the United States would dominate the Americas and weaker countries would gravitate towards her.

2 The Monroe Doctrine warned European colonial powers that the United States would not tolerate increased colonialism in the Americas.

3 The United States expected Cuba to gain independence from Spain and gravitate towards her.

4 From 1825 to 1859 the United States made several attempts to purchase Cuba.

5 European colonial powers were alarmed at the United States' designs on Cuba and their views were published in the Ostend Manifesto.

6 Between 1868 and 1898 the United States had the following reasons for military intervention in Cuba: protection of US investments; Spain's failure to emancipate slaves and grant internal self-government; other powers having imperialistic designs in the region; the blowing up of a US battleship in Havana harbour.

7 In 1898 the United States defeated Spain in ten weeks and Spain was forced to recognise Cuba's independence.

8 The United States occupied Cuba militarily from 1898 to 1903.

9 The Platt Amendment meant the United States had close control over Cuba after independence.

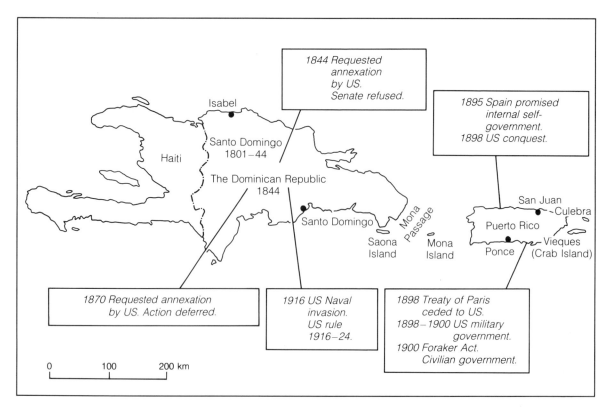

Map 7.4: United States involvement in the Dominican Republic and Puerto Rico

Map 7.4: United States involvement in the Dominican Republic and Puerto Rico in the nineteenth century

Dominican Republic

In the nineteenth century the Dominican Republic changed its name and changed its constitutional status and government several times. In 1801 it was taken over by Toussaint L'Ouverture of Haiti but soon recaptured by France in 1803. In 1808 the Spanish colonists rebelled against French rule and Santo Domingo became a colony of Spain again. In 1821 it proclaimed its independence but was immediately conquered by Haiti who ruled it from 1822 to 1844. In 1844 it proclaimed its independence and took the name 'Dominican Republic'. In 1861 President Santana returned it to Spain as he feared recapture by Haiti. The Dominican Republic regained its independence in the Dominican War of Independence, 1863–5.

Against this background of weakness and instability the Dominican people could see the benefits of annexation by the United States. It would give protection against Haiti and bring more material benefits than it was receiving from Spanish rule. So the Dominican Republic asked the United States to annex it in 1844. The United States sent a Commission of Inquiry which recommended annexation but the US Senate refused to ratify it.

In 1870 the Dominican Republic feared reconquest by Haiti and again asked the United States to annex it. The United States sent another Commission of Inquiry which acknowledged the vulnerability of the Dominican Republic and suggested that either the United States or another power should annex it, or that it should join an independent federation with Cuba and Puerto Rico. Nothing further was done and the Dominican Republic had to wait for US rule until 1916.

Puerto Rico

In the Spanish-American War of 1895–8 Spain promised Puerto Rico internal self-government and went as far as granting a constitution in 1897. However, a US expeditionary force captured Puerto Rico in 1898, probably with the good wishes of the people. By the Treaty of Paris, 1898, Puerto Rico was handed over to the United States which installed a military government for two years. In 1900 the Foraker Act established a civilian government but the officials were US appointees and political rights were denied to most Puerto Ricans.

Notes

1 The eastern part of Hispaniola passed from Haiti to France to Spain to independence in the first sixty years of the nineteenth century showing how unstable it was.

2 It became known as the 'Dominican Republic' in 1844.

3 It asked to be annexed by the United States in 1844 and 1870 but on both occasions nothing was done although the US Commissions of Inquiry were in favour of it.

4 Annexation by the United States offered the Dominican Republic protection against Haiti and material benefits.

5 United States rule eventually came in 1916.

6 Puerto Rico was conquered by the United States in the war of 1895–8 and a US military government took over.

7 When civilian government was established in 1900 the United States appointed officials and Puerto Ricans had little political power.

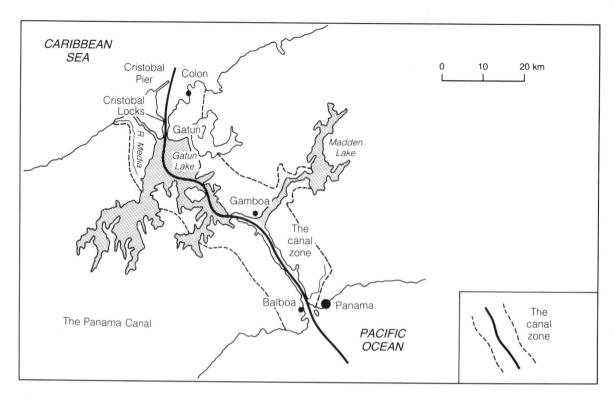

Map 7.5: The United States and the Panama Canal

Map 7.5: The United States and the Panama Canal

By 1850 the United States had reached California in its westward expansion and by 1898 it had acquired a Pacific and a Caribbean empire in the Philippines, Cuba and Puerto Rico. Easy and quick access by sea to both these areas was therefore very important to the United States and a canal through Central America was urgently needed. However, there were obstacles in the way of the United States building and controlling such a canal: a) by the Clayton-Bulwer Treaty of 1850 the United States and Britain had agreed to share in the construction and control of a canal; b) the French company formed by Ferdinand de Lesseps had sold out to another French company, the New Panama Canal Company which still held the rights for a canal from the Colombian Government until 1904; c) the route via Panama was through Colombian soil; d) the United States wanted the right to fortify a canal.

The United States overcame these obstacles one by one: *Obstacle a)* Britain freed the United States from the first obstacle, the Clayton-Bulwer Treaty, in 1901 by signing the Hay-Pauncefort Treaty which gave the United States the sole right to build, control and fortify a canal; *Obstacle b)* the New Panama Canal Company was anxious to sell the assets left behind by de Lesseps Company in 1881 and its rights from the Colombian Government before its treaty with Colombia expired in 1904. The United States was able to pay the New Panama Canal Company $40 000 000 for its rights to build a canal on Colombian soil; *Obstacle c)* In 1903 the United States paid the Colombian Government $10 000 000 down and promised $250 000 per year for a canal zone ten kilometres wide across the Isthmus of Panama; *Obstacle d)* the Hay-Pauncefort Treaty and the agreement with Panama cleared the way for the United States to fortify a canal.

However, the new Senate in Colombia revoked the agreement later in 1903 on the grounds that the compensation was not enough and that the Canal Zone would threaten Colombia's independence. President Roosevelt decided to instigate a revolution in Panama knowing that he would have the support of the French Company because they would not want to lose their $40 000 000 in compensation. The United States prevented Colombia from crushing the revolution by sending in marines to keep out the Colombian forces. Then the United States recognised the new government of Panama and paid it the monies it had agreed formerly to pay to Colombia.

The Panama Canal was built between 1904 and 1914 by Colonel George Goethals, a US army engineer, with mostly West Indian labour. Colonel W.C. Gorgas, an army medical officer, overcame the problems of malaria and yellow fever. The first ship passed through the Panama Canal on 15 August 1914. The United States was allowed to fortify the Canal Zone and she did this by stationing troops there. She also wanted to protect the approaches to the Canal which she did by establishing naval bases in Cuba as permitted under the Platt Amendment. Lastly she began to take a more active role in Latin American and Caribbean affairs. Justification for intervention was given by the 'Roosevelt Corollary' to the Monroe Doctrine under which the United States could claim 'police powers' in the Americas in cases of corruption, weakness and whatever the United States decided to term 'wrong-doing'.

Desire to safeguard the Panama Canal dominated US policy in the Caribbean in the twentieth century and led to her intervention in many Caribbean countries especially when she considered her routes were threatened in the First World War.

Notes

1 By 1898 the United States wanted a canal through Central America so that she could reach her West Coast and the Philippines quickly by sea.
2 Before the United States could build the canal she had to free herself from an agreement with Britain, buy the rights from a French company and obtain permission from the Colombian Government.
3 President Roosevelt instigated a revolution in Panama when Colombia revoked the agreement in 1903 to allow the United States to build a canal on Colombian soil.
4 The new Panamanian Government gave the United States a canal zone through its territory for $10 000 000 down and $250 000 per year.
5 The canal was started in 1904 and opened for shipping in 1914.
6 The Canal Zone was garrisoned by US marines.
7 The Panama Canal dominated US policy and strategy in the Caribbean in the twentieth century.

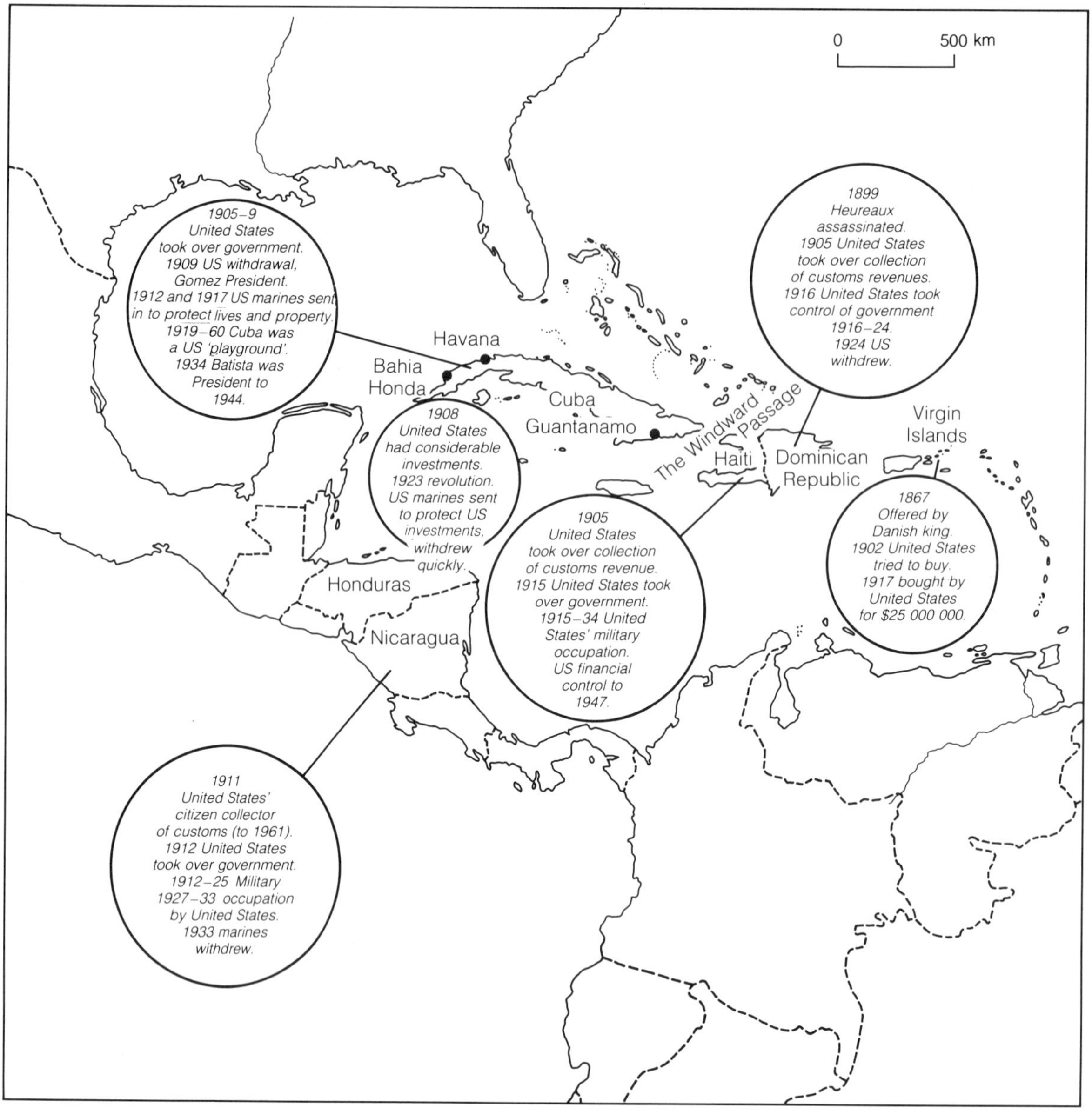
0
500 km
1905–9
United States
took over government.
1909 US withdrawal,
Gomez President.
1912 and 1917 US marines sent in to protect lives and property.
1919–60 Cuba was
a US 'playground'.
1934 Batista was
President to
1944.
Havana
Bahia
Honda
Cuba
Guantanamo
The Windward Passage
Haiti
Dominican
Republic
Virgin
Islands
Honduras
Nicaragua
1899
Heureaux
assassinated.
1905 United States
took over collection
of customs revenues.
1916 United States took
control of government
1916–24.
1924 US
withdrew.
1908
United States
had considerable
investments.
1923 revolution.
US marines sent
to protect US
investments,
withdrew
quickly.
1905
United States
took over collection
of customs revenue.
1915 United States took
over government.
1915–34 United
States' military
occupation.
US financial
control to
1947.
1867
Offered by
Danish king.
1902 United States
tried to buy.
1917 bought by
United States
for $25 000 000.
1911
United States'
citizen collector
of customs (to 1961).
1912 United States
took over government.
1912–25 Military
1927–33 occupation
by United States.
1933 marines
withdrew.

Map 7.6: Dollar Diplomacy

Map 7.6: Dollar Diplomacy

The policy called 'Dollar Diplomacy' is credited to William Howard Taft, US Secretary for War in 1904. It was the policy aimed at transferring the debts of Caribbean countries from European to United States creditors so that when Caribbean countries defaulted on their repayments the United States could have an excuse for intervention. The intervention followed a pattern until the United States gained complete control over the country. First, the United States would take control over the collection of customs revenues and use part of these revenues to pay off the debts to US citizens or banks. Then the United States would assume complete control over the country's finances. At the first sign of political instability the United States would take over the government. Finally the United States would send in marines and begin the military occupation of the country. Dollar Diplomacy was operated so successfully in the Caribbean between 1904 and 1930 that by 1924 the United States was controlling the financial affairs of Cuba, the Dominican Republic, Haiti, Nicaragua and Honduras and was either occupying those countries militarily or had done so at some time. In the First World War, 1914–18, the United States felt it necessary to intervene for strategic or security reasons, often to protect its sea lanes to and from the Panama Canal so much did the Panama Canal dominate US policy in the Caribbean.

Cuba

Throughout the nineteenth century the United States had been drawn into Cuban affairs because of its ideas of Manifest Destiny and its application of the Monroe Doctrine. The Platt Amendment of 1901 gave it the right to intervene in Cuba in the twentieth century, so 'Dollar Diplomacy' cannot be applied to Cuba in the same way as it can to the other four countries.

The Platt Amendment gave the United States the right to bases in Cuba. In 1903 the United States established two bases, Guantanamo in the south-east and Bahia Honda in the north-west, for a rent of $2000 per year. (Bahia Honda was given up in 1912 on condition that Guantanamo could be enlarged and the rent increased to $5000). These two bases made direct intervention by the US marines very easy.

In 1902 the pro-American President, Estrada Palma, wanted the United States to annex Cuba but he was forced to resign by the nationalists in 1905. The United States sent in Charles Magoon as Governor to restore stability. He stayed until 1909, administering Cuba according to its own constitution but with Americans in high office. Before he withdrew he supervised the 1908 elections which led to the very corrupt government of Jose Miguel Gomez from 1909 to 1912. When the opposition tried to remove the racism practised by this regime there was a revolution and US marines were sent in. Three thousand black Cubans died and discrimination continued. US investment in this period reached $60 000 000 and the US Government was keen to protect this. In the First World War, for the sake of stability, the United States supported the government of President Menocal although it was unpopular. In 1917 marines were sent in again to keep Menocal in power. When Menocal handed over the Presidency to Zayas in 1921 the United States intervened yet again when there was turmoil because the opposition accused Menocal of rigging the elections. The US General Crowder consulted with Menocal about the best ways of preserving political and economic stability, the latter being very necessary because sugar prices had crashed in 1921.

Over the past decade the United States had increased its domination of Cuba's economy. There had been a sugar boom in the First World War culminating in 'The Dance of the Millions' when Cuba put over 4 000 000 tonnes of sugar on the market at over $400 per tonne. Demand for sugar estates was so high that Cubans sold out to Americans at high prices. In 1921 sugar prices fell by 50 per cent and this time Cubans sold estates to Americans to clear their debts. Havana banks had made loans on the strength of sugar revenues and they were forced to rely heavily on US loans. The Cuban economy passed into the hands of US bankers.

At the same time American tourism to Cuba began on a large scale. Between 1919 and 1933 prohibition in the United States drove Americans to Cuba in search of liquor and gambling. Cuba built up its hotel, casino and night-club world and remained an American playground until 1959.

By 1923 sugar prices had begun to improve and in 1926–7 sugar revenues were high again, but this just showed the nationalists the dangers of monoculture especially when the sugar industry was in US hands and the economy controlled by US bankers. However, the US Government was determined not to intervene directly in Cuba again and showed its good intentions by giving up all claims to the Isle of Pines in 1926. In the 1930s the United States reaffirmed these intentions by withdrawing the Platt Amendment as a demonstration of its 'Good Neighbour' policy towards Cuba. In spite of some very brutal and corrupt regimes such as that of President Machado from 1923, and a communist-supported government which it did not like in 1944, and cases of 'chronic wrong-doing', the United States did not apply the Roosevelt Corollary ever again in Cuba.

Dominican Republic

There had been political stability and economic growth under the dictatorship of Ulises Heureaux from 1882 to 1895, but he was assassinated in 1899 resulting in turmoil. By 1905 there was considerable US investment in the Dominican Republic and the United States was its biggest trading partner. In 1905 the Dominican Republic could not pay its debts. The United States feared that European countries would intervene to protect their interests so she intervened first and took over the collection of customs revenues, setting some of these revenues aside to clear foreign debts. The Government asked the United States to continue doing this in 1907. This was the first application of Dollar Diplomacy and what followed was typical of this policy. In 1916 President Jimenez objected to further US control over the government and resigned making way for complete US takeover of the government. President Wilson thought that this was justified in the First World War to pre-empt any similar action by Germany.

US occupation of the Dominican Republic from 1916 to 1924 was politically unpopular but brought the country material benefits in the shape of new roads and schools, improved telephones and telegraphs, and health and sanitation reforms. It also brought the training of the army and police which was useful later to keep the dictator, Trujillo, in power.

In 1924 the United States withdrew from the Dominican Republic after supervising elections for civilian government.

Haiti

In 1905 the United States took over the collection of customs revenues in Haiti to enable the repayment of debts. Between 1905 and 1914 US investors increased their control over Haiti's economy.

Haiti's President was overthrown, put in prison and murdered by his political opponents in 1915. The United States took this as 'chronic wrong-doing' of the Roosevelt Corollary and intervened. The real reasons for intervention were strategic and economic. It was war-time and Haiti commanded the Windward Passage, an important sea lane for the United States between New York and Panama. Also US investors were demanding protection of their interests in Haiti.

The United States negotiated a ten-year occupation but the marines ignored the time limit and stayed until 1934. They were very unpopular with the black peasants because they recreated the old mulatto elite, introduced forced labour on the roads which recalled the slavery of Henri Christophe, allowed foreigners to own land which was very scarce to peasant small-holders and did not bring the material benefits which military occupation had brought to Cuba and the Dominican Republic. The black peasants revolted and two thousand were killed in the brutal repression.

Nicaragua

Nicaraguan citizens and institutions had borrowed heavily from US banks and could not repay their debts in 1911. A United States citizen was appointed Collector of Customs and this office stayed in American hands until 1961. In 1912 President Diaz asked the United States to take over the government because of political instability. This led to the military occupation of Nicaragua from 1912 to 1925 and again from 1927 to 1933 when the last marines withdrew after supervising the elections of 1932. US intervention in Nicaragua provides a very good example for the pattern of Dollar Diplomacy.

Honduras

In 1923 US investments were thought to be in danger because of a revolution so US marines were sent in. The marines soon withdrew but the United States continued to dominate the economy, so much so that by the 1950s the United States was taking almost all Honduran exports and supplying four-fifths of the imports.

The Danish Virgin Islands

US acquisition of these does not belong to Dollar Diplomacy but did occur at the same time as the policy was being operated elsewhere in the Caribbean.

In 1867 the Danish King offered to sell St Thomas, St John and St Croix to the United States but the offer was refused. In 1902 the United States tried to buy these islands but the Danish Government refused to sell. Finally in 1917 the United States bought the islands for $25 000 000 and they became the 'United States Virgin Islands'. In 1917 the strategic motive was strong as the Americans wanted a naval base on St Thomas.

Notes

1 Dollar Diplomacy was the policy of transferring the debts of Caribbean countries to US creditors in the expectation of default so that the United States could take over control of the finances.

2 Financial control would lead to control of the government and miltary occupation in typical cases.

3 Dollar Diplomacy was operated by the United States in the Caribbean between 1905 and 1930.

4 In the Dominican Republic Dollar Diplomacy led to US military occupation from 1916 to 1924.

5 In Haiti there was US military occupation from 1912 to 1934.

6 In Nicaragua the United States controlled the collection of customs from 1911 to 1961 and occupied the country militarily from 1912 to 1925 and from 1927 to 1933.

7 The United States bought the Danish Virgin Islands in 1917 for $25 000 000.

8 Dollar Diplomacy was the result of the US obsession with the need to protect the approaches to the Panama Canal.

Cuba:

9 The Platt Amendment of 1901 gave the United States the right to intervene in Cuba so cases of intervention in 1906, 1912, 1917 and 1921 cannot be put down to Dollar Diplomacy.

10 The United States had two naval bases in Cuba, Guantanamo and Bahia Honda.

11 After the First World War the Cuban sugar industry passed into the hands of Americans, being over 60 per cent American-owned, and the economy into the hands of US bankers.

12 From 1919 to 1959 Cuba was an American playground.

13 The Good Neighbour policy of the 1930s ended all direct US intervention in Cuba and the Platt Amendment was withdrawn in 1934.

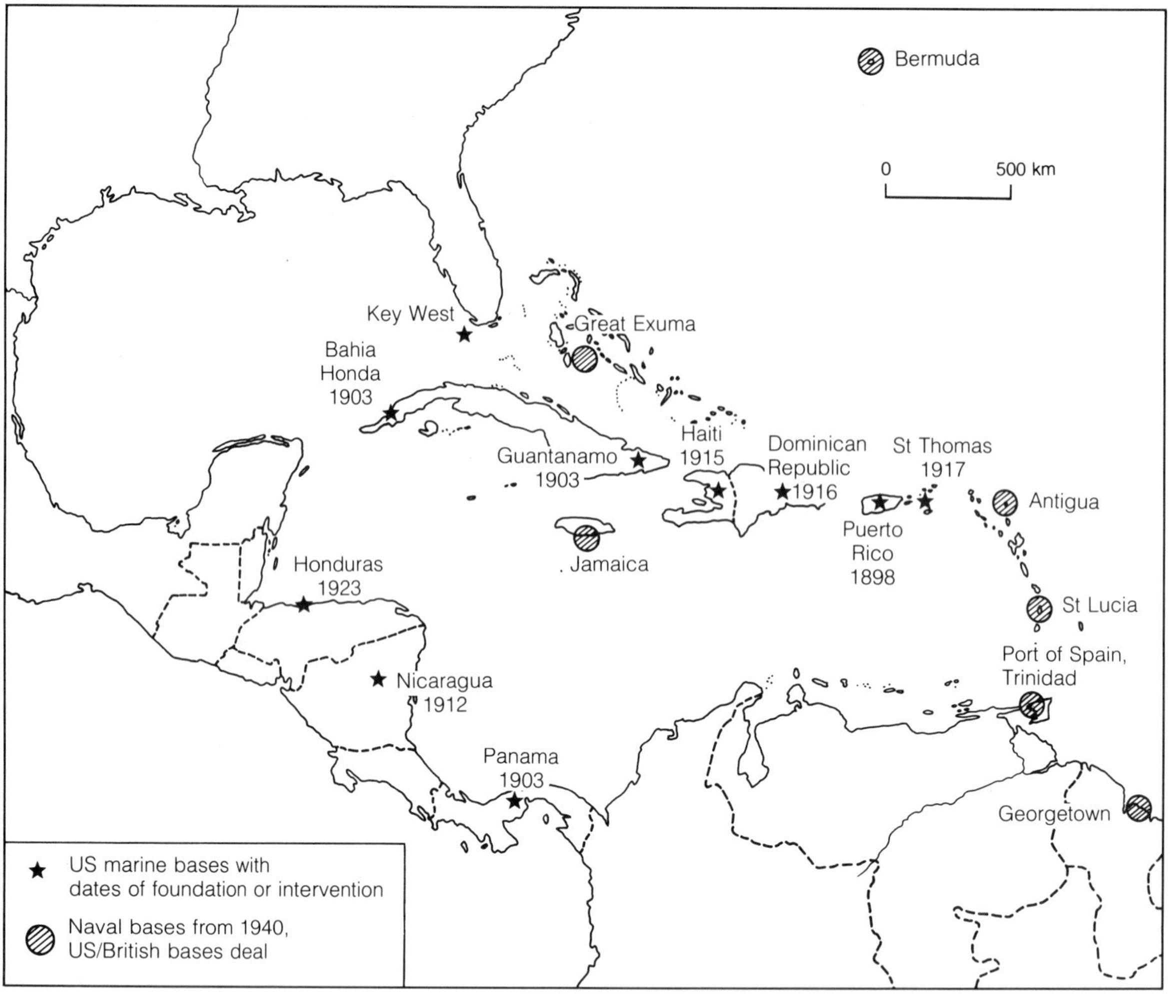
Bermuda
0
500 km
Key West
Great Exuma
Bahia
Honda
1903
Guantanamo
1903
Haiti
1915
Dominican
Republic
1916
St Thomas
1917
Antigua
Puerto
Rico
1898
Jamaica
Honduras
1923
St Lucia
Port of Spain,
Trinidad
Nicaragua
1912
Panama
1903
Georgetown
US marine bases with
dates of foundation or intervention
Naval bases from 1940,
US/British bases deal

Map 7.7: United States' marine and naval bases in the Caribbean

Map 7.7: United States' marine and naval bases in the Caribbean

In the section on Dollar Diplomacy we saw when and how the United States intervened militarily in the Spanish Caribbean and established the marine bases shown on Map 7.7. In this section we shall see the establishment of US naval bases in the British Caribbean.

Between 1939 and the end of 1941 the United States was neutral in the Second World War but resented the presence of the German navy in the Caribbean and its interference with neutral shipping. While professing neutrality the United States made a deal with Britain to exchange fifty destroyers for the right to build naval bases in the British Caribbean rent-free on 99-year leases. The United States wanted these to give further protection to their shipping lanes.

In 1942 German submarines sank peaceful shipping in the Caribbean, one near Barbados harbour and another in the harbour of Castries. This convinced most British West Indians that the bases were necessary. However, they were worried about the racial attitudes of marines towards blacks after the experiences of the local peoples of Cuba and Haiti. These worries were largely unfounded as relations between marines and residents proved to be good on the whole. The construction of the bases gave employment to thousands and brought in valuable US dollars to the local economy.

In 1958 the Government of the West Indies Federation wanted to re-negotiate the bases' deal with the United States. Trinidad wanted to negotiate separately as she had been particularly upset by the British deal because the base at Chaguaramas near Port of Spain had made hundreds homeless and had taken much more land than local residents thought necessary. However, by 1960 the United States had voluntarily withdrawn from some bases and by the agreement of 1961 agreed to give up most of the land held by the other bases. What was left was known as US Defence Areas.

Notes

1 By 1930 the United States had established marine bases throughout the Spanish Caribbean and Central America.
2 The United States was neutral at the beginning of the Second World War but resented the presence of the German navy in the Caribbean.
3 She negotiated a deal with the British Government in 1940 which gave the right for the United States to establish bases in the British Caribbean.
4 Most British West Indians saw the need for these bases when the Germans sank peaceful shipping.
5 The bases gave employment and brought in dollars to the local economy and relations between the US marines and local residents were usually good.
6 The West Indies Federation wanted to re-negotiate the bases' deal in 1958 and with or without formal agreement the United States ran down their bases.

Recent forms of United States' influence

Since independence the ex-British Caribbean has in some ways 'gravitated' towards the United States. The role of Britain has inevitably declined and geography has become the more important factor as the ex-British territories are conscious of being part of the Americas. They now look to the United States for protection. In 1967 Barbados and Trinidad, in 1968 Jamaica and by 1986 the Bahamas, Dominica, Grenada, St Kitts/Nevis, St Lucia and St Vincent have joined the Organisation of American States (OAS). This is a defence pact and anti-communist.

In 1965 Jamaica signed a defence agreement with the United States which implied the transference of responsibility of defence from Britain to the United States. Jamaica has since moved further into the US fold as the United States has taken over as Jamaica's biggest trading partner.

US tourists to the Caribbean have switched from Cuba to other parts of the Caribbean since 1959. Of course they go to Puerto Rico and the US Virgin Islands, but the Bahamas, Jamaica, Barbados, Antigua and the Cayman Islands also receive many US tourists. The cultural impact of the United States through tourism is considerable as the tourists want the life style, foods, drinks and entertainment they are used to.

Theme 8: Trade unions in the British Caribbean

Table 8.1: Early trade unionism in the British Caribbean

Territory	Trade union legislation		Early unions	Union leaders
Barbados	1939	Compulsory registration of unions	Barbados Progressive League 1937	
British Guiana	1921	Legal recognition Protection of funds No picketing	British Guiana Labour Union 1919	Critchlow
Jamaica	1919	Liable for claims for damages arising from trade disputes	Artisans Union 1899 Printers' Union 1907 Jamaica Trades and Labour Union 1908	Coombes, Bustamante
St Vincent	1933		Working Men's Association 1935	
Trinidad	1932		Trinidad Working Men's Association 1919.	Butler, Cipriani
British Honduras			Civil Service Association 1922	

Table 8.1: Early trade unionism in the British Caribbean

By 1910 workers in Britain had achieved the following legal position with regard to their unions: a) the right to form unions to improve their conditions; b) the right to withhold their labour (to strike) to strengthen their bargaining position; c) the right to persuade non-strikers to withhold their labour (to picket); d) immunity from claims for damages caused by workers during strikes.

However, their brother workers in the West Indies were unaware of these rights except for a few leaders. In any case in 1910 trade unions in the British Caribbean were still not recognised by law. Unions could still be held to be 'in restraint of trade' by their very existence and still more so by striking. Therefore the law might say that such workers were committing treason by undermining the peace and prosperity of the country. At that time there was little organised labour in the British Caribbean. Relations between employers and workers were still governed by the Masters'/Servants' Ordinances of individual colonies which stated hours, rates of pay and conditions and did not consider unionism. The first trade union legislation was passed in Jamaica in 1919 but unions did exist before then, for example the Artisans' Union of 1899 in Jamaica, without legal recognition.

The struggles of the nineteenth century unions in Britain did benefit the union movement in the British Caribbean because they saved West Indian workers from having to go through the same, and the rights achieved served as precedents for those who made the laws in the West Indies, i.e. British trade union legislation was partly accepted in the British Caribbean. The aim of trade union legislation in the British Caribbean was to encourage unionism so that labour unrest and strikes could be avoided by peaceful negotiation. However, the early legislation stopped short of the British position in that picketing was illegal and unions could face claims for damages done by striking workers.

Conditions in the British Caribbean were very different to those in Britain. There were no industrial towns with huge populations. Most workers were rural. Most were not solely dependent on wages for subsistence and to a certain extent were 'tied' to their cottages and grounds. It was difficult to organise scattered workers into unions. The first unions therefore were small craft unions of skilled workers like the Artisans' Union in Jamaica, the Printers' Union and the Tobacco Workers' Union. Even the Jamaica Trades and Labour Union of 1908 was a combination of skilled workers' unions. These small unions did not last long because: a) members were continually emigrating; b) conditions for skilled workers were relatively good; c) scattered agricultural workers could not easily combine into unions; d) employers were anti-union and employers dominated the legislatures; e) workers were ignorant of union legislation; f) lack of confidence in pressing their case made union leaders give up when problems arose.

The hardships and sufferings of the 1920s and 1930s, especially those which led to the riots and strikes between 1935 and 1938, brought a new unionism in which the unions were stronger, more militant, more informed and more confident of their power.

Notes

1   In the nineteenth century British workers had had a long struggle to win union rights.
2   Their struggles saved West Indian workers from having to undergo the same, as British West Indian Legislatives tended to follow British precedents.
3   In 1910 there was little or no organised labour in the British Caribbean and unions were not recognised by law.
4   The first unions in the British Caribbean were small unions of skilled workers and not recognised by law.
5   Trade unions were given legal recognition from 1919 in the British Caribbean because the authorities hoped that they would help improve workers' conditions without more serious trouble occurring.
6   The early unions faced too many difficulties and most were disbanded before 1930.
7   The riots and strikes, 1935–8, brought new, stronger unionism to the British Caribbean.

Table 8.2: Riots and strikes 1935–8

Territory	Date	Nature of disturbance	Reaction of authorities	Results
St Kitts	1935	Strike by sugar workers	Suppressed by police	
St Vincent	1935	Workers' protests against higher customs duties. Violence and damage	State of emergency Press censored	
St Lucia	1935	Castries' coal workers' strike	Suppressed by soldiers	
British Guiana	1935	Disputes and strikes on sugar estates for higher wages		Manpower Citizens' Association formed
	1937	Strikes and riots on sugar estates against mechanisation		Unions power conscious
	1938	Strikes on sugar estates		Labour conference called
Jamaica	1937	Unrest on sugar estates Strikes for higher wages	Police arrested leaders 4 rioters killed	
	1938	Strikes, riots and destruction at Frome Dockers' strike in Kingston	Bustamante arrested Brutal police suppression. 8 killed, 170 wounded Cruiser *Ajax* sent	Bustamante replaced Coombes Manley offered services as a lawyer
Trinidad	1937	Riots in oilfields	Police tried to arrest Uriah Butler Cruisers *Ajax* and *Exeter* landed troops	Butler became Labour leader Workers' demands heard
Barbados	1937	Workers' agitation Riots against Payne's deportation	Payne deported Brutal police suppression. 14 killed, 59 wounded	First trade unions Grantley Adams Labour leader

Table 8.2: Riots and strikes 1935-8

In the 1920s and 1930s employers took little notice of the hardships of the working classes in the British Caribbean. Unemployment was high, about 20 per cent in Barbados in 1925, rising to as high as 50 per cent in some territories in the 1930s after the Great Depression had struck. Those in employment received very low wages, no compensation for sickness or injury and no pensions. Health and education facilities were very poor and many workers lived in slums. Governments could not help because their revenues were inadequate to finance social services like health and education, to provide unemployment relief, or to finance labour-intensive projects like road-building. The workers were meant to help themselves but their employers in the private sector had to be made aware of their plight, pay them higher wages and give them better conditions. Men like Arthur Cipriani in Trinidad, Charles Duncan O'Neal in Barbados and Alfred Thorne in British Guiana did press the case of the working class but the riots and strikes of 1935-8 did more to show their grievances and desperation. They showed that effective unions representing the workers were needed.

In Map 6.6, we saw how the safety valve of emigration had ended in 1925. With no emigration unemployment rose and no money was being repatriated from abroad. In 1929 came the Great Depression. The United States and Britain reduced production, incomes fell and they imported less so BWI exports were also rapidly reduced and in the West Indies generally there was less production, lower incomes and unemployment. It was the Great Depression coming on top of the end of emigration which drove the workers to desperate measures in 1935 as shown in Table 8.2.

The reaction of the authorities was swift and often brutal. In St Kitts, St Lucia, Trinidad and Jamaica warships were sent. Police and soldiers suppressed the rioters so brutally that many were killed and many more wounded. This brutal suppression only made the people more determined to fight for better conditions. The first step was to call a meeting of working-class leaders to decide what to do. This was the British Guiana and West Indies Labour Congress which met in Georgetown in 1938. Many of the delegates were also nationalist politicians so they did not confine themselves to working-class grievances but also made political demands like universal suffrage, internal self-government and federation:

Labour demands	Political demands
1 Trade union immunity from claims for damages resulting from strikes.	1 Federation of the British West Indies.
2 Immunity from treason charges for union activities.	2 Universal suffrage to elect Legislative Assemblies.
3 Peaceful picketing.	3 Limitations on the powers of Governors.
4 Minimum wages.	4 Free compulsory education.
5 44-hour week.	5 Private sugar estates to be limited to twenty hectares.
6 Old-age pensions.	6 Nationalisation of the sugar industry.
7 National Health Insurance and Sickness Benefits.	7 Nationalisation of public utilities.
	8 Co-operative marketing of produce.

The delegates returned to their own countries after the 1938 Labour Congress determined to carry out these demands.

Notes

1 The economies of the British Caribbean could not finance social services. This led to the riots and strikes of 1935-8 which emphasized the need for effective trade unions.

2 The world-wide Great Depression added to the difficulties of the British Caribbean.

3 The brutal suppression of the riots increased the peoples' determination to fight for better conditions and led to the British Guiana and West Indies Labour Congress of 1938.

4 Both labour and political demands were made at the Congress by the nationalist leaders.

Table 8.3: New unionism 1938

Territory	Date	Union's name	Approx. size	Leaders
British Guiana	1937	Manpower and Citizens' Association	4000 (1939)	Ayube Edun
Trinidad	1938	Oil Workers' Trade Union		Butler
Jamaica	1939	Bustamante Industrial Trade Union	6000	Bustamante
Barbados	1939	Barbados Progressive League	23 000	Adams, Cummins, Crawford
Antigua	1940	Antigua Trades and Labour Union	12 000	Bird
St Kitts	1940	St Kitts Workers' League		Bradshaw

Table 8.3: New Unionism 1938

New trade unions were formed after the riots and strikes of 1935–8 larger than the early unions with a few thousand members each. This made their funds proportionally larger, their bargaining power greater and their strike threat more potent. However, most new unions were small, i.e. less than a thousand members, but these unions achieved strength through federations such as the Trade Union Advisory Council formed by Norman Manley in Jamaica in 1939. The unions had learnt that greater size meant greater strength.

The new unionism gathered momentum. In five years from 1938 fifty-eight new unions were registered with sixty-five thousand members. By 1945 there were sixty-five new unions with a membership of over one-hundred thousand. British Guiana had twenty-four unions in 1943. The Trade Union Council formed in British Guiana in 1941 represented fourteen unions by 1943. When the next Caribbean Labour Conference met in 1945 unionism was stronger in numbers, size of unions and finances. Their powers and rights had also been increased by new trade union legislation. West Indian laws had been brought into line with British laws in that peaceful picketing and immunity from claims for damages resulting from strikes were permitted, for example, by new trade union legislation in Jamaica in 1938 and in Barbados in 1942.

In 1942 Barbados and British Guiana also set up Labour Departments to control all employment and to negotiate in disputes between employers and employees if called upon in an attempt to improve industrial relations and to prevent further labour unrest.

Notes

1 New, larger and therefore more powerful unions were set up after 1938. Small unions often formed federations to increase their power.

2 In 1938 there were fifty-eight new unions with sixty-five thousand members. By 1945 there were sixty-five new unions with over one-hundred thousand members.

3 New trade union legislation in line with British laws was passed and Barbados and British Guiana set up Labour Departments to control and negotiate employment.

Map 8.1: Trade unions and political parties in the British Caribbean

In the British Caribbean trade unions have been very commonly linked with political parties. The 1938 Labour Congress began this link because the delegates voiced labour and political demands as if political affairs were part of their mandate. If the labour demands were to be translated into law, then politicians had to adopt these demands. Therefore the labour delegates often became politicians themselves. Politicians who were not unionists would be expected to carry out the demands of the unionists.

One of the political demands made at the 1938 Congress was universal suffrage. Once the vote had been extended to the working classes, any political party would need the support of the workers to win an election. Previously in the British Caribbean the people who made the laws were employers. After universal suffrage the employees' representatives would be making the laws. Therefore unions entered politics to take law-making out of the hands of the employers. If not, labour demands would never have been translated into law.

Nationalisation was a political demand of the trade union movement in the British Caribbean. Of course, the property-owning classes would never have proposed it. It was a socialist policy only likely to be put forward by a political party representing union opinion, such as the Barbados Labour Party.

There were three ways in which trade unions and political parties were linked:

1 The trade union and the political party were one and the same, for example, the Barbados Progressive League formed as a trade union in 1938 became registered as a political party; the St Kitts Workers' League was a trade union and a political party from 1940.
2 The political party was a wing of the trade union, for example, the Antigua Trades and Labour Union formed in 1940 established a Political Committee which became the Antigua Labour Party in 1946.
3 The trade union and the political party were separate but created the one or the other for mutual benefit. Sometimes the union came first and the party followed but sometimes it happened the other way round, as when the Busta-mante Industrial Trade Union was formed in 1939 and the Jamaica Labour Party which represented it was founded in 1944; and the other way round when the People's National Party was formed in 1938 by Norman Manley who also founded the National Workers' Union in 1952.

These links were important and strong when the unions needed their demands to be translated into law but once the demands had been satisfied the links became less important and weaker and sometimes broke. However, a political party still needed union support to win an election as in British Guiana when Dr Cheddi Jagan sought the support of the Guiana Industrial Workers' Union in the 1953 election.

Most of these links were made in the period from 1938 to 1952. There have been changes since as the mutual support became less necessary. For example, the Barbados Progressive League received recognition under a Trade Union Act of 1939. In 1942 more union demands were satisfied including a Workmen's Compensation Act. Thereafter political demands were given priority and the Barbados Progressive League split into union, the Barbados Workers' Union, and party, the Barbados Labour Party. The Party still represented the workers as when it passed the Trade Union and Factory Acts of 1951 and set up the Wages Board.

In Britain trade unions supported the Labour Party and the 1945–51 Labour Government gave the country the Welfare State. In the British Caribbean political parties could not hope to give the workers so much as the governments did not have sufficient funds, but they did manage to meet workers' demands such as: minimum wages, workmen's compensation, paid sick leave, holidays with pay, redundancy pay and pension schemes.

The links between the trade union movement in Britain and trade unions in the British Caribbean used to be very strong. Up to 1958 the British Trades Union Congress helped their Caribbean brothers financially and in other ways but as local funds grew such help became unnecessary. British Caribbean union leaders went to Britain for training but in the early 1960s the Trade Union Education Institute was opened in Jamaica and another link was ended.

As in other spheres US influence has been strong in trade unionism in the British Caribbean in recent times. For example, in the United States unions negotiate for the whole country and not industry by industry or company by company as in Britain. This removes the possibility of local

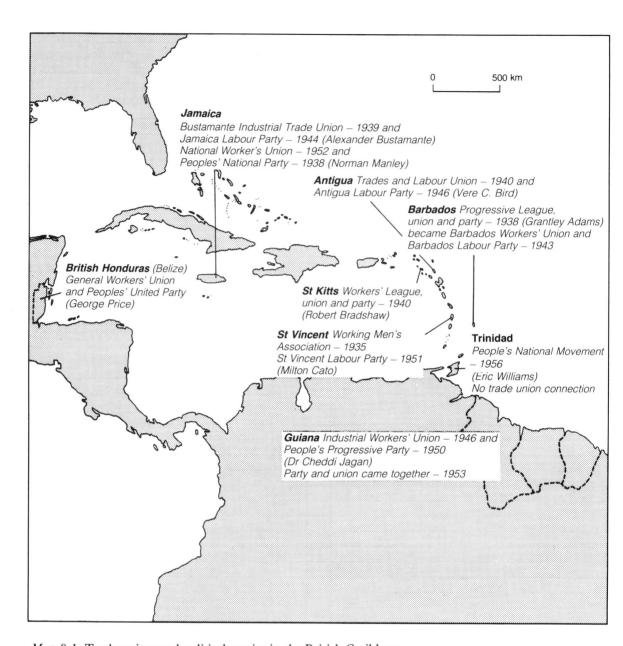

Jamaica
Bustamante Industrial Trade Union – 1939 and
Jamaica Labour Party – 1944 (Alexander Bustamante)
National Worker's Union – 1952 and
Peoples' National Party – 1938 (Norman Manley)

Antigua *Trades and Labour Union – 1940 and*
Antigua Labour Party – 1946 (Vere C. Bird)

Barbados *Progressive League,*
union and party – 1938 (Grantley Adams)
became Barbados Workers' Union and
Barbados Labour Party – 1943

British Honduras *(Belize)*
General Workers' Union
and Peoples' United Party
(George Price)

St Kitts *Workers' League,*
union and party – 1940
(Robert Bradshaw)

St Vincent *Working Men's*
Association – 1935
St Vincent Labour Party – 1951
(Milton Cato)

Trinidad
People's National Movement
– 1956
(Eric Williams)
No trade union connection

Guiana *Industrial Workers' Union – 1946 and*
People's Progressive Party – 1950
(Dr Cheddi Jagan)
Party and union came together – 1953

0   500 km

Map 8.1: Trade unions and political parties in the British Caribbean

discrepancies in pay and conditions and frequent local disputes and strikes. To a certain extent this has been adopted in the British Caribbean.

In developing countries strikes and trade disputes are illegal because they hinder economic progress. They are avoided at all costs. In the British Caribbean strikes in essential services are illegal. Also, because they are developing countries, the government intervenes in industrial disputes to try to keep production flowing. In a developed country like Britain direct government intervention would be the last resort and only when a national state . of emergency had been declared.

Notes

1   In the British Caribbean trade unions and political parties have been commonly linked.
2   The 1938 Labour Congress in British Guiana considered both labour and political demands.
3   Often union leaders were political leaders and founders of political parties.
4   Legislation was taken out of the hands of employers and put into the hands of employees' representatives.
5   Universal suffrage made support from the working classes very important in elections.
6   The links between trade unions and political parties became weaker once labour demands had been satisfied.
7   By the 1960s trade unions in the British Caribbean had achieved minimum wage legislation, workers' compensation, paid sick leave, holidays with pay, redundancy pay and pensions.
8   Links between trade unionism in Britain with trade unionism in the British Caribbean became very much weaker when financial support and training schemes ended by the early 1960s.
9   US influence, e.g. nationwide negotiation and bargaining, have had their effect in the British Caribbean.
10   The West Indies are developing countries and strikes and trade disputes are avoided at all costs even to the extent of declaring them illegal or accepting government intervention.

Theme 9: Movements to independence in the British Caribbean_____

Table 9.1: Constitutional developments in the British Caribbean to 1865

The first colonies were proprietary colonies, i.e. the King of England gave them to proprietors who were prominent nobles in England. The English Parliament had no control over these first colonies. The proprietors, such as the Earl of Carlisle, acted as patrons for the colonies. They sent out settlers and provisions, appointed Governors and carried out the King's instructions for the colonies. In return they hoped to reap some benefit when the colonies started production. When the King issued the royal 'Letters Patent' to the Earl of Carlisle in 1627 for the West Indies, his idea was to save himself the trouble and expense of administering these islands.

The Letters Patent gave the proprietor the authority to call the freemen of the colony (indentured servants and slaves were excluded) to an assembly to help make the laws. Thus the representative principle of government is very old in the British Caribbean, for example the Barbados Assembly was first called in 1639. Sometimes the assemblies were elected even from the beginning but sometimes the first assemblies were nominated. The rough rule is that assemblies were elected and legislative councils nominated by the Governor from among the leading citizens. These representative bodies, assemblies and councils increased their influence in the period of the Civil War and execution of the King in England, 1642–51.

On the Restoration of King Charles II in 1660 the idea of proprietary colonies was abandoned except in the case of the Bahamas which were handed over to the Lords Proprietors of Carolina in 1671. Between 1660 and 1663 the former proprietary colonies were handed over to a Committee of the Privy Council which later had various names, e.g. 'Council for Trade and Plantations', but whatever the name it was still a committee of the King's Privy Council. On behalf of the King the Committee appointed governors and charged them with the calling of assemblies and councils on the representative principle already established. Thus the representative principle continued.

Basically the constitution of a British West Indian colony from 1663 to 1763 (and in most cases later) was a Governor or Lieutenant-Governor representing the King; a Legislative Council consisting of members nominated by the Governor on account of their 'good estate' (property), corresponding with the House of Lords and acting as a court of appeal in the colony; and an Assembly to make minor laws and agree on taxation, corresponding with the House of Commons. The first assemblies were probably attended by all the freemen but as the colonies grew larger this was not possible and representatives had to be chosen, probably first by acclamation and later by show of hands. At first the assembly and council sat together and thus constituted what was known as a 'General Assembly'. However, there was a class distinction based on property which led to differences of opinion between assembly and council so these two bodies found it better to meet separately.

In the early days of the British Caribbean geographical knowledge was scanty from three to four thousand miles away and the colonies were strangely grouped, for example from 1627 to 1671 the Leewards were grouped with Barbados which was hundreds of miles away. Unions and associations were suggested for administrative convenience and were usually unpopular with the colonies who valued their independence such as Nevis which was only two miles from St Kitts but insisted on its own legislature and refused union with St Kitts in 1723. Union did not finally occur until 1882. New colonies like Dominica, small colonies like Turks and Caicos, and colonies which were still being contested like British Honduras were placed under the umbrella of a larger, established colony such as the Leewards, Bahamas and Jamaica respectively. Some colonies were so small, e.g. Anguilla and Barbuda, that they were

Table 9.1: Constitutional developments in the British Caribbean to 1865

Territory	Acquisition or conquest	Constitutional status	Legislature	Administrative association
Bahamas	1649 Settled by William Sayle and Company of Eleutherian Adventurers	Proprietary Colony even after 1670 when given to Lords Proprietors of Carolina	1666 Twelve elected to House of Assembly	First Commissions from Jamaica. Turks and Caicos under Bahamas to 1848
Barbados	1627 Captain John Powell's Settlement	1627–60 Proprietary Colony, then under Committee of P.C.	1639 Assembly (First Assembly in British Caribbean)	1672–1885 Governor of Barbados Governor-General of Windward Islands
British Guiana	1815 Ceded to Britain by Dutch. Unified as British Guiana 1831	Crown Colony by Order in Council	1815 Combined Court inherited from Dutch. Indirect election	
British Honduras	1666 Wallis's Settlement 1763 Partial recognition of British claims	1765 Burnaby's Laws. Settler Government 1862 Crown Colony	1752 Governed by 'Public Meeting' and later Legislative Assembly	To 1884 Under Governor of Jamaica. Jamaican Superintendent
Jamaica	1655 Conquered by England (Oliver Cromwell)	1655–61 Military Government 1651 Under Committee of Privy Council	1661 D'Oyley authorised to set up representative assembly	1848–73 Superintended Turks and Caicos. 1784–1884 Superintended British Honduras
Trinidad	1797 Conquered by Britain 1802 Ceded to Britain by Spain	Crown Colony. Crown retained right to legislate for Trinidad	1815 Crown refused Assembly	1838 In Windward Islands
The Leewards	1624–32 Settled by Thomas Warner and others	1627–60 Proprietary Colonies Removed from Barbados 1671	1674–1798 General Assembly of Leewards	1671 Leeward Island Act set up Leeward Island Government
St Kitts	1622–24 Settled by Thomas Warner	1627 Proprietary Colony 1660 Under Committee of Privy Council	1650 St Kitts Assembly	Anguilla annexed to St Kitts
Nevis	1628 Settled by Anthony Hilton	1627–60 Proprietary Colony	1664 (or earlier) Council and Assembly of Nevis	1723 Union with St Kitts refused
Antigua	1632 Colonised by Thomas Warner	1627–60 Proprietary Colony	1650 Assembly of Antigua	1860 Barbuda annexed to Antigua
Montserrat	1632 Settled by Irish 1783 Fully restored to Britain by France	1627–60 Proprietary Colony		
The Windwards	1763 Treaty of Paris. All except St Lucia (1815) ceded by France to Britain	Colonies under Committee of Privy Council with Representative Principle	1833 Federal Assembly of Windwards	1833 Barbados, Grenada, St Vincent, Tobago, plus 1838 St Lucia, Trinidad
Dominica	1763 Ceded to Britain 1783 Fully restored	1763 Governor appointed	1775 Assembly with Representative Principle accepted	1763 In Windwards 1771 Separate colony 1833 In Leewards
Grenada	1763 Ceded to Britain 1783 Fully restored	1763 Governor appointed	1766 Assembly with Representative Principle	In Windward Islands
St Vincent	1763 Ceded to Britain 1783 Fully restored	1763 Governor appointed, English Law applied	1763 Governor authorised to set up 'usual form of Assembly'	1833 Under Governor-General of Windwards
St Lucia	1815 Ceded to Britain	1815–38 Crown Colony 1838–85 Windward Islands	1814–16 Conseil Superior 1816–32 Governor's Privy Council (Abolished 1832)	1838–85 In Windward Islands Colony

annexed to larger colonies like St Kitts and Antigua respectively.

In 1763 in the Treaty of Paris Dominica, Grenada and St Vincent (Dominica and St Vincent had been 'Neutral Islands') were ceded to Britain by France. Immediately governors were sent to them with commissions authorising the usual form of representative institutions i.e. assemblies and councils. However, there was still insecurity from war and few settlers came so these institutions had to wait a few years, until 1775 in the case of Dominica.

Trinidad, acquired from Spain in 1802, Essequibo, Demerara and Berbice acquired from Holland in 1814, and St Lucia acquired from France in 1815, were made 'Crown Colonies', that is, they would be administered directly by the Crown through Orders-in-Council. Essequibo, Demerara and Berbice and St Lucia had experienced representative assemblies, the Court of Policy and the Combined Court in the former, and the Conseil Superior in the latter. However, the Crown did not want non-British citizens dominating the legislatures in these colonies. Also emancipation was being considered and the future of representative institutions was uncertain.

Emancipation in 1834–8 brought a big change in outlook towards the representative system. Newly emancipated slaves would be 'freemen' and would want representation. Even before emancipation the assemblies were no longer representative as most whites did not qualify for membership or a vote. After emancipation to talk of representation would be ridiculous as very few blacks, if any, would qualify by property. In any case the whites did not want to be dominated by the blacks in the assemblies. In Britain itself there was not universal suffrage so extending the vote to everyone in the colonies was not considered. Therefore the solution chosen for Trinidad, British Guiana and St Lucia was applied throughout the British Caribbean. Other events through the 1840s to the 1860s reinforced the decision to turn to Crown Colony Government.

Notes

1 The first English colonies were 'proprietary colonies' between 1627 and 1660. The proprietor was a powerful patron to administer the colony for the King.

2 Proprietors were encouraged to summon freemen to assemblies and councils so the representative system is very old in the British Caribbean.

3 Basically the assembly was elected by some means or other and the council was nominated on the basis of a property qualification.

4 On the Restoration of the King in 1660 the proprietary system was abandoned, but the representative system continued.

5 In a colony the Governor corresponded to the King, the Legislative Council to the House of Lords and the Assembly to the House of Commons.

6 The Crown wanted the colonies put into groups for administrative convenience, but the colonies usually resisted this.

7 Dominica, Grenada and St Vincent, all acquired by Britain in 1763, were encouraged to set up representative assemblies.

8 Trinidad, British Guiana and St Lucia, all acquired between 1802 and 1815, were made Crown Colonies because the representative system was thought inappropriate.

9 After emancipation the colonial assemblies were even less representative than they had been before as the vast majority of citizens had no political rights.

10 One of the reasons why Crown Colony Government was introduced was to avoid having to give blacks representation in the legislatures.

Map 9.1: The Morant Bay Rebellion 1865

The Morant Bay Rebellion in Jamaica was the immediate cause of the ending of the representative system of government in the British Caribbean. However, as we saw in the last section, the assemblies had ceased to be representative even before hundreds and thousands of emancipated slaves joined the citizenry. Crown Colony Government was thought to be the answer to all the troubles of the mid-nineteenth century.

In the 1850s and 1860s the general causes for rebellion were found in the economic problems of sugar. By 1854 the Equalisation of Sugar Duties Act of 1846 had brought down sugar prices by ten shillings per cwt and planters had been forced to sell up, throwing thousands out of work. Those in work had to accept wage reductions of 50 per cent or more. The Encumbered Estates Act of 1854 backfired as it also helped to reduce sugar prices and discouraged investment in the sugar industry. Therefore by the mid-1850s there was unemployment, low wages and considerable suffering amongst the poor classes.

The American Civil War, 1861–5, cut the supplies of salt fish, rice and other traditional foods for the poor. The shortage of supply made food prices rise at the same time as wages were falling.

Natural disasters contributed to the distress. Between 1851 and 1854 a cholera epidemic raged through the West Indies killing 40 000 in Jamaica in 1851. As breadwinners died more families were made destitute. Finally between 1863 and 1865 there were three years of drought in Jamaica.

West Indian governments had insufficient revenues to finance any relief so they were powerless to help the poor in their sufferings. Unfortunately they did not seem to have the will to help either as they repeatedly denied that there was a problem. The governments had become so unrepresentative that they probably did not know what was happening to the masses. This was definitely so in Jamaica. In 1862 Edward John Eyre was appointed Lieutenant-Governor. He associated with and took his advice from the leading planters in the island and he was completely lacking in sympathy for the poorer classes. The planters thought that compassion was a sign of weakness and so Eyre met the complaints of suffering with denials, accusation of exaggeration and brutal disregard.

Dr Edward Underhill, secretary of the Baptist Mission Council in England, made a report on the hardships and sufferings he had encountered in his two-year stay in Jamaica from 1863 to 1865. Eyre denied the findings of the report and said they were exaggerations. Similarly when the people of St Ann petitioned Queen Victoria in 1865 for relief from their poverty and the Secretary of State gave them a very unsympathetic reply known as the 'Queen's Advice', it was assumed that Eyre had influenced him. Basically the Queen's Advice told the poor to help themselves and to work hard for whatever wages were being offered. Eyre liked this reply and had 50 000 copies printed and displayed throughout Jamaica in June 1865. This made many people give up hope of help from the government.

On the side of the poor blacks were two outstanding leaders, George William Gordon and Paul Bogle. Gordon was a coloured who championed the blacks. He had the advantages of education, wealth and influence through politics and the press. He hated Governor Eyre and in 1863 denounced him with these words: 'I have never seen an animal more voracious for cruelty and power than the present Governor of Jamaica'. Gordon's attacks on the establishment and its lack of sympathy for the sufferings of the poor were published in his own newspaper, *The Watchman*. He addressed a crowded Underhill Meeting in Kingston in May 1865, on the same theme. It was later to be used in evidence against him.

Bogle was an ex-slave who had become a deacon in the Baptist Church with a chapel at Stony Gut in St Thomas in the East. Whereas Gordon favoured constitutional methods to right the wrongs, Bogle favoured more direct action and eventually violence. Bogle led a march from Stony Gut to Spanish Town to petition Governor Eyre in August 1865, but Eyre would not see him. Bogle returned to Stony Gut and throughout September he trained and armed his supporters. On 7 October Bogle's armed followers released a man from police custody at Morant Bay Court House and they returned to Stony Gut where they beat off attempts to arrest Bogle two days later.

The Morant Bay Rebellion began on 11 October 1865. Armed Volunteers attended the Vestry Meeting in Morant Bay to protect the whites who were expecting trouble. The blacks were provoked by this and attacked the police station from which they obtained arms. The Riot Act was read to the mob which only provoked further violence. The Volunteers opened fire but were driven back into the Court House which was then set on fire, kill-

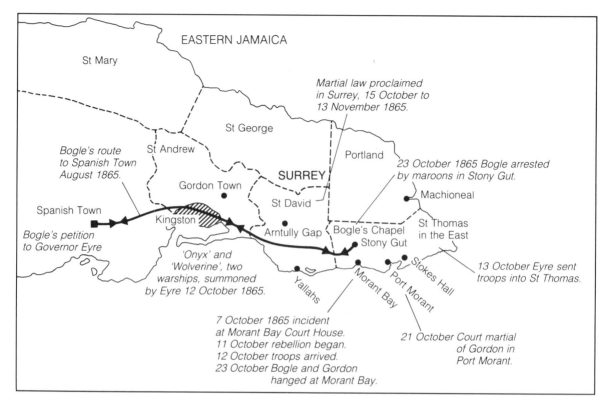

EASTERN JAMAICA

St Mary

St George

Martial law proclaimed in Surrey, 15 October to 13 November 1865.

Bogle's route to Spanish Town August 1865.

St Andrew

Portland

SURREY

23 October 1865 Bogle arrested by maroons in Stony Gut.

Gordon Town

St David

Machioneal

Spanish Town

Kingston

Arntully Gap

Bogle's Chapel

Stony Gut

St Thomas in the East

Bogle's petition to Governor Eyre

'Onyx' and 'Wolverine', two warships, summoned by Eyre 12 October 1865.

Yallahs

Morant Bay

Port Morant

Stokes Hall

13 October Eyre sent troops into St Thomas.

7 October 1865 incident at Morant Bay Court House. 11 October rebellion began. 12 October troops arrived. 23 October Bogle and Gordon hanged at Morant Bay.

21 October Court martial of Gordon in Port Morant.

Map 9.1: The Morant Bay Rebellion 1865

ing some of the Volunteers and magistrates. On that day the death toll was eighteen whites and seventeen blacks.

Bogle and his followers returned to Stony Gut. Rioting and looting soon spread to the plantations in St Thomas and more whites were killed. Troops of the West India Regiment arrived on 12 October and were surprisingly joined by the local maroons. Morant Bay Town was by then quiet so the troops were deployed in the countryside. The warships, *Onyx* and *Wolverine* arrived, having been summoned by Eyre. The Eastern part of Jamaica was put under martial law from 15 October to 13 November but the rebellion was really put down in the first week. It was suppressed with great cruelty. Fifty rebels were killed without trial and one thousand homes were burnt. Altogether two hundred and fifty-four were killed in the fighting, three hundred and fifty-four were executed and over six hundred were flogged. On 23 October Gordon and Bogle were hanged for treason on the site of the Morant Bay Court House. Gordon's involvement was questionable in that he did not incite the people to violence. He was in Kingston at the time of the rebellion and brought by Eyre into a martial law area so he could be sentenced by a court martial. This was illegal.

Eyre was praised by the Commission of Inquiry for putting down the rebellion so quickly and stopping its spread to the rest of the island and to other islands, but was criticised for the brutality of the suppression and the courts. However, the Secretary of State for the Colonies accused Eyre of lacking 'sound judgement' and removed him from office.

Notes

1   The collapse of the sugar industry in Jamaica brought unemployment, poverty and suffering to the poor classes.

2   The American Civil War added to their hardships by cutting the supplies of traditional foods and driving prices up.

3   Natural disasters, a cholera epidemic and droughts, plunged the poor into even further distress.

4   West Indian Governments were incapable and unwilling to give relief.

5   This was true of Jamaica's Governor Eyre who denied any hardships or said that they were exaggerated.

6   The poor had tried to petition Queen Victoria but received an unsympathetic reply, probably due to Eyre's influence.

7   Therefore by August 1865, the people of Jamaica were desperate.

8   The poor blacks were championed by George William Gordon and Paul Bogle.

9   In August Bogle led a march from Stony Gut to Spanish Town to petition Governor Eyre without any success.

10   Bogle and his followers decided that violence was the only way to improve their situation.

11   A tense situation where both sides were armed led to the rebellion in Morant Bay on 11 October 1865.

12   The Rebellion was suppressed with great cruelty and the loss of six hundred and eight lives.

13   Gordon and Bogle were hanged for treason, but Eyre was exonerated for his part except that the Secretary of State dismissed him for unsound judgement.

14   The Morant Bay Rebellion was the immediate cause for the change to Crown Colony Government

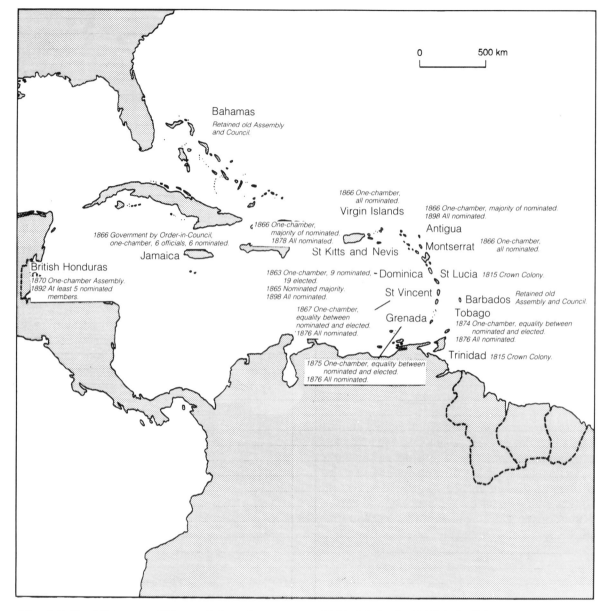

Bahamas
Retained old Assembly and Council.

0   500 km

1866 One-chamber, all nominated.
Virgin Islands

1866 One-chamber, majority of nominated.
1898 All nominated.
Antigua

1866 One-chamber, majority of nominated.
1878 All nominated.
St Kitts and Nevis

Montserrat   1866 One-chamber, all nominated.

1866 Government by Order-in-Council, one-chamber, 6 officials, 6 nominated.
Jamaica

British Honduras
1870 One-chamber Assembly.
1892 At least 5 nominated members.

1863 One-chamber, 9 nominated, 19 elected.
1865 Nominated majority.
1898 All nominated.
Dominica   St Lucia   1815 Crown Colony.

St Vincent

1867 One-chamber, equality between nominated and elected.
1876 All nominated.

Grenada

Barbados   *Retained old Assembly and Council.*

Tobago
1874 One-chamber, equality between nominated and elected.
1876 All nominated.

Trinidad   1815 Crown Colony.

1875 One-chamber, equality between nominated and elected.
1876 All nominated.

Map 9.2: Establishment of Crown Colony Government, 1866–98, in the British Caribbean

Map 9.2: Establishment of Crown Colony Government, 1866–98, in the British Caribbean

Crown Colony Government was thought desirable and necessary after the Morant Bay Rebellion because: a) strong government was necessary to deal with the violence threatened by poor blacks; b) if the representative system continued blacks would dominate whites in the assemblies; c) Crown Colony Government could raise taxes without the fear of opposition; d) taxes were necessary to provide the revenues needed for such forces as had been used to suppress the Morant Bay Rebellion; e) Crown Colony Government would cut out the delays caused by debates and votes in assemblies.

In Jamaica the Assembly dissolved itself in December 1865 and asked the British Government to give it a new constitution. Crown Colony Government was set up by Order-in-Council in 1866. The retiring Assembly had proposed a new Legislative Assembly of twelve nominated and twelve elected members but this was refused as it would re-introduce the elective principle which it had been decided to abandon. In June 1866, Jamaica received a Legislative Assembly of six official and six nominated members. The British Government retained the power to govern Jamaica by Orders-in-Council.

In 1867 St Vincent changed its own constitution by giving itself a new one-chamber Legislative Assembly of equal numbers of nominated and elected members, as did Grenada in 1875. In 1874 Tobago gave itself one chamber but with more elected than nominated members. However, all these three Windward Islands asked the British Government for a new constitution in 1876 and an Imperial Act gave them Legislative Assemblies of all nominated members.

In 1866 St Kitts, Nevis and Antigua established one-chamber assemblies with a majority of nominated members by local acts. In 1878 St Kitts and Nevis changed to all nominated members but Antigua and Dominica did not do this until 1898. British Honduras changed to a one-chamber assembly in 1870 and in 1892 added that there had to be at least five nominated members.

The Bahamas and Barbados were the only two colonies which did not adopt Crown Colony Government but kept their old assemblies. They felt that they were outside the mainstream of West Indian politics and free from the threat of racial unrest. The Barbados Assembly was the oldest in the British Caribbean and the people wanted to keep it. In Barbados the people felt that the way to reform was through the Assembly and gradually to let it become more representative. Barbados did nearly lose its Assembly but not because of the pressure to change after Morant Bay, but because of its refusal to do what Governor Pope-Hennessy wanted and join the Windward Islands Federation of 1876. The people rioted in support of their Assembly and Pope-Hennessy was removed.

Therefore, instead of more representation which was the trend of constitutional development, the British Caribbean, with the exception of the Bahamas and Barbados, abandoned the representative principle. Theorists spoke of 'effective government' which in the West Indian context meant that the Governor had the power to carry out his policies without any opposition in a subservient legislature whose members he had nominated himself. The officials worked for the government, thus the Attorney-General, Chief Secretary, and Financial Secretary always held seats along with the secretaries from the leading departments like Agriculture and Health. The nominated members were chosen to be 'yes-men' for the Governor.

The whites who had surrendered their rights thought that Crown Colony Government would preserve their privileged position, but the Colonial Office in London wanted Crown Colony Government to be above sectional interest and serve the whole population. It understood that representative government had neglected the needs of the whole community. Reforms like public works and social services were given priority. Nowhere was this better illustrated than by Jamaica where the Governor from 1866 to 1874, Sir John Peter Grant, first reformed the budget and then put the revenues to the needs of the people. He gave them district courts, a police force to replace the hated Volunteers, a Public Works Department, a Health Service, the Rio Cobre Irrigation Scheme, the disestablishment of the Church of England and many benefits for the peasants. Similar reforms were undertaken in other parts of the British Caribbean.

Notes

1 West Indian Colonial Assemblies dissolved themselves in the belief that Crown Colony Government would give strong, prompt and effective government, the need for which had been demonstrated by Morant Bay.

2 The representative principle had been discredited so the Colonial Office wanted no elected members in the Jamaican Legislature.

3 The Bahamas and Barbados alone did not adopt Crown Colony Government but retained their original assemblies.

4 All the other British Caribbean colonies adopted one-chamber legislatures.

5 All colonies except Jamaica at first included some elected members in their assemblies but by 1898 they had gone over to all nominated members except for British Honduras.

6 The new legislatures consisted of officials who were the leading civil servants and members nominated by the Governor for their loyal support.

7 Instead of favouring the whites the Colonial Office tried to govern in the interests of the whole community by introducing reforms which representative government had neglected.

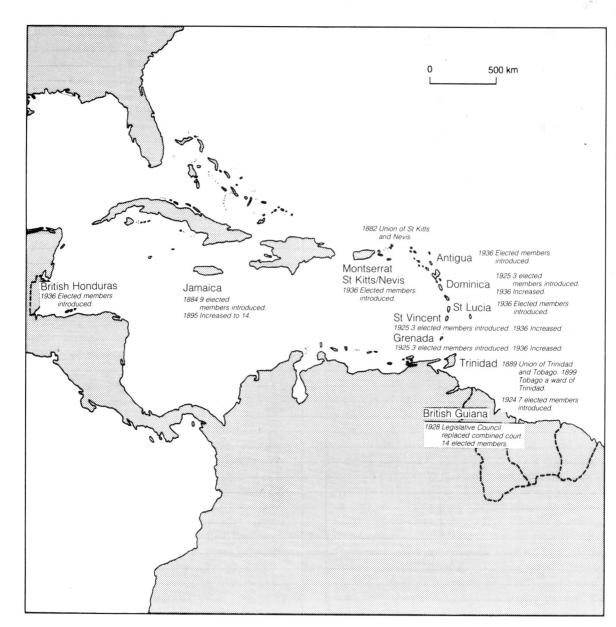

1882 Union of St Kitts
and Nevis.

Antigua   1936 Elected members
              introduced.

Montserrat
St Kitts/Nevis   Dominica   1925 3 elected
1936 Elected members   members introduced.
introduced.   1936 Increased.

                    St Lucia   1936 Elected members
                                   introduced.
St Vincent
1925 3 elected members introduced. 1936 Increased.
Grenada
1925 3 elected members introduced. 1936 Increased.

British Honduras   Trinidad   1889 Union of Trinidad
1936 Elected members   and Tobago. 1899
introduced.   Tobago a ward of
                                                   Trinidad.
Jamaica
1884 9 elected   1924 7 elected members
members introduced.   introduced.
1895 Increased to 14.
                    British Guiana
                    1928 Legislative Council
                      replaced combined court.
                      14 elected members.

Map 9.3: The re-introduction of the elective principle

Map 9.3: The re-introduction of the elective principle

West Indian nationalists looked on Crown Colony Government as a step backwards because they were further from governing themselves than they had been before 1866. Therefore they wanted to try some form of representation again. Crown Colony Government was out of touch with the masses because the Governor and officials were British citizens who came to the West Indies for short tours of duty and then departed. The 1935–8 disturbances made it clear how out of touch the officials had become.

The changes to Crown Colony Government were made gradually, that is a few elected members were introduced, then a few more, then a few more and so on. The Governor always retained over-riding control because up to 1944 he was always assured of a majority in the Legislative Council. Even this majority was not necessary as he could always over-rule the Council with his power of veto. The Legislative Councils began to consist of official members, nominated members and elected members. Of course, the official members voted with the Governor, but so did the nominated members because the Governor had appointed them. The Legislative Council gradually split into two sides, the official/nominated majority on one side and the elected members on the other. This was really the same as 'Government' and 'Opposition'. This was not apparent until much later when nationalism became strong in the British Caribbean.

In the late 1930s and 1940s the number of elected members in some territories became large enough to have an influence in politics so control of these members became important. Political parties sprang up to try to win these seats and have their policies put into effect. The re-introduction of the elective principle was a very important step in constitutional and political development.

The elective principle was re-introduced in Jamaica in 1884 when elected members equal in number to nominated and official members entered the Legislative Council. Its composition then was: four officials, five nominated and nine elected members. In 1895 the 'Government' side was increased to fifteen and the elected to fourteen.

Trinidad had been a Crown Colony since 1815 and it was over a hundred years before any modification came. In 1921 Major Wood of the Colonial Office recommended to the Secretary of State some measure of representation in West Indian legislatures. In 1924 seven elected members entered the Legislative Council in Trinidad and its composition was: twelve officials, six nominated and seven elected members, allowing the Government a comfortable majority.

In 1925 the elective principle was introduced again in Dominica, Grenada and St Vincent. In 1936 it was introduced in Antigua, St Kitts-Nevis, Montserrat, St Lucia and British Honduras. The Second World War, 1939–45, delayed further constitutional changes, but on the other hand it made the demands for change stronger and the Colonial Government more receptive to these demands.

Notes

1   Crown Colony Government was a step backwards in constitutional development because it made the Government even more out of touch with the masses.
2   Nationalists wanted the elective principle re-introduced but it was done gradually and the Governor's majority was always assured.
3   A large number of elected members could influence policy if they spoke with the same voice and therefore political parties emerged to control these seats.
4   The Colonial Office agreed to some form of representation in the British Caribbean after 1921 (N.B. Jamaica already had it).
5   The Second World War held back constitutional development.

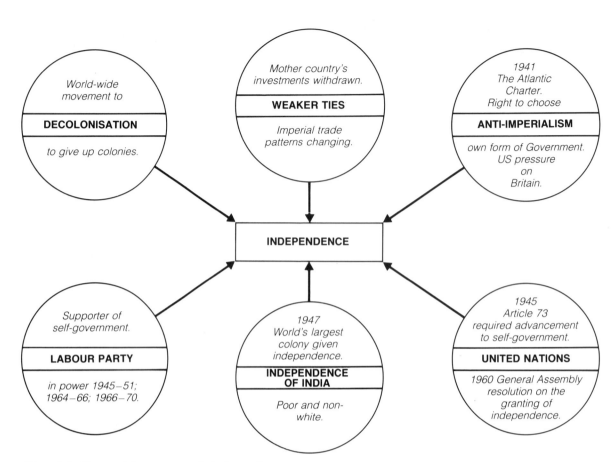

Chart 9.1: External forces towards independence

Chart 9.1: External forces towards independence

The Second World War changed the power structure of the world greatly. The United States was a super-power and imperial Britain relatively weak. Britain's victory was almost Pyrrhic in that the victor suffered as much as the vanquished. Britain had to bow to pressure from the super powers, the United States and Russia which were both anti-imperialist. Britain and the United States made an alliance in 1941, the Atlantic Charter. One of the conditions that the United States insisted on was that Britain should free her colonial peoples and the United States was expecting to see this carried out.

In 1945 the United Nations Organisation was born and it became the strongest force against colonialism. In its Charter it insisted on progress towards self-government and it watched what the colonial powers were doing towards Article 73 as it was called. The United Nations expected Britain to proceed much faster in decolonisation than she did. Russia in particular denounced imperialism in the United Nations and this attack was joined by more and more countries in the Communist Bloc and the Third World countries as they gained independence and took their places in the United Nations. India joined in 1947 and her support for decolonisation was particularly powerful as she had just been freed from Britain herself. In 1957 Ghana became Britain's first African colony to gain independence and her voice was also very important. The pressure on Britain to decolonise mounted and in 1960 an Afro-Asian resolution on independence condemning the colonial powers was adopted by 89 votes to nil in the General Assembly. Following this came the United Nations Committee on Colonisation in 1961. There followed the great wave of decolonisation in the early 1960s.

Britain's attitude had changed and she was more receptive to these demands, especially when a Labour Government was in power. Yet it was a Conservative Government which carried out the wave of decolonisation in Africa and the Caribbean between 1960 and 1964. Previously Britain had only given self-government to white-ruled dominions, Australia, Canada, New Zealand and South Africa. Soon after the Second World War she gave independence to India, a vast, very poor, non-white territory. Burma received independence a year later. The rest of the non-white empire took note that Britain was willing to give independence to under-developed black countries. At first economic viability mattered, i.e. the country should be able to stand on its own feet economically and not subject to 'economic imperialism' but later this did not seem to be a consideration. However, Britain did attempt to prepare her colonies for independence economically as well as in other ways.

In the twentieth century Britain had fought two world wars, 1914–18 and 1939–45, which had required calling in all her reserves of finance. These came from transferring investments from the colonies to the war effort. This weakened the ties between the Mother Country and her colonies. Also we have seen that trade from the colonies no longer automatically went to the Mother Country. There was 'imperial preference' but the colonies were able to trade in the world market, for example the British Caribbean increased its trade with the United States throughout the nineteenth century. Again this weakened colonial ties.

All other imperial powers, Spain, Portugal, France, Germany and Belgium had been caught in the tide of decolonisation. Spain had given up her American Empire in the nineteenth century. Germany had been forced to cede her colonies in the First World War. The Portuguese Empire had disappeared except in Africa (and Macao). After the Second World War France and Britain were the exceptions and could no longer reasonably resist the decolonisation pressure.

Notes

1 After the Second World War Britain was more likely to bow to pressure from countries like the United States and Russia which were much more powerful.
2 The United Nations was the strongest force against colonialism because at its meetings all anti-imperialist and ex-colonial countries attacked Britain for continuing to hold colonies.
3 The independence of India in 1947 showed that Britain was prepared to grant independence to poor, non-white colonies.
4 Britain's attitude had changed and both political parties played their part in decolonisation.
5 The two world wars drained Britain's resources and thereby weakened her ties to the colonies.
6 When decolonisation had taken place and was taking place in other countries Britain and France could not be the only ones not to decolonise.

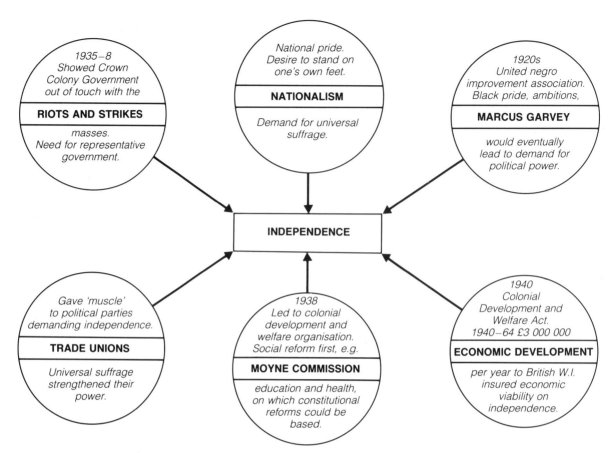

Chart 9.2: Internal forces towards independence in the British Caribbean

The circles in the chart contain the following text:

RIOTS AND STRIKES
1935–8
Showed Crown
Colony Government
out of touch with the
masses.
Need for representative
government.

NATIONALISM
National pride.
Desire to stand on
one's own feet.
Demand for universal
suffrage.

MARCUS GARVEY
1920s
United negro
improvement association.
Black pride, ambitions,
would eventually
lead to demand for
political power.

TRADE UNIONS
Gave 'muscle'
to political parties
demanding independence.
Universal suffrage
strengthened their
power.

MOYNE COMMISSION
1938
Led to colonial
development and
welfare organisation.
Social reform first, e.g.
education and health,
on which constitutional
reforms could be
based.

ECONOMIC DEVELOPMENT
1940
Colonial
Development and
Welfare Act.
1940–64 £3 000 000
per year to British W.I.
insured economic
viability on
independence.

INDEPENDENCE

Chart 9.2: Internal forces towards independence in the British Caribbean

In the 1920s most blacks in the British Caribbean had no political rights, for example they could neither vote nor hold political office because they did not have the property qualification and in any case lived under Crown Colony Government. They felt like second class citizens in their own countries. Marcus Garvey had an appeal to them because he gave them pride in themselves through his United Negro Improvement Association. The blacks were shown how productive they were and how West Indian economies depended on their labour as there was a reliance on primary production. When the blacks were organised into unions they had political 'muscle' even if they had no political rights. As soon as they became conscious of this and proud of it they demanded voting rights. Universal adult suffrage made them the most important class in politics.

The riots and strikes of 1935–8 shook the Colonial Government because the officials and nominated members in the Legislative Councils had been unaware of the unrest. The riots and strikes showed that Crown Colony Government was failing and must be changed. First of all the Councils had to be made more representative of the people. Whereas the strikers were interested in better working conditions and pay, their leaders were interested in social reforms and political demands.

The Moyne Commission came to the British West Indies to investigate the unrest. Its recommendation placed social reforms first but added that there should be more representation in the government. However, social reforms like more and better education would make the people more aware of the failings of the constitution and demand changes. Equal educational standards would lead to the demand for equal opportunities and political rights.

The Moyne Commission recommended the set- ting up of the Colonial Development and Welfare Organisation. This led to the Colonial Development and Welfare Act which in turn set up the Welfare Fund in 1940. From then to 1964 the British West Indies received an average of £3 000 000 per year from the Fund. This money was used to create the infrastructure necessary to enable the countries to be both economically and politically independent when the time for independence came.

Crown Colony Government made it clear to the people that they were being ruled by a foreign country. It bred resentment against this which led to nationalism. Nationalists wanted to throw off colonial rule and rule themselves. Greater contact with other countries as in the Second World War, strengthened nationalism. Anti-colonialism dominated the intellectual classes in the British Caribbean after the war. It was also strong in the trade union movement. Nationalist politicians with the backing of the masses could not be denied. Nationalism was the emotional force which brought independence.

Notes

1 In the 1920s Marcus Garvey's United Negro Improvement Association gave blacks in the British Caribbean pride in themselves and the confidence later to make political demands.
2 The riots and strikes of 1935–8 showed that Crown Colony Government was out of touch with the masses and would have to be changed.
3 The Moyne Commission recommended social reforms which were the foundation from which constitutional demands sprang.
4 It also recommended the setting up of the Colonial Development and Welfare Organisation which gave rise to the Welfare Fund which eventually helped British Caribbean countries to be economically independent.
5 Nationalism was the force which drove people to shake off colonial rule and to stand on their own feet politically.

Table 9.2: Constitutional development in Barbados, British Guiana, Jamaica and Trinidad at a glance.

Territory	Elective principle	Majority elected in Legislative Council	Party system	Universal adult suffrage	Ministerial system	Prime Minister or Premier	Cabinet government	Full internal self-government	Independence
Barbados			1946	1950	1954	1954	1958	1961	1966 (Nov)
British Guiana	1891 (Direct election)	1943	1947	1953	1957	1953 Chief Minister 1961 Premier	1961	1961	1966 (May)
Jamaica	1884	1944	1944	1944	1953	1953 Chief Minister	1957 Council of Ministers 1958 Cabinet	1959	1962 (Aug)
Trinidad	1924	1941	1946	1945	1950	1956 Chief Minister 1959 Premier	1959	1961	1962 (Aug)

Table 9.2: Explanation of terms in Table 9.2

1	*Elective principle*	The idea that the people should elect their own representatives in the legislature so that government might be more in accord with the wishes of the masses.
2	*Majority of Legislative Council elected*	The representatives of the people could out-vote the civil servants and the Governor's nominees in the Legislative Council.
3	*Party system*	Political parties are formed to capture the votes of the electorate and the party with most votes in a constituency wins that seat in the Legislative Council and the party with most seats forms the government.
4	*Universal adult suffrage*	Every man and woman over the age of twenty-one has a vote. (Later sometimes voting age reduced to eighteen.)
5	*Ministerial system*	An elected member of the Legislative Council belonging to the majority party is chosen to head a department of the Civil Service, e.g. agriculture. He is completely responsible for it and must answer for it in the Legislative Council.
6	*Prime Minister/ Chief Minister/ Premier*	The leader of the majority party in the Legislature who is asked by the Governor to form a government which he does by choosing certain colleagues in his party to accept ministerial posts.
7	*Cabinet government*	The Government's policy is decided upon and carried out by a committee selected by the Prime Minister and there are no officials or Governor's nominees.
8	*Full internal self-government*	The elected representatives of the people through a Prime Minister and Cabinet are in complete control of all affairs except foreign affairs and defence which remain under the Governor.
9	*Independence*	All internal and external affairs are under the complete control of the elected government. The colonial power has transferred the government totally to the citizens of the country.

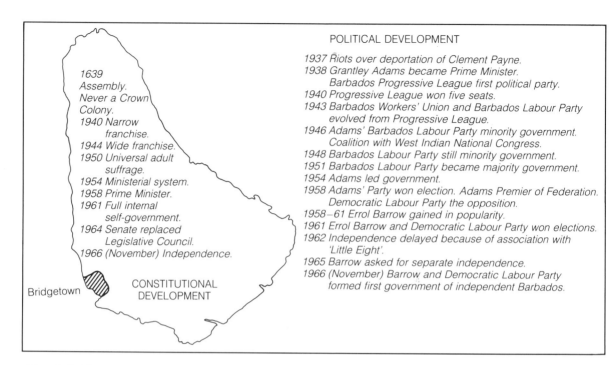

1639
Assembly.
Never a Crown
Colony.
1940 Narrow
franchise.
1944 Wide franchise.
1950 Universal adult
suffrage.
1954 Ministerial system.
1958 Prime Minister.
1961 Full internal
self-government.
1964 Senate replaced
Legislative Council.
1966 (November) Independence.

Bridgetown

CONSTITUTIONAL
DEVELOPMENT

1937 Riots over deportation of Clement Payne.
1938 Grantley Adams became Prime Minister.
Barbados Progressive League first political party.
1940 Progressive League won five seats.
1943 Barbados Workers' Union and Barbados Labour Party
evolved from Progressive League.
1946 Adams' Barbados Labour Party minority government.
Coalition with West Indian National Congress.
1948 Barbados Labour Party still minority government.
1951 Barbados Labour Party became majority government.
1954 Adams led government.
1958 Adams' Party won election. Adams Premier of Federation.
Democratic Labour Party the opposition.
1958–61 Errol Barrow gained in popularity.
1961 Errol Barrow and Democratic Labour Party won elections.
1962 Independence delayed because of association with
'Little Eight'.
1965 Barrow asked for separate independence.
1966 (November) Barrow and Democratic Labour Party
formed first government of independent Barbados.

Map 9.4: Movement to independence: Barbados

Map 9.4: Movement to independence: Barbados

Barbados had had a representative Assembly since 1639 and had never changed to Crown Colony Government. This meant that constitutional and political progress should have been smoother than in the Crown Colonies. To a certain extent this was true as Barbados in the nineteenth century had been free of racial disturbances like the Morant Bay Rebellion in Jamaica. However, Barbados did suffer from a serious riot in 1937 but then her constitutional and political position was just like that of the other British Caribbean colonies. There had been little coloured or black representation in the legislature in the nineteenth century and first quarter of the twentieth, and these riots and strikes showed that more representation was needed. As a result of the 1937 unrest Grantley Adams formed the Barbados Progressive League, at first registered as a political party. Its trade union legislation, including Workmen's Compensation, and nationalisation, appealed to the workers, and its demand for universal suffrage and self-government appealed to the nationalists. The Progressive League won only five seats in 1940 because few people had the vote.

Trade union legislation was passed in Barbados in 1942 and in the following year the union and the party were separated as they were following different goals, but the Barbados Workers' Union and the Barbados Labour Party still gave each other mutual support. After the vote was extended to many more people in 1944, the 1946 elections had much greater significance. Also the new Bushe Constitution meant that the winning party could have four elected members under the party leader in the Executive Council. However, Adams' Party did not win sufficient seats to exploit this chance of responsible government and he had to join a coalition with the West Indian National Congress and share the seats. Again in 1948 Adams found that he was leading a minority government and responsible government was still not possible. In the Legislative Council his policy of nationalisation was frustrated by white property-owners in 1949, but universal adult suffrage in 1950 strengthened his position. The Barbados Labour Party still had the support of the Workers' Union and with the workers' votes behind him Adams asked for constitutional reforms with a view to independence. After his victory in the 1951 elections he pressed for a ministerial system which would give responsible government to his party as he had a clear majority. He passed further trade union and factory legislation to fulfil his mandate from the Workers' Union.

Between 1953 and 1958 Adams lost the support of the Barbados Workers' Union because he abandoned the policy of nationalisation. The Union transferred its support to a new party, the Democratic Labour Party under Errol Barrow. Adams was not able to push ahead with his constitutional reforms. The Barbados Labour Party still won fifteen out of twenty-four seats in the 1956 election and when Cabinet Government was introduced in 1958 Adams could call himself Prime Minister of Barbados.

However, he chose to be Premier of the Federation and could not devote so much time to Barbadian politics. Barrow convinced the Secretary of State that the opposition was responsible enough to form a future government and he gained the confidence of the people. Adams lost further popularity over the unemployment issue following the Deep Water Harbour Scheme. The Democratic Labour Party easily won the 1961 elections and performed well in its first year in office. This party could lead the country to independence.

However, independence was delayed for four years. Jamaica and Trinidad chose to leave the Federation and take separate independence, but Barbados sacrificed separate independence for the economic benefits of a larger union with the 'Little Eight'. The 'Windfall Crisis' of 1964 hurt Barrow's prestige but in 1965 he still felt confident enough of his support to lead Barbados to independence. Barbados withdrew from the 'Little Eight'. The Lancaster House Conference set November 1966 as the date for independence and drew up a constitution. The Queen would be Head of State, represented in Barbados by a Governor. A Prime Minister as leader of the majority party would choose a Cabinet responsible to the House of Assembly and the Senate. Errol Barrow won the independence elections and became the first Prime Minister of independent Barbados.

Notes

1 The serious riot in Barbados in 1937 showed that more representation was needed.
2 Grantley Adams formed the Barbados Progressive League to carry out labour reforms and ask for universal adult suffrage.
3 Adams led minority governments between 1946 and 1950 and was not able to carry through his constitutional reforms.
4 Universal adult suffrage introduced in 1950 enabled Adams to achieve a ministerial system and to pass legislation on behalf of the workers.
5 Between 1953 and 1958 the Barbados Workers' Union transferred its support to the Democratic Labour Party because Adams dropped nationalisation from his programme.
6 In 1958 Adams still held a majority but he became Premier of the Federation in the same year and lost ground in Barbadian politics.
7 Barbados did not achieve independence in the same year as Jamaica and Trinidad because she remained a member of the 'Little Eight'.
8 Barbados left the 'Little Eight' in 1965 and gained her own independence in November 1966.
9 The Governor represented the Queen, and a Prime Minister and Cabinet responsible to the House of Assembly and Senate led the government.

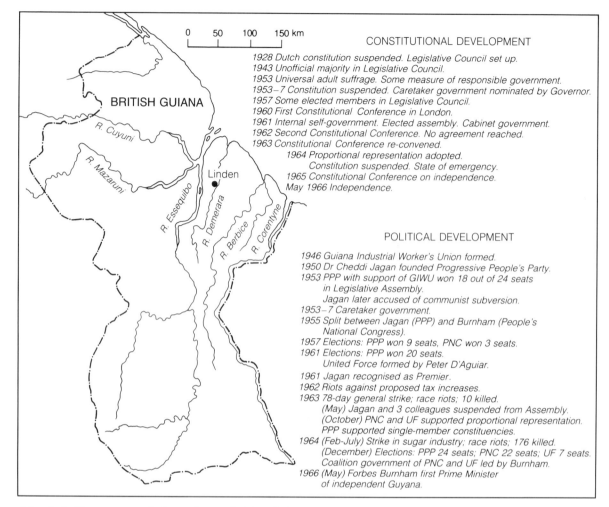

CONSTITUTIONAL DEVELOPMENT

1928 Dutch constitution suspended. Legislative Council set up.
1943 Unofficial majority in Legislative Council.
1953 Universal adult suffrage. Some measure of responsible government.
1953–7 Constitution suspended. Caretaker government nominated by Governor.
1957 Some elected members in Legislative Council.
1960 First Constitutional Conference in London.
1961 Internal self-government. Elected assembly. Cabinet government.
1962 Second Constitutional Conference. No agreement reached.
1963 Constitutional Conference re-convened.
1964 Proportional representation adopted.
     Constitution suspended. State of emergency.
1965 Constitutional Conference on independence.
May 1966 Independence.

POLITICAL DEVELOPMENT

1946 Guiana Industrial Worker's Union formed.
1950 Dr Cheddi Jagan founded Progressive People's Party.
1953 PPP with support of GIWU won 18 out of 24 seats
     in Legislative Assembly.
     Jagan later accused of communist subversion.
1953–7 Caretaker government.
1955 Split between Jagan (PPP) and Burnham (People's
     National Congress).
1957 Elections: PPP won 9 seats, PNC won 3 seats.
1961 Elections: PPP won 20 seats.
     United Force formed by Peter D'Aguiar.
1961 Jagan recognised as Premier.
1962 Riots against proposed tax increases.
1963 78-day general strike; race riots; 10 killed.
     (May) Jagan and 3 colleagues suspended from Assembly.
     (October) PNC and UF supported proportional representation.
     PPP supported single-member constituencies.
1964 (Feb-July) Strike in sugar industry; race riots; 176 killed.
     (December) Elections: PPP 24 seats; PNC 22 seats; UF 7 seats.
     Coalition government of PNC and UF led by Burnham.
1966 (May) Forbes Burnham first Prime Minister
     of independent Guyana.

Map 9.5: Movement to independence: British Guiana

Map 9.5: Movement to independence: British Guiana

In 1815 British Guiana inherited the old Dutch Constitution with a Court of Policy of four official and four unofficial members, and a Combined Court consisting of the Court of Policy and six Financial Representatives. The Combined Court had control over taxation and finance. Therefore British Guiana already had an advanced constitution with the elected members having control over financial affairs. In 1928 the Dutch Constitution was suspended and the Combined Court became the Legislative Council with some elected members. In 1943 the elected members became a majority in the Legislative Council.

The first political parties appeared in 1947. In 1950 Dr Cheddi Jagan formed the People's Pro-

gressive Party by merging his Political Affairs Committee wirh Dr J.B. Singh's British Guiana Labour Party. Jagan's People's Progressive Party had no union support so Jagan allied with the Guiana Industrial Workers' Union to contest the 1953 elections. In 1953 a new constitution introduced universal adult suffrage, a House of Assembly of twenty-four elected seats and three official, and a State Council of nine members. Six ministers each responsible for a government department came from the elected members of the House of Assembly but they were responsible to the Governor, not to the House of Assembly, so there was not responsible government.

Jagan's party won these important elections with eighteen out of twenty-four seats. He demanded self-government quickly but he offended the British Government with his Communist sympathies so the Governor suspended the Constitution and governed with a nominated caretaker government from 1953 to 1957. This held back British Guiana's constitutional progress.

In this period, in 1955, Forbes Burnham split from the People's Progressive Party and formed the People's National Congress. Burnham wanted self-government but he disagreed with Jagan's methods. He saw that there was nothing to be gained by antagonising the Colonial Government. Also Jagan was an Indian and Burnham was an African and this split introduced race into politics. Jagan was more to blame for this as he used *apan-jaht* (supporting one's race) into his party.

Jagan won the 1957 elections with nine seats against Burnham's three (only fourteen seats were being contested after the suspended constitution). He also won the 1961 elections with twenty seats against fourteen won by the other two parties together. A new, right-wing party, the United Force led by Peter d'Aguiar, had entered these elections.

In 1961 British Guiana gained internal self-government with a Prime Minister and a Cabinet responsible to a fully-elected House of Assembly. British Guiana was ready for independence in 1962, but Jagan's radical policies brought another setback. Amongst other measures he proposed to levy very high duties on all imported goods and to increase taxation of the wealthy. Prices would have risen sharply and there were strikes and race riots resulting in ten deaths in 1963. The Governor declared a State of Emergency and once again constitutional advance was delayed.

Another delay arose at the Constitutional Conference in London in 1962. The Conference had to be prorogued because the three political parties could not agree on an independence constitution. The People's National Congress and the United Force supported proportional representation with the whole of British Guiana as one constituency to avoid racial bias. The People's Progressive Party favoured single-member constituencies. The parties agreed to submit the decision to Duncan Sandys, the Secretary of State for the Colonies. He adopted proportional representation. Jagan refused to accept this decision and called a 'Freedom Rally' and a strike by the Guiana Agricultural

Workers' Union. Inter-racial violence flared up again and one hundred and seventy-six were killed in 1964. However, the British Government was determined to press on to independence.

In the 1964 elections Jagan won twenty-four seats but Burnham formed a coalition with the United Force giving him control of twenty-nine seats (PNC 22 seats, UF 7), so the Governor asked him to form a government. Jagan was furious at being out-manoeuvred and in a minority for the first time since 1947, and boycotted the 1965 elections to decide the government on independence. Therefore Forbes Burnham became the first Prime Minister of independent Guyana in May 1966.

Notes

1 The Dutch Constitution was representative, giving elected members financial control and was therefore an advanced constitution for the time.

2 In 1928 the Combined Court was replaced by the Legislative Council.

3 Jagan's Progressive People's Party won the 1953 elections with the support of the Guiana Industrial Workers' Union.

4 The Governor suspended the constitution and governed through a nominated caretaker government from 1953 to 1957 because he accused Jagan of Communist subversion.

5 In 1955 Forbes Burnham split from the Progressive People's Party and formed the People's National Congress.

6 Race was a factor in politics then because the People's Progressive Party was supported by Indians and the People's National Congress was supported by Africans.

7 Race riots in 1963 resulted in ten deaths, and in 1964 in 176 deaths.

8 The 1962 Independence Conference broke up without agreement on a constitution.

9 The Secretary of State decided on proportional representation as it would help to remove racial bias.

10 Forbes Burnham led a coalition government after the 1964 elections and this was the government which took British Guiana to independence in May, 1966.

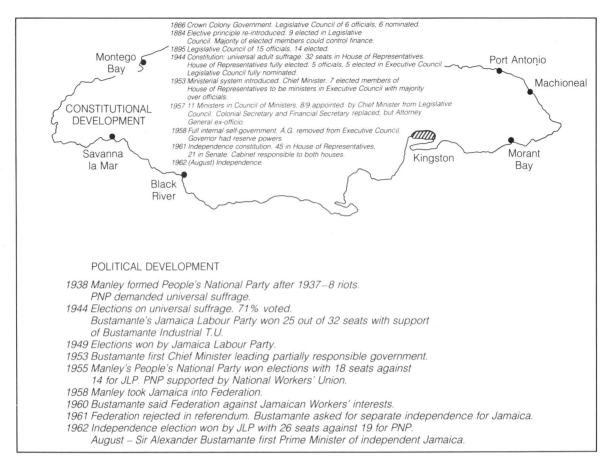

1866 Crown Colony Government. Legislative Council of 6 officials, 6 nominated.
1884 Elective principle re-introduced. 9 elected in Legislative
    Council. Majority of elected members could control finance.
1895 Legislative Council of 15 officials, 14 elected.
1944 Constitution: universal adult suffrage: 32 seats in House of Representatives.
    House of Representatives fully elected: 5 officials, 5 elected in Executive Council.
    Legislative Council fully nominated.
1953 Ministerial system introduced. Chief Minister. 7 elected members of
    House of Representatives to be ministers in Executive Council with majority
    over officials.
1957 11 Ministers in Council of Ministers, 8/9 appointed by Chief Minister from Legislative
    Council. Colonial Secretary and Financial Secretary replaced, but Attorney
    General ex-officio.
1958 Full internal self-government. A.G. removed from Executive Council.
    Governor had reserve powers.
1961 Independence constitution. 45 in House of Representatives,
    21 in Senate. Cabinet responsible to both houses.
1962 (August) Independence.

CONSTITUTIONAL DEVELOPMENT

Montego Bay · Port Antonio · Machioneal · Savanna la Mar · Black River · Kingston · Morant Bay

POLITICAL DEVELOPMENT

1938 Manley formed People's National Party after 1937–8 riots.
    PNP demanded universal suffrage.
1944 Elections on universal suffrage. 71% voted.
    Bustamante's Jamaica Labour Party won 25 out of 32 seats with support
    of Bustamante Industrial T.U.
1949 Elections won by Jamaica Labour Party.
1953 Bustamante first Chief Minister leading partially responsible government.
1955 Manley's People's National Party won elections with 18 seats against
    14 for JLP. PNP supported by National Workers' Union.
1958 Manley took Jamaica into Federation.
1960 Bustamante said Federation against Jamaican Workers' interests.
1961 Federation rejected in referendum. Bustamante asked for separate independence for Jamaica.
1962 Independence election won by JLP with 26 seats against 19 for PNP.
    August – Sir Alexander Bustamante first Prime Minister of independent Jamaica.

Map 9.6: Movement to independence: Jamaica

Map 9.6: Movement to independence: Jamaica

Crown Colony Government did not stop Jamaicans being politically active and they were anxious to return to some form of representation in the legislature. In 1884 nine elected members were introduced but more significantly five of these would have a casting vote in financial matters. These two principles, i.e. elected members and financial responsibility, were extended in 1895.

Major political developments took place as a result of the riots and strikes of 1937–8. Alexander Bustamante became the labour leader and first formed the Jamaica Workers' and Tradesmen's Union with A.G.S. Coombes. In 1937 Bustamante petitioned King George VI about the poor conditions and poverty of the Jamaican working classes. However, in 1938 he was imprisoned for his part in the strikes. Norman Manley acted as lawyer to secure his release. On his release Bustamante

formed the Bustamante Industrial Trade Union which later gave valuable support to his Jamaica Labour Party.

Meanwhile Manley had formed the People's National Party in 1938 and while Bustamante was imprisoned and later interned for another seventeen months at the start of the War, the PNP took over the administration of the BITU. In 1942 Bustamante resumed control of the BITU and refused a political alliance with Manley. Therefore Bustamante needed a party and Manley needed a union to achieve their political aims. Bustamante formed the Jamaica Labour Party to contest the 1944 elections but Manley stayed without a union behind his party. Jamaican politics were dominated by the rivalry between these two between 1944 and 1967, and the rivalry between their supporters frequently turned to violence, as when 19 were killed in 1946.

The 1944 constitutional changes made the elections of that year very important. Universal suffrage meant they would test political support comprehensively. A fully-elected House of Representatives gave the winning party a considerable voice in policy (but a fully-nominated Legislative Council would act as a check on that), and five elected members in the Executive Council was a preparation for responsible government.

There was a 72 per cent poll in 1944 and the Jamaican Labour Party won 25 out of 32 seats, demonstrating to Manley how badly he lacked union support. The JLP also won the 1949 elections but with a reduced majority. In 1952 Manley formed the National Workers' Union to back his PNP.

The 1953 constitution introduced some measure of responsible government in that the Chief Minister and seven other ministers chosen from elected members of the House of Representatives held a majority in the Executive Council. Full responsible government for the majority party was checked by the presence of the Attorney-General, the Colonial Secretary and the Financial Secretary as ex-officio members of the Executive Council. Bustamante was the Chief Minister.

With union support in the 1955 elections the PNP won eighteen seats against fourteen for the JLP. The 1957 constitution introduced a Council of Ministers of eleven of which Manley could choose eight or nine from his party in the Legislative Council. Still the Attorney-General remained in the Executive Council but the Financial and Colonial Secretaries were removed.

The Attorney-General was removed from the Executive Council by the 1958 Constitution. This brought full internal self-government because an elected government had control over everything except foreign affairs and defence which were still in the hands of the Governor. The Governor also had reserve powers to suspend the Constitution, which was disputed by the politicians.

Federation was a crucial issue in Jamaican politics. Manley strongly supported Jamaica's membership of the Federation but Bustamante suspected it was a device by the British Government to withhold independence so he asked for a guarantee of Jamaica's self-government inside or outside the Federation. He also thought that Jamaica would be 'subsidising' the smaller islands. Therefore he supported membership with reservations. Later Bustamante told the Jamaican workers that Federation was against their interests thus making Federation unpopular in Jamaica. When Manley agreed to a referendum on Federation in 1961, Bustamante knew that Federation would be rejected and Manley discredited. Jamaica withdrew from the Federation and Bustamante insisted on separate independence as Britain had agreed.

The Independence Constitution gave a House of Representatives of forty-five members and a Senate of twenty-one, of whom thirteen would be the Prime Minister's nominees and eight the Leader of the Opposition's. A Governor-General would represent the Queen. A Prime Minister and Cabinet responsible to both Houses would form the government.

The Jamaica Labour Party won the pre-independence elections with twenty-six seats against nineteen for the People's National Party. Sir Alexander Bustamante (he was knighted in 1955) became the first Prime Minister of independent Jamaica in August 1962.

Notes

1 The elective principle was partially re-introduced into the Jamaican Constitution in 1884.
2 Bustamante emerged as a leader out of the riots and strikes of 1937–8.
3 Bustamante led the Bustamante Industrial Workers' Union and Jamaica Labour Party.
4 Manley led the People's National Party and the National Workers' Union.
5 From 1944 the Jamaica Labour Party was in power and Bustamante was Chief Minister.
6 The 1944 Constitution introduced universal adult suffrage and a fully elected House of Representatives of 32 seats.
7 The 1953 and 1957 Constitutions gave partially responsible government but the ex-officio members of the Executive Council prevented full responsibility.
8 Full internal self-government was granted in 1958.
9 Bustamante was able to use the Federation issue to bring down Manley and the PNP in 1961.
10 The Independence Constitution gave a House of Representatives of forty-five, a Senate of twenty-one and a Prime Minister and Cabinet responsible to both Houses.
11 Jamaica achieved independence on 6 August 1962.

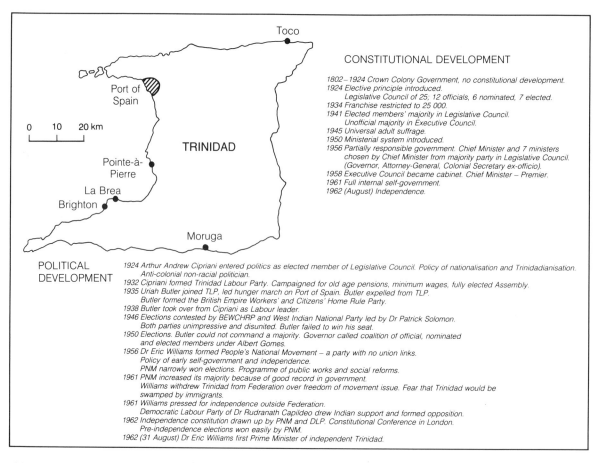

Map 9.7: Movement to independence: Trinidad

Map 9.7: Movement to independence: Trinidad

Arthur Andrew Cipriani was the father of politics in Trinidad. He first entered politics in 1922. In those days there was no talk of independence but Cipriani paved the way for the movement by his anti-colonialism and his wish to replace foreigners by Trinidadians in the top jobs. In 1932 he formed the Trinidad Labour Party and campaigned for old age pensions, minimum wages and other labour and social reforms. This made him the workers' champion. His political demand was for a fully-elected Assembly. In 1924 seven elected members had been introduced into a Legislative Council of twenty-five.

However, the riots and strikes in the oilfields brought forward another labour leader, Uriah Butler, who was more militant than Cipriani. He joined the TLP in 1935 but was expelled from it for leading a workers' hunger march on Port of Spain. He then formed his own party, the British Empire Workers' and Citizens' Home Rule Party, but he was not a good organiser and his party was never able to form a government.

In 1941 there was a majority of elected members in the Legislative Council but Butler was interned for the duration of the War and unable to lead his party. Universal adult suffrage was introduced in 1945 but in the 1946 elections Butler was unable to win a seat for himself so his party was leaderless. He won a seat in the 1950 elections but his party was unable to command a majority. The other political party, the West Indian National Party led by Dr Patrick Solomon, was also disunited so the Governor called a coalition of official, nominated and elected members under Albert Gomes to form a government. In 1950 a ministerial system had been introduced but with officials in the government it made little practical difference.

1956 was an important year in Trinidad's constitutional and political progress as a new constitution was introduced and a new political party was formed. The Chief Minister could choose seven ministers from his party in the Legislative Council to form a government. It was only partially responsible government because the Attorney-General and the Colonial Secretary were ex-officio in the Executive Council.

Dr Eric Williams formed the new party, the People's National Movement. It had no union links and was meant to be non-racial although its chief backing was from Africans. Williams pressed for early self-government and independence. He was the first Chief Minister of Trinidad. In 1956 his government had only a narrow majority but it did well with a programme of public works and social reforms. This term coincided with a period of economic prosperity from 1955 to 1961 which contributed to the PNM's increased majority in 1961 (Butler lost his seat and retired from politics).

Cabinet Government was introduced in 1958 and 'Chief Minister' became 'Premier'. Williams led Trinidad into the Federation but it was felt that his support for it was lukewarm when he himself did not stand in the Federal elections. The proposal for freedom of movement within the Federation worried him as he thought that Trinidad would be swamped by immigrants coming to share in Trinidad's growing prosperity. He withdrew Trinidad from the Federation in 1961 and demanded separate independence. In that year Trinidad was given full internal self-government.

Dr Rudranath Capildeo had formed an Indian-backed political party, the Democratic Labour Party, which contested the 1961 elections. The PNM and the DLP drew up an independence constitution which was put before a constitutional conference in London in 1962.

The People's National Movement easily won the pre-independence elections and on 31 August 1962, Dr Eric Williams became the first Prime Minister of independent Trinidad.

Notes

1 Arthur Andrew Cipriani, the father of Trinidadian politics, came before the era of independence movements but he did foreshadow the movement with his anti-colonialism and Trinidadianisation.
2 Uriah Butler took over the leadership of the labour movement from Cipriani because he had more appeal to the workers.
3 Butler formed the British Empire Workers' and Citizens' Home Rule Party but it was never able to form a government even when it won the elections in 1950.
4 In 1956 a new constitution brought in a Chief Minister and seven ministers.
5 In 1956 Dr Eric Williams formed the People's National Movement, a party committed to independence.
6 Trinidad withdrew from the Federation over freedom of movement.
7 The People's National Movement easily overcame the Indian-backed Democratic Labour Party of Dr Rudranath Capildeo in the pre-independence elections.
8 On 31 August 1962, Dr Eric Williams became the first Prime Minister of independent Trinidad.

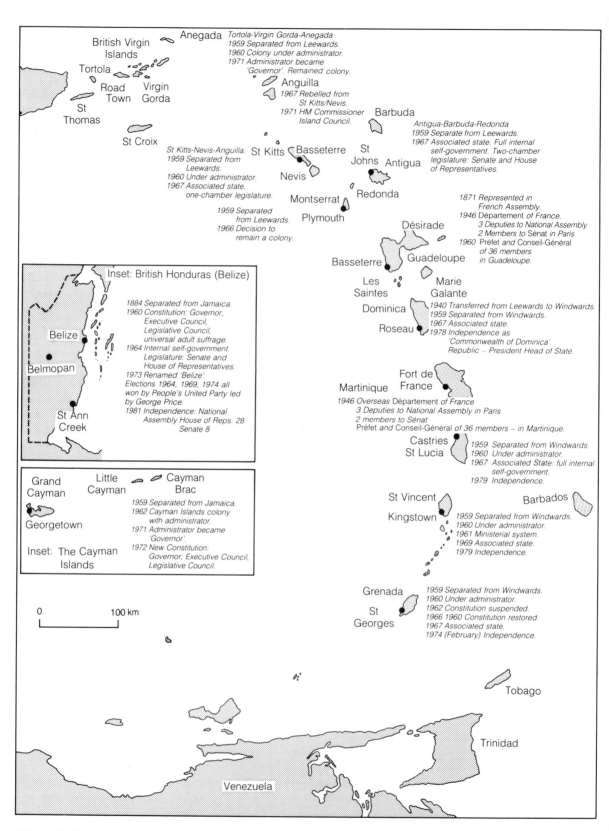

Map 9.8: Constitutional development in the Eastern Caribbean after 1959

Map 9.8: Constitutional development in the Eastern Caribbean after 1959

The territories considered in Map 9.8 are: 1 The British Virgin Islands; 2 Antigua-Barbuda-Redonda; 3 St Kitts-Nevis-Anguilla; 4 Montserrat; 5 Dominica; 6 St Lucia; 7 St Vincent; 8 Grenada; 9 The Cayman Islands; 10 British Honduras (Belize); 11 Guadeloupe and Martinique.

1 The British Virgin Islands (Tortola, Virgin Gorda and Anegada) separated from the Leeward Islands Colony in 1959 and became a separate colony under an Administrator who represented the Queen. In 1967 they were given a ministerial system with the Chief Minister and two other ministers in the Executive Council. In 1971 the Administrator changed in title to 'Governor'. They remained a colony with officials of the colonial government in both councils.

2 Antigua-Barbuda-Redonda are administered together from Antigua which has 98 per cent of the population. In 1936 the elective principle was re-introduced and universal adult suffrage was granted in 1951. At that time Antigua was a Presidency of the Leeward Island Colony. When this was dissolved in 1959 Antigua was given separate administration. An Administrator represented the Queen and he governed with an Executive Council consisting of the Chief Minister, four other ministers and one official; and a Legislative Council consisting of one official, three nominated and ten elected members.

In 1967 Antigua became an Associated State with full internal self-government. There was a Governor and a two-chamber legislature consisting of a House of Representatives of seventeen elected members and a Senate of ten members appointed by the Governor on the advice of the Premier. Britain retained responsibility for External Affairs and Defence and appointed the Governor.

In 1946 the Antigua Labour Party led by Vere C. Bird came to power and stayed in power until 1971. The 1971 elections were the first held under internal self-government and were won by the Progressive Labour Movement led by George Walter. However, Bird's Antigua Labour Movement regained power in the 1976 elections.

3 St Kitts-Nevis-Anguilla became a separate colony in 1959 when the Leeward Islands Colony dissolved and was given its own Administrator.

In 1967 St Kitts became an Associated State. Britain appointed the Governor who retained responsibility for External Affairs and Defence. Otherwise St Kitts had full internal self-government. The one-chamber legislature was the House of Assembly with ten elected and three nominated members. The executive was under a Premier and Cabinet of four ministers and one official.

(Anguilla rebelled against the Government of St Kitts in 1967. The British Government opposed this but could not find a solution agreeable to all parties. Therefore in 1971 Britain assumed direct resposibility for Anguilla and appointed a Commissioner and a Council for Anguilla.)

4 Montserrat also became a separate administration in 1959 and was given an Administrator who became 'Governor' in 1971. He governed with an Executive Council consisting of the Chief Minister and three other ministers and two officials; and a Legislative Council of two officials, one nominated member and seven elected. In 1966 Montserrat chose to remain a colony and retain its present constitution.

5 Dominica had been in the Leeward Islands Colony from 1833 to 1940 when it was transferred to the Windwards. It gained separate administration from the Windwards in 1959.

In March 1967, Dominica became an Associated State with an Administrator and a one-chamber legislature, the House of Assembly of twenty elected members; and an executive consisting of the Premier and a Cabinet of five, the Attorney-General and, of course, the Administrator. Britain retained control over External Affairs and Defence. Otherwise Dominica was fully self-governing.

The Dominica Labour Party won the 1975 elections and decided to ask for independence for 1978. In 1978 Dominica became independent as 'The Commonwealth of Dominica'. It chose to be a republic with an Executive President elected by the Legislature. Government was by a Prime Minister and an eight-member Cabinet. The one-chamber legislature was the House of Assembly of twenty-four members, twenty-one elected and three nominated by the Prime Minister.

6   In 1838 St Lucia became part of the Windward Islands Group in which it remained until 1959. In 1960 an Administrator represented the Queen and governed with an Executive Council consisting of the Chief Minister and three other ministers, and one official; and a Legislative Council of one official, two nominated and ten elected members.

In March, 1967, St Lucia became an Associated State with full internal self-government while Britain retained control of External Affairs and Defence. It had a one-chamber legislature, the House of Assembly consisting of ten elected, three nominated and one official member; and an executive consisting of the Premier, Cabinet of five ministers and the Attorney-General ex-officio.

In the 1974 elections the elected seats in the Assembly were increased to seventeen. John Compton and his United Workers' Party won with ten seats. He decided to press for independence in five years' time. In 1979 St Lucia became independent. It had a two-chamber legislature consisting of a seventeen-member House of Assembly and an eleven-member Senate. The executive was led by the Prime Minister and a Cabinet of ten ministers.

7   In 1959 St Vincent also separated from the Windwards and was given an Administrator, an Executive Council consisting of the Chief Minister and five other ministers and one official; and a Legislative Council of one official two nominated and thirteen elected members.

In 1969 the Statehood Constitution gave St Vincent full internal self-government with power to declare independence at some date in the future. At that time St Vincent was an Associated State with Britain in control of External Affairs and Defence.

Milton Cato, leader of the St Vincent Labour Party, was Premier. He chose independence in 1979 and it was granted. The Prime Minister and Cabinet led the executive and the legislature consisted of the one-chamber House of Assembly of thirteen elected members and six senators appointed by the Governor-General on the advice of the Prime Minister.

8   In 1959 Grenada separated from the Windwards and was given an Administrator, an Executive Council consisting of a Chief Minister, three other ministers and one official; and a Legislative Council of one official, two nominated and ten elected members.

In 1962 this constitution was suspended and the Administrator took over full control of the government. The 1960 Constitution was restored in 1966. In the following year Grenada became an Associated State with an Administrator and a two-chamber legislature consisting of a twelve-member Senate and a fifteen-member House of Representatives. The Chief Minister and Cabinet led the executive. Thus Grenada had full internal self-government while Britain retained control over External Affairs and Defence.

In 1972, Eric Gairy, leader of the Grenada United Labour Party, decided to ask for independence without going to the people in a referendum. Independence was granted in February 1974, so Grenada became the first of the Associated States to gain independence. It kept its existing constitution.

9   The Cayman Islands were a dependency of Jamaica until 1959. From 1959 to 1962 the Governor-General of Jamaica had reserved powers over Cayman and laws passed by the Jamaican Legislature specifically for Cayman had to be enforced. Otherwise Cayman had its own Administrator and Legislative Assembly.

In 1962 Jamaica became independent and the Cayman Islands became a separate Colony under the Colonial Office. They had a Governor, an Executive Council of two official, one nominated and two chosen from the elected members of the Legislative Assembly; and a Legislative Assembly of two/three officials, two/three nominated and twelve elected members. In 1972 the constitution was revised and the Cayman Islands chose to remain a British Colony.

10 British Honduras had no constitutional government until the Burnaby Code of 1765 when Admiral Burnaby formalised the 'Regulations and Usages' under which the set-

tlers had been living. The Governor of Jamaica was in charge until 1786 when a Superintendent responsible to the Governor of Jamaica was appointed. In 1862 British Honduras was given its own Lieutenant-Governor and in 1884 it became a separate colony with its own Governor.

Since then the constitution gradually developed towards self-government and independence. The 1960 constitution gave a Governor, an Executive Council consisting of two officials, six elected unofficials (ministers) and one nominated member; and a Legislative Council of two official, five nominated and eighteen elected members.

In January 1964, British Honduras received full internal self-government. The two-chamber legislature consisted of a fully-elected House of Representatives of eighteen and a Senate of eight appointed by the Governor. A Premier and Cabinet replaced the Executive Council. British Honduras's advance to independence was delayed by the threat to its sovereignty posed by Guatemala. While Britain was responsible for External Affairs and Defence, British Honduras could feel secure. A defence agreement with Britain was necessary to safeguard independence.

In 1973 British Honduras took the name 'Belize'. Independence was given in 1981. The Independence Constitution gave Belize a Governor, the Prime Minister and Cabinet leading the executive and a two-chamber legislature consisting of an elected House of Representatives of twenty-eight members, and a Senate of twelve members appointed by the Governor on the advice of the Prime Minister and Leader of the Opposition.

11 Guadeloupe consists of Guadeloupe itself and its dependencies of Marie Galante, La Désirade, Les Saintes, Saint Bartélémy and Saint Martin. Martinique has no dependencies.

Both Guadeloupe and Martinique were colonies of France. From 1871 Guadeloupe had been continuously represented in the French Assembly in Paris. In 1946 both became overseas *départements* of France under the Constitution of the Fifth Republic. This gave them equal status with the metropolitan *départements* of France. Therefore French laws apply to and are fully enforced in Guadeloupe and Martinique. They can each send three deputies to the National Assembly in Paris and two members to the *Sénat*.

In both *départements* a *Préfet* is the local representative of the French Government. He presides over the *Conseil-Général* of thirty-six members.

France maintains that it is irrelevant to talk of independence as Guadeloupe and Martinique are not colonies but parts of France.

Notes

1 In 1959 most of the islands in the Eastern Caribbean became separate administrative units because the Leeward Islands Colony and the Windward Islands Group were dissolved. Jamaica also gave up its control over some of its dependencies.

2 The Leeward Islands Colony gave way to four separate units: Antigua-Barbuda-Redonda; The British Virgin Islands; Montserrat; and St Kitts-Nevis-Anguilla.

3 The Windward Group yielded: Dominica; St Lucia; St Vincent and Grenada.

4 The Cayman Islands began their separation from Jamaica.

5 From 1959 to 1966 they all remained colonies with similar constitutions the only differences being due to differences in the size of the colonies.

6 In March 1967, the Associated States Constitution began. Under this Constitution the State was given full internal self-government but Britain retained control over External Affairs and Defence.

7 From this status the former Windward Group evolved to independence in the 1970s, Grenada achieving this first in 1974.

8 British Honduras (Belize) waited for independence until 1981 when she felt secure from the threats of Guatemala because of a defence agreement with Britain.

9 In 1946 Guadeloupe and Martinique ceased to be colonies and constitutionally became part of France (overseas *départements*) and therefore independence was irrelevant.

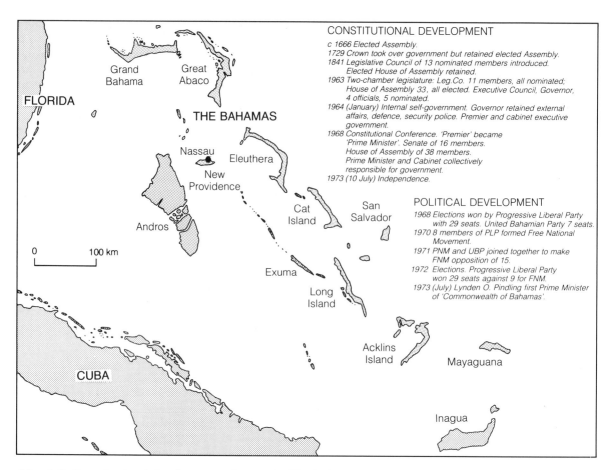

CONSTITUTIONAL DEVELOPMENT

c 1666 Elected Assembly.
1729 Crown took over government but retained elected Assembly.
1841 Legislative Council of 13 nominated members introduced. Elected House of Assembly retained.
1963 Two-chamber legislature: Leg.Co. 11 members, all nominated; House of Assembly 33, all elected. Executive Council, Governor, 4 officials, 5 nominated.
1964 (January) Internal self-government. Governor retained external affairs, defence, security police. Premier and cabinet executive government.
1968 Constitutional Conference. 'Premier' became 'Prime Minister'. Senate of 16 members. House of Assembly of 38 members. Prime Minister and Cabinet collectively responsible for government.
1973 (10 July) Independence.

POLITICAL DEVELOPMENT

1968 Elections won by Progressive Liberal Party with 29 seats. United Bahamian Party 7 seats.
1970 8 members of PLP formed Free National Movement.
1971 PNM and UBP joined together to make FNM opposition of 15.
1972 Elections. Progressive Liberal Party won 29 seats against 9 for FNM.
1973 (July) Lynden O. Pindling first Prime Minister of 'Commonwealth of Bahamas'.

Map 9.9: Constitutional development after 1960: The Bahamas

Map 9.9: Constitutional development after 1960: The Bahamas

The representative system of government has had an unbroken history in the Bahamas since about 1666 when the commission from Sir Thomas Modyford, Governor of Jamaica, allowed for an elected House of Assembly. Even when the Crown took over the government in 1729, the elected Assembly was retained.

In 1841 a Legislative Council of thirteen members nominated by the Governor was introduced but it was separated from the House of Assembly. As we have seen the Bahamas avoided Crown Colony Government after 1866 as it was outside the mainstream of West Indian politics. The constitution evolved without major changes until 1963.

The 1963 Constitution retained the two-chamber legislature consisting of a Legislative Council of eleven members, all nominated by the Governor, and an elected House of Assembly of thirty-three members, all elected. The Executive Council was formalised to include the Governor, Attorney-General, Colonial Secretary, Receiver-General and Treasurer ex-officio, and five nominated members.

In January 1964, the Bahamas were given internal self-government. A Cabinet chosen by the Premier and responsible to both Houses, would conduct the executive government. The Governor retained control over External Affairs, Defence, Internal Security and the Police.

The Constitution drafted by the Constitutional Conference of 1968 was basically that adopted at independence. The Premier became the 'Prime Minister'. The Senate, consisting of sixteen members, nine chosen by the PM, four by the Leader of the Opposition, and three jointly by the PM and Governor after consultation. The PM and Cabinet were collectively responsible to both Houses.

There was one major political development after the 1968 elections which were won by the Progressive Liberal Party under Lynden Pindling with twenty-nine seats against seven for the United Bahamian Party and one for the Labour Party. In 1970 eight members broke away from the PLP and formed the Free National Movement. They were joined in 1971 by the old opposition, the UBP to make an opposition of fifteen against the PLP government of twenty-one. However in the pre-independence elections of 1972 the Progressive Liberal Party regained its twenty-nine seats and the Free National Movement won nine. Therefore Lynden O. Pindling became the first Prime Minister of the Commonwealth of the Bahamas on 10 July 1973.

Notes

1 The representative system of government in the Bahamas was unbroken from about 1666 to independence,
2 After 1866 the Bahamas avoided Crown Colony Government because it was outside the mainstream of West Indian politics.
3 In January 1964, the Bahamas were given internal self-government.
4 The Progressive Liberal Party under Lynden Pindling led the government but in 1971 the opposition parties united to give the Free National Movement fifteen seats.
5 Lynden O. Pindling became the first Prime Minister of the Commonwealth of the Bahamas in July 1973.

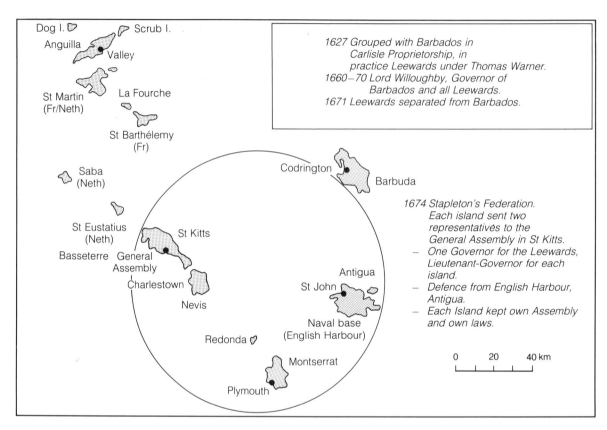

Dog I.   Scrub I.

Anguilla
    Valley

St Martin   La Fourche
(Fr/Neth)

St Barthélemy
(Fr)

Saba
(Neth)

Codrington   Barbuda

St Eustatius
(Neth)
    St Kitts

Basseterre   General
          Assembly
       Charlestown

Nevis

Antigua

St John

Naval base
(English Harbour)

Redonda

Montserrat

Plymouth

*1627 Grouped with Barbados in
      Carlisle Proprietorship, in
      practice Leewards under Thomas Warner.
1660–70 Lord Willoughby, Governor of
       Barbados and all Leewards.
1671 Leewards separated from Barbados.*

*1674 Stapleton's Federation.
     Each island sent two
     representatives to the
     General Assembly in St Kitts.*
— *One Governor for the Leewards,
    Lieutenant-Governor for each
    island.*
— *Defence from English Harbour,
    Antigua.*
— *Each Island kept own Assembly
    and own laws.*

0   20   40 km

Map 10.1: The Leewards – early groupings

Map 10.1: The Leewards – early groupings

The British Government favoured groups of colonies because they were easier and cheaper to administer. Less colonial officials were needed and less salaries had to be paid. Also colonial assemblies tended to give trouble by opposing the British Government's policies and decisions, and groups cut down the number of assemblies. Before 1838 the free populations of most colonies hardly justified separate administrations. However, the colonies themselves tended to be against groups as they wanted autonomy and feared sacrificing it to a central body. British West Indian islands were fiercely independent, for example Nevis was separated from St Kitts by two miles of sea but it was not united to it until 1882.

In the Carlisle proprietorship of 1627 Barbados and the Leewards were grouped together, but in practice it was difficult to administer them together and Thomas Warner governed the Leewards only. In 1660 Lord Willoughby, as Governor of Barbados, governed all the Eastern Caribbean until 1670. This was appreciated by the Leewards as they needed the help of Barbados in the Second Dutch War. After the War the Leewards returned in 1671 to having their own Governor.

The Leewards had the first federation in the British Caribbean. It was established by Sir William Stapleton in 1674 and was never really dissolved but replaced by other arrangements. Stapleton set up a General Assembly of the Leewards in St Kitts. Antigua, Montserrat, Nevis and St Kitts each sent two representatives. The federation was active from 1674 to 1685 when Stapleton was Governor and the General Assembly met regularly until 1711. After that it only met once again in 1798. The federation was unpopular and in 1683 the Leewards rejected the proposal for one government and one set of laws. In the eighteenth century each island had its own assembly and made its own laws but they shared one Governor and one Attorney-General. They were protected by the naval base at English Harbour, Antigua.

Notes

1 The Carlisle proprietorship placed Barbados and the Leewards under one administration in 1627.

2 However, in practice Barbados and the Leewards were administered separately.

3 From 1660 to 1670 the Leewards were under the Governor of Barbados.

4 In 1674 Sir William Stapleton gave one Governor and a General Assembly to the Leewards which was the first form of federation in the British Caribbean.

5 Each island kept its own assembly and resisted a common set of laws.

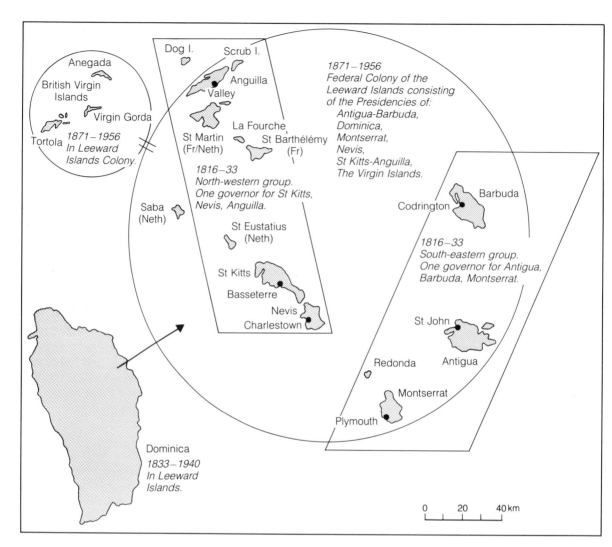

Dog I.

Scrub I.

Anegada

British Virgin Islands

Virgin Gorda

Tortola

1871–1956
In Leeward
Islands Colony.

Anguilla
Valley

St Martin
(Fr/Neth)

La Fourche

St Barthélémy
(Fr)

1871–1956
Federal Colony of the
Leeward Islands consisting
of the Presidencies of:
Antigua-Barbuda,
Dominica,
Montserrat,
Nevis,
St Kitts-Anguilla,
The Virgin Islands.

Saba
(Neth)

1816–33
North-western group.
One governor for St Kitts,
Nevis, Anguilla.

St Eustatius
(Neth)

St Kitts

Basseterre

Nevis
Charlestown

Codrington

Barbuda

1816–33
South-eastern group.
One governor for Antigua,
Barbuda, Montserrat.

St John

Antigua

Redonda

Montserrat

Plymouth

Dominica
1833–1940
In Leeward
Islands.

0   20   40 km

Map 10.2: The Leeward Islands Colony, 1871 to 1956

Map 10.2: The Leeward Islands Colony, 1871 to 1956

Between 1816 and 1833 the Leeward Islands were divided into two groups: St Kitts, Nevis and Anguilla were in a north-west group, and Antigua, Barbuda and Montserrat were in a south-east group. Each group had its own Governor. In 1833 all the Leewards were brought together again and Dominica was added to the Leeward Islands until 1940. As mentioned earlier, the free population of each island was too small to justify a separate administration. After emancipation in 1838, the ex-slaves were without political rights and so the assemblies were completely unrepresentative. In 1871 the British Government passed the Leeward Islands Act to set up the Federal Colony of the Leeward Islands whereby all the islands were under one Governor and one set of laws. The British Government hoped that this arrangement would serve the interests of the majority of the population. Each island was called a 'Presidency' under its own Administrator or Commissioner. As usual with the early groupings, this federation was unpopular but it was not dissolved until 1956 when it made way for the Federation of the West Indies.

Notes

1 Between 1816 and 1833 the Leewards were divided into two groups, each group having its own Governor.
2 In 1833 all the Leewards came together again and Dominica joined the group.
3 From 1871 to 1956 there was the Federal Colony of the Leeward Islands more commonly called 'The Leeward Islands Colony' under one Governor and one set of laws.
4 Each unit was called a 'Presidency'.

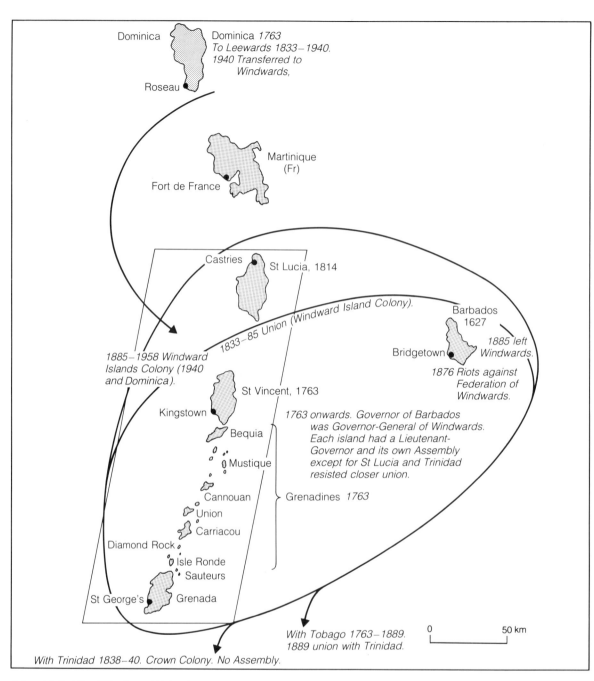

Dominica

Dominica *1763*
To Leewards 1833–1940.
1940 Transferred to
Windwards,

Roseau

Martinique
(Fr)

Fort de France

Castries

St Lucia, 1814

1833–85 Union (Windward Island Colony).

Barbados
1627

1885 left
Windwards.

Bridgetown

1876 Riots against
Federation of
Windwards.

1885–1958 Windward
Islands Colony (1940
and Dominica).

St Vincent, 1763

Kingstown

1763 onwards. Governor of Barbados
was Governor-General of Windwards.
Each island had a Lieutenant-
Governor and its own Assembly
except for St Lucia and Trinidad
resisted closer union.

Bequia

Mustique

Cannouan

Union

Grenadines *1763*

Carriacou

Diamond Rock

Isle Ronde

Sauteurs

St George's

Grenada

With Tobago 1763–1889.
1889 union with Trinidad.

0   50 km

With Trinidad 1838–40. Crown Colony. No Assembly.

Map 10.3: The Windward Islands

Map 10.3: The Windward Islands

Barbados was the most windward of the Windwards and well outside the chain of the Eastern Caribbean islands. However, in 1763 she was put in charge of the new colonies acquired in the Seven Years' War because she was well established. The Governor of Barbados became Governor-General of Grenada and the Grenadines, St Vincent and Tobago although communication from west to east was very difficult for these islands in the days of sail. Each island had its own Lieutenant-Governor.

Trinidad, acquired from Spain in 1802, and St Lucia, acquired from France in 1814, were administered separately as Crown Colonies at first until in 1838 they were brought into the Windwards. However they were not given their own assemblies. (Trinidad separated from the group in 1840). From 1833 to 1885 the Windwards were a formal union known as 'The Windward Islands Colony'.

Barbados had been a colony for one hundred and thirty-six years before Britain acquired another Windward colony. Barbados had ancient institutions and wanted to keep its separateness. The other colonies did not enjoy the association with Barbados but needed it for defence against France until 1815. Therefore Barbados and the other colonies resisted the British Government's attempts to bring them into closer union. Barbados especially was determined to resist federation and the whites fought to keep their own Assembly. In 1876 they rioted when the Governor, Pope-Hennessy, wanted to enforce federation. He tried to dissolve the Assembly and failed. He had underestimated the opposition and was transferred to Hong Kong in 1876. The Governor of Barbados remained the Governor-General of the Windwards until 1885 when Barbados finally left the Windwards.

From 1885 to 1958 the Windward Island Colony consisted of Grenada and the Grenadines, St Vincent and St Lucia for the whole period. Tobago was in the group until 1889 when she formed a union with Trinidad. Dominica was transferred from the Leewards to the Windwards in 1940. The Windward Island Colony was under one Governor-General based in Grenada and each island had a Lieutenant-Governor and its own assembly as before. They always resisted attempts to establish a federal assembly. The Windward Island Colony broke up in 1958 when each island chose to join the Federation of the West Indies separately.

Notes

1 Barbados was geographically windward but outside the chain of the Eastern Caribbean islands.
2 Barbados was one hundred and thirty-six years older as a colony than any of the other British Windward Island colonies.
3 From 1763 the Governor of Barbados acted as Governor-General of the Windwards but neither party liked this association.
4 Each island kept its own assembly except for Trinidad and St Lucia which joined the group as Crown Colonies without assemblies.
5 Riots in Barbados in 1876 persuaded the British Government that the Assembly did not want a Windward federation.
6 Barbados left the Windward Islands Colony in 1885.
7 The Windward Island Colony ended when each island joined the West Indies Federation as a separate unit.

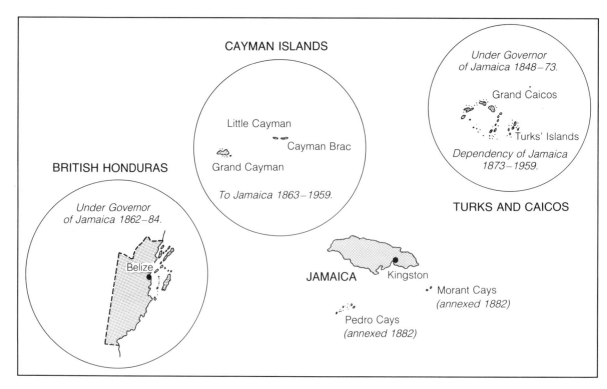

Map 10.4: Jamaica and her dependencies

Map 10.4: Jamaica and her dependencies

The remaining British colonies in the Caribbean (except for British Guiana) were grouped under Jamaica at some time in their history although they had no geographical relationship with her. British Honduras, surrounded by hostile Spanish colonies, needed Jamaica's protection. The Cayman Islands and the Turks and Caicos were too small to justify separate administrations.

British Honduras was a dependency of Jamaica and directly under Jamaica from 1763. The Governor of Jamaica appointed a Superintendent for British Honduras. In 1862 it became a Crown Colony and was placed under the Governor of Jamaica with its own Lieutenant-Governor. In 1884 it finally broke its administrative ties with Jamaica.

The Cayman Islands were a dependency of Jamaica from 1863 to 1959 and were rather like a parish of Jamaica with nominated justices of the peace and elected vestrymen in their Legislature.

The Governor of Jamaica appointed a Commissioner for the Islands. From 1959 to 1962 the Governor of Jamaica had reserve powers over Cayman but on Jamaica's independence in 1962 Cayman broke its administrative links with Jamaica.

In 1848 the Turks and Caicos broke their association with the Bahamas and became a separate colony with a Superintendent appointed from Jamaica until 1873. They were then made a dependency of Jamaica with a Commissioner and a Legislative Board. In 1959 they became a separate colony.

Notes

1   Other British colonies were placed under Jamaica not because of any geographical relationship but because Jamaica was the dominant British possession.
2   British Honduras needed Jamaica's protection against the Spanish colonies.
3   The Cayman Islands and the Turks and Caicos were too small for separate administrations.

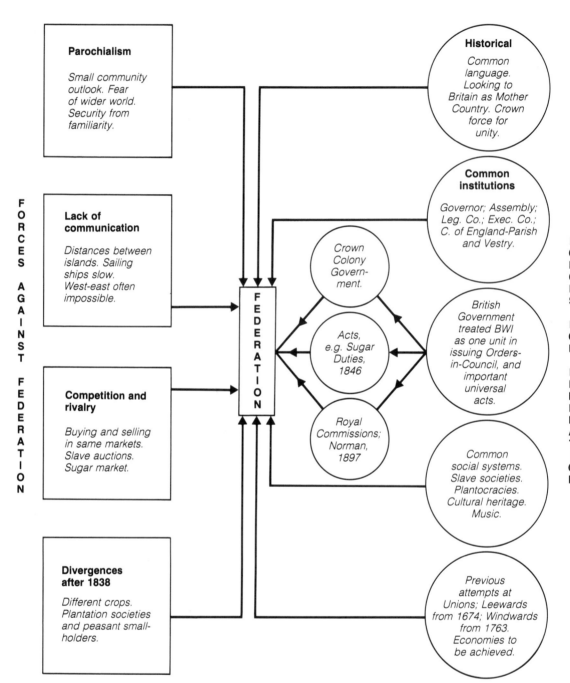

Chart 10.1: Forces for and against federation

Chart 10.1: Forces for and against federation

The Federal Colony of the Leeward Islands, 1871–1956, and the Windward Island Colony, 1833–1958, had both shown that the forces against closer union were stronger than the forces for it. In both federations the individual colonies had insisted on keeping their own assemblies. Pressure from the British Government had created these unions and held them together but the islands themselves dissolved them at the earliest convenient time.

British West Indian islands were unwilling to sacrifice their autonomy. Each island felt that its conditions and interests were different and could only be looked after by their own representatives. In this respect they were selfish and narrow-minded. They could not see that the greater benefits of membership of a larger union could outweigh the sacrifices of some local interests. This small community outlook is parochialism. It had been made stronger by lack of communication in the days of sail. The islands could not easily communicate with one another so they grew further apart and more insular. It was especially difficult for Jamaica to communicate with the Eastern Caribbean because of the contrary winds. When steam came and then air travel the parochialism was too deeply rooted to be broken down suddenly.

Economic rivalry was also strong. Islands bid against each other in the slave markets and high demand from one island drove up the prices for another. The islands also competed against each other in selling their crops and the success of one island could mean the failure of another. The older colonies did not want Trinidad and St Lucia to grow sugar on a large scale because they could adversely affect their own sales.

Before emancipation the economic and social structure of the British islands had been the same, but after emancipation divergences appeared. Differences in wage rates between Barbados and Trinidad brought differences in living standards. The availability of land in Jamaica led to a class of free peasantry whereas most Barbadians remained plantation labourers. Emancipation heightened the differences between islands rather than lessened them.

On the other hand the British islands spoke the same language with minorities speaking French in St Lucia and Spanish in Trinidad. This was a huge advantage towards closer union. In spite of disagreements from time to time with the British Government, as over amelioration and emancipation, the islands still held allegiance to the Crown and looked to Britain for protection. The presence of the Royal Navy in time of war reminded them that they were on the same side. The plantocracy felt the links with the Mother Country more than the other classes through factors like absenteeism, education and retirement. The West India Committee in London represented all the British Caribbean and parochialism did not exist in its business.

Pressure for closer union came from the British Government for administrative convenience. The British Government wanted to deal with the British West Indies as one unit. It was convenient for it to pass one law for all, such as Amelioration in 1823 and Emancipation in 1833, without regard for different local conditions. Crown Colony Government was the extreme of convenience: direct rule from London by Order-in-Council laying down one law for all with no local opposition. The Commissions of 1883, 1897 (Norman), and 1938 (Moyne) also treated the British Caribbean as one unit but did identify local issues where necessary.

Until the Second World War, the forces against closer union were stronger than the forces for it, but in the 1930s the Great Depression, the riots and strikes of 1935–8, the trade union movement and the West Indian Labour Conference changed attitudes towards federation.

Notes

1 Early attempts at local federations, such as the Leewards and the Windwards, had not been popular with the citizens.
2 British West Indian islands had developed a small-community-outlook which poor communications had fostered.
3 In commerce the islands were competitors and this hindered political union.
4 The common heritage of language, institutions, Crown and Church, helped to bring the colonies together.
5 The British Government was the greatest force towards federation because it had always tried to treat the British West Indies as one unit.
6 However, until 1939, the forces against closer union seemed to be stronger than the forces for it.

Table 10.1: Unifying bodies in the British Caribbean

Name of body	Date	Location	Purpose
Imperial Department of Tropical Agriculture	1898	Barbados	To co-ordinate the work of the Botanical Departments in all islands.
West Indies Court of Appeal	1919	Jamaica	To hear appeals from colonial courts. To make decisions and practices uniform in judiciaries.
Imperial College of Tropical Agriculture	1922	Trinidad	To promote study of tropical agriculture for the benefit of all islands.
West Indian Standing Conference on Federation	1926/ 1929	London/ Barbados	To work towards federation.
Associated West Indian Chambers of Commerce	1929	Barbados	To urge governments to establish a free trade area and to promote federation.
West Indian Press Association	1929	Barbados	To act as a news agency for the British Caribbean.
West Indian Unofficial Conference	1932	Dominica	To help Eastern Caribbean islands achieve independence through federation.
British Guiana and West Indian Labour Conference	1938	British Guiana	To foster trade unionism, improve labour and social conditions and to make political demands, including federation.
The Moyne Commission	1938	British West Indies	To investigate and report on labour unrest and social grievances.
The Colonial Development and Welfare Act	1940	London	To set up a common fund for economic development in the British West Indies.
Colonial Development and Welfare Organisation	1940	Barbados	To co-ordinate the development plans of all the islands and create a body of expertise.
The University of the West Indies	1949	Jamaica/ Trinidad/ Barbados (1963)	To provide higher education for the British West Indies.
West India Regiment	1795		To serve in every colony in its defence and assist Britain in two World Wars.

Table 10.1: Unifying bodies in the British Caribbean

In the first half of the twentieth century there were some bodies which demonstrated that the individual colonies were able to come together. These gave encouraging signs for federation and in the case of the Colonial Development and Welfare Organisation actually laid a foundation.

The bodies which put federation as their aim did not achieve much. The West Indian Standing Conference on federation met from 1926 to 1929 and achieved nothing positive. The West Indian Unofficial Conference was positive in that it suggested a constitution and listed the responsibilities of a federal government but it was only for the Eastern Caribbean. It disagreed with T. Marryshow of Grenada, the champion of federation, by putting federation first and independence later.

The Associated West Indian Chambers of Commerce, the Caribbean equivalent of the West Indies Committee, linked the idea of a free trade area with federation, thus emphasizing the economic benefits of closer union. The Moyne Commission of 1938 (Report published in 1945) also recommended federation. Finally, the British Guiana and West Indian Labour Conference of 1938 was in favour of federation, but later the labour movement was not consistent in its support.

The other bodies gave examples of closer union but not in the political sphere. The West India Regiment, founded in 1795, had brought the colonies together in the defence of the West Indies as a whole and soldiers from the different islands served alongside each other. Service in the two World Wars broadened the soldiers' outlooks and showed their common interests. It helped to create the West Indian identity.

The Imperial Department of Tropical Agriculture in Barbados arose out of the recommendations of the Norman Commission and was to serve all the islands. The Imperial College of Tropical Agriculture in Trinidad, which later became the Faculty of Agriculture of the University of the West Indies, showed inter-colony co-operation. The University of the West Indies, given its charter in 1949, was a forerunner of federation both in its concept of cost economy and as a practical institution of federation. Another institution which did this was the West Indies Court of Appeal.

The Colonial Development and Welfare Act of 1940 gave rise to the Colonial Development and Welfare Organisation based in Barbados. As said earlier, this body laid a foundation for federation because the Comptroller in Barbados administered the common fund and co-ordinated the development plans for all the individual colonies. This organisation developed a body of expertise which was taken over by the Federation in 1958.

Notes

1   Some bodies were formed with the aim of federation, such us the West Indian Standing Conference on Federation and the West Indian Unofficial Conference but these bodies achieved little.

2   Other bodies had federation on their agenda, for example the British Guiana and West Indian Labour Conference and the Associated West Indian Chambers of Commerce.

3   Other bodies gave positive proof that the British West Indian colonies could work together, such as the West India Regiment, the Imperial Department of Tropical Agriculture and the West Indies Court of Appeal.

4   Other bodies, like the University of the West Indies, were forerunners of federation.

5   The Colonial Development and Welfare Organisation in particular paved the way for federation because it helped towards economic viability and trained a body of experts to serve the Federation.

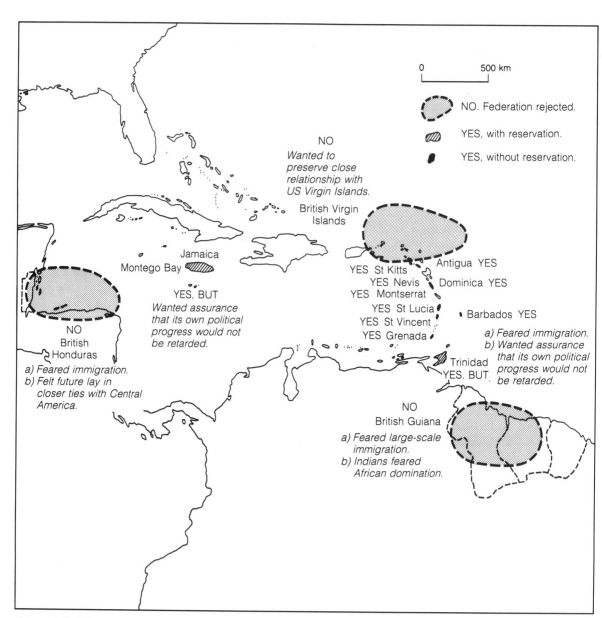

0   500 km

NO. Federation rejected.

YES, with reservation.

YES, without reservation.

NO
Wanted to
preserve close
relationship with
US Virgin Islands.

British Virgin
Islands

Jamaica
Montego Bay

YES St Kitts   Antigua YES
YES Nevis   Dominica YES
YES Montserrat
YES St Lucia
YES St Vincent   Barbados YES
YES Grenada

YES, BUT
Wanted assurance
that its own political
progress would not
be retarded.

a) Feared immigration.
b) Wanted assurance
that its own political
progress would not
be retarded.

NO
British
Honduras

a) Feared immigration.
b) Felt future lay in
closer ties with Central
America.

Trinidad
YES. BUT.

NO
British Guiana

a) Feared large-scale
immigration.
b) Indians feared
African domination.

Map 10.5: The Montego Bay Conference on federation

Map 10.5: The Montego Bay Conference on federation

The British Government had been discouraged by the attitude of the colonies towards its attempts to create federations in the British Caribbean. However, between the Wood Report of 1921 and the Moyne Commission of 1938 (Report, 1945) the attitude of the colonies changed. The Great Depression may have made the colonies realize the need for help against external economic forces beyond their control.

T. Marryshow of Grenada showed the British Government that West Indian politicians supported federation and it understood his reservation that the individual colonies should proceed towards their own independence before demanding federation rather than have federation enforced on them while they were still colonies (referred to as 'Crown Colony Federation'). Jamaican and Trinidadian politicians wanted assurance that their own political and constitutional progress would not be delayed by federation. By 1945 the British Government's attitude to decolonisation was changing and it was prepared to give these assurances.

In 1945 the West Indian Labour Conference, then led by Marryshow, the Barbados Progressive League led by Adams, the People's National Party in Jamaica led by Manley and the Associated West Indian Chambers of Commerce urged the British Government to create a federation. Colonel Oliver Stanley, the Secretary of State for the Colonies, agreed to establish a federation for the whole of the British West Indies. His successor, Arthur Creech Jones, called a conference in Montego Bay, Jamaica, for September 1947. Every colony except the Bahamas sent delegates from their legislatures. At that stage they all approved of some form of closer union. Committees were established to work out the details.

In March 1950, the Standing Closer Association Committee reported. Eight colonies had accepted federation without reservation. Jamaica and Trini-dad received assurances that their own progress to independence would not be affected by joining the Federation and they then accepted. British Guiana rejected federation on the grounds that free movement within the Federation would lead to large-scale immigration, the Indian population in particular feeling strongly about this. British Honduras rejected federation as it felt that as a mainland Central American colony it should look to better relations with its neighbours. The British Virgin Islands rejected federation as they thought it would prejudice their good relations with the US Virgin Islands.

The delegates at Montego Bay agreed with the British Government that federation would bring greater efficiency in government, purer democracy, the promotion of West Indians in government and more talented government. They agreed with the Associated West Indian Chambers of Commerce that federation would create a larger market, remove duties and expand production.

Notes

1 Between the Wood Report of 1921 and the Moyne Commission of 1938, the West Indian attitude turned in favour of federation.
2 West Indian politicians like Marryshow, Adams and Manley convinced the British Government that federation would be supported.
3 Arthur Creech Jones, the Secretary of State for the Colonies, called the Montego Bay Conference on federation for the British West Indies in 1947.
4 All the colonies except the Bahamas attended.
5 The Standing Closer Association Committee assured Jamaica and Trinidad that they would be able to achieve independence individually.
6 British Guiana, British Honduras and the British Virgin Islands rejected federation.
7 The Montego Bay Conference argued that federation would bring the political benefits of greater efficiency and West Indianisation, and the economic benefits of expanded production and a free trade area.

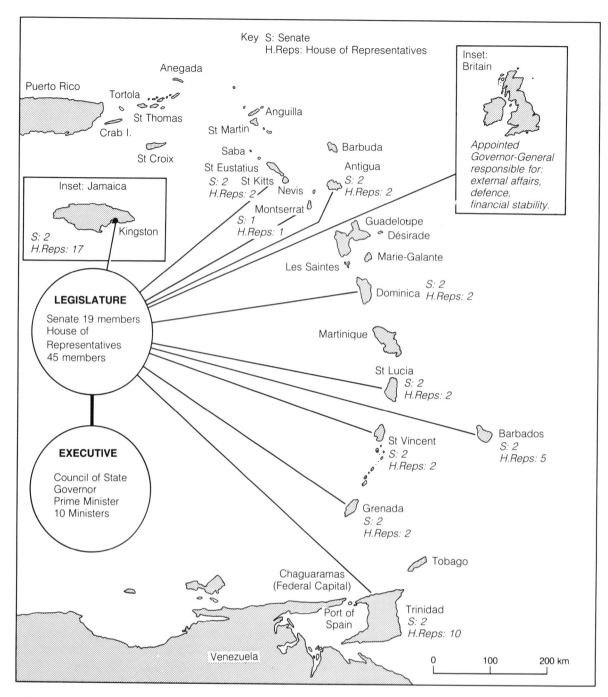

Inset:
Britain

Appointed
Governor-General
responsible for:
external affairs,
defence,
financial stability.

Anegada

Puerto Rico

Tortola

St Thomas

Crab I.

St Croix

Anguilla

St Martin

Saba

Barbuda

St Eustatius

Antigua

S: 2   St Kitts
H.Reps: 2   Nevis

S: 2
H.Reps: 2

Montserrat
S: 1
H.Reps: 1

Guadeloupe

Désirade

Marie-Galante

Les Saintes

Inset: Jamaica

S: 2
H.Reps: 17

Kingston

Dominica   S: 2
H.Reps: 2

LEGISLATURE

Senate 19 members
House of
Representatives
45 members

Martinique

St Lucia
S: 2
H.Reps: 2

St Vincent
S: 2
H.Reps: 2

Barbados
S: 2
H.Reps: 5

EXECUTIVE

Council of State
Governor
Prime Minister
10 Ministers

Grenada
S: 2
H.Reps: 2

Tobago

Chaguaramas
(Federal Capital)

Port of
Spain

Trinidad
S: 2
H.Reps: 10

Venezuela

0   100   200 km

Map 10.6: The Constitution of the Federation of the West Indies

Map 10.6: The Constitution of the Federation of the West Indies

After Montego Bay there were three more conferences on federation held in London. The 1953 Conference heard the reports of the committees which had been appointed at Montego Bay and sent the reports to the colonial legislatures for approval.

The 1955 Conference discussed finance, in particular the raising of revenue through taxation. Grantley Adams considered that the Federal Government should have the power of taxation but Norman Manley disagreed. The revenue issue still had not been settled by the time the Federation came into being in 1958.

The 1956 Conference agreed on the Constitution for the Federation. Then the British Government established the Federation of the West Indies by Order-in-Council. The British Government would be responsible for External Affairs, Defence and Financial Stability. The Crown would appoint the Governor-General. The Legislature would consist of: a) a Senate of nineteen members, one from Montserrat, and two from each of the other colonies; and, b) a House of Representatives of forty-five members, seventeen from Jamaica, ten from Trinidad, five from Barbados, one from Montserrat and two from each of the other colonies. The Executive would be a Council of State, not a Cabinet, and would consist of the Governor-General, the Prime Minister, and ten other Ministers. The Civil Service would be under the Federal Secretary and in practice it consisted of colonial servants who had been working in the Colonial Development and Welfare Organisation. The Federal Capital would be at Chaguaramas in Trinidad and Britain agreed to contribute £1 000 000 towards the construction.

Notes

1 The conferences before the Federation came into being failed to decide how money should be raised to finance the Federal administration.
2 The British Government retained control over External Affairs, Defence and Financial Stability. It also appointed the Governor-General.
3 The Legislature consisted of a nineteen-member Senate and a forty-five-member House of Representatives.
4 The Governor-General, a British appointee, led the Executive.
5 It was called a 'Crown Colony Federation' because of the powers retained by the Colonial Government and the importance of the Governor-General.
6 The Federal Capital was to be at Chaguaramas in Trinidad.

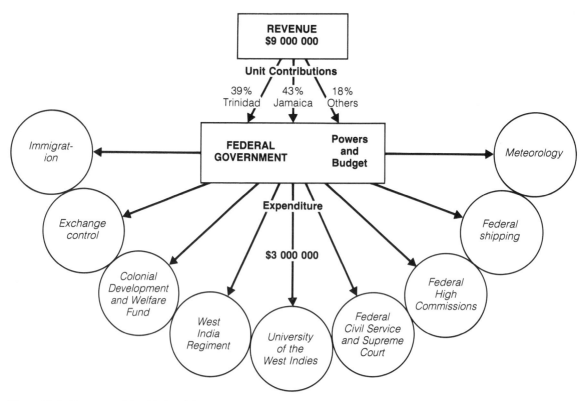

Chart 10.2: Powers of the Federal Government

Chart 10.2: Powers of the Federal Government

The Federal Government was very weak in both its powers and budget. It was only given residual powers, that is, responsibility for affairs which the unit governments did not consider important. The Federal Government was given these powers ('subjects'): a) administering the funds of the Colonial Development and Welfare Act; b) the West India Regiment; c) the University of the West Indies' administration costs; d) the Federal Civil Service and Supreme Court; e) Federal Shipping, Meteorology, Immigration and Exchange Control. The unit governments retained control over such important matters as taxation, education, health and agriculture. Therefore the Federal Government had no control over economic development.

The Federal Government's revenue was only $9 000 000 (BWI dollars). The revenue came from unit contributions assessed on the size of the unit's national income; e.g. Jamaica contributed 43 per cent; Trinidad 39 per cent; and the others 18 per cent. $3 000 000 of the expenditure went on the administration costs of the University of the West Indies and the remaining $6 000 000 was spread over its other subjects like maintaining Federal High Commissions in Britain, Canada and Venezuela.

Notes

1 The Federal Government only had residual powers.
2 The unit governments retained control of taxation, education, health and agriculture.
3 The Federal Government had no control over economic development.
4 Revenue came from unit contributions assessed on the size of the unit's national income.

Table 10.2: The dissolution of the Federation, May 1962

Built-in causes	General causes	Immediate causes
British Government agreed to units' constitutional and political progress separate from the Federation. Units could negotiate their own independence	Federal Elections of March 1958, gave victory to WIFLP with 26 seats, 17 out of 19 of opposition DLP's seats were from Jamaica and Trinidad. Therefore largest units were in opposition to Federal Government. Small units controlled government and had most Ministers. Prime Minister, Grantley Adams from Barbados.	The secession of Jamaica and Trinidad brought the Federation to an end. They both had specific causes for their withdrawal.
Federation was so weak there was no point in its continuing. Only given residual powers. Nothing of importance. Very little revenue and no possibility of increasing it as it had no control over taxation.	Manley of Jamaica and Williams of Trinidad did not stand. Federal Government lost prestige.	*Jamaica* One of the aims of the Federation was a Customs' Union and free-trade area. Jamaica received most of her revenue from duties and opposed this.
It was a 'Crown Colony Federation'. West Indians felt insulted. Cabinet Government, August 1960, too late to save Federation.	Jamaica and Trinidad had reservations about the Federation. Strongest units did not give it full support.	Jamaica insisted on control of her own economic development. Grantley Adams and Federal Government wanted control over all economic development. Jamaica developed oil refinery in 1960 and gave tax concessions to oil company.
Backward Constitution. Barbados, Jamaica and Trinidad all more advanced constitutionally than Federation in 1958 because they had inter-self-government.	Attitude that Federation had to be 'all ten, or not at all'. If one seceded, the whole would collapse.	Adams proposed retroactive legislation to be used against Jamaica and her illegal tax concessions. Jamaica would be made to pay back taxes.
Jamaica and Trinidad, the largest units with approximately 80 per cent of population, land and resources, were under-represented, even after constitutional revision of September 1959. Federation dominated by small islands through House of Representatives and especially the Senate.	Conflict between Jamaica and Trinidad over major issues like power of taxation insurmountable.	*Trinidad* Trinidad's per capita income twice that of next richest unit. Trinidad feared large-scale immigration which would result from 'freedom of movement' without which Federation would lose its point.
No possibility of economic development because budget was too small and it was not a 'subject' for the Federal Government.	Bustamante's fear that Jamaica was being asked to support Eastern Caribbean seemed to be justified. Used to good effect in Jamaican referendum on Federation.	The site of the Federal Capital was the Chaguaramas Peninsula in Trinidad, then leased to United States. Williams negotiated with US and Britain as if lease was a domestic issue. Adams felt it was a Federal issue. Williams accused of trying to make political capital.

Table 10.2: The dissolution of the Federation, May 1962

Politically the Federal Government was dominated by the smaller islands because of the results of the Federal Elections of March 1958. The West Indies Federal Labour Party won these with twenty-six seats against nineteen seats for the Democratic Labour Party which became the opposition. The DLP won eleven of Jamaica's seventeen seats and six of Trinidad's ten. Therefore the two biggest units supported the opposition while the government drew its support from the smaller islands. The smaller islands also had the majority of Ministerial posts in the Council of State and the Prime Minister was Grantley Adams from Barbados. This sowed the seed of conflict between the two large units and the Eastern Caribbean.

The WIFLP's Chairman was Norman Manley of Jamaica, and another of its prominent members was Dr Eric Williams, Prime Minister of Trinidad. Both of these did not stand in the Federal Elections. This made West Indians feel that the Federal Government was of secondary importance to the leading politicians of Jamaica and Trinidad which was probably true in view of subsequent events. The leadership of the WIFLP in the House passed to Grantley Adams who certainly put the Federal Government before his political career in Barbados.

In 1958 Barbados, Jamaica and Trinidad had internal self-government whereas the Federation was still a Crown Colony with the Governor-General as leader of the executive with more power than the Prime Minister. The Federation was more backward constitutionally than its leading units and was therefore labelled a 'Crown Colony Federation'. Williams of Trinidad pressed for Cabinet Government which the British Government agreed to in August 1960. This brought its constitution into line with the three leading units but by that time Jamaica and Trinidad were becoming unenthusiastic about the Federation and thinking about separate independence.

Jamaica and Trinidad together contributed 73 per cent of the population, 83 per cent of the land area and 82 per cent of the revenue of the Federation yet they only held 60 per cent of the seats in the House of Representatives and 20 per cent of the members of the Senate. They were proportionally under-represented, especially in the Senate where Antigua had equal representation with Jamaica. Jamaica and Trinidad pressed for a constitutional revision which the British Government agreed to in September 1959. The House was increased to sixty-four seats of which Jamaica had thirty and Trinidad fifteen, 70 per cent of the seats between the two. They were still under-represented, again much more so in the Senate. The smaller islands and the British Government had to accept the new allocation of seats because the Federation could not survive without its two most powerful members and there was the idea of 'all ten, or not at all' for the Federation. In spite of the revision Jamaica and Trinidad were still dissatisfied with their representation and the fact that the Federation seemed to favour the smaller islands.

The powers of the Federal Government were a persistent problem. The Federation was weak, with only residual powers. Williams wanted a strong Federation, in particular the power to levy taxes, control economic development and set up a customs union. Adams wanted the first two of these. Jamaica opposed all of them and wanted a weak Federation. Jamaica and Trinidad's conflict over these points was not good for the Federation. While the Federation was so weak there seemed to be no point in continuing with it.

Manley went to London in January 1960, to begin separate negotiations for Jamaica's independence which the British Government had allowed for as early as the Montego Bay Conference. Trinidad began similar moves soon after which certainly undermined the Federation. The smaller islands saw their best chance of independence within the Federation. Thus the two largest islands thought that their association with the smaller islands in the Federation would hold back their own constitutional progress.

There were five immediate causes for the breakdown of the Federation. It is unthinkable to have a federation without freedom of movement from one part to another. The small islands insisted on freedom of movement. However, British Guiana and British Honduras had not joined originally because of this condition. When it arose again in 1961 Trinidad opposed it because her per capita income was twice that of the next richest unit. Trinidad was relatively under-populated in comparison with Barbados. Trinidad felt that she would suffer from large-scale immigration which she would be powerless to prevent. This was the main cause of Trinidad's withdrawal. A second conflict between Trinidad and the Federal Government was over the Chaguaramas site for the Federal Capital. The Peninsula had been leased to the United States for ninety-nine years under the 'destroyers-for-bases' deal of 1940. Britain had promised £1 000 000 towards the Federal Capital. Williams negotiated with the United States and Britain for the revoking of the lease on the grounds that the Trinidadian people had not been consulted. He regarded it as a domestic issue. Adams regarded it as a Federal issue as it involved the Federal Capital and that the Federal Government should negotiate. Williams was accused of trying to make political capital by successfully negotiating the restoration of Chaguaramas to Trinidad.

There were three immediate causes for Jamaica's secession. The Federation, it was hoped, would develop into a customs union and free trade area, with tariffs on goods from outside the Federation. Most of Jamaica's revenue derived from customs duties so she opposed the customs' union. Trinidad wanted her exports to move freely throughout the area so she supported free trade. Most members argued that a customs' union would lead to the expansion of trade and production and would benefit all. Jamaica withdrew when it became obvious that the Federal Government's policy was to introduce a customs' union.

Jamaica wanted a weak Federation and wanted to control her own economic development. The Federal Government wanted to control all economic development and did not want any unit to develop faster than another. Jamaica's economy was expanding faster than all other units' except Trinidad. In 1960 Jamaica allowed an oil company to build an oil refinery in Jamaica and gave the company tax concessions. This conflicted with the Federal Government's policy of controlling all economic development and also Trinidad's advantage in oil-refining. Adams held that the tax concessions that had been granted were illegal as he wanted the Federal Government to have control over taxation. He also argued that this special tax arrangement had helped Jamaica's industrial development at the expense of the other units. Economic development became linked with the last cause of Jamaica's secession, that of retro-active legislation. Adams said that taxation would become a Federal subject and that when retro-active legislation was passed in 1963 he would back-date the law to cover Jamaica's illegal tax concessions and make Jamaica pay the back taxes. Bustamante demanded secession.

In May 1961, Sir Alexander Bustamante, leader of Jamaica's Democratic Labour Party, demanded a referendum of the Jamaican people on membership of the Federation. He had always had reservations about the Federation, suspecting it to be a device of the British Government for withholding independence from Jamaica. He also saw Federation as a device whereby Britain would transfer responsibility for the smaller islands from herself to Jamaica. He felt that Jamaica was being asked to subsidise the smaller islands. Jamaica's contributions to revenue certainly seemed to prove his point. He was able to convince organised labour in Jamaica that they were supporting the Eastern Caribbean and the referendum rejected Federation. Manley subsequently lost the 1961 elections and Jamaica seceded from the Federation of the West Indies and proceeded with separate independence. Trinidad did the same. The Federation could not continue without its two most powerful members and in May 1962, the British Government formally dissolved the Federation.

Notes

1 Although Jamaica and Trinidad were the largest units, the smaller islands dominated the Federal Government politically and had most ministers including the Prime Minister, Grantley Adams.
2 Manley of Jamaica and Williams of Trinidad did not stand in the Federal Elections of March 1958 thus weakening the standing of the Federal Government.
3 The Federation was weak, with only residual powers and no control over levying taxes, economic development or having a customs union.
4 Both Trinidad and Jamaica continued to pursue their moves to independence which undermined the Federation.
5 Trinidad withdrew from the Federation mainly in opposition to freedom of movement and over the site of the Federal Capital at Chaguaramas.
6 Jamaica withdrew through opposition to the proposed customs union, her desire to control her own economic development, and possible Federal action over her 'illegal' tax concessions.
7 Both Jamaica and Trinidad seceded from the Federation in 1961. As it could not continue without its two most powerful members, the Federation was dissolved in May 1962.

Map 10.7: The 'Little Eight', CARIFTA, and CARICOM

'Little Eight'

In May 1962, the Eastern Caribbean islands except Trinidad tried to preserve some form of closer union at a Conference in London. Barbados, the dominant partner by population and resources, was at first enthusiastic and tried to hold the 'Little Eight' together by calling conferences in Barbados in 1963 and 1964. However, by 1965 Barbados decided to seek separate independence and the 'Little Eight' broke up.

CARIFTA

Antigua, Barbados and Guyana wanted the benefits of membership of a larger trading area and began negotiations in 1965. They were joined by Trinidad as the first signatories to the Treaty of Antigua which set up the Caribbean Free Trade Association (CARIFTA) in May 1968. Between July and August 1968, the remainder of the British Caribbean joined except for British Honduras which did so in 1971. Therefore there were twelve members of CARIFTA.

The general aims were to expand production in the whole area, thus creating full employment and higher living standards, by encouraging trade by the removal of customs duties on goods traded between members. Unlike the Federation, CARIFTA intended to co-ordinate economic development for the whole area. Once again Jamaica's reliance on customs duties for revenue was the major problem and a period of adjustment had to be allowed before duties could be removed. Some duties were removed immediately, others over a five-year period, and, in the case of less developed countries, over a ten-year period. By 1974 CARIFTA was almost a free trade area and was working successfully.

Its Constitution was: a) the Conference of Heads of Government to decide policy; b) a Council of Ministers to put specific schemes into practice; c) a Commonwealth Regional Secretariat based in Georgetown, Guyana, as a permanent body to administer the development projects decided on by the Council of Ministers.

CARICOM

The Caribbean Common Market (CARICOM) was more ambitious but the logical extension of CARIFTA. Barbados, Guyana, Jamaica and Trinidad signed the Treaty of Chaguaramas which set up CARICOM on 4 July 1973. In July 1974, the remaining CARIFTA members joined.

CARICOM'S aims were to replace CARIFTA and extend its work into the political sphere. The Common Market would integrate economic development and the Caribbean Community would establish certain common services and co-ordinate foreign policy. There would be a common tariff on goods from outside the Common Market to protect native industry. Free trade between members had almost been achieved by CARIFTA. Industry would be encouraged by attracting outside investment and channelling it into development projects, and by giving tax concessions and incentives. The less developed members of CARICOM would be given special consideration and, unlike the Federation, the rich members of CARICOM were prepared to support the poorer. Common services which were soon set up were in health, agriculture, transport and meteorology, some being more important subjects than the Federal Government was given control of. In the next round responsibility for education, industry, labour, finance and mines was added. (Students will be interested to know that the Caribbean Examinations Council was a CARICOM institution set up at this time.) Foreign affairs also came under the control of the Community.

CARICOM constitutionally consisted of: a) a Heads of Government Conference which was the final authority and determined policy. It concluded treaties and negotiated with foreign governments on behalf of its members. It also had control over finance; b) the Common Market Council consisted of one Minister from each member state and was responsible for the day-to-day running of the Common Market. It acted on the directives of the Conference; c) the Permanent Secretariat in Georgetown, Guyana, was divided into a Trade and Integration Department, and General Services and Administration.

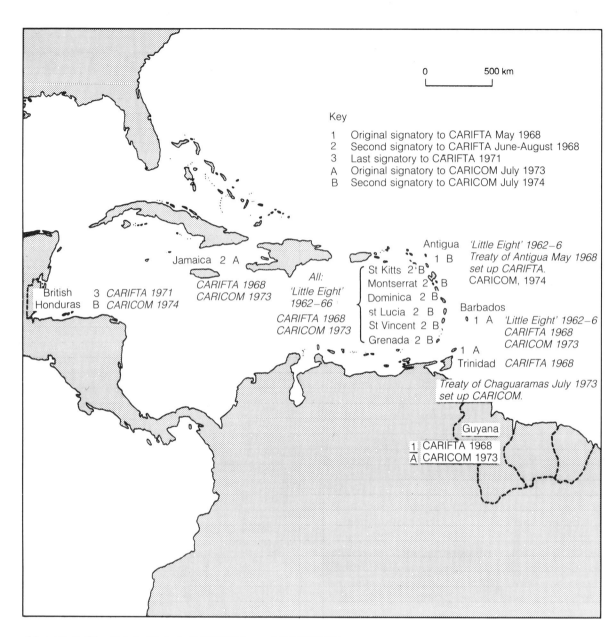

1 Original signatory to CARIFTA May 1968
2 Second signatory to CARIFTA June-August 1968
3 Last signatory to CARIFTA 1971
A Original signatory to CARICOM July 1973
B Second signatory to CARICOM July 1974

0   500 km

Antigua   'Little Eight' 1962–6
• 1 B   Treaty of Antigua May 1968
        set up CARIFTA.
        CARICOM, 1974

Jamaica 2 A

CARIFTA 1968
CARICOM 1973

All:
'Little Eight'
1962–66

CARIFTA 1968
CARICOM 1973

St Kitts 2 B
Montserrat 2 B
Dominica 2 B
st Lucia 2 B
St Vincent 2 B
Grenada 2 B

Barbados
° 1 A   'Little Eight' 1962–6
        CARIFTA 1968
        CARICOM 1973

1 A
Trinidad   CARIFTA 1968

British   3 CARIFTA 1971
Honduras   B CARICOM 1974

Treaty of Chaguaramas July 1973
set up CARICOM.

Guyana
1 CARIFTA 1968
A CARICOM 1973

Map 10.7: The 'Little Eight', CARIFTA, and CARICOM

Notes

1 The 'Little Eight' was an attempt by Barbados and the other Eastern Caribbean islands except Trinidad to preserve the Federation but it broke down when Barbados withdrew to seek separate independence in 1965.

2 CARIFTA was an attempt to achieve the benefits of a larger trading area by removing customs duties to stimulate trade and production amongst members.

3 It lasted from 1968 to 1973/4 and had twelve members from the British Caribbean.

4 Between 1973 and 1974 CARIFTA was replaced by CARICOM which was a more ambitious association politically and economically as it intended to set up a Common Market and a Community which would take over certain common services and foreign affairs.

5 The constitutions of CARIFTA and CARICOM were similar and consisted of a Heads of State Conference, a Council of Ministers (Common Market Council) and a Secretariat.

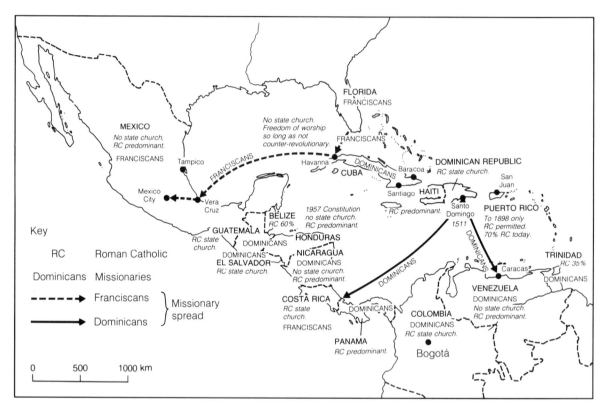

Map 11.1: Roman Catholicism in the Spanish Caribbean

Map 11.1: Roman Catholicism in the Spanish Caribbean

The Pope required the settlers to convert the heathen to Christianity. Indeed he would not give his blessing for the voyage unless they undertook to do so. By the 'Bulls of Donation' of 1493 and 1506 in which the Pope gave the lands of the New World to the Spanish Crown, it was the sacred trust of the King to see that the Indians were converted to Christianity. However, the early settlers were not interested in conversion. The clergy of the Roman Catholic Church was divided into 'secular' and 'regular'. The secular clergy conducted the work in the parishes, holding masses, preaching, etc., ministering to the settlers and paying little attention to the Indians.

The regular clergy were those who had taken the vows of a certain order, such as the Dominican or Franciscan Order. They were the missionaries who came to convert the Indians. In the Spanish Caribbean the Dominicans dominated but there were some Franciscans in Mexico. Montesinos and Las Casas were both Dominicans who devoted themselves to the conversion of Indians. They were opposed by the settlers. The missionaries wanted the conversion of the Indians and the settlers wanted the Indians for labour. At first the Crown put the economic development of the Indies first and the settlers had their way in spite of the Papal Donations.

The Indians were the subjects of the King of Spain and they could not be enslaved. However, by about 1640 the Indians had been wiped out in the Spanish Indies. Then came the problem of the Catholic Church and African slavery. The Church avoided this by saying that Africans were subjects of foreign princes at war with Spain and therefore could be enslaved. Also the argument that it was better to be a Christian slave than pagan free was used, especially in the French Islands. Spain encouraged Christianity for slaves. *Las Siete Partidas*, the Spanish Slave Code, required a master to baptise his slaves, instruct them in Christianity, allow them to go to Church and to marry. However, even baptism was usually no more than a token gesture. The Spanish thought Christian instruction would be dangerous to the slave system with its ideas of brotherhood and equality before God.

However, when emancipation came Spanish ex-slaves were already members of the Church. This explains why the Roman Catholic Church had almost one hundred per cent membership among blacks in the Spanish Caribbean. To-day Roman Catholicism dominates the Americas and it is easily the dominant Christian denomination in the Caribbean.

Notes

1 The Pope required the settlers in the Spanish Empire to convert the Indians to Christianity but the settlers were only interested in Indians for labour.
2 The secular clergy ministered to the settlers and did little about conversion.
3 The regular clergy, especially the Dominicans, undertook the conversion of Indians in the Spanish Caribbean.
4 Montesinos and Las Casas were the two most famous Dominican missionaries.
5 Indians, as subjects of the King of Spain, could not be enslaved by law, but Africans as subjects of foreign princes could be and the Catholic Church saw nothing wrong in this.
6 The Spanish encouraged the conversion of slaves and almost all were baptised but Christian instruction usually did not go beyond this.
7 As all the slaves had been baptised into the Catholic Church, on emancipation the Catholic Church had almost one hundred per cent membership from the ex-slaves.
8 Roman Catholicism is easily the predominant religion in the Caribbean today because the Spanish Caribbean is highest in proportion of population and the Roman Catholic Church has 70–80 per cent membership.

Chart 11.1: Organisation of the Church of England in the British Caribbean

A   Overall organisation:

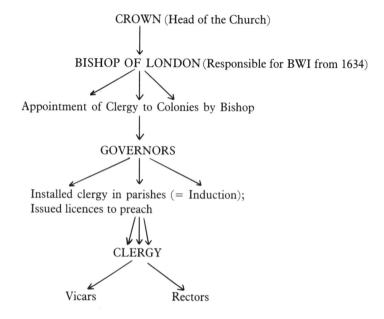

CROWN (Head of the Church)

BISHOP OF LONDON (Responsible for BWI from 1634)

Appointment of Clergy to Colonies by Bishop

GOVERNORS

Installed clergy in parishes (= Induction);
Issued licences to preach

CLERGY

Vicars   Rectors

Paid by Central Government;
Supplemented by a)   Mother Church in England
                 b)   Bequests, donations, alms
                 c)   Income from Church lands
                      (Rectors only)
(Vicar's stipend could reach £300 per annum.)

B   Organisation within Colony:

COLONY

PARISHES

VESTRY   – Membership: Clergy ex-officio
                              Elected parishioners

Responsible for Government

CHURCH   LOCAL GOVERNMENT
Conduct of services   ↔ Registration ↔ Tax collection
Baptism, marriage, burial   of   Conduct of elections
(Births, deaths, marriages) Parishioners Publishing laws
                                          Local Government Offices

Chart 11.1: Organisation of the Church of England in the British Caribbean

The Church of England was the 'Established Church'. This means that it was the official Church of the State and the Crown was the Head of the Church of England. Therefore the Church of England became the official Church of the West Indian colonies. In practice this meant that the clergy of the Church of England in the West Indies were appointed from England (by the Bishop of London from 1634) and assigned to parishes by Governors of colonies; only the latter could issue licences to preach. The Church of England clergy were paid out of government funds and by 1870 one-tenth of government funds was going towards the Church of England. Finally, as the Established Church it meant that the Church of England, through the parishes, was the instrument of local government.

However, having an Established Church did not mean that other denominations were excluded although in the early days of the British Caribbean colonies other churches were uncommon. In 1641 Captain Philip Bell introduced the Church of England officially into Barbados by making attendance at Sunday service compulsory and punishing Dissenters (those outside the Church of England). And a series of laws from England between 1661 and 1665 brought the crime of Dissension to the British Caribbean and the persecution of Quakers in Barbados followed. The Glorious Revolution of 1688–9 restored religious toleration and persecution disappeared not returning to the British Caribbean until the time of abolition and emancipation when the slave owners blamed the dissenting churches for undermining the slave system.

However, being the Established Church meant that it was the church of the 'Establishment', that is, of the Governor himself, the colonial officials, of the leading planters and the armed forces. The leaders of society were members of the Church of England and the clergy enjoyed this high social status and sometimes enjoyed incomes befiting this status. For example £300 per annum in the sixteenth and seventeenth centuries was a very good income in the British Caribbean. The clergy were either 'vicars' or 'rectors'. Rectors received income from Church lands in the parish. Parishes were sub-divisions of British colonies and were used by the government to carry out local government. Thus they had church duties and government duties. Parishes were controlled by Vestries. Under church duties came baptism, marriage and burial. Under local government duties came tax collection, conduct of elections, publication of laws and running local government offices.

Notes

1   The Church of England, as the official Church of the State, also became the official Church of the West Indian colonies, with clergy appointed by the Bishop of London from 1634, and licensed and assigned to parishes by the Governors.
2   From 1661 Dissension became a crime in the British Caribbean, for example, the Quakers were persecuted in Barbados. Even after 1689 and religious toleration, the dissenting churches were blamed for undermining the slave system.
3   Being the Established Church gave the clergy social standing and a role in local government through the Vestry.

Map 11.2: Nonconformist Churches before emancipation

Churches which did not agree with the doctrine and ritual of the Church of England became known as 'Nonconformist Churches', i.e. they did not conform to the Church of England. They have some things in common with each other but also have individual characteristics. They broke away from the Church of England because they did not like the hierarchical, episcopalian (through

bishops) structure of the Established Church; nor its ritual; nor some of its doctrine. Most wanted a more personal relationship between the worshipper and God without the priest intervening. Therefore they played down the role of the clergy. Four Nonconformist groups were prominent in the British West Indies.

Quakers were founded between 1647 and 1666 by George Fox. They sought a more personal knowledge of God by each individual. Their worship took place in a 'meeting' where they had a period of 'silent waitng' for an 'inward light'

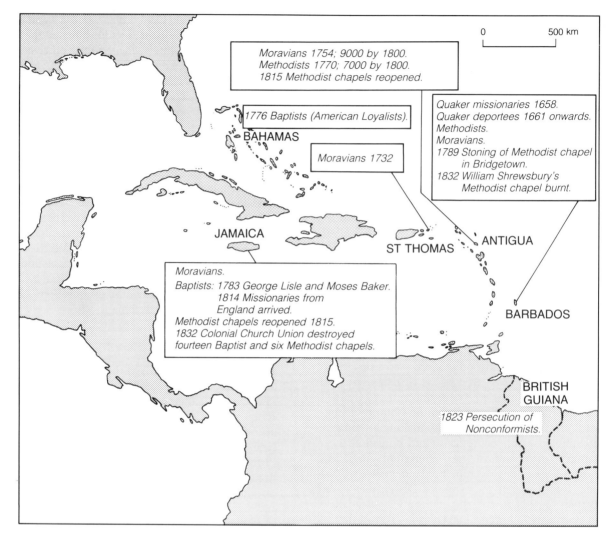

Map 11.2: Nonconformist Churches before emancipation

which would give rise to a 'concern' and then discussion by the rest of the meeting. This was how Quaker opposition to slavery arose. It was the concern of a single group which spread to the whole movement. They rejected formal prayers, creeds, clergy and ritual.

In 1658 Quaker missionaries arrived in Barbados. Then Quakers were deported to Barbados as indentured servants. They rejected much of West Indian life, like the militia (Quakers were forbidden to bear arms), Church of England services, tithes to the Church, dress and later, slavery. In 1676 the Barbados legislature passed anti-Quaker laws and persecution began.

The Moravians became united in East Germany in 1727 and the first group arrived at St Thomas in the Virgin Islands in 1732. They were welcome in the West Indies for their piety which people could not object to. Also they kept to themselves on self-contained estates. They tried to imitate Jesus and took the Bible as their authority for all conduct. Missionary work was very important to them and this gave the impetus to other Nonconformist Churches to come to the West Indies also. The Moravians were most active in Antigua where they reached 9000 in number by 1800. They were also active in Jamaica and Barbados.

Wesleyan Methodists became the third largest denomination in the Caribbean after Roman Catholics and Anglicans. They began to move away from the Church of England after 1729. They sought a personal relationship with God through Bible study and simple forms of worship. They believed that the Holy Spirit helped to achieve this relationship with God. They played down the role of the clergy and made them partners with the laity. They emphasised salvation through good works and so they were very active in helping the poor and under-privileged. Thus they appealed to slaves and their missionary work in the West Indies was very important. They held informal meetings for slaves as well as formal services and they preached against the evils of the social system. They first reached Antigua in 1770 and by 1800 there were 7000 Methodists there. In 1789 their leading missionary, Thomas Coke, visited the West Indies and as a result twelve more missionaries were sent out by the Methodist Missionary Society. Methodism was very popular with slaves and unpopular with planters.

In Jamaica the most popular Nonconformist denomination was the Baptists. The sect that came to the West Indies were the General Baptists who believed that Christ died for all men not just the 'Chosen'. They also believed in salvation by good works. American Loyalists brought the Baptist Movement to the West Indies, first to the Bahamas. The Bible was their supreme authority for belief and conduct. The Church was composed of believers only and only believers could be baptised. Therefore they practised adult baptism. This was by total immersion. As they held that religion was a matter of man's conscience they separated the Church and State. In the West Indies they built plain, simple chapels in which there was little ritual or set prayers. Indeed prayers could be introduced at any time and the words varied from one occasion to another. Hymn-singing was important.

American Loyalists brought their servants with them and two such, George Lisle and Moses Baker, brought the Baptist Movement to Jamaica in 1776. George Lisle was given a licence to preach and built a large chapel in Kingston. It easily became the most popular Church for ex-slaves after 1838. The Baptist Missionary Society sent out missionaries from England in 1814.

Nonconformist ministers received licences without difficulty at first but when they were accused of undermining the slave system with ideas of equality and Christian brotherhood their licences were hedged with conditions which made it almost impossible to reach the slaves, for example they could not preach between sunrise and sunset. However, they thrived on hardship and as the planters became even more worried about their success the persecution took the form of violence as abolition and emancipation drew near. In 1789 the Methodist Chapel in Bridgetown was stoned. The most famous case of persecution was when the Colonial Church Union, a militant group formed by the planters, destroyed fourteen Baptist and six Methodist chapels in Jamaica in 1832. Frequently in Jamaica and Barbados Nonconformist ministers and preachers were beaten up.

Notes

1 Nonconformist Churches broke away from the Church of England because they would not agree to follow the government, doctrine or ritual.
2 As they put much emphasis on good works they were prominent in the missionary field.
3 The Quakers were most active in Barbados where they were frequently persecuted because they would not accept attendance at the Church of England, service in the militia and later the institution of slavery.
4 Moravians were encouraged to come to the British Caribbean because of the good example they set in piety, hard work and self-sufficiency.
5 Moravians believed in equality and blacks and whites worked alongside each other in the fields on Moravian estates.
6 Wesleyan Methodists were the most enthusiastic missionaries and they helped the poor, oppressed and under-privileged and slaves were in need of their ministry.
7 Baptists came to Jamaica at first from the United States. They became the most popular church with the slaves as they preached that Christ died for all men. Their services were particularly easy to follow and any member of the congregation could offer prayers.
8 As abolition and emancipation approached the Nonconformists were persecuted for undermining the slave system with the doctrines of equality before God and Christian brotherhood.

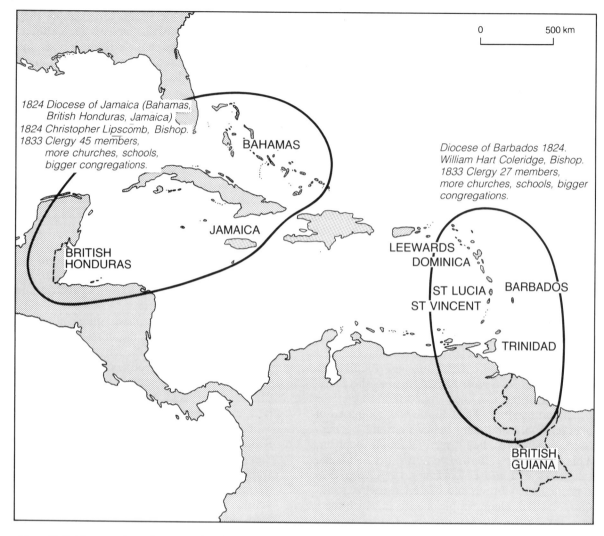

1824 Diocese of Jamaica (Bahamas, British Honduras, Jamaica)
1824 Christopher Lipscomb, Bishop.
1833 Clergy 45 members, more churches, schools, bigger congregations.

Diocese of Barbados 1824.
William Hart Coleridge, Bishop.
1833 Clergy 27 members, more churches, schools, bigger congregations.

Map 11.3: Preparations for emancipation by the Church of England

Map 11.3: Preparations for emancipation by the Church of England

The Church of England was unprepared for emancipation and did little to reform until too late. It had stressed obedience which also implied obedience by slaves to their masters. It had encouraged slaves to accept their station in life and not seek equality. When the Church was accused of not working for emancipation or preparing for it, it answered its critics by saying that the doctrines of obedience and accepting one's station in life would help emancipation to pass off peacefully. This was in sharp contrast to the Nonconformist Churches which had preached equality before God and Christian brotherhood and had actively campaigned for emancipation.

The Church of England in the West Indies had been weak and poorly served. The settlers and planters who made up the majority of the congregation were generally irreligious and rarely attended church. They were opposed to slaves becoming Christians and so the majority of the population was kept out of the Church. The organisation of the Church of England was poor. The Bishop of London never visited the West Indies and was too far away to know what was going on. He appointed the clergy but never checked on their work or dismissed those who were incompetent or corrupt. The West Indian clergy never held synods (meetings) and so were never able to discuss Church affairs or keep up with new practices. Consequently there were many local variations in doctrines and practices in the Church in the West Indies. The clergy were generally poor, being attracted by the income and social status rather than by the calling. They were not prepared to oppose the planters over slavery. Indeed they were slave-owners themselves and enjoyed the social system that went with slave-owning. The Church of England rejected the slaves before emancipation so on emancipation it is not surprising that the slaves rejected the Church of England.

The main missionary societies of the Church of England, the Church Missionary Society founded in 1799, and the British and Foreign Bible Society founded in 1803, directed their activities towards Africa, Asia and the Pacific and neglected the West Indies. However it is doubtful that they would have opposed the plantocracy over slavery. The Society for the Propagation of the Gospel, founded much earlier, had tried to convert slaves but had little impact in the nineteenth century against the vested interests.

The Church of England was losing ground to the Nonconformist Churches and knew that it had to reform. The reforms came too late and after emancipation it lost even more ground even though it remained the Established Church in most islands until 1870.

About 1800 the Church tried to ensure that each parish had a church in good repair and a clergyman. Bishop Porteus of London established a court of five rectors in Jamaica to discipline the clergy. He also tried to encourage Sunday Schools but the churches lacked competent laity. In 1824 the first local bishop was appointed, the Bishop of Jamaica. He was to lead the Church in the British Caribbean on the spot. In the same year in an effort to attract blacks into the Church, baptism fees were reduced from twenty shillings to two shillings and for slaves were done away with completely. However, by this time slaves were being baptised into other churches.

In 1824 the British Caribbean was divided into two dioceses. Jamaica included British Honduras and the Bahamas. Barbados included the Eastern Caribbean and British Guiana. Christopher Lips-

comb was the first Bishop of Jamaica and William Hart Coleridge of Barbados. They were instructed to improve the clergy and report on what had been done to Christianise the slaves.

By increasing the grant to the Church in the Caribbean to £20 000 the British Government enabled it to recruit more clergy, and the total went up from forth-eight in 1800 to seventy-two in 1833, forty-five in the Diocese of Jamaica and twenty-seven in Barbados. However, there were still no locally-recruited clergy until Codrington College, Barbados, held its first ordinations in 1834.

Therefore by emancipation the Church of England had more churches, clergy, congregations and schools yet still failed to attract blacks except in Barbados.

Notes

1   The Church of England had not been willing to change the slave society and therefore had not prepared for emancipation.
2   It was in a poor state before 1800 with its members irreligious, its organisation poor and neglected, its clergy few and of poor quality and its churches in disrepair.
3   By teaching obedience and accepting one's station in life the Church had been teaching the slaves to accept servitude rather than challenge it.
4   The Nonconformist Churches had been stressing equality before God and Christian brotherhood which was much more acceptable to slaves seeking their freedom.
5   The Missionary Societies of the Church of England had turned away from the British Caribbean and were unlikely to have challenged the plantocracy.
6   The Church of England knew too late that it had to reform.
7   In 1824 the British Caribbean was divided into the Dioceses of Barbados and Jamaica and the new Bishops were told to improve the clergy.
8   The number of churches, congregations, clergy and schools increased by 1833, but still the slaves rejected the Church of England on emancipation.

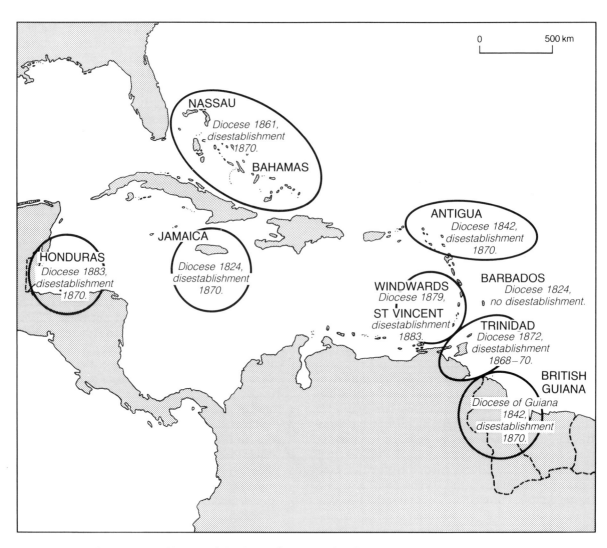

Map 11.4: Reforms in the Church of England after emancipation

Map 11.4: Reforms in the Church of England after emancipation

In 1834 the Church of England, through the Society for the Propagation of the Gospel, contributed to the Negro Education Grant for schools in the British West Indies. Most of the Society's funds of £200 000 went towards education. This was an immediate response to emancipation. The Central Governments also voted more money for the Established Church and the Vestries used some of this money on education but put more into recruiting more clergy. By 1845 there were ninety clergy in Jamaica and seventy in Barbados Dioceses, too many for two Bishops to control. So new Dioceses were created: Antigua and Guiana in 1842; Nassau in 1861; Trinidad in 1872; the Windward Islands in 1879; and British Honduras in 1883. All these new Bishops helped to improve the standards of the clergy.

The British Government wanted the disestablishment of the Church of England throughout the Empire. In the British Caribbean an Established Church which was not the church of the majority was an anachronism. Emancipation had made it an anachronism. It had been the Church of the white ruling class. It had rejected the blacks and the blacks rejected it after emancipation. By 1870 the Church of England had the support of only one-third of the population of the British Caribbean except in Barbados where it had majority support.

There were other less important reasons for disestablishment. One tenth of government funds went on the Church and the British Government thought that the Church of England should pay for itself out of local funds as the other churches did. Having an Established Church was causing social and racial divisions.

In 1868 the British Government stopped its grant of £20 000 per year to the Church of England in the West Indies. Its intention was obviously disestablishment but it wanted the local legislatures to vote it for themselves. Most British West Indian Governments passed Disestablishment Acts between 1868 and 1870, except for Barbados which kept the Established Church and St Vincent who delayed it until 1883 because it needed government funds for its Church. For example, by the Jamaican Disestablishment Act of 1870 all churches, rectories, vicarages and schools were transferred to a corporation of the Church. The local churches then had to pay the stipends of the clergy as each former incumbent died. It was very expensive when the stipend had been £400 per year and many parishes could not support a rector or a vicar so the numbers of clergymen fell. However, the Church of England remained the Church of the leaders of colonial society in spite of disestablishment.

In the British Caribbean Barbados was the only colony to retain the Established Church. There it was the Church of the majority, perhaps 70 per cent of the population with strong support from the blacks. It was not causing social and racial divisions because most people were its members. The Church of England clergy were locally born and trained in Codrington College. This, together with the popular efforts of the early bishops, ensured that the Church was of the people. Therefore after resisting Crown Colony Government successfully the Barbados Legislature felt strong enough to resist the British Government again. In 1872 it confirmed the Church of England as the Established Church and the Government continued to pay the clergy.

Notes

1 The Church of England made an immediate effort to help the ex-slaves by contributing to the Negro Education Grant.
2 The British Government also put more money into the Established Church which was channelled through the Vestries largely to recruiting more clergy.
3 Between 1842 and 1883 six new dioceses were created in the British Caribbean in an attempt to improve the organisation and standards of the Church of England.
4 After emancipation the Church of England could not remain the Established Church because it was not the church of the majority.
5 It had not catered for the blacks before emancipation so the blacks did not join it after emancipation.
6 Disestablishment took place between 1868 and 1870 in most colonies.
7 Barbados retained the Church of England as the Established Church.
8 After disestablishment the local churches had to pay the stipends of the clergy, hence the delay in disestablishment in St Vincent.
9 In Barbados the Church of England was the church of the majority. It was popular because there were no racial or social divisions caused by the Church and the clergy were locally trained at Codrington College.

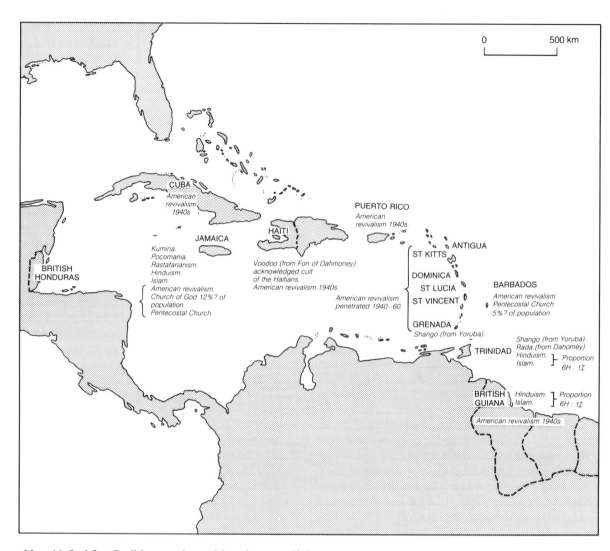

0   500 km

CUBA
*American
revivalism
1940s*

PUERTO RICO
*American
revivalism 1940s.*

JAMAICA
*Kumina.
Pocomania.
Rastafarianism.
Hinduism.
Islam.
American revivalism.
Church of God 12%? of
population.
Pentecostal Church.*

HAITI
*Voodoo (from Fon of Dahmoney)
acknowledged cult
of the Haitians.
American revivalism 1940s.*

ANTIGUA

ST KITTS

DOMINICA

ST LUCIA

ST VINCENT

*American revivalism
penetrated 1940–60.*

BARBADOS
*American revivalism.
Pentecostal Church
5%? of population.*

GRENADA
Shango (from Yoruba).

BRITISH
HONDURAS

TRINIDAD
*Shango (from Yoruba).
Rada (from Dahomey).
Hinduism.]
Islam.*   *Proportion
6H : 1I*

BRITISH
GUIANA
*Hinduism.]
Islam.*   *Proportion
6H : 1I*

American revivalism 1940s.

Map 11.5: Afro-Caribbean cults and immigrant religions

Map 11.5: Afro-Caribbean cults and immigrant religions

Afro-Caribbean cults

African slaves brought animist beliefs which evolved into Afro-Caribbean cults with the geographical separation from Africa and the passage of time. Usually they were a mixing of animist beliefs and Christianity, as in Voodoo, the most famous example of an Afro-Caribbean cult. Often a West Indian would hold two beliefs, his Afro-Caribbean cult and Christianity, at the same time. Belief in the Afro-Caribbean cult would usually be the stronger in a time of crisis.

Afro-Caribbean cults conflict with Christianity in that the latter has no place for superstition and magic, spirit-worship, etc. However, Christian church leaders often accept two beliefs among their congregations rather than having to reject the holders completely.

Dahomey was the source of most animist beliefs that crossed the Atlantic but Nigeria and Ghana have also been sources. Voodoo came to Haiti with the slaves when it was St Domingue. The French imported slaves on such a large scale and so quickly after 1670 that little assimilation into French culture and religion could take place and Voodoo was able to flourish secretly among the slaves. Over one hundred years later the Haitian Revolution cut Haiti off from the outside world and it became a country where animist beliefs became almost universal so that today Voodoo is the acknowledged religion of the country although on paper most profess Roman Catholicism.

'Voodoo' derives from 'Vodun', the tribal god of the Fon of Dahomey. In Haiti he became one of the gods presided over by 'Bondieu'; the others are called 'loa'. Voodoo families worship their own loa whom they identify with African gods, spirits of ancestors or Catholic saints. The loa are meant to protect families by their magic powers which enter the worshippers in trances brought on by ritual dances. Voodoo services are conducted by 'hourigans' (male priests) while 'mambos' (female attendants) keep away evil spirits.

In Trinidad and Grenada Shango, the Yoruba god of thunder and lightning, is worshipped by many blacks. He was the god the slaves remembered while forgetting many others like Ogun and Oisha Oko. A few blacks in Trinidad also follow the Rada cult from Dahomey.

The maroons of Jamaica preserved their animist beliefs from Africa when they were outlaws and cut off from Christianity. In the cult of Kumina the followers are possessed by spirits who save them from sickness and death. Pocomania has overtaken Kumina in the last hundred years as the chief Afro-Caribbean cult in Jamaica. It is a typical mixture of animism and Christianity. In their worship the followers are possessed by spirits during their drumming and dancing.

Rastafarianism in Jamaica began as a religious cult with the worship of Haile Selassie, the Emperor of Ethiopia, as the Messiah of the black race who would lead the blacks back to Africa. While Haile Selassie, a direct descendant of King Solomon, was alive he kept the emphasis on the religious side of Rastafarianism, but after his death, and even as a result of his disappointing visit to Jamaica, the movement had become more social and political.

Belief in Obeah is widespread in the Caribbean but it is not a religious cult but more of a superstition. 'Obeah' derives from 'Obi', the Ashanti word for a priest and an obeahman is believed to work spells.

American revivalism

Between 1933 and 1963 Protestant revivalist movements grew strong in the United States and had a great impact on religion in the Caribbean. Revivalists felt that many of the Christian churches needed 'purifying' because of their excessive emphasis on the importance of the clergy as in episcopacy, on sacraments, ritual, liturgy and adornment. In other words, revivalists felt that these churches had become corrupted. Their answer was to restore the Bible as the supreme authority for belief and conduct; to imitate Jesus Christ; to achieve salvation through good works; to achieve a personal relationship with God through prayer; and to prepare for the Second Coming of Jesus Christ to earth (this was the central theme of most revivalist belief).

Not only did they consider that some Christian churches had become corrupt, but also they disliked the liberal society of the twentieth century. In the Caribbean revivalists tended to segregate themselves from the rest of society by their rigid abstention from dancing, drinking, smoking and movie-going. Their women wore plain, long dresses and no cosmetics. In the Caribbean their good works have been largely through finance and not by going out amongst the poor and oppressed which they have left to the Salvation Army.

American revivalism came to the Caribbean in

the 1940s through Cuba, Haiti and Puerto Rico where it attracted those who rejected Roman Catholicism. It penetrated Jamaica and the Eastern Caribbean as far as British Guiana before 1960. In the Caribbean American revivalism has two branches:

1 The Holiness Churches consist of the Church of God, the Church of the Nazarene, the Church of Christ and Pilgrim Holiness.
2 The Pentecostal Church.

Holiness Churches believe that the Holy Spirit enters the heart of a believer in prayer and gives him a 'holiness' (second blessing). Their services are quiet and simple. Because of this the Pentecostals broke away, wanting much more active, physical participation in their services such as shouting and stamping during prayers.

Indian religions

The Indian immigrants who arrived in the Caribbean between 1838 and 1917 brought two religions, Hinduism and Islam. They were allowed to practise their religions because there was freedom of worship but they met with racial discrimination because Hinduism and Islam were social systems as well as religions. They were also discriminated against legally in that non-Christian marriages were not recognised so their children were illegitimate and not allowed to inherit property. They were excluded from Christian schools, but even when education became secular, Indians often chose not to send their children to state schools where they felt they would become corrupted by western immorality. Therefore Indians of both religions tended to cut themselves off from other West Indians.

The Church of England tried to convert Indians to Christianity through the Society for the Propagation of the Gospel. They were more successful in the British Caribbean than elsewhere in the Empire where Indians had settled, but nevertheless Hinduism and Islam still claim almost universal adherence amongst Indians. In the British Caribbean Hindus outnumber Moslems by about six to one.

Hinduism

Hinduism is polytheistic (there are many gods). The chief gods are Siva and Vishnu (Brahma declined in importance about AD 800) whom Hindus worship as the highest form of existence. Siva is the Destroyer but also the Creator because whatever is destroyed must have been created in the first place. Siva is bloodthirsty and can work miracles. Vishnu is the Protector and Preserver who upholds order in the world.

Hnduism is a social system as well as a religion. Society is divided rigidly into castes. The caste system has resisted all attempts to break it down, especially in India. Caste determines occupation and marriage and conveys a multitude of rules and conventions.

Hindus believe that the soul passes from one life to another, even from an animal to a human, in its earthly existence. If it has been godly and moral after its earthly cycle, the soul passes into 'Nirvana' or Everlasting Bliss. This belief is known as the transmigration of souls and the reincarnation of the soul. It explains why Hindus are not allowed to take life or eat meat in most forms.

Hindu festivals are conspicuous outward displays of the religion and are now tolerated in the West Indies although at first they were confined to Indian villages because they were apt to cause conflict. The chief festivals are: 1 *Diwali* (late October) in which Laksmi, the goddess of wealth, is honoured by the merchant community. It also commemorates the start of a new financial year. Westerners call *Diwali* the 'Hindu Christmas'. 2 *Holi* (February or March) is the Spring festival in which the god Krishna is particularly remembered. During this festival caste divisions are set aside and everyone is joyful, throwing coloured waters and powders and setting off fireworks. 3 *Mahasivarati* is the 'Great Night of Siva' (between January and March). It is the major festival of Sivaites, the followers of Siva. It starts off as a very solemn festival on the first afternoon and evening but on the next day there is feasting and exchanging gifts.

Islam

Muhammed founded Islam on 'Five Pillars' of compulsory doctrine:

1 Belief in one God, Allah. Muhammed is His prophet who explains God's message.
2 Prayers must be said five times a day. The prayer mat must be placed facing Mecca. The Friday midday service is the most important in the mosque.
3 Moslems must give alms which are assessed by the wealth of the giver.
4 Moslems must make the 'Haj' or pilgrimage to Mecca at least once in their lifetime.
5 Moslems must make peace with Allah and ask

for forgiveness of sins in the month of atonement known as 'Ramadan'.

Islam is also a social and legal system. Moslem law is laid down in the Koran, the Holy Book of Moslems. Polygamy of up to four wives is permitted. In strict Moslem societies women are not emancipated. Moslem festivals are not so conspicuous as Hindu ones except for Ramadan. In this month Moslems must abstain from food, drink and sexual intercourse from two hours before sunrise to after sunset, a severe discipline in a hot climate. Ramadan is a very solemn period of atonement which ends on the twenty-seventh day with a joyous festival called '*Id-el-Fitr*' when gifts are exchanged.

Notes

1 Belief in spirits (animism) was brought to the Caribbean from West Africa by slaves and mixing with some Christian beliefs produced Afro-Caribbean cults.

2 Voodoo, which originated in Dahomey, is the most famous example of an Afro-Caribbean cult. Voodoo is practised in Haiti where it is the dominant belief although most Haitians outwardly profess Christianity.

3 Rastafarianism in Jamaica started off in the 1930s as a religious cult but is now more of a social and political movement.

4 Many West Indians have two beliefs, Christianity and Afro-Caribbean cult, and in a crisis it is usually the Afro-Caribbean cult which is called upon.

5 American revivalism came to the Caribbean in the 1940s by way of Cuba, Haiti and Puerto Rico.

6 Revivalist churches require a purer form of worship stressing the authority of the Bible, the imitation of Jesus Christ, the power of prayer and little reliance on the minister.

7 The Second Coming of Jesus Christ to Earth is an essential belief.

8 Revivalists shun drinking, dancing, smoking and movie-going as corrupt.

9 The Indian immigrants brought Hinduism and Islam to the Caribbean.

10 Hinduism and Islam are more than religions. They are social systems which have tended to set Indians apart from the rest of West Indian society.

11 Hinduism is polytheistic with Siva and Vishnu as the chief deities.

12 Hindu festivals are very conspicuous and used to cause trouble in West Indian society.

13 Islam is monotheistic and Allah is the God and Muhammed is His prophet.

14 Moslem belief is based on the 'Five Pillars' laid down by Muhammed.

15 The chief Moslem festival is Ramadan, a month of abstinence and atonement in which forgiveness of sins is asked.

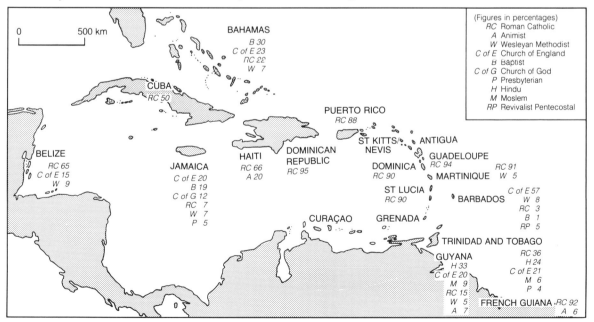

Map 11.6: Religions and religious denominations in the principal Caribbean territories c.1970.

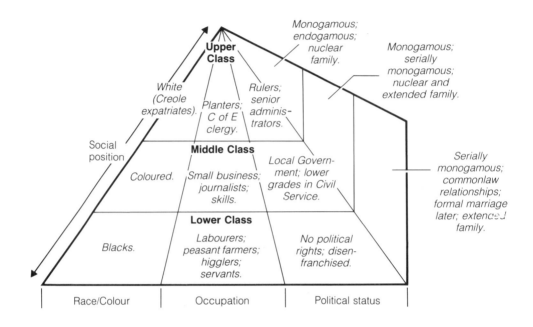

Chart 12.1: The social pyramid in the British West Indies

Chart 12.1: The social pyramid in the British West Indies

'A race has been freed, but a society has not been formed' (Lord Harris, Governor of Trinidad, 1848). Emancipation made a legal change but not a social change. The basic structure of West Indian society remained unchanged after emancipation. The ex-slaves remained at the bottom of the social pyramid and the whites at the top. There were several reasons why such a radical constitutional change as emancipation had no social impact for a long time. Emancipation was done at the stroke of a pen in London and was not produced by a revolutionary class and race struggle in which roles were reversed. In the Eastern Caribbean especially, e.g. in Barbados, there was little disruption in the old life style of the plantation economy. After three hundred years of slavery the idea of inferiority had been indoctrinated into blacks and after emancipation they were resigned to the lowest social position. Blacks still lacked material benefits but did not rebel to win them. West Indian agricultural economies were very conservative. 'White is right' led to the imitative society which lasted a long time in the West Indies. Crown Colony Government after 1860 reinforced the social structure because the whites ruled even more obviously than before and the expatriate white rulers allied with the planters.

Therefore emancipation brought no social changes at first. In the nineteenth century social changes came gradually as the blacks acquired land and education. The first generation after emancipation was of ex-slaves. The second generation was born-free. The ex-slave grandfathers died and eventually there was the class of blacks which had lost contact with slavery. The white population declined absolutely and relatively while the coloured and black populations increased. The tertiary sector had vacancies for journalists, lawyers, teachers, accountants, etc. but it took a long time for blacks to fill these.

Notes

1 Emancipation was a legal change but not a social change and the basic structure of British West Indian society remained the same as before emancipation.
2 This was chiefly because emancipation was not effected by violent revolution in which society was turned upside-down.
3 Crown Colony Government reinforced the social structure because there was no representation.
4 Social change occurred very slowly in the nineteenth century as old ideas died hard.

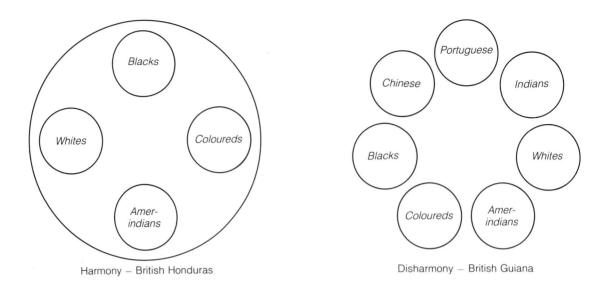

Harmony – British Honduras

Disharmony – British Guiana

Chart 12.2: Racial segregation and friction in the nineteenth century.

Chart 12.2: Racial segregation and friction in the nineteenth century

Most British West Indian societies in the nineteenth century were racially mixed except for a small island like Carriacou in the Grenadines which was predominantly black. Most societies were basically the white/coloured/black mix but some like British Guiana were more complex because of the Amerindian population and nineteenth-century immigrants. The societies were mixed but the races did not integrate. The immigrants, especially the Indians, remained completely outside the West Indian social system and kept to their own caste and class structures. They also kept out of the educational system. In other words they were separate societies.

Colour determined everything, occupation, social status, marriage, recreation and residence. There was no attempt to achieve integration in the nineteenth century. Segregation was encouraged from the top and accepted at the bottom. Desegregation often occurs in towns and cities, but not so in the nineteenth-century British West Indies where the towns had segregated housing. The immigrants were deliberately kept apart in 'Indian Villages' to increase the chance of re-indenture. Therefore there was racial discrimination and racial friction.

Chart 12.2 attempts to show two colonies at opposite ends of racial attitude. British Honduras had never been a plantocracy. Relations between master and slaves had been perhaps the best in the Caribbean. Yet the races did not integrate in British Honduras although race relations were relatively harmonious. The whites were the rulers and the blacks were the labourers as in a typical British West Indian society. On the other hand in British Guiana, the racial segregation was accompanied by racial disharmony, not just black/white friction but black/Indian friction and any other combination causing friction.

There was no social mobility, that is in the pyramid it was not possible to move upwards at first. Administrative posts were held by whites. Lower executive posts were held by light-skinned coloureds perhaps and menial jobs were performed by blacks. Even moving vertically downwards in the pyramid would have been impossible, for example, a white could not perform manual labour. There was no law about occupational immobility but purely social forces prevented it from happening. Also it is doubtful that the ruling classes practised 'divide and rule' except perhaps in British Guiana where one class was played off against another. Class divisions just happened and non-integration of races and classes was observed by the top and bottom of the social pyramid.

Notes

1 British West Indian Societies were racially mixed but not racially integrated in the nineteenth century.
2 There was racial discrimination built in to the social, political and economic life of the colonies through the social structure inherited from pre-emancipation days.
3 Sometimes there was friction between races but usually most people accepted their position in society and did not rebel.
4 Indians had their own social systems and were completely outside the rest of West Indian society.
5 British Honduras illustrates racial harmony but no racial integration.
6 British Guiana illustrates racial segregation with some racial friction.
7 There was no social mobility in the British West Indies for many years after emancipation.

Table 12.1: Family life in the nineteenth century

Marriage	Children	Parental allegiance	Family/kinship	Community
Monogamous	Legitimate	To both. Inheritance through father	Nuclear among whites	Self-reliant
Serially monogamous	Illegitimate	To mother	Extended – mother may collect children from different fathers.	Matri-focal and 'yard'. For support and benefit.
Common-law	Illegitimate	To mother	Extended. Family gathers round grandmother	Matri-focal and 'yard'
Common-law later formalised	Legitimate. Formalised to make children legitmate	To both. Inheritance through father	Extended but could become nuclear if formalised	

Table 12.1: Family life in the nineteenth century

After emancipation Christian marriage was the ideal and open to ex-slaves. However few could enter into formal marriage for economic reasons and so other unions were formed. The upper classes practised monogamy not so much because of their Christian beliefs but because of the social pressures. Also they were the propertied class whose children would inherit. Their marriages can be called 'endogamous', that is within their class in this case and the permanent unions were often made for convenience. In the imitative culture monogamy was the ideal to be followed and it often came late in life when the man's economic circumstances permitted.

In the middle class serial monogamy was a West Indian phenomenon. A man would have the same partner for some years, perhaps six, and then take another partner for a similar period. The children produced in these unions were illegitimate but may be legitimised later when the man wanted to honour the mother or when his circumstances had improved enough. The children from these unions had allegiance to the mother because the father most often was the one to leave. These unions were responsible for the matri-focal families that were common in the nineteenth-century West Indies.

Common-law marriage is a marriage recognised by society but not by the Church. It was just as binding as a church marriage and the man accepted his responsibilities for support of wife and children as in a formal marriage. The children were illegitimate and held their first allegiance to their mother or grandmother as the focus of the family. Such unions amongst the lower classes account for the high figure of about 70 per cent illegitimate births which is given for the British West Indies in the nineteenth century.

Matri-focal families were common when property and inheritance were irrelevant. The mother assumed the role usually played by the father in western societies. This dated back to the days of slavery where Christian marriage was impossible and it was continued in the nineteenth century for other reasons, e.g. a) when the father was not known; b) when the father would not support the children; c) when the father was a migrant worker; d) when the woman wanted to keep the children; e) when daughters went away to work and left the children with their grandmother; f) when the father's economic circumstances made him unable to support the children.

The upper classes followed the pattern of the nuclear family, that is when the children make their own marriages and leave the parental home to set up their own home. The parents have then no obligation for further support. The lower classes could follow this pattern but the extended family arrangement was more common. In this the children find that they have not the means to set up their own home and so bring their partners back to the parental home. Then each unit in the extended family contributes his or her share to the home. Kinship is wide. The system brings obligations of support but it also confers benefits like security, companionship and affection all through life.

The lower classes tended to have even wider relationships through the 'yard', a social phenomenon which arose out of communal living as slaves. Several families grouped together round the yard in the countryside but also when they moved to the towns. The yard community brought security to the members, prevented loneliness, provided recreation and gave care to the sick and aged. The members were obliged to help each other, to work together and to give voluntary service to the community.

Notes

1 Christian marriage was the ideal but was often impractical for economic reasons.
2 Serial monogamy and common-law marriage led to the high rate of illegitimacy in the British West Indies in the nineteenth century.
3 Serial monogamy and common-law marriage also resulted in matri-focal families which were common in the nineteenth-century West Indies.
4 The nuclear family was the rule among the upper classes while the extended family was more common amongst the lower classes.
5 Many families frequently grouped around the 'yard' which created an even wider community than the extended family.

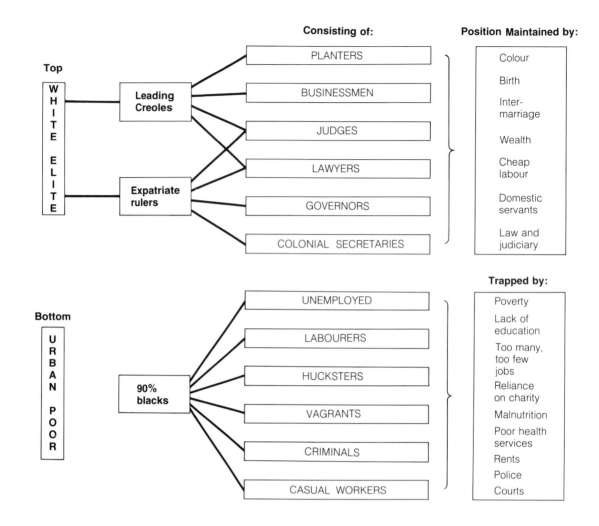

Chart 12.3: Top and bottom of the social scale in the nineteenth-century British Caribbean

Chart 12.3: Top and bottom of the social scale in the nineteenth-century British Caribbean

The contrast between those at the top and those at the bottom of the social scale was stark. The white elite enjoyed an extremely high standard of living and maintained this position by exclusivism. The urban poor lived in some of the most squalid conditions in the western hemisphere and were trapped in their poverty.

The white elite kept their class small by keeping others out (exclusivism). Family name was important. Marrying within the same class (endogamy) was also a means of keeping it exclusive. Dynastic marriages between powerful families increased family fortunes and strengthened the class. They built up an hierarchy in business and the land. They helped each other prosper and they were to a certain extent immune from the law because the law and the courts were controlled by their class. They worked, played, entertained and relaxed together and were a tightly-knit group.

However, this position was maintained not only by birth and exclusivism. They did have ability and talent in business and the professions through superior education. The leading schools in the British Caribbean in the nineteenth century were the preserve of whites. Often sons of the white elite were educated in Britain. Visits to Europe and absenteeism kept the white elite in touch with high society and gave them the social graces. Their households in towns and on their estates set the fashion and kept them at the top of the social ladder.

At the bottom the urban poor lived in ghettoes which had grown up as a result of the urban drift after emancipation. The blacks wanted to break their bondage to the soil so they fled the countryside. They were attracted to the towns by employment opportunities, better education and health services, communal living with its care and benefits, the excitement of gambling, entertainment and vice, and the prospects of economic betterment offered by trading. However, once in the cities they were in a trap. Too many were chasing too few jobs so most were unemployed. Many turned to vagrancy and were forced to depend on charity and could not leave the community which fed and sheltered them. Often the temptation of easy gains from crime and prostitution proved too strong. Illegitimacy left many children without support. Street gangs developed, especially in Trinidad in the late-nineteenth century, and conflicts with the police were common. Urban poor sometimes ended up before the courts and sentenced to prison. Although the police were of the same colour and sympathised with them, they were distrusted and violence against the police was common. This led to certain areas of cities like Port of Spain and Kingston becoming 'no-go' areas for the police.

Notes

1. In the nineteenth century the British Caribbean territories showed stark contrasts between the top and bottom of the social scale.
2. The white elite kept their class exclusive to certain families.
3. They also maintained their position by their domination of the land, business and the professions.
4. After emancipation the drift from the countryside to the towns gave rise to a class of urban blacks.
5. In the towns too many chasing too few jobs led to large-scale unemployment and vagrancy.
6. Once in the towns the blacks were trapped because their only means of support had become the community.
7. Crime and vice resulted and the urban blacks often found themselves on the wrong side of the law.

Table 12.2: Newspapers in the nineteenth-century British Caribbean

Territory	Newspaper	Voice of:	Political allegiance
Barbados	*Barbados Gazette*	Establishment/plantocracy	Colonial Government
	The Liberal	Working class/ smallholders/coloureds and blacks	Liberal Party. In opposition to the Assembly
British Guiana	*The Colonist*	Plantocracy/white elite	The Assembly. Anti-black.
	The Daily Chronicle	White liberals	British Guiana Political Reform Club. Opposed to plantocracy
Jamaica	*Jamaica Courant*	Plantocracy	The Assembly
	The Watchman	Coloureds and blacks	Opposed to the Assembly
Trinidad	*Port of Spain Gazette*	Establishment/white elite	Local Assembly and anti-colonial later
	Recorder	Coloureds and blacks	Liberal Opposition

Table 12.2: Newspapers in the nineteenth-century British Caribbean

The *Jamica Courant*, first published in 1722, was the earliest newspaper in the British Caribbean. It was the voice of the ruling class as were the early newspapers in all the islands. They were often the means by which the Government published information about appointments, laws and policy. They were at first not much more than 'fact-sheets' and were commonly called *Gazette* which is still the name used for official news publications. Later they sometimes carried the social news of the white elite.

For about one hundred years they voiced the news and views of the white elite and there was no conflict with the colonial government. However, when the question of emancipation arose, the plantocracies opposed the colonial government. Then freedom of the press became important and has remained a very strongly-held principle in the British West Indies ever since.

After emancipation newspapers like *The Colonist* in British Guiana became anti-black in opinion over issues like black education, employment and labour conditions. The coloureds and blacks wanted to answer and have their own voice so newspapers like *The Watchman* in Jamaica and the *Recorder* in Trinidad appeared. These gave social and political support to the working classes and opposed the Assemblies. *The Liberal* in Barbados was actually the organ of the Liberal Party which was like an unofficial opposition to the Government. Freedom of the press still prevailed and permitted these newspapers to attack the Government no matter how much the ruling classes resented them. In 1832 Edward Jordan, the editor of *The Watchman* was arrested when his newspaper attacked the Government over emancipation, but the case was dropped, a famous victory for freedom of expression in Jamaica.

Towards the end of the nineteenth century all newspapers, both conservative and liberal, became 'local' in that they were anti-colonial in opinion. They campaigned for political reform, such as representation in the Assembly, and were influential and successful in their campaigns. *The Liberal* in Barbados helped to achieve coloured representation in the Barbados Assembly.

Notes

1 Early newspapers acted as the voice of the ruling classes.
2 *Gazette* was the common name for government fact-sheets.
3 Over the issue of emancipation most local newspapers supported their own assemblies against the colonial government and the principle of 'freedom of the press' insured that their opinions would be heard.
4 After emancipation the newspapers of the coloureds and blacks attacked local assemblies and again freedom of the press operated.
5 British Caribbean newspapers of all social and political classes became 'local' in that they were anti-colonial towards the end of the nineteenth century.

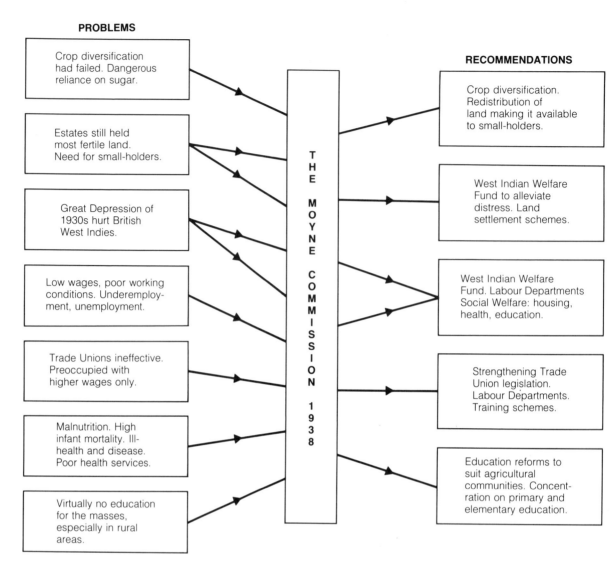

PROBLEMS

Crop diversification had failed. Dangerous reliance on sugar.

Estates still held most fertile land. Need for small-holders.

Great Depression of 1930s hurt British West Indies.

Low wages, poor working conditions. Underemployment, unemployment.

Trade Unions ineffective. Preoccupied with higher wages only.

Malnutrition. High infant mortality. Ill-health and disease. Poor health services.

Virtually no education for the masses, especially in rural areas.

THE MOYNE COMMISSION 1938

RECOMMENDATIONS

Crop diversification. Redistribution of land making it available to small-holders.

West Indian Welfare Fund to alleviate distress. Land settlement schemes.

West Indian Welfare Fund. Labour Departments Social Welfare: housing, health, education.

Strengthening Trade Union legislation. Labour Departments. Training schemes.

Education reforms to suit agricultural communities. Concentration on primary and elementary education.

Chart 12.4: The Moyne Commission: a) Problems

Chart 12.4: The Moyne Commission: a) Problems

Problems

The Moyne Commission of 1938 investigated all aspects of life in the British Caribbean both economic and social and exposed the reasons why most of the population was being denied the basic rights of work, health and education.

Monoculture The British Caribbean was still dangerously dependent on sugar. Although the Norman Commission of 1898 had stressed the need for diversification, sugar still seemed to be the safest crop on which the colonies could pin their economic hopes. The diversification that had taken place, such as spices in Grenada, coffee in Dominica and sea-island cotton in Antigua, had not provided viable alternatives. Successful alternative crops like cocoa in Trinidad and bananas in Jamaica had failed to boost those economies enough to avoid the social unrest which broke out between 1935 and 1938. Barbados still provided the best example of monoculture and there the working and living conditions were the most depressed in the British Caribbean.

The Norman Commission and the Oliver Commission of 1929 had both recommended the redistribution of land yet in 1938 most of the fertile land was still held by the sugar estates. Estate owners were reluctant to sell land to small-holders as they thought this would undermine their labour supply. Both Commissions had pointed out that the best prospects for the British Caribbean lay in the land being farmed by peasant small-holders. In 1938 it was obvious that small-holders were enjoying a better standard of living than unskilled wage earners.

Trade Unions Undoubtedly the sugar and oil companies were exploiting cheap labour. The worst of the riots and strikes in Jamaica and Trinidad were on the Tate and Lyle sugar estates at Frome and the oilfields at Fyzabad. The companies were making large profits and distributing them to their shareholders in the form of dividends and not passing them on to the workers in the form of higher wages. In 1938 the trade unions were powerless to squeeze these abnormal profits because of the high level of unemployment which existed and their own weakness and inexperience.

The trade unions needed strengthening. The Passfield Memorandum of 1937 and the Orde-Browne Report both pointed out the inadequacies of the existing unions and what could be achieved by stronger unions. Trade union leaders were inexperienced. Strike power was limited because peaceful picketing was not allowed and the unions would be liable for damages caused by striking workers. Passfield criticised the preoccupation of unions with higher wages instead of urging employers to improve working conditions and give fringe benefits. He felt unions should press governments to provide or improve the social services. Orde-Browne also wanted the co-operation of unions and governments to have social legislation passed. Perhaps more experienced leaders would have urged governments to increase company taxes and allocate the revenues to the social services.

Wages The Colonial Office sent Major Orde-Browne to the British West Indies in 1938 because of the trouble that had flared up in 1935–8 as a result of poor labour conditions. He produced the Orde-Browne Report on Labour Conditions in the British West Indies.

Wages for agricultural workers were very low and had risen very little on average over the previous hundred years. This Report endorsed the Passfield Memorandum about the preoccupation of the unions with higher wages which had produced unemployment. The Memorandum recommended that unions should strive to make jobs secure and improve working conditions and social services. The Orde-Browne Report provided the

evidence that the Moyne Commission used on labour conditions. It compared the wages of unskilled workers in the sugar industry between 1838 and 1938 as being fairly representative of agricultural wages throughout the British Caribbean.

On average wages rose in those hundred years by 27 per cent. However, as prices had risen by a greater percentage, real wages (what goods and services money can buy) had actually fallen, leading to all the distress of the late 1930s. It was calculated that expenditure on food must have taken up all the wages of most agricultural workers by 1938. Even then the food that most agricultural workers could afford was of low nutritional value and contributed to poor health.

In Barbados wages had not risen at all to 1898 and in the twentieth century to 1938 rose only from 10d per day to 1/3. Here the working and living conditions were the worst because wages were low and no land was available for subsistence.

In Trinidad agricultural wages actually fell from 2/- to 1/6 but unskilled oilfield workers were receiving about 3/- per day. Land was available for subsistence in Trinidad yet both oilfield wages and agricultural were so low that there were riots and strikes.

Unemployment Wages were low for unskilled workers because there was so much unemployed labour willing to work for whatever was offered. This was especially true in the smaller islands like Barbados. However, even in the larger territories unemployment was high and considerably higher than the 12 to 20 per cent suggested by the governments. All the figures really say is that 80 per cent of the labour force had had some employment at some time in the year. This employment could have been part-time or rotational, both common in the sugar industry which was still the biggest employer in the British Caribbean in 1938. Employment on sugar estates was seasonal and full employment existed only in crop time. Only 10 per cent of unskilled labour and 40 per cent of skilled labour were employed full time throughout the year, and the rest were unemployed or underemployed. Rotational labour saved labour costs for the employer but made it appear that more workers were being employed. Instead of employing one worker for five days, the employer employed two workers for two days each, thus saving the wages of one day and making it appear that two men were being employed instead of one.

On the other hand, only those employed for

wages were recorded as being employed and subsistence farmers appeared as unemployed. This fact made unemployment higher than it really was. Yet if subsistence farmers accepted any paid employment at any time of the year they would go down as being employed. Therefore the unemployment statistics of the 1930s must be taken with reservations.

Nevertheless unemployment was high, perhaps as high as 50 per cent, and contributed greatly to the unrest of the late 1930s. The Great Depression of the decade meant that foreign demand for West Indian produce was greatly reduced. This meant less production in the British Caribbean, leading to less employment and lower incomes. There was a multiplied effect throughout the whole Caribbean as less income meant less demand, and so on. Also by 1925 emigration had ceased so the unemployed could no longer seek work outside the British Caribbean. To make matters worse, Cuba sent back immigrant workers from the British Caribbean to swell the numbers of the unemployed.

Unemployment would have been relieved by the redistribution of land to small-holders. British Guiana had created about 10 000 small-holders by such a scheme, but was the only territory to do so. Trinidad had land available but had no settlement scheme, found itself with 20 000 unemployed and only 5000 small-holders in 1938.

Health The British Caribbean should have been self-sufficient in food by 1938 yet all the territories were importing food. For example, Trinidad imported three-quarters of its food even though it had much land available for agriculture. There was a lack of small farmers and still a reliance on the earnings of sugar exports to pay for imported food. We have seen that the poor had to spend all their wages on food and that they could only afford cheap, low-nutrition foods. However, rice and maize from the United States were so cheap that the British Caribbean could not have competed in production and prices. Only British Guiana was beginning to export rice in 1938. Ideally the British Caribbean should have been producing high-protein foods like eggs, meat, milk and fish, and importing the cheap staples.

The blacks tried to continue the diet they had been used to as slaves, i.e. salt-fish and maize, fish for protein and maize for carbohydrate (rice was often substituted for maize in the late-nineteenth and early-twentieth centuries). However it was difficult to maintain this diet and most of the rural poor rarely tasted meat or milk.

Malnutrition was the chief cause of infant mortality and lack of resistance to disease. The health of the masses was poor. In 1938 infant mortality in the British Caribbean was about 17 per cent as against 6 per cent for developed countries. This figure was for the first year of life and many more died before they were four years old. Malnourished mothers cannot give birth to healthy babies; malnourished babies succumb to disease. Food was at the root of the problem.

Poor living conditions led to diseases like hookworm and tuberculosis. Hookworm induces lethargy which leads to low productivity. It also lowers resistance to other diseases. Tuberculosis, however, was the biggest single cause of death after infancy in the 1930s, accounting for 15 per cent of all deaths. There were also the other diseases endemic in tropical areas and probably every adult in the rural areas was, or had been, affected by one or other of the serious diseases which had an adverse effect on productivity not only by shortening their working life, but also by reducing the output-per-man-hour.

Sanitary and health services were non-existent for the poor. In towns over-crowding placed too much demand on running water and latrines so hygiene suffered. People suffered from diseases resulting from dirt and from urinating and defecating in the open. The Orde-Browne Report noted the serious lack of medical services as being most urgently needed to improve the standard of living of the poor. The governments under the control of the upper classes hesitated to give free or subsidized medical services on the grounds that they would not be morally good for the poor. The doctors wanted a fee-paying service but that would have been beyond the reach of the poor. In the second half of the nineteenth century Boards of Health had been set up to provide free or subsidised medical services but by the 1930s they were only serving the towns and inadequately at that. The dispensaries in the rural areas were few and far between and lacking trained staff. Therefore the poor lacked medical services, and, as the Moyne Commission concluded: 'Barbados has to thank God for health, not the medical profession'.

Education The plantocracy considered that education would make blacks dissatisfied with their position and thus deprive the estates of labour. Under pressure they conceded that a basic literacy and numeracy should be granted, but not any agricultural science. The planters wanted a subservient labour force who could understand and obey instructions and give correct measurements and quantities.

In the 1930s education received low priority in governments' budgets, ranging from only 5 per cent in British Guiana to 15 per cent in Barbados. Expenditure was proportionally higher in towns than in the country, higher on boys than on girls, higher on secondary than primary, and directed towards a few selected schools for whites and coloureds. Primary-school-aged girls in the rural areas suffered most from lack of educational opportunities. In the 1930s illiteracy ranged from about 30 per cent in Barbados to 90 per cent in the Grenadines. In spite of compulsory primary education under the 1876 Education Ordinance illiteracy was about 60 per cent in British Guiana. Planters attracted child labour although it was illegal because the parents wanted the money. However, it was possible for a child to pass through primary education without learning how to read or write.

For 'white-collar' jobs education was essential in reading, writing and arithmetic, but for rural labour education in hygiene, domestic science and agricultural science was more important. The curriculum in most schools was attacked by the Moyne Commission as being too literary and not geared to the needs of British Caribbean economies. However, in the 1930s primary education of whatever sort was unavailable for most of the poor, or declined because of economic constraints like having to send the children out to work, or having to keep the children at home to care for the household while the mother went out to work. Secondary education was completely beyond the reach of the poor, the prerogative of the whites and coloureds.

Lack of education re-inforced the trap that the blacks found themselves in at the bottom of the social scale. They could not rise because they lacked education and they could not receive education because they could not afford it.

Notes

1   The alternative crops suggested by the Norman Commission of 1838 had failed to provide satisfactory bases for BWI economies which were still dangerously dependent on sugar in 1938.

2   The Norman Commission and the Oliver Commission of 1929 had recommended the redistribution of some estate land to small-holders as the best foundation for BWI economies, but it had not been carried out except in British Guiana.

3   In 1938 trade unions had little power because the high level of unemployment meant that cheap, unskilled labour was readily available.

4   Trade unions were preoccupied with higher wages and did not demand better working conditions or social services from governments.

5   In the hundred years since emancipation wages had risen by only 27 per cent on average throughout the British Caribbean.

6   Prices had risen faster than wages in this period, therefore real wages had fallen.

7   The sugar industry was still the biggest single employer of labour in the British Caribbean.

8   Unemployment was considerably higher than the figures suggest because of the practices of part-time and rotational labour.

9   Subsistence farmers were counted as unemployed unless they did any casual labour for wages.

10   The Great Depression of the 1930s contributed to high unemployment in the British Caribbean.

11   The redistribution of land to small-holders would have been the solution to the high unemployment.

12   Malnutrition made infant mortality as high as 17 per cent in the British Caribbean in the 1930s.

13   The British Caribbean territories still imported food in the 1930s.

14   Diseases associated with squalid living conditions were rife.

15   Medical services were inadequate or non-existent, especially in the rural areas.

16   Poor health led to the low productivity of labour.

17   Education was of low priority to BWI governments because the planters wanted to keep the labour force uneducated.

18   The curriculum in primary schools was literary and not suited to the needs of agricultural communities.

19   Most expenditure on education was directed towards a few secondary schools for whites and coloureds.

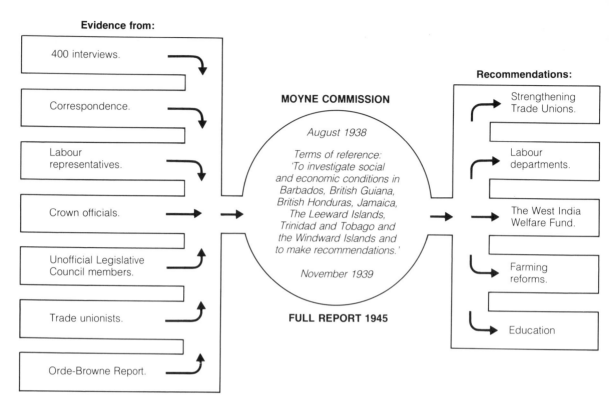

Evidence from:

400 interviews.

Correspondence.

Labour representatives.

Crown officials.

Unofficial Legislative Council members.

Trade unionists.

Orde-Browne Report.

MOYNE COMMISSION

August 1938

*Terms of reference:
'To investigate social and economic conditions in Barbados, British Guiana, British Honduras, Jamaica, The Leeward Islands, Trinidad and Tobago and the Windward Islands and to make recommendations.'*

November 1939

FULL REPORT 1945

Recommendations:

Strengthening Trade Unions.

Labour departments.

The West India Welfare Fund.

Farming reforms.

Education

Chart 12.5: The Moyne Commission

Chart 12.5: The Moyne Commission

The Moyne Commission sat for fifteen months from August 1938 to November 1939. It was most thorough in its investigations into labour relations, working and social conditions. However, most West Indian nationalists ignored its value and dismissed it because its constitutional and political recommendations did not go nearly far enough.

Major Orde-Browne, who had recently been appointed Labour Adviser to the West Indies, was influential on working conditions, while Walter Citrine, a leading British trade unionist, was influential on labour relations.

The collection of evidence was slow and wide-ranging from Crown Officials to members of the general public. Then the evidence had to be sifted for the compilation of the significant facts. Some of the evidence came through letters. Finally the recommendations had to be carefully considered. Consequently only an incomplete draft was ready for publication in February 1940. The full report was published in 1945.

The Moyne Commission dealt with the British West Indies as Crown Colonies yet by the time the full report was published in 1945 decolonization was in the air. It could be said therefore to have been out-of-date and it was certainly unacceptable to West Indian nationalists. However, its value can be judged by the fact that so many of its economic and social recommendations were implemented by the colonial governments.

Notes

1   The Moyne Commission sat from August 1938 to November 1939.
2   The collection of evidence was wide-ranging from Crown officials to members of the general public.
3   Its investigations covered labour relations, working and social conditions.
4   The full report was published in 1945 by which time decolonization was in the air.
5   Although regarded as out-of-date many of its economic and social recommendations were implemented by the colonial governments.

Table 12.3: The Moyne Commission: b) Recommendations

Recommendations	Reasons	Implementation
1 Strengthening trade unions	Present unions ineffective; no strike power; leaders inexperienced; wages too low and working conditions poor.	Labour leaders sent to England for training. Labour Departments to help unions. Legislation passed for workmen's compensation, holidays with pay, severance pay and inspection of factories, etc.
2 Labour Departments	Unemployment high. Trade unions needed help in negotiations and disputes. Need for better statistics.	1939 Jamaican Labour Department. Other colonies followed.
3 West Indian Welfare Fund	Deep social distress caused by poor health and housing, lack of land for subsistence, unemployment and low wages and poor education services.	1940 Colonial Development and Welfare Act set up fund. Administered in Barbados by Comptroller and permanent staff.
4 Farming reforms	British West Indies food importers. Need for self-sufficiency in food. Land settlement to relieve unemployment.	Little reforms followed.
5 Education	Widespread illiteracy. Curriculum irrelevant to needs of agricultural communities.	Concentration on basic literacy and numeracy at primary and elementary levels.

Table 12.3: The Moyne Commission: b) Recommendations

1 Strengthening trade unions

The Moyne Commission encouraged more trade unions to register and the public and private sector employers to be prepared to recognise and work with more trade unions, especially in the agricultural sector where unions were most lacking as the conditions were the most depressed.

The unions that existed had little muscle, except in British Guiana, chiefly because peaceful picketing was not allowed and unions could be held liable for damages caused by their workers during strikes. The Moyne Commission recommended that these gaps in trade union laws be filled to strengthen the strike power of unions. It also recommended that trade union leaders be sent to England for training to overcome their inexperience, and that they should be democratically elected so that they would truly represent the wishes of their members.

The following improvements in working conditions recommended by the Moyne Commission were put into effect: a) workmen's compensation (for injuries received at work); b) holidays with pay (Governors could decree this in most colonies); c) severance pay (in the event of the employers closing down the business); d) inspection of factories and conditions for agricultural workers.

2 Labour Departments

The Moyne Commission recommended that Labour Departments be set up in each of the colonies to regulate wages, to register trade unions, to audit union accounts, to negotiate with employers, to help in industrial disputes, to see that union rights were observed and to collect labour statistics.

The Moyne Commission recommended minimum wage legislation until trade unions were strong enough to negotiate satisfactory wage agreements themselves. If governments refused to implement minimum wage legislation, wage boards should be set up to fix wages throughout the colony.

3 The West Indian Welfare Fund

This was recommended by the Moyne Commission to provide £1 000 000 per year for twenty years to cover education, health, housing, land settlement, labour departments and social welfare, the chief causes of distress in the British Caribbean. This recommendation was quickly taken up when the British Government passed the Colonial Development and Welfare Act in 1940. The British West Indies benefited more than proportionally to their size and population. A Comptroller with a permanent staff was established in Barbados to administer the Fund for the British West Indies.

4 Farming reforms

The Moyne Commission recommended that agricultural production aimed at self-sufficiency should be based on small farmers. The West Indian colonies should turn from being food importers to food exporters. A Caribbean market should meet the demands of the various islands and any surplus could find an export market outside the Caribbean. Caribbean shipping lines should handle the distribution of food between the colonies.

Land settlement schemes would alleviate unemployment and raise living standards as the Commission noted that small farmers enjoyed a much better standard of living than wage labourers on estates.

5 Education

The Moyne Commission was pessimistic about education as it thought that standards could not improve until social and economic conditions improved. It criticised the curricula as being un-suited to the needs of agricultural communities because they were too literary. It did recommend basic literacy and numeracy, health and agricultural sciences for the West Indian colonies. It pointed out that the deficiency in secondary and further education was not a serious problem as few students had the educational attainment to go on to higher levels. Therefore the Commission recommended concentrating on primary and elementary education.

Notes

1 More trade unions should be registered and employers, both public and private, should be prepared to negotiate with them.
2 Trade unions were most needed in the agricultural sector.
3 Trade unions should have their strike power increased.
4 Trade union leaders should be sent to England for training.
5 Labour Departments should be established in each colony to assist trade unions and improve working conditions.
6 Minimum wage legislation should be passed, or Wages Boards established, while trade unions were still ineffective.
7 A West Indian Welfare Fund should be set up to alleviate the main causes of social distress.
8 Small farmers should form the backbone of agriculture and help to make the British Caribbean self-sufficient in food production.
9 A British Caribbean market should channel demand and supply to enable the colonies to achieve this self-sufficiency.
10 Education could not improve until social and economic conditions improved.
11 The present curricula were irrelevant to the needs of agricultural communities.
12 Governments should concentrate on basic literacy and numeracy in primary and elementary education.

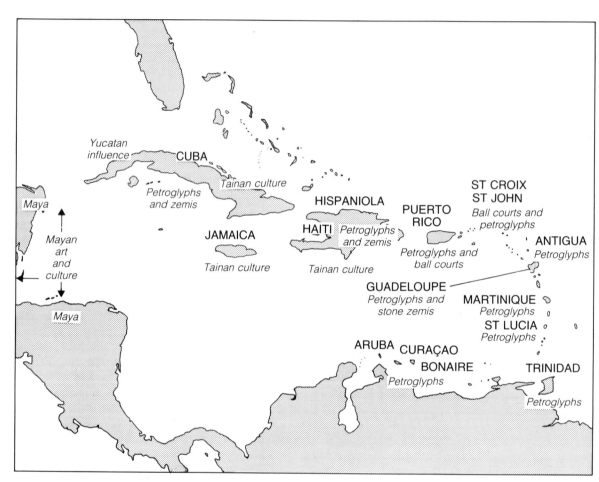

Map 13.1: Pre-history cultural and artistic relics

Map 13.1: Pre-history cultural and artistic relics

Archaeological sites from about 5000–3000 BC have been found in the Caribbean islands but most of the relics of an artistic nature date from around AD 200. *Petroglyphs* (rock carvings) are common throughout most of the islands. *Zemis* carved in wood or stone have also been common finds but jewellery, probably because it was made of gold, has not been found which made some archaeologists decide that Arawaks did not have jewellery. However, we know of *caracou* (necklaces) and *rassada* (bracelets). Painted ceramic pottery has also been found even in Carib sites but in these cases it is thought that the Caribs captured it from the Arawaks.

Notes

1 Most artistic relics date from around AD 200.
2 Rock carvings, zemis, necklaces, bracelets and painted ceramic pottery are the main finds.

1 Haiti

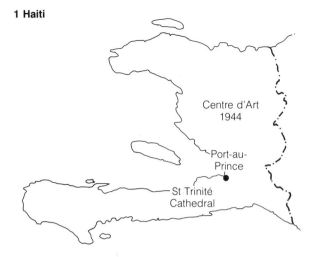

Centre d'Art
1944

Port-au-
Prince

St Trinité
Cathedral

*Early nineteenth century sculptures of
Toussaint l'Ouverture and Dessalines by
Normil Charles. In 1867 Louis Laforest-
erie exhibited sculptures in Paris.*

---

*1944 Centre d'Art founded by De Witt
Peters. Included famous artists
like Hector Hyppolite and Philomené
Obin; and sculptors like Odilon
Duperier and Jasmin Joseph.*
*1947 Haitian artists prominent at UNESCO
International Exhibition in Paris.*
*c.1950 Primitive murals commissioned
for St Trinité Cathedral in Port-au-Prince.*
*1950 Foyer des Arts Plastiques founded
by Max Pinchinat, Roland Dorcély and
Luce Tournier.*

*From that time Haiti has been the most
prolific and innovative centre in art.*

2 Jamaica

*1931–7 Edna Manley pioneered
a movement in Jamaica for
more social and political
awareness in art. Institute
of Jamaica encouraged art
with teaching and
exhibitions.*
*1940 First All-Jamaica Exhibition
of paintings.*
*1950 Jamaica School of Art
founded.*
*1960s Mallica Reynolds (KAPO)
began Jamaica group of
Primitives who emphasised the
African heritage.*

*Albert Huie from the early period
remained recognised as Jamaica's
outstanding painter.*

Institute of
Jamaica 1930s

Jamaican School
of Art 1950

Kingston

3 Trinidad

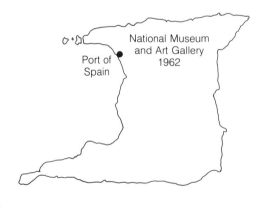

National Museum
and Art Gallery
1962

Port of
Spain

*c.1850 Jean Michel Cazabon's water colours
of Port of Spain and other Trinidadian
scenes in European style.*

---

*1930s Hugh Styollmeyer and Amy Leong Pang
began native Trinidadian movement.*
*1943 Trinidad Art Society founded with Mildred
Faulkner, Sybil Atteck, Albert Gomes as
members.*
*1944 Annual Art Exhibition began. Boscoe Holder
famous early exhibitor*
*1948–55 Nina Lamming Squires pioneered
Trinidadian abstract painting.*
*1955–60 Reaction against abstract
painting by P. Alladin, Noel Vaucresson
and Joseph Cromwell. Native Trinidadian
style.*
*1962 National Museum and Art Gallery founded for
permanent and special exhibitions.*

Map 13.2: Three centres of art: Haiti, Jamaica and Trinidad

Map 13.2: Three centres of art: Haiti, Jamaica and Trinidad

In colonial times Caribbean art was imitative, in that it followed the themes and styles of Europe, such as watercolour landscapes. It was realistic as for example, the water colours of English Harbour, Antigua and scenes on the sugar estates in the early-nineteenth century by William Clark, from which we can learn much about the cultivation and production of sugar. Art was imitative because it was commissioned by Europeans and hung in their houses in the West Indies and Europe. There were no art galleries or museums in the Caribbean in the nineteenth century and works of Caribbean painters only appeared in European exhibitions. The appeal had to be to Europeans and this strengthened imitativeness. Jean Michel Cazabon, the mid-nineteenth century painter from Trinidad, turned from medicine to painting while in Europe. The watercolours he produced of Port of Spain and other Trinidadian scenes were imitative in style.

When nationalism became a force in the 1930s, and thereafter when colonialism was coming to an end after the Second World War, native Caribbean movements in art began and flourished. Imitative art still existed, as with Albert Huie, the outstanding Jamaican painter who followed the post-impressionist school and was strongly influenced by the work of Cezanne. The first hint of change came when Caribbean artists took up local themes depicting social issues and political causes like nationalism. Leading this movement was Edna Manley whose works between 1931 and 1937 reflect the social and political awareness that was growing in Jamaica. Her success was the inspiration for others to follow.

African influence became very strong, especially in Haiti. The themes chosen were frequently animals, but more often people and many people in crowds. Grotesque forms were sometimes used symbolising humanity in all its shapes and forms, what in modern African carving is commonly called the 'Family Tree'. In most cases the backgrounds were bright and bold.

In two British islands, Jamaica and Trinidad, native artists came to be grouped into three styles, the Primitives, the Representationalists and the Abstractionists. The Primitives were self-taught amateurs who often concentrated on African themes and styles. Each artist was an individual in style but animals, people and bright bold backgrounds formed a common link. The most famous exponent of this school was probably Mallica Reynolds (KAPO) of Jamaica who flourished in the late 1960s. His influence led others to concentrate on the African heritage of Jamaica.

The Representationalists were earlier. In the mid-1940s Boscoe Holder held popular exhibitions in Trinidad before he emigrated to the United States. In Jamaica Albert Huie was very well known. He painted portraits and landscapes with figures using light and shade subtly in the post-impressionist style. Representationalists were professionals who had had formal training, often in Europe or the United States. They included sculptors like Alvin Marriot who sculptured Jamaica's National Monument. One Jamaican artist, Karl Parboosingh, was strongly influenced by Mexican realism. His works were varied, but his themes were frequently mundane scenes like cement factories and streets, drawn in his individual perspective.

The Abstractionists were part of a world-wide school whose works' only connection with the Caribbean was that their authors were West Indian. They were concerned with the formal and technical problems of art. Nina Lamming Squires started this school of painting in Trinidad in the late 1940s and provoked a reaction from later Trinidadian artists like P. Alladin, Noel Vaucresson and Joseph Cromwell who tried to make Trinidadian art relate to Trinidad. Abstractionists in Jamaica like Eugene Hyde, Milton Hawley and Leonard Fergusson removed their work from the current social and political influences.

In Jamaica and Trinidad artists were taught and encouraged by the institutions which developed with nationalism. In 1943 the Trinidad Art Society was founded and from 1944 it held annual exhibitions of local art. This brought works of art before the public, helped the artists sell their paintings and made foreign institutions like UNESCO and the British Council interested in Caribbean art. Artists then received scholarships to study at home and abroad and their successes inspired others. In Jamaica the First All Jamaica Exhibition of Painting was held in 1940 and the successful annual exhibitions helped to show the need for an art school. In 1950 the Jamaican School of Art was founded. This relieved the Institute of Jamaica of its earlier responsibilities for training and encouraging artists. On independence the national museums and art galleries became very important centres for art. The National Museum and Art Gallery of Trinidad was founded in 1962 and it now permanently displays Trinidadian works of art, one-man shows and other special exhibitions.

However, most artists in the British Caribbean are amateurs who have to rely on full-time occupations like commercial art or art teaching for their incomes. Some are still self-taught but an increasing number are professionally taught. It is impossible to calculate the contribution which Edna Manley has made to art in Jamaica. She 'set the ball rolling' and it is gathering speed.

Haiti

Haiti has been the most prolific and innovative art centre in the Caribbean. In 1944 De Witt Peters, an American artist, founded the *Centre d'Art* in Port-au-Prince. This began an art revival in Haiti. Artists who had previously taught themselves received training, encouragement and material help from the *Centre*. Of the ten original artists at the *Centre* in 1944, perhaps the most famous were Hector Hippolyte and Philomené Obin. They were encouraged to paint their own themes in their own styles so individualism is one of the bases of Haitian art. The work of the *Centre d'Art* found international recognition at the UNESCO International Exhibition in Paris in 1947.

Haitian art is full of African influence. The paintings are frequently of animals and people against vivid backgrounds. The scenes are crowded and vibrant with life. They also show the influence of the spirit world of Voodoo. Haitian artists like Prefete Duffaut, Philippe Vieux, Jean-Baptiste Jacques, Louines Mestor and Saint-Brice have exhibited and sold paintings all over the world. The *Centre d'Art* also encouraged sculptors like Odilon Duperier and Jasmin Joseph who did terracotta sculptures and carved the choir screen for St Trinité Cathedral in Port-au-Prince. This Cathedral became a permanent gallery for the Primitives of Philomené Obin, Wilson Bigaud and Castera Bazile.

In 1950 the *Foyer des Arts Plastiques* was formed by a splinter group from the *Centre d'Art* consisting of Max Pinchinat, Roland Dorcély and Luce Tournier. This was a healthy sign for Haitian art showing that it was active and flourishing rather than damaged by internal conflicts.

Notes

1 Imitative Caribbean art followed European themes and styles to satisfy its patrons who were Creole Europeans.
2 Nationalism was a force which made artists adopt local themes and styles which frequently reflected social and political problems of the Caribbean.
3 Edna Manley in Jamaica in the 1930s gave the lead and inspiration to a local movement.
4 African influence became strong in these local movements especially in Haiti.
5 The African influence is apparent in paintings of animals and people against bold, bright backgrounds.
6 Caribbean artists can be grouped into the Primitives, the Representationalists and the Abstractionists.
7 Towards the end of the Second World War and after, the first institutions which encouraged and taught art appeared in the British Caribbean. Previously most local artists had been self-taught.
8 Haiti had a revival of art when the *Centre d'Art* was founded in Port-au Prince in 1944.
9 This revival has resulted in Haiti becoming the most prolific and innovative art centre in the Caribbean.

Map 13.3: Architecture in the Caribbean

There was no distinctive Caribbean style of architecture. In colonial times the style followed that of the colonial masters, Spanish, British, Dutch or French. Modifications had to be made for the tropics, such as high ceilings and many large windows. Also slave quarters had to be incorporated into the estates but their buildings were well away from the main structure. Churches were always important as those were the buildings which were usually given the most care and attention. Roman Catholic churches were ornate, full of side chapels, statues and stained glass, and sometimes displaying works of art as at St Trinité Cathedral in Port-au-Prince. At the other extreme, the Pentecostal chapels of the mid-twentieth century were plain and purely functional.

Spanish architecture

Santo Domingo, founded by Bartholomew Columbus in 1498, was the first colonial town in the New World. Spanish towns had a cathedral, a plaza (cathedral square), government buildings and then dwellings radiating out from the town centre in decreasing order of importance. Santo Domingo had the Cathedral of Santa Maria de Menor, 1514, which was a mixture of Gothic and baroque architecture and very ornate.

The Spanish built solidly in stone with thick walls, high ceilings and many windows, louvred for shade during the day and shuttered for security at night. The rich built their houses round gardens in the classical Greek or Roman style. The Casa de Tostado, Casa del Cordon and the Alcazar, buildings in Santo Domingo dating from Columbus' and Ovando's time, are now tourist attractions.

The castle of El Morro which guards San Juan harbour is probably the most famous Spanish colonial building in the Caribbean. It was started in 1584. It was massive and functional as a fort but also contained courtyards and arches round the living quarters. It blended in well with the rocky coast and protected San Juan effectively for two hundred years.

British architecture

The British Caribbean's greatest architectural contribution lies in the 'Great Houses' of the sugar estates. They were built from the fortunes made from sugar and often literally grew with these fortunes, i.e. as more money came in, more was added to the house. Typically they were three storeys high. The ground floor was used for storage and had a stone floor for coolness. The first floor contained reception rooms and the master bedroom. The top floor contained the other bedrooms. The floors were linked by magnificent curving staircases. These houses were usually built of stone in the Palladian or Georgian styles. 'Palladian' means following the style of Andrea Palladio, a sixteenth-century Italian architect who had great influence in England. The style followed the Greek and Roman public buildings with porticos arranged symmetrically round a central hall and supported by classical columns. Such building in the eighteenth-century British Caribbean should properly be called 'neo-Palladian'. In Jamaica Devon House is neo-Palladian while Rose Hall is more typically Georgian. 'Georgian' refers to the architecture from the reigns of the four Georges, Kings of England from 1714 to 1830. It was modelled on Palladian principles and is sometimes referred to as the 'Greek Revival'. The houses were square or octagonal with bold perpendicular lines, and faced with many large, square windows. There were no curved lines in conspicuous places. The fronts were often characterised by tall, classical columns.

The styles came from Europe but the materials and builders were local. The craftsmanship was superb especially with regard to the woodwork, exemplified in the fine, carved staircases and furniture. These houses were large as their owners entertained large parties for long periods, as well as for special functions like weddings. The plantocracies of different islands were united by their class and when visiting each other hundreds of miles away from home, they would take up residence for weeks or even months.

'Great Houses' existed in all the British islands. Clarence House in Antigua, built in 1787, is a fine example, as is Montpelier in Nevis. Codrington College in Barbados is not an example of a great house, but is well known from photographs and is largely Georgian in its original architecture.

Also from the British Caribbean are examples of forts, e.g. Brimstone Hill in St Kitts and St Anne's Fort in Barbados. Their architecture is functional in the main. Churches are also noteworthy: St John's Cathedral in Antigua, the Anglican Cathedral in Georgetown, British Guiana, and St John's Church, Bridgetown, which was modelled on a typical English country church.

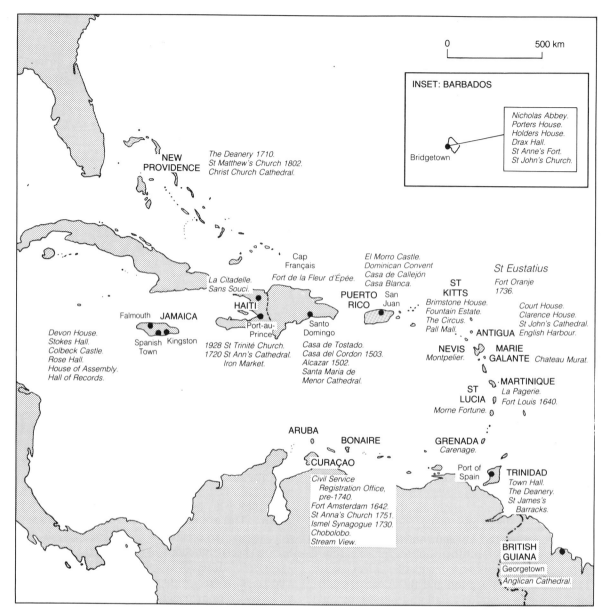

0   500 km

INSET: BARBADOS

Bridgetown

Nicholas Abbey.
Porters House.
Holders House.
Drax Hall.
St Anne's Fort.
St John's Church.

NEW
PROVIDENCE

The Deanery 1710.
St Matthew's Church 1802.
Christ Church Cathedral.

Cap
Français

Fort de la Fleur d'Épée.

El Morro Castle.
Dominican Convent
Casa de Callejón
Casa Blanca.

St Eustatius

Fort Oranje
1736.

La Citadelle.
Sans Souci.

ST
KITTS

HAITI

PUERTO
RICO

San
Juan

Brimstone House.
Fountain Estate.
The Circus.
Pall Mall.

Court House.
Clarence House.
St John's Cathedral.
English Harbour.

Falmouth   JAMAICA

Devon House.
Stokes Hall.
Colbeck Castle.
Rose Hall.
House of Assembly.
Hall of Records.

Spanish   Kingston
Town

Port-au-
Prince

ANTIGUA

Santo
Domingo

1928 St Trinité Church.
1720 St Ann's Cathedral.
Iron Market.

Casa de Tostado.
Casa del Cordon 1503.
Alcazar 1502.
Santa Maria de
Menor Cathedral.

NEVIS
Montpelier.

MARIE
GALANTE   Chateau Murat.

ST
LUCIA

Morne Fortune.

MARTINIQUE
La Pagerie.
Fort Louis 1640.

ARUBA

BONAIRE

CURAÇAO

Civil Service
Registration Office,
pre-1740.
Fort Amsterdam 1642.
St Anna's Church 1751.
Ismel Synagogue 1730.
Chobolobo.
Stream View.

GRENADA
Carenage.

Port of
Spain

TRINIDAD
Town Hall.
The Deanery.
St James's
Barracks.

BRITISH
GUIANA
Georgetown
Anglican Cathedral.

Map 13.3: Architecture in the Caribbean

Certain whole towns in the British Caribbean are noteworthy for their architecture. Basseterre in St Kitts has many Georgian buildings in the streets of The Circus and Pall Mall. However, their Georgianism is modified by overhanging balconies decorated with carved woodwork. Falmouth, near Montego Bay in Jamaica, was mostly built in the nineteenth century and is unusual in that all the houses are different in style but in common they have decorated ironwork and carved woodwork on their balconies. St John's, Antigua, dating from the late-eighteenth century, was built largely of wood, with the wooden columns being deceptively like stone. The wide main streets are linked by narrow passages. Nassau in New Providence, Bahamas, has architectural features from the seventeenth to the nineteenth centuries, as well as the twentieth-century banks, of course.

In the British Caribbean the sugar estates were intended to be self-contained. As sugar production was the source of great incomes the buildings were of great importance and built sturdily with little regard for architectural merit. At Orange Valley in Jamaica it is possible to see an almost complete group of sugar estate buildings, all of stone, ranging from the Great House to the slave hospital.

French architecture

French influence in architecture in Europe as well as the Caribbean was particularly strong in the seventeenth and eighteenth centuries. Cap Français in St Domingue, which unfortunately was partly destroyed by terrorism between 1791 and 1803, and then by the earthquake of 1840, was called 'the Paris of the Antilles', a nickname now given to Point-à-Pitre in Guadeloupe. Fort de la Fleur d'Epée commanded the harbour, but all that can be seen of it to-day are the gardens and parts below the surface, the dungeons and the moat. The Cathedral, reinforced with iron to withstand earthquakes, is covered with yellow stucco and very ornate. Many three-storeyed houses with steep roofs also remain today. However, most of what we see today is the Cap Haitien built after the 1840 earthquake.

Port-au-Prince is mainly a nineteenth-century city, a little like New Orleans, Louisiana, in its architectural style. The houses are faced with ornate iron balconies closely fronting the streets. Many are festooned with creepers and give the impression of stillness and coolness. The upper storeys have their windows built out of steeply-sloping roofs (dormer windows). St Ann's Cathedral, built in 1720, no longer exists, but St Trinité Episcopal Cathedral, referred to in the section on Caribbean art, is a tourist attraction because of its murals.

Perhaps the most famous buildings in the Caribbean were the Palace of Sans Souci and La Citadelle, built by Henri Christophe at Milot inland from Cap Haitien. Sans Souci was lavishly appointed with tapestries and silks lining its walls, and polished mahogany panelling. Unfortunately this was destroyed by an earthquake in 1842. One thousand metres above Sans Souci was La Citadelle, intended to house a garrison of fifteen thousand soldiers and withstand a siege of three years. The walls are forty metres high and three metres thick. It was designed by La Ferrière, a French engineer and architect, and built by thousands of labourers who had to carry all the materials up the rocky cliffs or drive donkeys with their loads.

Like the British, the French also built their 'Great Houses' of which one is very famous and still remains in good condition. Chateau Murat in Marie-Galante is neo-Palladian in the style of its façade but less elaborate behind. It was surrounded by formal gardens like a French chateau. Unfortunately La Pagerie in Martinique, the home of Napoleon's Josephine, is not in good repair, and Fountain Estate in St Kitt's, built by de Poincy in 1640, is also largely in ruins above the ground.

Apart from Fort de la Fleur d'Epée, mentioned above, other noteworthy French forts were Fort St Louis in Martinique and Morne Fortune in St Lucia. Fort St Louis was begun by du Parquet in 1640 like a mediaeval castle with a moat and underground passages. It was added to in the early-eighteenth century and much of it can be seen today. Morne Fortune is today used as a school and a branch of the University of the West Indies. It is French and British in its construction. It consists of two-storeyed buildings with cloister-like colonnades on the ground floor supporting balconies above and topped by steeply-sloping roofs.

Dutch architecture

Dutch architecture appears clearly in the island of Curaçao because even the older buildings are in remarkably good condition. As in Amsterdam in Holland, many town buildings are tall with a narrow street frontage. Some rise to five storeys and are topped by very steep roofs. If not actually joined, such buildings stand very close together. The Civil Registration Office in Willemstad is a good example of such architecture.

In the Dutch West Indies Fort Oranje in St Eustatius is of particular interest. It was built overlooking Oranjestad and was very strongly fortified and so well built that it is almost completely intact today. Inside are a variety of buildings from the Commander's house to the prison cells. 'Stream View' in Curaçao is an octagonal, eighteenth-century house with its main floor projecting over the ground floor. Also in Curaçao St Anna's Catholic Church dating from 1751, and the Ismel Synagogue from 1730, the oldest synagogue in the West Indies, are noteworthy.

Notes

1 In colonial times architecture in the West Indies followed the styles of the colonial rulers with modifications made to take into account the heat of the tropics.
2 In the Roman Catholic islands most care was put into the building of the churches.
3 The Spanish built solidly in stone so that Santo Domingo, founded in 1498 and the oldest town in the Caribbean, has some of its oldest buildings still standing like Santa Maria de Menor Cathedral.
4 Spanish houses of the wealthy were often built round shaded courtyards.
5 The Castle of El Morro, San Juan, Puerto Rico, is an imposing construction from the sea, but inside has pleasant living quarters and courtyards.
6 The Great Houses of the sugar estates provide the most noteworthy architectural features of the British Caribbean.
7 The Great Houses were frequently built in the neo-Palladian or Georgian style.
8 The materials and craftsmanship of the Great Houses were local.
9 The craftsmanship put into the woodwork of staircases and furniture was particularly fine.
10 Basseterre in St Kitts, Falmouth in Jamaica and St John's in Antigua are whole towns of architectural interest in the British Caribbean.
11 Cap Français in St Domingue was the pride of French architecture in the Caribbean until it was destroyed by an earthquake in 1840.
12 Port-au-Prince bears some resemblance to New Orleans, Louisiana, in the style of some of its houses with their ironwork balconies close to the street.
13 Sans Souci and La Citadelle, built by Henri Christophe between 1804 and 1818, were both remarkable, the former for its lavishness and the latter for the engineering feats necessary in its construction.
14 Chateau Murat in Marie-Galante is probably the best-known French 'Great House' still standing.
15 Many of the town buildings of Willemstad, Curaçao, follow the architecture of seventeenth-century town buildings in Amsterdam, with narrow frontages rising to five storeys.

Map 13.4: Caribbean music

Caribbean music has developed from African, Asian and European music, with African music playing the dominant role. Caribbean music is far more distinctive than either Caribbean art or Caribbean architecture, for instance, the rhumba, calypso and reggae belong to the Caribbean and nowhere else. Only Haitian art has any comparable claim to be distinctively Caribbean.

In spite of the lack of proper instruments and attempts by the authorities at suppression, African drum rhythms were retained by the slaves, especially in Haiti. The African characteristics in Caribbean music are:
a) close relationship between melody and speech tone;
b) spontaneity in rhythm and melody;
c) willingness of performers to extemporise, and their ability to do so;
d) polyphony; the emphasis on many voices and parts in music, and the bringing of these voices and parts together in harmony, or keeping them separate;
e) arrangement of complicated rhythms.

Thus Haitian music demonstrates the complicated and syncopated rhythms of the Yoruba of Nigeria. One rhythm is followed until the accent is suddenly placed on another beat, or the first rhythm is interrupted by another. Early reggae, and some of Bob Marley's reggae, use the syncopated rhythms of Africa.

Relationship between melody and speech tones is found in the early calypsoes of The Mighty Sparrow. The syncopation here involves the displacement of beats and accents in the melodies. However, it is not just in melody that calypsoes follow African patterns, but also in the themes. The lyrics are often intentionally ambiguous, having an innocent meaning for the uninitiated while lampooning at the same time.

European influence is strong, especially in instrumentation in Spanish Caribbean music. The trumpet, clarinet, saxophone and the guitar feature prominently. Asian influence is more local, being confined mainly to Trinidad and British Guiana, where the sitar has been 'borrowed' for Caribbean music.

Instruments

The percussion instruments originated in West Africa: drums, xylophones, claves, clappers, rattles, scrapers, thumb pianos and bones have all been used in Caribbean music. Well-known local variations of these instruments are: tamboo-bamboo in Trinidad (related to the xylophone); maracas, which are probably native to America, but are like African gourds with the seeds left inside; turtle shells cut into ridges which are akin to African gourds with their stems cut into notches; and marimba which are the Cuban equivalent of the thumb piano.

Music from Trinidad

Steel bands   From the social distress of the 1930s came steel band music. The tamboo-bamboo was banned as the canes could be used as offensive weapons. The musicians turned to oil drums which were plentiful in Trinidad in areas of waste ground. They beat out their rhythms on them. These places became known as 'panyards', one of which was occupied by the 'Invaders', perhaps the most famous early steel band.

The rise of the steel bands shows much creativity. At first any steel utensils were used, but soon the forty-four gallon oil drum became the chief instrument made of steel in regular use. The drums were then cut into cross sections of varying depths and became known as 'pans'. The deepest was the bass-pan, an oil drum with only the bung end cut off. The cellopan was cut thirty to thirty-seven centimetres from the bung end. The guitar-pan was cut fifty centimetres from the bung end. Finally the highest note was obtained from the ping-pong which was only twenty centimetres deep at the most.

Ellie Mannette of the 'Invaders' discovered that these pans could be tuned. His first tuned pan was a ping-pong. He hammered its surface into a convex shape which he then marked into circles with a cold chisel. He hammered these circles into domes or bosses which produced notes of different pitches. Such tuning was called 'Ellie's technique'. Then this sort of tuning was applied to all sizes of pan. Soon the number of notes on each pan was regularised, the bass-pan having four notes, the cellopan, six, the guitar pan, fourteen, and the ping-pong between twenty-six and thirty-two. The 'Invaders' were probably the first to use all four pans with the complete range of notes, but other bands soon copied them. Then steel bands all had a range of about thirty-six notes which produced the famous 'liquid sound' of steel band music.

On 8 May 1945, musicians came out of the 'hellyard' beating their pans in celebration of the victory over Germany in the Second World War.

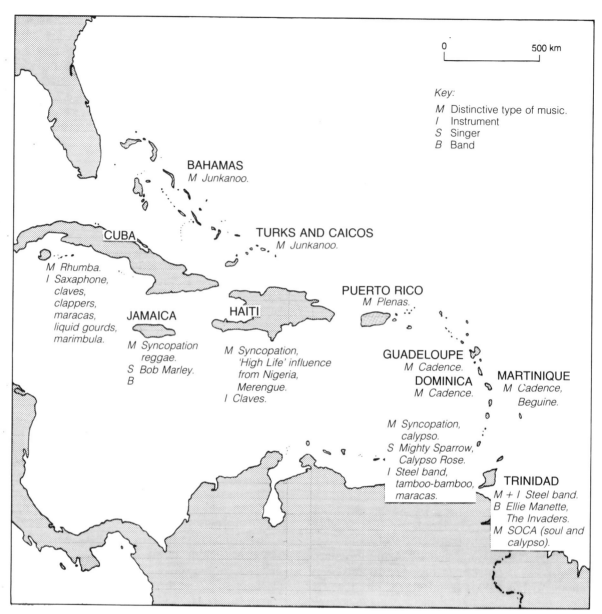

Key:
M Distinctive type of music.
I Instrument
S Singer
B Band

BAHAMAS
M Junkanoo.

TURKS AND CAICOS
M Junkanoo.

CUBA
M Rhumba.
I Saxaphone,
claves,
clappers,
maracas,
liquid gourds,
marimbula.

JAMAICA
M Syncopation
reggae.
S Bob Marley.
B

HAITI
M Syncopation,
'High Life' influence
from Nigeria,
Merengue.
I Claves.

PUERTO RICO
M Plenas.

GUADELOUPE
M Cadence.

DOMINICA
M Cadence.

MARTINIQUE
M Cadence,
Beguine.

M Syncopation,
calypso.
S Mighty Sparrow,
Calypso Rose.
I Steel band,
tamboo-bamboo,
maracas.

TRINIDAD
M + I Steel band.
B Ellie Manette,
The Invaders.
M SOCA (soul and
calypso).

Map 13.4: Caribbean music

There had not been a carnival for five years and the people were in joyous mood. The success of the Victory Parade secured the future of steel bands. In 1945 apart from 'Hellyard' there was another band, 'Bar-29' led by Scribo Maloney who introduced the 'cut-and-tumble' beat. Gangs of hooligans marred the success of steel bands in those early years between 1945 and 1950, but by 1950 the true musicians were winning through and Ellie Mannette's 'Invaders' performed before the Governor. Also in 1950 was the first steel band competition which was won by the Casablanca Steel Orchestra playing 'The Bells of St Mary's' with the hubcap as solo instrument. They also rendered Chopin's 'Nocturne in E-flat' arranged by their leader, Russell Manning. This demonstrated the versatility of steel bands for now their music was ranging from calypsoes to marches to classics. The reputation of steel bands was carried overseas, chiefly to Britain, by the emigrants of the 1950s, and the cricket tour of 1950 when the calypso about the spin bowlers, Ramadhin and Valentine, was accompanied by a steel band. Since 1951 steel band music has continuously gained in popularity. Bands became orchestras of over one hundred instruments like the Catelli Trinidad All Stars Steel Orchestra which was capable of giving a full-length concert of classical music. However, most steel bands consist of three to six bass pans, two or three pairs of cellopans, two to four guitar pans and one or two ping-pongs. Today many of the bandsmen still cannot read music, but learn by heart and play by ear.

The Calypso A calypso theme is often like a ballad, a simple song with musical accompaniment. This is the European influence. The African influence lies in the melody following speech tones and when the theme is a lampoon on leading characters in society. Calypsoes nowadays are often accompanied by steel bands but they are a hundred years older in origin than steel bands. At the time of emancipation the slaves made up songs about their supporters or their opponents and the singing groups were led by the composers called 'shatwell'. The calypso flourished at carnival in Trinidad. Carnival formalised calypso, whether to follow the conventional calypso melody or to make up a new one. For carnival calypso singers adopted popular names like 'The Mighty Sparrow' and 'Calypso Rose', the King and Queen of Calypso in the carnival of 1979.

Some calypso lyrics incorporate Spanish, Yoruba, Ashanti and Creole words which make it hard for a foreigner to Trinidad to understand. Calypsoes used to be accompanied by tamboo-bamboo, shak-shak (maracas), guitar and 'cuatre', instruments particularly associated with Trinidad.

Soca The word 'Soca' derives from 'soul' and 'calypso' put together. Thus soca blends the jazz of the 'Deep South' of the United States with the calypso, and it uses the sitar, mandolin and tabla, East Indian instruments, sometimes for accompaniment. Thus it is a typical Caribbean mixing of cultures, black American, West Indian and Indian.

Music from Jamaica

Reggae is Jamaican folk music, comparable to the position of calypso in Trinidad. Its themes vary from the militancy of black power, through the message of Rastafarianism to happy Jamaican folk songs. Pure reggae lyrics are difficult for outsiders to understand as they are in a distinct Jamaica patois, but modern commercial reggae has adapted to gain universal appeal, for instance it is very popular in Malawi where this book is being written. The late Bob Marley is something of a hero in parts of Africa. Of course, reggae features very strongly in the 'pop' music world in Britain. Bob Marley's music and lyrics reflect pure reggae but have also met with great commercial success.

Musical forms in other parts of the Caribbean

Cadence from Guadeloupe, Dominica and Martinique has become internationally known in the 1980s. In the Caribbean its chief exponents are the Dominican bands which play in the neighbouring French islands. In London and Paris it has become fashionable at night clubs. So its appeal ranges from the unemployed youth of the Eastern Caribbean to the rich young night-club set in Europe.

Junkanoo is local to the Bahamas and Turks and Caicos; **Merengue** to Haiti; **Beguine** to Martinique; **Plenas** to Puerto Rico; and, of course, we must not forget the **Rhumba** of Cuba. No other part of the world is as rich as the Caribbean in musical forms and performers.

Notes

1 African musical patterns have had most influence on Caribbean music.
2 Syncopated rhythms in calypso and reggae

provide very good illustrations of African influence.

3   The instruments used in much Caribbean music are also based on African originals although European musical instruments are also in common use especially in Spanish Caribbean music.

4   Steel band music began in the back streets of Port of Spain, Trinidad, in the depression of the 1930s.

5   From the basic oil drum to the sophistication of a steel orchestra required much creativity.

6   Ellie Mannette was the first to tune pans.

7   Nowadays a typical steel band has about fourteen instruments and a range of about thirty-six notes.

8   Calypso is a distinctive Trinidadian musical form in which the melody follows speech tones and the lyrics lampoon social figures.

9   Calypso flourished at carnival where singers nowadays compete for the titles for 'King' and 'Queen' of Calypso.

10   Reggae is Jamaican folk music with a message, often political or social.

11   The most famous exponent of reggae was the late Bob Marley whose reggae not only pleases the purists but has also had great commercial success.

12   No other part of the world is as rich as the Caribbean in musical forms.